Legal Cases of the Civil War

Legal Cases
of the Civil War

Robert Bruce Murray

STACKPOLE
BOOKS

Published by
STACKPOLE BOOKS
5067 Ritter Road
Mechanicsburg, PA 17055
www.stackpolebooks.com

Printed in the United States of America

10 9 8 7 6 5 4 3 2 1

FIRST EDITION

Library of Congress Cataloging-in-Publication Data

Murray, Robert Bruce, 1927-
  Legal cases of the Civil War / by Robert Bruce Murray.— 1st ed.
      p. cm.
  Includes bibliographical references.
  ISBN 0-8117-0059-3
  1. United States—History—Civil War, 1861–1865—Law and legislation.
  2. War and emergency legislation—United States—History—19th century. I. Title.
KF7221.M87 2003
349.73'09'34—dc21

2002156350

To Marge,
my beloved partner in life

CONTENTS

ACKNOWLEDGMENTS

Today an author does not just put down his pencil and, in a sigh of relief, send his manuscript off to the publisher. Now an author's manuscript must be profiled, formatted, and placed on disks. To accomplish this task, I am indebted to Michele Free and J. D. Reza. They were totally dedicated to this task and to getting it right. I give you both my sincere thanks.

INTRODUCTION

The Civil War was fought not only on the land and sea, but also in the courts of the nation. This book examines many of these legal cases, both the important constitutional cases and those that involved average citizens and their problems. Cases were filed by people in the military and civilians, by men and women, by whites and blacks, by citizens of the United States and of the Confederacy, and by corporate entities. They ranged from cases such as one filed by a Union private who believed he was entitled to a military bonus that he had not received to those that determined control of large corporations.

After carefully reviewing 185 such cases that reached the docket of and were heard by the Supreme Court of the United States, I selected a number of these cases for the book that are representative of the subject matter in the categories indicated by the chapters. The situations leading to these cases reflected the turmoil created by the war in the lives of the people. The arguments made by counsel indicate the urgency and the intrigue used to meet and overcome the new and unusual situations created by the war.

During this period of our history, the statutes permitting appeal to the Supreme Court were liberal. The court also had a limited number of rules governing how appeals should be docketed and handled. The parties were required to file briefs incorporating their arguments just a few days before the oral arguments were scheduled to be made. Although the oral arguments reflected the assertions made in the briefs, at times they did not seem to reply to one another. This is because one party may have combated assertions in the other party's brief when that party may have abandoned the argument or just had not set it out in his oral argument.

The cases have been taken from the *U.S. Supreme Court Reports, Lawyers' Edition,* originally published in 1884 by the Lawyers' Cooperative Publishing Company, Rochester, New York. This set of reports presents the official opinions of the court as written by reporters of the court, along with summaries of the oral arguments the attorneys made to the court. In Appendix B, this set is cited in the format "67 *U.S. Supreme Court Reports,* 459," meaning that the case appeared in volume 67 of the *U.S. Supreme Court Reports, Lawyers' Edition,* beginning at page 459. Where the *U.S. Supreme Court Reports* appear in the endnotes, these citations are also to the *Lawyers Edition.*

The volumes listed in the Bibliography are the sources of the background history of the cases.

Information relative to the justices and chief justices of the U.S. Supreme Court for the Civil War period is provided in Appendix A, and brief summaries of the Civil War cases are contained in Appendix B.

Robert Bruce Murray
September 23, 2002

Chapter One

Defining the Conflict:
The Prize Cases

When President Lincoln assumed the office of the presidency on March 4, 1861, the Confederate States of America had been formed and Jefferson Davis had assumed its provisional presidency. Before Lincoln had a chance to establish an operating and effective administration, the Confederate States' military fired upon Fort Sumter. Three days later, on April 15, 1861, Lincoln issued a proclamation stating that the laws of the United States were being opposed and their execution obstructed by "combinations too powerful to be suppressed" in the normal course of law enforcement. He called the militia of the several states of the Union to active duty to the extent of seventy-five thousand men, "in order to suppress said combinations, and to cause the laws to be duly executed." Congress was called into extraordinary session beginning on July 4, 1861, to consider and determine what measures should be taken to meet the emergency. The states named in which these combinations were situated were South Carolina, Georgia, Alabama, Florida, Mississippi, Louisiana, and Texas.

Recognizing that an insurrection had broken out in the states mentioned in the first proclamation, President Lincoln followed with a second proclamation on April 19, 1861. It stated that the collection of revenue could not be "effectually executed" in these states, and that a "combination of persons" in these states had threatened to grant "pretended" letters of marque that would result in assaults on the lives and property of citizens of the country who lawfully engaged in commerce on the high seas. This statement was in direct reply to Jefferson Davis's proclamation of April 17, 1861, in which he had encouraged volunteers to take out letters of marque from the Confederacy with the avowed purpose of raiding Union shipping.

For years, letters of marque, referred to in Article I, Section 8 of the Constitution of the United States as "Letters of Marque and Reprisal," found their basis in international law, the law that governs the rights among sovereign nations. This law is not codified, but relies upon custom derived from the decrees of cases determined in courts of the countries of the world. Under this law, these letters were granted during wartime by a belligerent to its citizens who owned armed vessels, commissioning them to raid the enemy's shipping. In 1856, the Declaration of Paris abolished such privateering. The United States was not a signatory to the declaration, but later accepted the principles therein to govern its conduct during the Civil War.

Lincoln's second proclamation furthermore called for a blockade of all ports in the states involved in the insurrection in order to encourage peace and protect the lives and property of citizens, until Congress could meet to consider the issues created by the insurrection. The blockading vessels were to stop any vessel approaching or leaving these ports and notify it of the blockade by inscribing the date of the warning on the vessel's register. Thereafter, if the same vessel attempted to enter or leave a blockaded port again, it would be captured and subject to legal proceedings as a prize.

International law defines the terms *prize* and *prize of war* as the successful judicial condemnation of property following its capture at sea. To be subject to prize procedures, the property must have been movable and in the hands of, owned by, or destined to the enemy and used or intended to be used for hostile purposes. Prize courts exist still in all maritime nations to determine whether captured property falls into this classification and is subject to condemnation.

An integral aspect of prize law at that time was that if the condemnation proceeding was successful, the proceeds of subsequent sales were apportioned among the crew of the capturing vessel. Pursuant to a law passed by the U.S. Congress in 1862, if the capturing vessel was of a superior force to the one captured, its crew received half of the net proceeds, and the United States received the balance. If, however, the capturing vessel was of an inferior force to the one captured, the entire proceeds after necessary costs went to the crew. Before this time, only commissioned privateers shared in condemnation proceeds.

Article III, Section 2 of the U.S. Constitution gives jurisdiction of prize court proceedings, maritime cases, and cases in admiralty to the Federal courts. The Federal District Courts, which are trial courts, have jurisdiction over prize cases under the Judiciary Act of 1789. These are courts of original jurisdiction in prize cases without considering the factors that determine federal jurisdiction in other cases, such as the amount involved, the subject of the controversy, or diversity of citizenship. In prize proceedings, the judge normally determines the facts and how the law should be applied without the benefit of a jury.

President Lincoln ended the proclamation by stating that if any person, under letters of marque or under any other pretense, should molest a vessel of the United States or any person or cargo on board such a vessel, this person would be subject to the laws of the country for the prevention and punishment of piracy. This proclamation was amended by another proclamation on April 27, 1861, which added Virginia and North Carolina to the list of states participating in the insurrection.

Controversy and disagreement arose among Lincoln's advisors regarding the installation of a blockade. Lincoln and members of his cabinet deemed it important not to recognize the Confederate States as sovereign. If they did, they would be acknowledging that the Southern states had seceded. This could have serious international consequences. However, under international law, a blockade normally is recognized only between two sovereign powers that are at war. Lincoln therefore faced a dilemma. On one hand, he insisted that the conflict with the South was not a war, but an insurrection. On the other hand, he needed a classification of war to support a legally valid blockade.

The British assisted the Lincoln administration in reconciling this dilemma when they communicated through their minister in Washington that any procedure other than a blockade might force an English recognition of the Confederacy.[1] The British recognized the blockade as a legitimate tactic to be used in maritime war but had difficulty determining how to protect their interests in any other procedure that would close the Southern ports without full recognition of the Confederacy.

The status of the blockade affected thousands of citizens on both sides of the lines of battle. The owners of the vessels and cargoes first captured by the blockading forces seized on the issue that no war existed and therefore the blockade was illegal. In the first Civil War cases to come before the U.S. Supreme Court, the court had to determine whether the blockade was legal. To answer this question, the court was forced to define the nature of the conflict: Was it a war, an insurrection, or something else? The court then had to determine the ramifications of this classification under international law. The decision of the court would set the course of the war and how the North, South, and the other nations of the world would treat the conflict.

The issue was brought before the court in the form of four separate maritime prize cases, which were consolidated into a single appeal. The importance of these cases warrants a careful consideration of their facts, history, and treatment before the Supreme Court. Though each case possessed a separate name and was a distinctive case unto itself, the combined appeal appeared on the court docket as the *Prize Cases.*[2]

The first of the four cases concerned the *Brilliante,* a Mexican merchant schooner that sailed from Sisal on the Yucatán coast for New Orleans in early June 1861. The crew was unaware of the problems awaiting her and expected a smooth voyage. A Mexican mercantile company, Preciat & Gaul of Campeachy, owned most of the cargo, which probably consisted of products grown in the Yucatán. This company also owned the vessel. Part of the cargo was owned by Ybana & Donde, another mercantile house situated in Sisal. Don Rafael Preciat, the owner's partner, was a passenger on board the vessel. He expected to enjoy a profitable trip.

As the vessel approached New Orleans, it was intercepted by the Union steam sloop USS *Brooklyn,* which was blockading the Mississippi River at Pass à Loutre. An officer of the *Brooklyn* informed the officers of the *Brilliante* that Federal naval forces were enforcing a blockade of the Southern ports, and they would not allow the vessel to enter the river and proceed to New Orleans.

This was a serious blow to Preciat, so he changed his approach. He explained to the commander of the *Brooklyn* that he had a son at Spring Hill College, close to Mobile, and he wanted to pick him up to get him away from the deteriorating conditions in the South. Receptive to the problem, the commander of the *Brooklyn* gave Preciat a letter addressed to the commander of the USS *Niagara*, the ship that was blockading Mobile Bay, permitting the *Brilliante* to land there and pick up Preciat's son.

As the vessel proceeded toward the *Niagara*, the crew of the *Brilliante* became restless and refused to take the ship to Mobile. Instead, they turned the vessel, entered Lake Pontchartrain, and docked at New Orleans. There they unloaded the ship and took on a new cargo consisting of 600 barrels of flour. Heading back to Sisal, the *Brilliante* was captured attempting to run the blockade. The USS *Massachusetts* captured the vessel in Biloxi Bay, north of Ship Island between Pass Christian and Pascagoula Bay, on June 23, 1861.

The vessel and cargo were taken to Key West, where they were libeled in the District Court for the Southern District of Florida. Because Key West remained in control of the Union throughout the war, this court became the site of numerous cases involving blockade running. The term *libel* was used at that time to describe the initial pleading in a maritime condemnation case. That pleading was filed with the court, asking that the vessel and cargo be condemned under the proclamation of the president, legislation of Congress, and the rules of international law. The court was sympathetic to the pleading. Without written opinion, or at least one that has been preserved, the vessel and cargo were condemned as a prize of war. This decision was not appealed to the Circuit Court. Instead, the appeal was taken directly to the Supreme Court of the United States.

The *Crenshaw* was the second vessel to become part of the Prize Cases. She sailed from New York on April 19, 1861, arriving at her destination of City Point, the port of Richmond, on April 22. She completed the discharge of her cargo on April 27. On May 13, she received orders to load for Liverpool, England. The loading was completed on May 15, and the vessel proceeded downriver. The clearance papers were signed by R. H. Lortin, collector of the port of Richmond, Confederate States of America.

The *Crenshaw*'s cargo was tobacco. Part of that cargo, 108 hogsheads and 49 half hogsheads of tobacco, was owned by John and James Caskie, who resided in Richmond. A hogshead was a sixty-three-gallon cask pressed full of tobacco leaves. John Currie and other Virginia citizens owned the vessel.

The balance of the cargo consisted of forty tierces of tobacco strips. Irvin & Company of New York claimed thirty tierces, purchased before April 12, 1861. Ten tierces were claimed by Henry Ludlum of Rhode Island, G. F. Watson of Richmond, and Lear & Son of Liverpool, England. One tierce is the amount of tobacco equal to one-third pipe, or thirty-five gallons. Tobacco measured in this fashion was also pressed into casks.

On May 17, the vessel was captured off Newport News by the USS *Star*, under command of Flag Officer Silas H. Stringham, the recently appointed commander of the Atlantic Blockading Squadron. The vessel was taken to New York as a prize of war and libeled in the U.S. District Court for the Southern District of New York. The vessel and cargo were condemned except for the interest of Lear & Son. The Circuit Court affirmed the decision, and the losing claimants appealed the case to the U.S. Supreme Court.

During the course of this appeal, John and James Caskie filed a motion with the court for an order to deliver their tobacco to them. The Caskies claimed that the tobacco was suffering severe deterioration in value from its exposure to the elements and its confinement in the hold of the vessel. The Caskies offered to stipulate to account for the proceeds derived from any sale of the tobacco in the event that the court held against them.

The *Crenshaw* lay at the wharf of the Union Stores in the city of Brooklyn. The Caskies argued that they were forced to hire someone to guard and take care of the tobacco to prevent further damage. They pointed out to the court that the market value of the tobacco had increased substantially, and that it would be to the interest of all parties to take advantage of the increase in the market value.

Circuit Judge Samuel Nelson, who also sat as a justice of the Supreme Court, denied the motion. However, he thought that the arguments presented by the Caskies were sound. He appointed two commissioners to appraise the tobacco, and then ordered the U.S. marshal to sell the tobacco at a public sale under supervision of the commissioners. The proceeds of the sale would not be turned over to the Caskies, residents of the Confederacy, but instead would be deposited with the court for disbursal according to the final determination of the case.

The third vessel in the case, the *Hiawatha,* was captured on May 20, 1861, by the Union flagship *Minnesota* in Hampton Roads off Fortress Monroe. British citizens owned and manned the vessel and cargo. The vessel had sailed from Liverpool with a cargo of salt destined for City Point, the port of Richmond. She reached Hampton Roads on April 23, made her way upriver, and completed the unloading of her cargo by May 10.

The U.S. secretary of the navy had allowed neutral vessels fifteen days to leave blockaded ports after the April 30 declaration that the blockade was in effect, so the master of the *Hiawatha* could have withdrawn from the port safely within this period with whatever cargo was on board, adding nothing to the cargo. However, the British owners were operating under the erroneous impression that the effective date of the blockade was May 2.

The British owners feverishly worked the crew to load for the outgoing trip. By May 15, the vessel had taken on a full load of cotton and tobacco. She was ready to depart the next day, but no steam tug could be found in port to tow her downriver. On May 17, she was taken in tow by the steam tug *David Currie*. But this tug did not have sufficient power, and the *Hiawatha* was forced to anchor. On May 18, the steam tug *William Allison* towed her to sea. Two days later, the *Hiawatha* was captured and taken with her cargo to New York, where she was condemned as a prize of war in the U.S. District Court of the Southern District of New York. The Circuit Court affirmed the decision. The British owners and claimants appealed to the U.S. Supreme Court.

As in the case of the *Crenshaw,* the Circuit Court was requested to enter an order to permit the public sale of the *Hiawatha*'s cargo of tobacco. In this case, the claimants did not request the order; this was done by the prize commissioners whose job it was to oversee the ship and cargo. The commissioners reported to the court that the *Hiawatha* was lying at the Atlantic dock in Brooklyn. They provided proof satisfactory to the court that the tobacco was perishing.

The court entered an order to sell the tobacco, then followed with an order that each claimant's parcel be separated and appraised according to the bills of lading. This was quite a task, since there were thirty-three claimants. Following the sale, the proceeds were paid into the registry fund of the court, and each claimant was advised of the amount in the registry that would be disbursed to him in the event that the claimants were victorious in the case. Judge Samuel Nelson, a justice of the U.S. Supreme Court, entered these orders.

The brig *Amy Warwick* was the fourth vessel involved in this case. After departing from Rio de Janiero on May 29, the vessel headed for Hampton Roads with a cargo of coffee. The U.S. gunboat *Quaker City* captured her on the high seas on July 10, 1861. The brig and her cargo were libeled in the U.S. District Court for the District of Massachusetts.

David Currie and others claimed the brig. Edmund Davenport & Company claimed 400 bags of coffee; Dunlap, Moncure & Company claimed 4,700 bags. All claimants lived in Richmond and were engaged in business there. At the initial hearing, the titles of the claimants were conceded, but the property was nevertheless condemned. The Circuit Court affirmed, and the case was appealed to the U.S. Supreme Court.

Though it was and remains a rare procedure, the Supreme Court combined these four cases for the purposes of appeal. The cases remained separate; only the appeal was joined. The cases were thought to be an excellent test of the legality of the proclamations pertaining to the blockade and of the status of the maritime law as the conflict began. The *Brilliante* posed the question of the status of a neutral vessel and cargo attempting to run the blockade; the *Crenshaw,* the status of a vessel and cargo, or most of the cargo, owned by residents of the Confederacy; the *Hiawatha,* a vessel and cargo owned by a neutral where the violation of the blockade was claimed to be unintentional; and the *Amy Warwick,* a vessel and cargo owned by residents of the Confederacy but captured on the high seas. However, all the issues created by the different situations were secondary to the prime issue of whether the blockade was legal. These cases were also important because other cases with similar facts were held up by the courts pending the decision of the Supreme Court in the Prize Cases.

Samuel Nelson, the judge who had affirmed the *Crenshaw* and the *Hiawatha* District Court cases at the Circuit Court level, ironically now sat as a justice on the Supreme Court, reviewing and disagreeing with his own decisions and prior affirmances in those two cases. This is an interesting and little-known aspect of the cases. This unusual situation arose due to the organization of the court system.

The passage of the Judiciary Act of 1789 had completed the organization of the Supreme Court and divided the country into thirteen districts, each with a District Court and one judge assigned to each district. The districts were apportioned into three circuits: the Eastern, Middle, and Southern, each of which roughly encompassed the states in its area. Circuit Courts sat twice a year in each district. Each was presided over by two justices of the Supreme Court, assigned according to the circuits, and the district judge where the Circuit Court was sitting. The Circuit Courts, among other jurisdictions, handled appeals from the District Courts. The Supreme Court justices found that "riding the circuit" under this arrangement was a hardship beyond their endurance. Congress attempted to help them in 1793 by passing legislation amending the Judiciary Act of 1789, assigning only one Supreme Court justice to each Circuit Court.

By 1861, additional districts, district courts, and circuit courts had been added. During the Prize Cases, Justice Nelson was assigned to the Eastern Circuit, which covered the Southern District of New York. When the appeals in the *Crenshaw* and *Hiawatha* cases arrived there, they were just two cases among several. To facilitate a hearing at the Supreme Court level, Judge Nelson of the Circuit Court affirmed the District Court opinions without delivering or otherwise expressing an opinion. This rushed the cases to the Supreme Court so that a decision could be obtained on the legality of the blockade. When the cases formally reached the Supreme Court, Nelson sat as a justice. Thus when he reviewed the decisions of the Circuit Court, he was in the unusual position of reviewing his own decisions.

The *Amy Warwick* case likewise came to the Supreme Court without a Circuit Court opinion, though it was noted in the *Federal Cases* that there was an affirmance at that level. The *Brilliante* does not have a published opinion at either the District Court or Circuit Court level. How it became part of the *Prize Cases* will remain an interesting historical mystery.

THE ARGUMENTS BEFORE THE COURT

The cases were argued to the court for twelve days, beginning on February 10, 1863. Representing the United States were Attorney General Edward Bates and members of his staff, Charles Eames, William M. Evarts, R. H. Dana, Jr., W. D. Booth, and C. B. Sedgwick. Counsel for the claimants were J. M. Carlisle in the case of the *Brilliante;* Daniel Lord, C. Donohue, and Charles Edwards in the case of the *Crenshaw;* Charles Edwards also in the case of the *Hiawatha;* and Edward Bangs in the case of the *Amy Warwick.*

J. M. Carlisle, speaking on behalf of the claimants in the *Brilliante* case, gave the opening argument. Citing Article 17 of the Treaty of Guadalupe Hidalgo, he insisted that the port of New Orleans had been open to trade with Mexico on June 23, 1861, the date the vessel was captured. If the port had not been open, he questioned how it had achieved the status of a closed port. He argued that such a status could have been achieved only by the domestic laws of the United States or by the effect of international law.

Carlisle then asserted that a closing of the port could not have been achieved by domestic laws. Congress had not acted before the date of the vessel's capture. Therefore, if the port had been closed, it could have taken place only by virtue of the president's constitutional powers. Carlisle insisted that the president's so-called implied powers were strictly limited and did not include the power to close a port. He argued that the guarantees of personal liberty and rights in the Constitution were designed to prevail in times of tumult, public danger, and disorder; that the president had no authority to suspend these liberties; and that the president did not possess the power to attain the rights and privileges of the people set out in the Preamble of the Constitution, but that these objects were reserved for other means of attainment. Carlisle pressed his view that the president's powers were clearly limited to defending the Constitution and executing the office of the presidency. Therefore, he argued, the president must abstain from exercising powers given to the legislature and judiciary. At this point in his argument, Carlisle reviewed the president's enumerated powers, pointing out to the court that none of them gave the president the authority to close the port of New Orleans.

As to the president's role of commander-in-chief of the military, Carlisle insisted that this meant nothing more than having command of the army, navy, and militia in actual service in time of war. This command did not involve any power to suspend or repeal any law. "He is to act as Commander-in-Chief, not as a legislator or emperor."

To say that the president can declare war because of his position of commander-in-chief was absurd, said Carlisle. The Constitution granted Congress the power to declare war, and by this grant, this power was denied to the other branches of government. Carlisle indicated that this interpretation was clearly set forth in the Articles of Confederation, in the Federalist Papers, in the works of William Blackstone, and in the works of prominent authorities in the field of constitutional law. He argued against the "modern idea" that a state of war may exist by executive act, without a declaration of war by Congress, because of how and when it arose, reiterating that the fixing of a state of war was the role of Congress no matter how the war situation evolved.

Carlisle then made reference to the war with Mexico. Although the conflict was ongoing at the time, he pointed out that a legal state of war did not exist until May 13, 1846, when Congress passed the act recognizing that a war existed. It was recognized, he argued, that the powers to repel invasion, to suppress insurrection, and to cause the laws to be faithfully executed were purely provisional executive powers to be used temporarily to prevent injury in exceptional cases where prompt and temporary action was necessary. These temporary powers were not meant to upset the distribution of powers set out in the Constitution.

If the president had the power to close ports, Carlisle asked, what action had he taken to close them prior to June 23, 1861? Carlisle cited the president's proclamations, pointing out that he had never recognized a state of war, but treated the armed activity as an evil perpetrated by a combination of persons. This, Carlisle argued, was not even an acceptance of war. He acknowledged that the president did, indeed, set on foot a blockade pursuant to the laws of nations. What these laws were, he asserted, were not to be discovered.

Carlisle maintained that the temporary blockade was to last only until Congress could act. Congress acted on July 13, 1861, with legislation that purported to accomplish and ratify what the president had already done. However, this legislation treated the Southern ports as ports of the United States, not as ports of a foreign nation or belligerent. In addition, the act passed by Congress took effect on July 13, 1861; it had no retroactive application. Neither did the act include forfeitures or penalties for violating the blockade.

He argued further that the provisions of the president's proclamations were not followed, because no endorsement was made upon the vessel's register. Therefore, the capture of the vessel was nothing more than a mere trespass.

Carlisle ended with a summation that the decree of condemnation of the *Brilliante* had to be based upon one of two grounds: either the seizure was pursuant to the domestic laws of the United States, or the vessel was captured under international law for violating the blockade. If the seizure was under the domestic laws of the United States, it was based upon a usurpation of power by the president, because he could not make, alter, or suspend the laws of the United States, this clearly being denied by the Constitution. If the seizure was based upon the belligerent right of blockade under the law of nations, such seizure was invalid, because at the time it was made, the sovereign power of the United States had neither declared nor recognized the existence of war. Therefore the blockade was not legal, and the seizure of the vessel was a nullity. Carlisle relied, at least in part, upon the works of the Swiss jurist Emmerich de Vattel and the American legal scholar James Kent to illustrate that only the sovereign could declare war, such power being lodged "singly in Congress."

William M. Evarts and R. H. Dana, Jr., replied to Carlisle's arguments on behalf of the United States. Evarts spoke first. He appeared to be very upset, even frustrated, by Carlisle's arguments that the actions of the president were a usurpation of power. He described the extensiveness of the war at the time of the capture of the *Brilliante*. Under any definition, he argued, it was a public war, citing world-recognized scholars in the field of international law. He maintained that a public war attributes all the rights of war to the sovereign. Among them were the rights to blockade and do maritime capture. Therefore, he argued, war was a question of actualities. It was no less a war because it arose without solemnities or because it arose from within the nation against the government. The right of the government to use war powers was defined only by the wartime actions brought against the government. To hold otherwise would mean the government was incapable of defending itself. It was vain to insist that only Congress could declare war, or that a true war could exist only among or between sovereign nations, or that the only actions the government was able to take against a rebellion were peaceful measures. Such arguments, Evarts insisted, all aided and abetted the rebellion and paralyzed government, for they proclaimed in advance success to military assaults upon constitutional government. These assertions ended in the absurdity that weapons and power of war could not be met with similar weapons and power of war until a declaration of war that recognizes the rebellious group as a belligerent nationality was made. This in itself, Evarts argued, would accomplish the objects of the revolt for the rebellious group: recognition as a sovereign. Any draftsman of a declaration of war would therefore obliterate the cause of the war while he was penning its announcement; he would be a "herald of its close."

He insisted it was manifest upon reason that when in a rebellion, the president would be able to wield the military and naval power of the nation without action of the legislature. Evarts cited other matters in which the president was entitled to act without legislative authority, such as taking acts to curb treason. The president had to be free to use his own judgment in emergencies of this type. It had already been argued that initiating a blockade in itself did not include the right to confiscate property for its breach. Again showing his frustration, Evarts stated forcefully that such a distinction was insensible. A power to blockade without sanction was nugatory, making the blockade ridiculous.

Changing the subject, Evarts stated that it had been argued in the lower courts that residence of the property owners in the revolted areas, or even citizenship there, was not sufficient to make their property prizes of war without additional proof that the property owners were espousing rebellion. He countered this argument by asserting that whatever became part of the commercial property of the area in rebellion could be used to further the rebellion and was subject to capture and condemnation regardless of the individual sentiments or disposition of the owners. Therefore, there was no need to inquire into whether the owners remained loyal to the Union. If a war existed, the classification of "enemy" was ascribed to all who lived in the revolting area, regardless of their beliefs. Even loyal citizens living in the revolting area may lose their property. The American Congress and the British Parliament both adhered to this stand during the American Revolution.

Evarts closed his argument by stating that the decisions in the lower courts that condemned the properties under consideration as prizes of war conformed to the law of nations and the previous holdings of the Prize Court. He requested that the Supreme Court affirm them.

At this point, Dana continued the argument on behalf of the United States. He did not become as emotionally involved as Evarts. He took a professorial approach and began his argument by lecturing the court as to the laws governing the capture of property during wartime. He defined war as the acts of a public body or power to obtain a purpose through the coercion of the power against which one acts. Whenever private property was captured or destroyed under international law, it was because the property was of such a character that its confiscation was a justifiable means of coercion.

He went on to state that if the property in question was of the type used in war, it was liable to capture. In such a case, who owned the property was immaterial. Privately owned property not usable in war was not confiscated when on land, because a certain amount of this type of property was necessary to support the life of noncombatant persons and animals. However, this reason did not apply to property on the high seas, which were a common field of war and commerce. The object of this commerce was the enrichment of the owner. The property was the source of revenue to the government under which the owner resided. For this reason, coercion by capture was therefore applied to private property at sea. Such capture did not rest upon the criminality or hostility of the owner, but solely on whether the owner or the property was in the control of the enemy.

Here Dana cited several cases in support of his argument and at least two authorities on international law. He indicated that these sources sustained the propositions that it was immaterial whether the owner of the property had taken part in the war or was a citizen of the enemy. In addition, the sources held that the property, when captured, need not be on a voyage to or from the enemy's country.

Where a capture was based solely on the ground that the owner was a resident or under control of the enemy, Dana said, the jurisdiction or control of the enemy was sufficient if the territory was in the occupation of the enemy with the intent to hold the territory for so long as the war should enable the enemy to do so. In support of this statement, he cited a case arising from the war between England and Russia wherein the British court had enunciated this proposition.[3] Dana maintained that there was no doubt that Richmond was enemy territory, because at the time of the capture of the *Crenshaw, Hiawatha,* and *Amy Warwick,* the Confederacy claimed jurisdiction over the area on a permanent basis. He brought this issue to a close by stating that the claimants who were residents of Richmond, clearly enemy territory, had the onus to show the court why their property should not be condemned.

Dana then posed what he termed to be the main issue of the cases: whether the principles governing the captures of prizes of war enunciated in his arguments, and which are applicable to sovereigns at war, are equally applicable to participants in wars that are civil, domestic, or internal. To answer this question, he applied his previous definition of war as an exercise of force against each other by bodies politic. He argued that the Confederacy had established a separate nation and resorted to arms against the sovereign. Foreign nations had recognized this as a state of war and had conceded to each power the rights of belligerents. There was no need for Congress to declare war, because it was the actual state of things and not a legislative act that created the war.

If a foreign power made war upon the United States during a recess of Congress, Dana asked, could the president repel war with war, or was that illegal? He answered by declaring that it was enough to state the proposition. If a president could not do so, there would be no protection to the state.

Dana argued further that a declaration of war was not appropriate to civil wars, because a civil war was caused by rebels. A declaration of war could be interpreted as recognizing them as an independent sovereign. A sovereign held the right to determine whether to meet rebellion by a civil or military act, to grant the rebels the privileges of a belligerent, or to treat them as traitors. Part of a proper military response to a rebellion was the maritime capture of property, which could be used against the sovereign.

He acknowledged that there were allegations that Congress, in the first instant, must act in some fashion to authorize the war. He answered this with another question: If in the first instant Congress must act, why not through the entire war? Because the war changes from day to day, Congress would be a council of war in continuous session.

In answer to Carlisle's contention that the action of Congress that ratified the acts of the president establishing the blockade was retroactive, and therefore illegal, Dana asserted that the legislation did not, in its terms, contemplate a retroactive effect, but rather the reverse. There was nothing inconsistent with the legislation declining to act upon the past exercise of the war powers of the president and providing for legislation on similar matters to be effective in the future.

Dana summarized the essence of his argument by stating that the right to capture property on the high seas of persons who resided in enemy territory existed in civil or domestic war. This right had been exercised by an authority that the court must deem competent, and Richmond was territory of the enemy within the meaning of the prize law at the time of the vessels' capture. Dana then requested that the court confirm the lower courts' decisions in all the cases. The arguments on behalf of the United States were thus concluded.

Daniel Lord then gave a short closing rebuttal on behalf of the claimants. He opened by stating that the Prize Court had made a serious error in classifying citizens of Virginia as enemies. An international war was territorial; people living in the territory identified with the sovereign. In a civil war, on the other hand, all the territory remained the domain of the government. Resistance to the government was personal, not territorial. People who resisted the government were committing a criminal act, such as treason. A criminal act could not be imputed from mere residence. It was therefore improper, Lord asserted, to apply international principles to a civil war.

Further, said Lord, an international war had the object of destroying and subduing subjects; the object of a civil war was only to subdue the rebellion with the least damage possible. The court should consider that in a civil war, those who did not take part in the rebellion were still entitled to the rights of loyal citizens. No government had the right to classify them as enemies, and neither did the president. Only Congress had the right to declare war, and this had not been done.

When the *Crenshaw* was captured, a territorial war did not exist. When the governor of Virginia declared that the state had seceded, this was the governor's treason, and it did not make enemies of others who did not act with him. The governor did not represent the claimants. Similarly, it was illegal for the Virginia Legislature to pass an ordinance of secession, because the legislature did not have this power. This legislative act did not represent or bind the claimants.

The only power the president possessed was to use force to put down the rebellion. He could not do anything beyond this, such as confiscate property. Only Congress could do this with a declaration of war. Lord concluded his argument with the request that all properties be returned to the claimants.

THE OPINION OF THE COURT

The judges of the court considered these arguments carefully. On March 10, 1863, the court rendered its decision in an opinion written by Justice Robert C. Grier.

The court was comprised of nine judges at the time of the Prize Cases. President Andrew Jackson had appointed three: Justice James Moore Wayne, Chief Justice Roger B. Taney, and Justice John Catron. President John Tyler had appointed Justice Samuel Nelson, President James K. Polk had appointed Justice Robert C. Grier, and President James Buchanan had appointed Justice Nathan Clifford. President Abraham Lincoln had appointed three to the court: Justices Noah H. Swayne, Samuel F. Miller, and David Davis.

All of these justices were from Northern or border states except Wayne, who came from Georgia. When the Civil War began, Justice John Archibald Campbell from Alabama resigned from the court because of his loyalty to his native state, but Wayne refused to resign. Although Wayne was a slaveowner and felt a loyalty to his native Georgia, he was a fervent supporter of the Union. He and Samuel Nelson were the two justices expert in admiralty law, and this specialty was in particular need at this time. Despite the Northern composition of the court, a majority of the court's members either supported slavery or had Southern leanings.

Justice Grier began his opinion by defining the issues presented by the parties. The first issue was whether the president had the right to institute the blockade based upon the principles of international law. The second issue was whether the property of persons residing within the insurgent states was subject to capture at sea as enemy property.

The facts that the blockade physically existed and that the president was the proper person to institute it had not been disputed, said Grier. The right to prize and capture, however, had to be judged under the law of nations. For a capture to be legitimate, a war must have existed and a neutral must have had notice or other knowledge that one of the parties intended to use this means of coercion against a port in possession of the other.

Did a war exist? Grier pointed out that a normal public war was engaged in by independent nations. However, it was not necessary that both parties should be acknowledged as sovereign states. A war may exist where one of the states claimed sovereign rights against the other. Grier cited as authority Emmerich de Vattel, the Swiss jurist first cited by J. M. Carlisle in his argument on behalf of the claimants. Vattel wrote a book, *The Law of Nations*, in 1758, wherein he applied natural law principles to international relations. His use of natural law to develop a basis for liberty and equality in the law of nations found a wide and sympathetic audience in America. He was considered the authority on international law in the United States, although his major work appeared over 100 years before Grier wrote his decision.

Grier cited Vattel's work to show that a civil war produces in a nation "two independent parties, who consider each as other enemies. . . . Those two parties, therefore, must necessarily, be considered as constituting, at least for a time, two separate bodies, two distinct societies." Vattel went on to describe that these two societies stood precisely in the "same predicament" as two separate nations engaging in war. Vattel emphasized how important it was for these two societies in a civil war to act as nations and adhere to the common laws of war, "those maxims of humanity, moderation and honor."

A civil war was never publicly proclaimed, said Grier, but its actual existence was a fact that the court was bound to notice, in effect taking judicial notice of the war's existence. The true test of a war's existence was that if the regular course of justice was interrupted by insurrection to the point that the courts could not be kept open, then civil war existed. Further, Grier stated that although Congress alone had the power to declare war, there was no clause in the Constitution permitting Congress to declare war against a state or group of states. However, the president, as commander-in-chief of the army, navy, and militia, had the authority to suppress a rebellion under the Acts of Congress passed in 1795 and in 1807. Not only did the president have the authority, but he also was bound to resist an invading force with force without waiting for any special legislative authority. If the hostile force existed as states organized in rebellion, it was nonetheless a war.

Grier pointed out that the battles of Palo Alto and Resaca de la Palma had been fought before Congress declared that a state of war existed with Mexico. Further, it was not necessary that the independence of the revolted states be recognized in order for these states to be considered a belligerent party according to the law of nations. This was affirmed because foreign nations recognized the conflict as a war by their declarations of neutrality. Once a foreign nation had declared its neutrality in the conflict, that nation, or a citizen of that nation, was estopped to deny the existence of war.

The president was the sole judge as to whether the hostility that the nation had encountered was of such alarming proportion as would necessitate the classification of the hostile group as belligerents, said Grier. The court would be controlled by this decision made in the political department of the government where it was entrusted. Grier then stated that the proclamation of a blockade was, in itself, conclusive evidence that a state of war existed that authorized recourse to such a measure. If this were not enough, Congress, at its extraordinary session, ratified all acts of the president as though they were made by Congress itself. If there were any defects in the way the president acted, this ratification by Congress cured these defects. This cure, if needed, acted retroactively.

In answer to the first issue, the court was of the opinion that the president had the right to institute a blockade of ports in possession of the states in rebellion that neutral countries were bound to honor. Grier therefore held that the civil conflict, a conflict not between sovereigns, was a war as defined by international law, and that the blockade was legal beginning with Lincoln's proclamation of April 19, 1861.

Then Grier turned to the question of what was included in the term *enemy's* property. He referred to the claimants' argument that the term *enemy* could be applied only to those subjects or citizens of a foreign sovereign at war with our own country. The claimants cited ancient common law for this definition. The claimants further contended that insurrection is an individual thing, that confiscation of property cannot be accomplished unless that individual was convicted of some offense. Further, state secession ordinances were not effective in changing an individual's allegiance to the national government. The rights given by the national government were still effective to these individuals. Therefore, it would be unconstitutional to condemn the property of these citizens.

In response, Grier cited the Constitution, which states that although citizens owe supreme allegiance to the Federal government, they owe "qualified allegiance" to the state in which they live, and their person and property are subject to that state's laws. Grier pointed out that the states, which claimed to have jurisdiction over all persons and property within their borders, had asserted the right to sever the relations of all their citizens from their allegiance to the Federal government. These states had attempted to form a new sovereign state claiming recognition from other nations. The boundary of these states was marked by lines of bayonets that could be crossed only by the use of force. "South of this line is enemies' territory," said Grier, "because it is claimed and held in possession by an organized, hostile and belligerent power."

All persons residing within this territory whose property lent strength to the hostile power were liable to be treated as enemies, Grier continued. Whether the capture of this property was legal did not depend on the personal allegiance of the owner. It was the nature of the traffic that classified it as illegal and stamped the property as enemy property. It made no difference if the property was owned by an ally or a citizen of the North.

In answer to the second question of what was classified as enemy property, Grier stated, "The produce of the soil of the hostile territory, as well as other property engaged in the commerce of the hostile power, as the source of its wealth and strength, are always regarded as legitimate prize, without regard to the domicile of the owner, and much more so if he reside and trade within their territory." He then applied these principles to the specific captures before the court.

In the case of the *Brilliante,* Grier indicated that the vessel had adequate warning of the blockade from the officers of the USS *Brooklyn* who first apprehended her. The arguments that the warning of the blockade was not noted on the *Brilliante*'s register were ineffective in this instance. Grier stated that it could not be supposed that the only evidence of warning was the ship's register.

The vessel could destroy a register, or it could keep several registers and destroy the one with the endorsement. Grier held that the *Brilliante* was justly condemned as neutral property for running the blockade, "and which she had once successfully violated."

Regarding the *Crenshaw,* Grier indicated that this was a question of "enemies' property, pure and simple." He held that such of the cargo that came within the definition of enemy property was rightfully condemned. The true owners of the tobacco were difficult to ascertain from the evidence; all of the claimants asserted to be bona fide holders of the bill of lading. It was consistent with the evidence that Ludlum and Watson were the real owners of the primary cargo. Since Ludlum and Watson did business in Richmond, and Watson resided there, Grier held that the property was classified by his status and was enemy property.

The Prize Court had decreed that Lear & Sons were the owners of the ten tierces of tobacco and that it should be restored to them. Grier indicated that this was a poor decision, but since the government had not appealed this decision, it would be affirmed and the ten tierces returned to Lear & Sons of Liverpool. The claim to the thirty tierces of tobacco by Irvin & Company of New York was a more difficult problem. The evidence showed that Irvin & Company had purchased this tobacco before the war broke out, with their own resources, and that the principles in the company were citizens and residents of New York. The government claimed that this property should be condemned because its purchase constituted illegal traffic with the enemy. This was not a sound argument, said Grier, because the tobacco was bought and paid for before the war began. Grier also stated that the secretary of the navy's order permitting fifteen days to withdraw from the blockaded ports should apply to "one of our own citizens" as well as to cargo owned by neutrals. He held that the thirty tierces should be restored to Irvin & Company.

As for the *Hiawatha,* Grier stated that the evidence clearly showed that the Navy and State Departments had given all neutral vessels in the blockaded ports license to depart with their cargoes within fifteen days after the blockade was established. He indicated that all reasonable doubts should be resolved in favor of the claimants; however, the blockade had been effective on April 30, 1861, and a vessel in a blockaded port is presumed to have notice of the effective date of a blockade under the rules of the law of nations. The British Consul had set May 2, 1861, as the effective date of the blockade. Under either date, the vessel was guilty of a breach of the blockade. Grier said that "those concerned, notwithstanding the warnings they received, in their eagerness to realize the profits of a full cargo, took the hazards of the adventure, and must now bear the consequences." He again dismissed the argument that there had been no warning endorsed on her register, saying that this applies only to vessels approaching a line of blockade in ignorance of its existence. Grier held that the cargo must share the fate of the vessel, affirming the Circuit Court's judgment condemning the vessel and cargo.

Considering the *Amy Warwick,* Grier observed that all of the claimants at the time of capture, and for a long time before, were residents of Richmond and were engaged in business there. Grier held that the vessel and cargo were enemy property, affirming the judgment of the Circuit Court condemning the property.

Justice Samuel Nelson wrote a long opinion dissenting from Grier's opinion as it applied to the *Hiawatha.* He insisted that a neutral vessel, according to international law, could not have legal notice of a blockade until it had been warned off. A lawful seizure could not be made until a vessel, once warned, made a second attempt to enter or leave a port. Nelson also stressed a second point. According to the law of nations, there was no existing war between the United States and the states in insurrection until it was recognized by Congress on July 13, 1861. Nelson insisted that the president does not possess the powers to declare war, or even to recognize its existence within the meaning of the law of nations and create belligerent rights. Consequently, Nelson insisted, the president had no right to create a blockade causing the capture of vessels and cargoes. Therefore, it was his opinion that all captures prior to July 13 were illegal and void, and because the decrees of condemnation in the cases before the court all applied to captures prior to that date, the vessels and cargoes should be returned to the claimants.

Chief Justice Roger B. Taney, Justice John Catron, Justice Nathan Clifford, and Justice Samuel Nelson all dissented from the majority in the case of the *Brilliante,* but without opinion.

Historians and political scientists have widely held to the conclusion that the decision in the Prize Cases was a close five-to-four decision on the issue of whether the blockade was valid between April 19 and July 13, 1861, from the date of President Lincoln's proclamation of the blockade to the date when Congress ratified the president's acts. The issue of presidential powers often becomes involved in these analyses.

This apparently is not a true reflection of what took place in the court's proceedings, however. Nelson's dissent, rendered in the *Hiawatha* case but by its wording applicable to all four cases, supported the argument that a legal blockade did not go into effect until Congress recognized that a war existed in its special session of July 13. However, the dissents of Taney, Catron, and Clifford were not in concurrence with Nelson's dissent in the *Hiawatha* case; rather, they were given in the *Brilliante* case, and Nelson entered into a second dissent with the other three dissenting justices in that case.

Since these dissents were not supported by written opinions, we do not know the actual basis of their objections to the majority. It is interesting to note that there was one matter that distinguished the *Brilliante* case from the others, that being Carlisle's pleading that the Treaty of Guadalupe Hidalgo of 1848 with Mexico guaranteed that the ports would be open to trade with Mexico. The justices who dissented may have been reluctant to participate in a decision that could have violated the terms of that treaty.

Therefore, although the vote of the court in the *Brilliante* case was five to four, the other cases were all eight-to-one decisions supporting the majority.

This decision upheld the legality of the blockade of the Southern ports and allowed it to continue. This was one of the more important decisions reached by the court. If the court had held otherwise—that a war in the international sense did not exist in a civil conflict, and therefore the acts of war, such as the blockade, were illegal—Congress would have had no alternative but to declare war under its constitutional powers. Had this been done, it would have raised the specter of the recognition of the Confederate States of America as a sovereign power. This in turn could have influenced the formal recognition of the Confederacy by England, France, and other foreign powers. If these recognitions, with their implications, had been forthcoming, the outcome of the war may have been very different.

Chapter Two

Running the Blockade

When President Lincoln initiated the blockade of all ports of the states involved in the insurrection on April 19, 1861, the U.S. Navy was not in good enough condition to enforce such a large assignment.

The Union navy possessed approximately ninety vessels. Half of these were sailing vessels, considered obsolete for blockade service. The rest were steam-driven ships, but most of the fighting ships were either out of commission or assigned to foreign duty.[1]

One of the first tasks of the new secretary of the navy, Gideon Welles, was to acquire vessels as fast as possible and equip them for blockade duty. Agents of the navy acquired anything that could float and be mounted with one or two cannons. A strange conglomeration of former fishing schooners, tugs, whalers, and ferryboats set out to enforce the blockade.

In the meantime, the navy ordered twenty-four 500-ton vessels (each of which could be fully constructed in three months), the so-called "90 day gunboats," several deep-sea cruisers, and forty-seven "double enders," vessels with rudders and pilot houses at both ends. These vessels were suitable to pursue blockade runners into river channels where it was difficult to turn about. They undertook the task of enforcing the blockade along the 3,500 miles of the Southern coastline and were assigned to squadrons divided among the North Atlantic, the South Atlantic, and the Gulf.

At first, businesses in the Confederacy, with full approval of the government, inadvertently aided the blockade by developing a policy to withhold the exporting of cotton. Confederate leaders, convinced that "cotton was king," believed that this policy would cause the English mills to run short of cotton. The Confederacy would then be in a position to demand recognition of the Confederate States of America before they would resume shipments. This policy failed. During the years prior to the war, England had built up a large surplus of cotton, so the embargo became meaningless.

Nevertheless, this failed policy did not prevent the Union from claiming that the reduction in cotton reaching all European ports was because of the

Vessels built as blockade runners were sleek sidewheelers, fast and of low draft, painted gray to blend with the ocean colors. Their captains burned anthracite coal, if they could acquire it, so that they would not leave a smoke trail. The blockade runners could not tolerate the weight of armaments, nor did they have the space for them.

effectiveness of the blockade. This was important, because under international law, a blockade must be effective to be legal; it couldn't be just a blockade on paper.

It did not take long for the citizens of the Confederacy and other countries to discover that large profits could be made from successfully running the blockade. Soon vessels were constructed specially for that purpose, primarily in England and Scotland. They were sleek sidewheelers, fast and of low draft, painted gray to blend with ocean colors. If possible, they burned anthracite coal, which didn't leave telltale smoke. Because these vessels could not tolerate the weight of armaments, or afford the space they would occupy, the ships were totally unarmed.

The profit earned from one or two successful trips by one of these vessels could pay the entire cost of the vessel itself. The problem to the Confederacy, however, was that this profit was most easily gained from importing luxuries to be sold to citizens who could afford their high prices. The type of imports the blockade runners tried to bring into the Southern ports were products to make the Southern citizens' lives more comfortable. This did not help the war effort.

The Confederacy attempted to remedy this problem by acquiring government ownership of blockade-running vessels. In 1864, President Davis decreed that private blockade runners must reserve up to 50 percent of their space for products that aided the war effort. In addition, the Confederate Congress passed legislation prohibiting the importation of luxuries. However, these attempts to control imports through the blockade were largely unsuccessful.

The status of any vessel in relationship to the blockade was determined by international law: The blocking forces could not legally intercept any vessel owned by citizens of a neutral country destined for a port in another neutral country. Because of this law, the blockade runners from England and other neutral countries would list their destinations as Halifax, Bermuda, Nassau, Havana, or Matamoros, all neutral ports. Many vessels would touch at these ports, then go on to a Confederate port. Others would unload at these ports and transfer their cargo to a blockade runner, which would head for a blockaded port.

The blockaders were not misled by these deceptions, but Prize Courts were confronted with bending the long-standing doctrines of international law to fit these situations. Soon the U.S. attorney's staff argued to the Prize Courts that if it could be proven that a vessel intended to violate the blockade, even if she was neutral and headed for a neutral port, the vessel and cargo should be subject to a legal capture. And if it could be proven that a neutral vessel was destined for the Confederacy, no matter how she planned to get there, the vessel and her cargo should be subject to a legal capture. This came to be termed the Doctrine of Continuous Voyage.

THE CASE OF THE *CIRCASSIAN*

One of the first such cases concerned a vessel captured in Cuban waters prior to the opinion handed down in the *Prize Cases.* The case involved one of the first sleek blockade runners, the *Circassian.* The ship was named for the people of Circassia, a country in the Caucasus where people were renowned for their physical beauty. She was captured by the *Somerset,* a converted ferryboat that was part of the strange menagerie of early blockading vessels. The *Circassian* tried to evade the former ferryboat but surrendered after Lt. Earl English, captain of the *Somerset,* ordered the placement of two shells fore and aft of the *Circassian,* and a third in her rigging.

A sleek vessel of 1,500 tons displacement, the *Circassian* was of British registry. Zachariah Charles Pearson of London was the listed owner, and Edward Hunter was her master. The vessel was chartered in Paris on February 11, 1862, by J. Soubry, an agent for several merchants. According to the charter agreement, the vessel was to dock at Havre or Bordeaux, load, then proceed with her cargo to Havana, Nassau, or Bermuda. Then, if so ordered by the freighters, she was to continue on to a port in America and run the blockade.

The vessel sailed to Bordeaux, took on a very valuable cargo of merchandise, and departed for Havana. On May 4, 1862, the *Somerset* apprehended her when she passed Matanzas, Cuba, thirty miles east of Havana. Escorted to Key West, the vessel was libeled upon by the United States in the Federal District Court for the Southern District of Florida. District Judge William Marvin, an expert in admiralty law serving his fifteenth year on this court's bench, heard the trial of the case.

Trials in prize cases, except in rare occasions, were heard by a judge without a jury. After carefully considering all the evidence, Judge Marvin gave his decision.[2] He first noted that to be guilty of running the blockade, it was not necessary to attempt to sail through a cordon of blockading vessels. If a vessel sailed for a blockaded port with knowledge and intent to run the blockade, this alone was sufficient grounds for it to be found guilty of attempting to break the blockade. However, the capture had to be made *in delicto*, or while the vessel was committing the illegal act. This was because up until the act was actually being committed, the master could change his mind and commit the vessel to a legal purpose. So whether or not the vessel was captured *in delicto* depended entirely on the provable facts. This law had ample basis in English and American case law and texts on the subject.

Marvin found that the evidence clearly indicated that the ship's owner, master, freighters, and underwriters intended for the vessel to run the blockade of New Orleans, and therefore it was captured *in delicto*. This evidence consisted mainly of letters and papers found on board the vessel. Facts proved that the master had ordered certain papers thrown overboard and had others burned before the officers of the *Somerset* came on board. These actions did not reflect well on the case of those who claimed that the vessel and cargo should go free.

Apparently believing that the letters and papers still on board were harmless personal messages, the master had not destroyed them. This proved to be a mistake. One letter from a businessman in Bordeaux to Carriere & Company in New Orleans stated that a British steamer was to load 1,000 tons of cargo "for your port." The letter went on to detail the cargo of wine, brandy, coffee, and preserved meats. It stated, "This steamer will endeavor to force the blockade." The letter then spoke of insurance rates. The writer indicated that he was sending nothing on the voyage because the voyage was not secret, it being generally known in Paris, London, and Bordeaux that the vessel intended to attempt to run the blockade. Because this was so extensively known in Europe, the writer believed that the Americans would also find out. Other letters, some by the shippers of cargo goods, also stated that the *Circassian* intended to run the blockade.

Along with the letters found on board was a memorandum of affreightment, signed with the authority of the responsible party. It said that the merchandise would be disembarked at New Orleans after engaging to force the blockade. None of the bills of lading, also found with the letters, called for a delivery of the goods to Havana.

Marvin closed his opinion by stating that the parties involved had undertaken a risk and a speculation. Had they been successful, their profits would have been great. However, they had failed and been caught *in delicto*. Therefore, it was not unreasonable for them to submit to the incurred losses. The judge issued a decree condemning the ship and cargo.

The trial of the case was heard by Judge Marvin shortly after the vessel's capture, which took place on May 4, 1862. The claimants, working through the ship's master, Edward Hunter, appealed the decision of condemnation to the U.S. Supreme Court. Because Civil War cases were beginning to crowd the court's docket, the case was not argued until December 20, 1864.[3]

The Arguments before the Court

At this appeal, the claimants were the owners of the ship and cargo. They were represented by three attorneys: Jeremiah Larocque, A. F. Smith, and E. G. Benedict. These attorneys constructed a clever argument, alleging that New Orleans was not subject to a blockade when the *Circassian* was captured. This argument violated one of the prime rules governing appeals: that one cannot argue a point in the Supreme Court that was not at issue at the trial level. The argument of whether there was a legal blockade on New Orleans at the time the *Circassian* was captured had not been mentioned at the trial level. How did the claimants' attorneys get around this?

Judge Marvin had held that the capture of the *Circassian* had to be *in delicto* to be a valid capture. This meant that the vessel actually had to be discovered violating the blockade when apprehended. Marvin had held that clear and unequivocal knowledge and intent to violate the blockade was the equivalent of actually, physically running the blockade.

The claimants' attorneys jumped on this finding. How, they asked, could the capture of the *Circassian* be *in delicto* under the definition given by Judge Marvin if no blockade existed? By raising the issue in this manner, they succeeded in getting the challenge of the blockade's existence before the court.

They argued that the city of New Orleans fell to the Union naval forces on April 25, 1862, and that Forts Jackson and St. Philip, which guarded the river approaches to New Orleans, had fallen two days earlier. On May 1, Gen. Benjamin F. Butler announced by proclamation that the city and its environs, with all of its interior and exterior defenses, had surrendered to the Union forces. This was three days prior to the capture of the *Circassian;* however, this information apparently had not been available when the attorneys were preparing for the condemnation trial before Judge Marvin.

The attorneys argued that a belligerent could not blockade its own ports against a neutral, because under international law this was an embargo, an act of war. They maintained that no matter how guilty the plans of the *Circassian* were, the blockade of New Orleans had ceased with the Union occupation and put an end to the right of capture.

They treated the issue of intent by arguing that even if the blockade had been in existence, the *Somerset* had no right to capture the *Circassian,* because there was no unlawful intent to force the blockade until the decision to run the blockade was made in Havana. Until the *Circassian* reached Havana, its destination was a neutral port. Since the *Circassian* never reached Havana because of her capture, a decision to run the blockade had never been made. This fact alone was sufficient defense against her capture.

The claimants also argued that the *Circassian* had been entitled to a warning that would be entered on her log. She was subject to capture only while forcing the blockade after this warning. They cited President Lincoln's April 19, 1861, proclamation as support.

In closing, they reiterated their main point, that the blockade had come to an end prior to the capture of the *Circassian,* and therefore the vessel was not taken *in delicto* and was not subject to capture. They requested the court to overrule Judge Marvin's District Court decree of condemnation.

Attorney General Edward Bates and a member of his staff, Charles Eames, appeared on behalf of the United States to answer the arguments of the claimants. (Eames used his first initial as his given name.)

First they brought the court's attention to the holding in the *Amy Warwick* case in the Prize Cases that, however the court holds, the cargo consigned to merchants in New Orleans was enemy property subject to condemnation.

Their second point was that under international law, the destruction of the *Circassian*'s papers when the ship was captured, taken in connection with other evidence, provided sufficient grounds to support condemnation.

The government stressed that the *Circassian* was not entitled to first have a warning of the blockade noted on her register. The intended purpose of this warning was to notify a vessel that a blockade existed. Here the requirement had no application, because the *Circassian* had been fully apprised of the blockade before she left Bordeaux.

The balance of the government attorneys' argument rebutted the claimants' argument that the blockade had not existed. The blockade was initiated by President Lincoln's proclamation of April 19, 1861. Once a blockade was so proclaimed by a belligerent government, it continued as long as the blockading forces were present and until a similar proclamation of its termination was made by the blockading government. The president of the United States issued such a proclamation on May 12, 1862, eight days following the capture of the *Circassian.* This showed that the blockade had been in force on the date of the proclamation and would remain in force until June 1. The government's attorneys argued that the content of this proclamation was conclusive upon all the Prize Courts of the United States. The proclamation was issued pursuant to the 5th Section of the Act of Congress on July 13, 1861. The government concluded with this statement.

The Opinion of the Court

The justices took the case under advisement and issued their opinion on January 30, 1865. The opinion was given by Chief Justice Salmon P. Chase, who had taken his oath of office on December 15, 1864, just five days before the arguments in the case were heard. Chase had been appointed to the court as chief justice by President Lincoln to replace Chief Justice Roger B. Taney, who died on October 12, 1864.

The court had also been changed since the *Prize Cases* with the appointment of Justice Stephen J. Field, who had taken his oath of office on December 7, 1863. Field was a well-known attorney, judge, and active politician in

California. He occupied the tenth seat on the court, which was authorized by Congress in 1863. The court was composed of ten justices from the date of Field's oath of office to the death of Justice John Catron on May 30, 1865, except for the two-month period between Taney's death and Chase's appointment. This was the only period in history in which the court was composed of more than nine justices.

Chase first cited the *Prize Cases* to illustrate that a true Civil War existed and that the validity of the blockade could no longer be questioned. No one could complain if the government of the United States had merely closed all the ports seized by the Confederacy; however, out of deference to the principal commercial nations, a commercial blockade defined by international law was instituted. It was expected that such a blockade would be scrupulously respected by neutral nations.

The chief justice then set forth the issues of the case as he perceived them: whether New Orleans was blockaded on May 4, 1862, and whether the *Circassian* intended to violate the blockade.

Regarding the first issue, he posed the question of whether the capture of the river forts and the city itself had terminated the blockade. He answered that the capture of the forts did not terminate the blockade, but made the blockade more complete and absolute. At the time of the capture of the *Circassian,* only the city of New Orleans was occupied, not the port of New Orleans. The city was still hostile, with Confederate forces in the neighborhood. Such an occupation could not suspend the blockade.

Chase described the differences between a simple blockade and a public blockade: A simple blockade could be established by an officer acting under direction of his superiors, whereas a public blockade was established by the government notifying other governments. In the case of a simple blockade, the captors had the burden of proof to show the court that a blockade existed. In the case of a public blockade, the claimants of the ship and cargo had to prove that the blockade was discontinued. The blockade of New Orleans was a public blockade and was not released until its revocation was conveyed to other governments. The chief justice cited English cases to support the proposition that the blockade existed until other governments were notified by the U.S. government. Since this was not done until May 12, 1862, and the notification stated that the blockade of New Orleans would not be lifted until June 1, the blockade had still been in effect when the *Circassian* was captured.

The court then considered whether the *Circassian* had been subject to capture for a violation of the blockade on May 4, 1862. Chase again cited U.S. and English cases. These cases held that a vessel sailing from a neutral port with knowledge that a blockade existed and intent to enter a blockaded port subjected that vessel and cargo to capture and condemnation. The chief justice approved that rule, stating that steam and electricity had made all nations neighbors. Further, blockade running from neutral ports had become a profession, so such a rule was necessary to protect belligerent rights.

Chase recited the facts as revealed by evidence presented to Judge Marvin in the trial court. These facts, combined with the destruction of other records at the time of capture, compelled a belief of guilty intent at the time of sailing and capture. It was possible that the owners of the vessel and cargo may have changed their minds in Havana and decided not to run the blockade. This, however, did not change the fact that the *Circassian* had intended to run the blockade at the time that it was captured. This intention was all that was necessary to permit a legal capture and condemnation. The decree of the District Court given by Judge Marvin condemning the *Circassian* and her cargo as a lawful prize of war was affirmed.

Justice Samuel Nelson gave a dissenting opinion. First, he recited that the evidence was certainly sufficient to show that the *Circassian* intended to run the blockade, and that this had been the intent from the inception of the voyage. The basis of his dissent was that he believed no blockade existed at New Orleans at the time of the *Circassian*'s seizure. Nelson recited the dates of the military occupation of the environs of New Orleans and of the city itself. He pointed out that General Butler announced by proclamation on May 1, 1862, that the city of New Orleans and its exterior and interior defenses had surrendered to the combined land and naval forces of the United States. Nelson insisted that to continue the blockade beyond the military occupation was inconsistent with international law, citing an 1807 English case as support for this view. He said that no proclamation terminating the blockade was necessary. The recapture of the city was public and notorious, and foreign nations were bound to take notice of the change of status.

Nelson then demonstrated an interesting long-term approach to the issues. He stated that a belligerent tends to press the right of blockade beyond its proper limits. This unwittingly aided in the establishment of rules that were later found to be a hardship when the belligerent became a neutral. He felt that the doctrine set out by the majority of the court was a step in that direction, so he was unwilling to concur in the opinion of the majority.

It is interesting to note that the U.S. Navy converted the *Circassian* to a supply ship, carrying needed ammunition and provisions to all the squadrons of the blockading forces. Her home port was Boston, and she served in this capacity until the end of the war.

In the *Circassian* case, the court held that if the evidence of the case clearly indicated that the vessel intended to run the blockade, even though the vessel was of neutral register destined for a neutral port, the vessel and cargo were subject to legal capture and condemnation.

But what if evidence of intent to run the blockade was not present, yet the vessel's cargo was of such a suspicious nature that even an unbiased person would conclude that the cargo was destined for the Confederacy? This situation was the basis for the establishment of the Doctrine of Continuous Voyage. The first and leading case establishing this doctrine for the Civil War period was that of the steamship *Bermuda*.

THE CASE OF THE *BERMUDA*

The *Bermuda* was built in 1861 at Stockton-upon-Tees, on the east coast of England. In August of that year, Edwin Haigh filed a declaration of ownership, required by the British Merchants' Shipping Act of 1854. In this declaration, he listed himself as a citizen of England and the sole and exclusive owner of the vessel. E. L. Tessier was listed as master of the vessel. A certificate of registry was issued based upon this information.

Shortly thereafter, Haigh executed a power of attorney authorizing Allen S. Hanckel or George A. Trenholm of Charleston, South Carolina, to sell the vessel within a twelve-month period anywhere outside the kingdom. The price was left up to Hanckel or Trenholm. This power of attorney was sent to Charleston to John Foster & Company, a shipping and banking firm. Trenholm was a partner in Fraser, Trenholm & Company, the Liverpool branch of this firm.

To generate business and demonstrate to English merchants that the Union blockade was ineffective, the *Bermuda* was sent to Charleston on her first voyage, laden with weapons and general supplies. Apparently finding the port too well guarded by blockading vessels, the *Bermuda* went on to Savannah, where it slipped into the port without being seen. The vessel returned triumphantly to England in January 1862, making a sizable profit for the merchants who had participated in the voyage.

The *Bermuda* was loaded at Liverpool in February 1862 to undertake her second voyage under direction of Fraser, Trenholm & Company, whose Charleston branch of John Fraser & Company had become a depository and agent of the Confederacy at Richmond. A man by the name of Westendorff, who had arrived in Liverpool from Charleston in the previous December, replaced Tessier as master of the vessel. Tessier had become master of the *Bahama,* which three months later supplied guns and munitions to the Confederate raider *Alabama.* Most people connected with the second voyage regarded Fraser, Trenholm & Company as the *Bermuda*'s owner.

The *Bermuda*'s cargo consisted of eighty tons of cannons, guns in cases, shells, fuses, and carriages for guns. In addition, there were seven cases of pistols, twenty-one cases of swords, seventy barrels of cartridges, and 300 whole barrels, 78 half barrels, and 280 quarter barrels of gunpowder. The vessel also carried printing presses with printing materials, paper, and Confederate States postage stamps, which were obtained in Scotland by an agent of the Confederate government. Accompanying the printing equipment were several printers and engravers, who were referred to as "government passengers" and were added to the crew list under assumed names.

The *Bermuda* departed Liverpool on March 1, 1862, headed for the island of Bermuda. The cargo was to be delivered in Bermuda to specific designees or their assigns according to the bills of lading. The ship arrived at the port of St. George in Bermuda on March 19. She remained there for five weeks, awaiting further orders. The orders came from Fraser, Trenholm & Company on April 1, instructing Westendorff to take the *Bermuda* to Nassau. The *Bermuda* departed for Nassau on April 23. Four days out of St. George, the *Bermuda* was captured prior to reaching her Nassau destination.

When captured, the crew of the *Bermuda* threw two small boxes of papers and a package overboard. The boxes purportedly contained bills of lading and invoices; the package held Confederate postage stamps. In addition, a bag of letters was burned by the master's brother under the direction of the master. One of the passengers also burned letters.

The vessel was taken to the port of Philadelphia and libeled upon in the District Court of the United States for the Eastern District of Pennsylvania as a prize of war. The evidence was presented in a hearing before Judge John Cadwalader. He condemned both cargo and vessel, reserving for a future proceeding whether more evidence would be permitted pertaining to a residue of the cargo. This reservation was apparently caused by Alexander T. Blakely, who claimed that he, not Fraser, Trenholm & Company, owned the cannons on the *Bermuda*. He requested the right to submit further proof of his ownership and proof that the cannons were supposed to be legitimately unloaded at one of the neutral ports. Despite this reservation, this decree was considered final, and Edwin Haigh, who claimed the vessel, and Alexander T. Blakely and Fraser, Trenholm & Company, who claimed the cargo, appealed to the U.S. Supreme Court.[4]

The Arguments before the Court

Attorneys George M. Wharton and W. B. Reed represented the claimants Edwin Haigh, Alexander T. Blakely, and Fraser, Trenholm & Company. Attorney General James Speed and a deputy from his office, Titian J. Coffey, represented the United States.

The arguments on behalf of both parties were first made during the term of court that began in December 1864. The court acknowledged that the issues were fully and ably argued, but admitted that certain issues of fact and law were troubling. Because the justices of the court deemed these issues very important, they ordered the counsel of the parties to reargue the case in the term of the court that began in December 1865. Pursuant to this order, counsel appeared before the court and reargued the case on January 9, 1866.

Wharton and Reed began by stressing one of the more important rules of international law: that a neutral vessel traveling from one neutral port to another neutral port was not liable to capture by a belligerent. Edwin Haigh, a natural-born British subject, was listed as owner of the *Bermuda* on the vessel's certificate of registry. Further, the *Bermuda* was sailing from St. George to Nassau, both neutral ports. To be eligible for capture, the *Bermuda* would have to have been headed for Charleston or another blockaded port, with the clear intent to run the blockade. Furthermore, the capture of the *Bermuda* while the vessel was between the two neutral ports was consistent with the assertion of a blockade of Nassau. This could not be done, because a belligerent can never blockade a neutral port under international law. The *Bermuda* should have been at perfect liberty to navigate among all the ports of the British West India Islands without threat of capture.

They argued that there could be no assertion of a continued voyage unless there was clear evidence that the *Bermuda* was on its way to a blockaded port, with Nassau merely an intermediate stop. There was no such evidence. The shipping articles and the captain's letter of instructions clearly indicated that a violation of the blockade was not planned.

The claimants' attorneys argued that British merchants had the right to trade between their own ports, even in military stores. They also had the right to sell goods of all sorts to the Confederacy at any of their ports, even if these merchants knew that these goods would be used in a war against the United States. The rules of international law permitted a neutral to sell munitions of war to either belligerent in his own territory. Applying this to the *Bermuda,* no questions could be raised pertaining to the military supplies carried by the *Bermuda* unless the vessel was on a voyage to a blockaded port.

Moving on, they insisted that the control exhibited by John Fraser & Company of Charleston over the voyage of the vessel did not clothe that company with ownership. The power of attorney from Edwin Haigh was recognized, but not coupled with an interest in the sense that it granted an interest in the *Bermuda* to the agents. This was stressed to the court, because if it had been coupled with an interest, the power of attorney would have been irrevocable. Not accompanied with an interest, it was revocable at any time. Since the evidence did not show any transfer of funds to Edwin Haigh as consideration for the sale of the vessel, it was likely that the power of attorney had been revoked.

Wharton and Reed admitted that the spoliation of the papers was cause in itself for condemnation of the vessel and cargo. However, this constituted proof only against the parties committing the spoliation if they had an interest in the vessel or cargo. Because there was no proof whatsoever that the spoliation of the papers was authorized by Haigh, or that it was conducted for his benefit, the spoliation of the papers should not be considered as determinative of condemnation of the vessel and cargo.

The attorneys for the claimants delved deeply into ancient international law. They argued that the capture of the *Bermuda* was not justified for the following reasons: It was made within the range of modern cannon shot from British territory; it was made within the space made by a line drawn due south from the nearest headland on the island of Abaco to just above the place of capture; it was made in channel waters between islands owned by Great Britain; and it was made before actual search of the vessel. They closed their argument by citing numerous cases, texts, and legal works that they believed supported their arguments.

Attorney General James Speed and Titian J. Coffey replied to the claimants' arguments on behalf of the United States. Their first point was a vigorous attack on the claimants' insistence that the *Bermuda* was protected from capture because it was a neutral vessel carrying a neutral cargo to a neutral port. They argued that Edwin Haigh was not the owner of the vessel, but had transferred ownership of the vessel to John Fraser & Company by means of the power of attorney given to George A. Trenholm and Allen S. Hanckel, citizens of the Confederacy living in Charleston, South Carolina.

The attorneys for the government pointed out that it was George A. Trenholm's firm, Fraser, Trenholm & Company, a branch of John Fraser & Company, that initiated and planned the voyage. The chief engineer and firemen of the *Bermuda* testified in depositions that Fraser, Trenholm & Company was the true owner of the vessel. If Edwin Haigh were the owner, there would have to be something in writing showing that Fraser, Trenholm & Company were Haigh's agents. Nothing like this ever existed.

They argued that if all the papers had been preserved, not thrown overboard or burned, the true ownership of the vessel and cargo would have been disclosed. Certainly, if these papers had been favorable to the claimants, showing Edwin Haigh as the vessel's owner, they wouldn't have been destroyed. The shipping articles were the only papers left on board that showed Haigh as the vessel's owner, but these were falsified by listing the printing and engraving employees of the Confederacy as crew members under assumed names.

Even if Haigh were the owner of the vessel, they argued, the *Bermuda* was still subject to capture. The *Bermuda* could qualify as a neutral ship proceeding to a neutral port only if her cargo were meant to be unloaded at its destination and become part of the mass of goods at that port. If, however, the vessel had taken on a contraband cargo destined in reality for a belligerent port, it was subject to capture because the continuity of the voyage could not be interrupted by touching at an intermediate neutral port.

As to the rules of international law cited by the claimants' attorneys that the *Bermuda* was illegally captured because the capture took place within the range of modern cannon shot from British territory, and the related arguments, the U.S. attorneys argued that no facts had been introduced at the trial level that would enable the court to rule on these points. Consequently, Speed and Coffey concluded by requesting the court not to consider these arguments.

The Opinion of the Court
Chief Justice Salmon P. Chase gave the opinion of the court on March 12, 1866.[5] He opened by referring to the court's request that counsel for the parties were ordered to argue the case twice. This had caused an exhaustive and thorough discussion of the questions of fact and law presented by the case. He assured counsel that the issues raised had been given the most deliberate consideration by the court.

First the chief justice wanted to dispose of questions concerning the steamship's ownership. He reviewed the vessel's history and acknowledged that Edwin Haigh was listed as the vessel's owner on the certificate of registry. The power of attorney given to residents of Charleston, South Carolina, had been granted for a term of twelve months, and there was no evidence in the court file that it had ever been revoked.

These acts certainly brought the ownership of the vessel into doubt. Haigh may have been the true owner of the *Bermuda* initially, but it was strange that he was in such haste to remove the vessel from his own neutral control to the control and absolute power of the enemies of the United States. From this early date on, Fraser, Trenholm & Company made all of the decisions pertaining to the ship and was regarded as the vessel's owners by the people who dealt with the company. The insistence of Fraser, Trenholm & Company that Edwin Haigh was the real owner of the vessel was questionable, because the company had no charter or other written authority to represent Haigh.

The facts showed that John Fraser & Company or its Liverpool branch, Fraser, Trenholm & Company, directed the voyage of the *Bermuda* by means of a series of letters. No ownership could have exercised more absolute control over the ship and cargo than these companies demonstrated.

Chase said that if the vessel's papers had not been destroyed, the true ownership of the vessel would have been revealed. This act of spoliation was an unusual aggravation and warranted the most unfavorable inferences as to the *Bermuda*'s ownership, employment, and destination.

When the evidence was taken as a whole, it clearly indicated that the vessel had been sold in Charleston under the power of attorney to John Fraser & Company. The apparent title reflected by the British papers remained in the name of Edwin Haigh as a pretense and cover. Under these conditions, the chief justice held that the vessel and cargo were rightly condemned as enemy property.

Then Chase followed the suggested direction of the U.S. attorneys. He posed the question of the status of the condemnation of the *Bermuda* if Haigh were assumed to be the vessel's true owner. He agreed that neutral trade was entitled to protection in all courts. Neutral ships were permitted to convey any goods, including contraband, from one neutral port to another neutral port if they were intended for actual delivery at the port of destination and would become part of the common stock of the country or port of destination. However, a neutral ship could not take contraband ostensibly to a neutral port when in actuality the contraband was destined for a belligerent port by either the same ship or another ship. This subjected the vessel to seizure from the commencement to the end of the voyage. The character of the *Bermuda*'s cargo made it obvious that she was headed to a Rebel port. Transshipment at Nassau, if such were intended, could not break the continuity of the voyage.

The chief justice reviewed the history of this doctrine. In considering whether the neutral port was the actual port of destination, he cited a famous British judge. In a case in 1800,[6] Sir William Scott held that the landing and warehousing of goods and the payment of importation duties were sufficient to make that port a destination of the original voyage. A subsequent exportation to a belligerent port was then lawful. In an 1806 case,[7] Sir William Grant reviewed all the cases with these facts and held that the landing of goods and payment of duties did not interrupt the continuity of the voyage unless there was an honest intention to bring the cargo into the common stock of the country. Chase held that this was still the law that governed the ultimate fate of the cargo of the *Bermuda*.

The status of the *Bermuda* itself was separate from its cargo. In a situation such as the *Bermuda* found itself in, it was possible that the owner of the vessel was ignorant of the ulterior destination and had not chartered his ship with a belligerent destination in mind. In this situation, the vessel could not be condemned.

That was not, however, the situation with the *Bermuda*. First, the contraband cargo was ready for immediate use in battle. Second, Haigh turned over the vessel to enemies of the United States without even denying knowledge of their intentions. It was highly probable that the vessel was actually in the service of the Confederate government.

Chase held that the *Bermuda,* despite her stop at a neutral port and her intended stop at a second neutral port, was on one continuous voyage from Liverpool to a blockaded port. It was therefore subject to capture at any time following its departure from Liverpool.

As to the allegations made by the claimants that the *Bermuda* was captured within cannon shot range of neutral territory, he agreed with the attorneys for the United States and indicated that it was not necessary to examine these questions because there was nothing in the evidence that could prove that the *Bermuda* was within this range.

The chief justice confirmed the condemnation of the *Bermuda* and its cargo, even if both were neutral. Thus the decree of the U.S. District Court for the Eastern District of Pennsylvania was affirmed.

District Court Judge John Cadwalader had reserved a final judgment pertaining to part of the *Bermuda*'s cargo pending the results of the Supreme Court appeal. This part of the case was returned to Judge Cadwalader following the opinion of Chief Justice Chase. This reservation was based on an affidavit filed by Alexander T. Blakely, in which he claimed he was the rightful owner of the cannons on board the *Bermuda,* and that it was his honest intent that they be unloaded at one of the neutral ports. Blakely had requested that he be allowed to submit more evidence in this regard. Cadwalader observed that the matters in the affidavit had no substance, because the cannons were carried in the hold of the vessel and used as ballast. To unload the cannons, the entire cargo would have to be unloaded first. Cadwalader held that he didn't need further proof, because Blakely's entire claim of ownership was unbelievable, and condemned the balance of the cargo that consisted of the cannons. Thus the epic of the *Bermuda* came to an end.

The *Bermuda* case solidified the Doctrine of Continuous Voyage for the Civil War period. In cases that followed, the captured vessels' owners were careful to plead that they were unaware of the ultimate destinations of the cargoes. Based upon Chief Justice Chase's statements in the *Bermuda* case that such owners should not lose their vessels to condemnation, many owners emerged from the proceedings with the vessels returned to them, though their cargoes were confiscated.

THE CASE OF THE *GREY JACKET*

Another defense that claimants used to attempt to maintain the ownership of their vessels and cargoes was that they somehow were justified in attempting to run the blockade. This defense took many forms. Occasionally the owner of a vessel captured in the area of the Rio Grande would claim that he had anchored in neutral water to unload a cargo destined for Matamoros, but the wind blew his ship into Texas waters. Several owners claimed that they had a license to break the blockade given by some official of the government. Others, citing international law, claimed that their vessels had sustained storm damage so severe that it was an unavoidable necessity that they put into a blockaded port for repairs. But the rules of the Prize Courts made a defense of justification particularly difficult to plead successfully.

Prize Courts were like no other courts in the United States. Their procedures more closely resembled the civil courts of Europe than those of Anglo-American common law. Prize Courts applied international law to the facts before them, relying on cases decided in Prize Courts of other nations as well as the United States. The decisions rendered in the U.S. Prize Courts became influential in the determination of cases in the Prize Courts of all maritime countries.

International law dictated that a vessel captured while running a blockade must be "taken home." Home normally was the closest U.S. port that had a Prize Court or one close by. To accomplish this, the captain of the capturing vessel would appoint a prize master and prize crew from his own crew to run the ship to port. The capturing vessel would take possession of all the captured vessel's papers and records, and accompany the vessel to port.

When the captured vessel put into port, it was the duty of the prize master to report to the Prize Court, probably by calling upon the U.S. attorney. The Prize Court would immediately appoint one or two prize commissioners to take possession of the captured vessel. The U.S. attorney would then file a libel, the first pleading with the court, asking that the vessel be condemned as a prize of war. Contemporaneously, preparatorios, or interrogatories and depositions, would be taken from the captured vessels' officers, some seamen, and the claimants. These consisted of testimony or the answering of questions under oath, reduced to writing. The court would issue and publish monitions, or notices, as to the time and place of the hearing to everyone who may have an interest in the case.

The hearing was held promptly. The capturing vessel was expected to be back on blockade duty as rapidly as possible. Also, the captain and crew of the captured vessel, if no basis could be found to condemn the ship and its cargo, wanted to resume their trip as soon as a decree was rendered. The hearing was therefore what is termed a "summary" hearing. The only evidence that the court would consider was the captured vessel's papers and the depositions and interrogatories taken in preparatorio. The claimants, who consisted of the owners of the vessel and cargo, had the burden of proving that the ship was not subject to condemnation. The judge would examine the ship's papers and the interrogatories and depositions, listen to the arguments of the attorneys pertaining to this evidence, and make his decision. If the judge did not feel that he could make a decision based upon this evidence, he would require the parties to submit further proof. The judge would stay the hearing until this further proof, usually additional affidavits and other documents such as letters and invoices found on the captured vessel, could be produced.

One or more of the parties to the case could move the court for the opportunity to submit further proof. However, the Prize Courts were very reluctant to require further proof or to grant motions by the parties to submit further proof. This is what made pleading of a justification for running the blockade difficult. A justification, of whatever type, would normally not be reflected in the ship's papers, and possibly only cursorily in the depositions. The only way a party could get the facts pertaining to justification would be to file a motion for further proof, but these motions were normally denied.

The decision of the court was *in rem,* meaning that it affected property only. In these cases, this included the vessels and cargoes. The decisions made in these cases had nothing to do with people. If a decision was made to condemn the captured vessel and its cargo, the original ownership was transferred to the United States.

One of the more interesting cases where justification for running the blockade was used as a defense is that of the steamboat *Grey Jacket.*

Timothy Meaher was born in Maine. He had made his home in Alabama for thirty years, his permanent home in Mobile. An imaginative and hard-working man, he developed and operated a successful cotton plantation and commercial sawmill.

In 1862, he developed a novel and unique marketing strategy with his brother, "J. M." Meaher. Their plan included the building of a steam vessel on Timothy's land. When launched, they intended to load it with cotton from Timothy's plantation, together with additional cotton that they would buy, and ship the cotton to market at Havana, Cuba. Timothy Meaher's true motives are not clear, though he may have been having difficulty selling his cotton.

The brothers wasted no time and undertook the construction of a vessel they named the *Grey Jacket.* They cut the lumber in Timothy's sawmill from their own forest stands. This activity was soon brought to the attention of the Confederate government.

The brothers were soon visited by a Confederate ordnance officer named Meyers. Meyers warned Timothy that the *Grey Jacket,* if completed, would not be cleared to exit the Mobile harbor unless the Meahers entered into a contract with the Confederate government agreeing that half the cotton carried by the vessel would be owned by the Confederate government. Meyers offered Confederate cotton, but the Meahers agreed to share their cotton, which was already baled and in place, ready to load.

The contract called for the *Grey Jacket* to take the cotton to Havana and then return to Mobile or some other Confederate port. On the return trip, half of the carrying capacity of the vessel was to be reserved to carry essential military cargo that would be used in the Confederate war effort. Realizing they had no choice, the Meahers signed the contract.

The brothers launched the *Grey Jacket* successfully and made ready for the journey. They hired a crew, with Timothy Meaher as master. The crew loaded the vessel, now of 200 tons displacement, with 513 bales of cotton, twenty-five boxes of rosin, and small amounts of turpentine and tobacco.

The *Grey Jacket* slipped out of Mobile Bay under cover of darkness on December 30, 1863. The exits from the bay were closely guarded by the vessels of the Union Southern Blockading Squadron. The watch on one of these vessels, the US steamer *Kennebeck,* thought he detected shadows of an exiting vessel and decided to investigate by pursuing the sighting. The next morning, the *Kennebeck* overtook the *Grey Jacket* about sixty miles from Mobile Bay, headed directly for Havana. Lieutenant Commander McCann, captain of the *Kennebeck,* ordered a shot across the bow of the *Grey Jacket.*

The crew hauled down its colors and hove to. The *Kennebeck* took possession of the vessel and turned it over to a prize crew under a prize master named Emerson. The prize crew took the *Grey Jacket* into New Orleans, where she was libeled on February 26, 1864, as a prize of war in the U.S. District Court for the Eastern District of Louisiana.

The notices were duly issued. Timothy Meaher intervened as a claimant of the vessel and cargo on March 21. Though his intervening documents were meant to be a true claim, Meaher included several allegations that were in the nature of an answer in a domestic civil suit. This did not conform to Prize Court practice, and on the motion of the U.S. attorney, Meaher's allegations in the nature of an answer were stricken from the record. The judge, however, gave Meaher leave to file an affidavit in addition to his previous in preparatorio deposition. This affidavit was filed on August 29, after the District Court hearing.

The case was heard on the basis of the depositions and other preparatory proofs and papers. Meaher testified in his deposition, a different document from the affidavit, that the *Grey Jacket* had been bound for Havana, where the trip would end. However, if he had arrived safely in Havana, he had intended to ship the cotton to a port where he could obtain a better price. Meaher also testified that he was the sole owner of the vessel and cargo. But depositions of the mate and engineer of the vessel stated that Meaher and his brother owned the vessel, and that the Confederacy owned half of the cargo. The mate, named Flynn, testified that the *Grey Jacket* tried to leave the Port of Mobile secretly.

At the close of the hearing, Meaher moved the court for leave to introduce further proof. This motion was denied. The court then entered a judgment condemning both the vessel and cargo. Timothy Meaher appealed to the U.S. Supreme Court.[8]

The Appeal to the Supreme Court
Timothy Meaher's appeal to the U.S. Supreme Court in the *Grey Jacket* case was one of the more unusual appeals made to this court. It was not clear whether the affidavit the District Court gave Meaher leave to file was filed before or after the District Court hearing. Since it was filed six months after the

libel, and the District Court did not refer to the second affidavit during the course of its hearing, it is likely that it was filed either after the hearing or just before the hearing, and that it formed the basis of Meaher's motion for leave to introduce further proof. This motion was denied.

Following the District Court hearing, Meaher applied to the U.S. secretary of the Treasury, an unusual move. Meaher convinced the secretary that he was a loyal citizen of the United States, that he had taken the oath of loyalty to the United States pursuant to the president's proclamation of December 8, 1863, and that he was simply attempting to move his cotton out of the Confederacy to a loyal state. Meaher stated that he intended to disavow the contract with the Confederate government as soon as he was out of the jurisdiction of Confederate laws. Under terms of the Federal statute of July 13, 1861, the secretary of the Treasury believed he could remit all of the rights of the United States to the condemned vessel and cargo to Meaher. After considering the information submitted by Meaher, this was done by the secretary of the Treasury by warrant under his hand and the seal of his office.

With his remission and his second affidavit as a basis, Meaher petitioned the Supreme Court itself for an order for further proof. In a very unusual move, the Supreme Court consented to receive the petition and hear arguments as to whether it would permit further proof. This consent was clearly contrary to the court's traditions and its own rules, and was probably made because another department of the government was involved. Because the secretary of the Treasury wanted to defend its decision to remit the vessel and cargo to Meaher, a decision that would effectively overrule the District Court before the Supreme Court heard the case, the secretary of the Treasury desired that its point of view be argued in the Supreme Court hearing. This could be done only if an attorney for the Treasury Department was allowed to argue the secretary of the Treasury's case. To allow a new principal party in the case at the Supreme Court level also did not comply with the court's own rules.

To overcome this hurdle, the Treasury Department filed a separate case in the District Court asking that an attorney for the Treasury Department be allowed to appear in the condemnation case appeal on behalf of Timothy Meaher. This request was summarily denied by the District Court. The Treasury Department then appealed this case to the Supreme Court. The arguments in that case were heard and decided on the same day as, but prior to, the condemnation case. Chief Justice Salmon P. Chase gave the opinion on behalf of a unanimous court. He held in a two-paragraph opinion that in cases where the United States was a party and was represented by the attorney general or an attorney under the attorney general, no counsel could be heard in opposition on behalf of any other department of the government. In this case, however, because it was the impression of the bar that counsel representing the Treasury Department would be heard, and the court was desirous to receive "all the light that can be derived from the fullest discussion," the court held that counsel for the Treasury Department could be heard in the appeal of the condemnation case.

Thus, in addition to the other strange aspects of this case, two separate departments of the U.S. government opposed each other: the Justice Department, represented by the U.S. attorney general, and the Department of the Treasury, represented by its own counsel. The attorney general's office fought to maintain and affirm the judgment of the District Court condemning the *Grey Jacket* and cargo, while the Treasury Department, representing Timothy Meaher, strove to overturn the District Court and uphold the remission entered by the secretary of the Treasury. Timothy Meaher also was represented by his own attorneys. The crew of the *Kennebeck,* as captors, were also represented by their own counsel in their attempts to share in the prize money.

The Arguments before the Court

The arguments to the Supreme Court were made on April 22, 1867. The case for Timothy Meaher was argued first by his private attorneys, B. F. Butler and Miles Taylor. It appears from the formal published court opinion that Butler gave the argument.

Butler began his argument by setting forth what Meaher would prove to the court if his offer for further proof was accepted. He recited the facts of the case, then indicated that Meaher was, and always had been, a loyal citizen of the United States. He claimed that Meaher had never aided the Rebellion, but had always unobtrusively taken care of his business. Having a great deal of property, Meaher wanted to save what he could, Butler alleged, and remove it to the safety of the United States. Meaher was forced to deal with the Confederate government concerning the shipment of cotton and the reservation of space on the return trip to enable him to leave Mobile Bay. Meaher intended to repudiate this contract as soon as he was beyond the limits of Confederate power. When Meaher observed the *Kennebeck* pursuing him, he did not alter his course and try to escape. Meaher had proved all of these assertions to the satisfaction of the secretary of the Treasury, who had remitted all the condemned property to Meaher pursuant to his powers under the Act of Congress of July 13, 1863.

Butler acknowledged to the court that the arguments he made to this point were contained in a petition for further proof. It was undoubtedly clear to the court that these arguments contradicted the statements made by Meaher in the preparatorio documents. This would make their acceptance by the court an uphill climb. Butler endeavored to cover himself by arguing that if the court held to its usual Prize Court rules, only the original documents could be considered by the court. Then there still were errors in the District Court hearing that nevertheless should overturn the case.

As part of these errors, Butler stressed that the District Court had admitted documents that were not part of the original documents the court would normally consider. In that proceeding, the report of the prize commissioners, the testimony of the prize master, and the letter from the commander of the *Kennebeck* should not have been considered by the District Court. Simple residence in the rebellious territory did not make a loyal citizen an enemy. Butler gave an emotional argument that was designed to bring forth the patriotism of the Supreme Court justices. He claimed that Meaher had secretly protected his own American flag, and that the *Grey Jacket* was sailing under this flag. Any status that Meaher had as an enemy changed when he formed an intention to return to the United States and moved to carry out that intention. Raising the American flag demonstrated that Meaher was no longer an enemy, but a free American citizen. His property changed status with him.

This argument may have moved the justices of the court, but the only evidence before the court on this subject was contained in the deposition of the mate, Flynn, who testified that the *Grey Jacket* was flying an English flag.

Continuing this argument, Butler pressed the point that the president of the United States had invited all rebellious enemies to return to their allegiance. The president's proclamation of December 8, 1863, promised such individuals full pardon and amnesty upon taking the prescribed oath. By taking this oath, Meaher had a full restoration of his property rights, except for slaves. Because of the change of status and the president's proclamation, Meaher had a right to withdraw himself and his property through the blockade. Furthermore, Meaher had a license to run the blockade, because to do what ought to be, and was meritorious to be done, should be permitted in these circumstances. This was not just a presumed, but a proclaimed, license to run the blockade.

Butler closed his argument with a long dissertation setting out the right of the secretary of the Treasury to remit the property to Meaher, even though it was libeled upon as a maritime prize of war. Under the circumstances there set forth, he requested that a new claim, or a new answer, or both, could appropriately be made as further proof in the Supreme Court. It was solely up to the discretion of the court whether the request should be granted.

Butler and Taylor gave an ably presented argument. They requested the Supreme Court to overrule the District Court and to order the return of the *Grey Jacket* and its cargo to Timothy Meaher. They based this request either on the merits of the case itself or upon the new material and evidence submitted in their petition for further proof, which would include an acceptance of Meaher's second affidavit and the warrant of the secretary of the Treasury remitting the vessel and cargo to Timothy Meaher.

The United States and the crew of the *Kennebeck* then argued for the upholding of the decree of the District Court. Attorney General Henry Stanbery and members of his staff, J. Hubley Ashton and T. J. Coffey, represented the United States. Charles Eames appeared on behalf of the *Kennebeck*'s crew, which was interested in the outcome of the case because of the prize money. If the decree of condemnation was upheld, the crew would apportion among themselves at least half the proceeds from the sale of the *Grey Jacket*.

Ashton and Eames presented the argument in answer to the allegations made by Meaher's counsel. The historical evidence is not clear, but Eames, representing the crew of the *Kennebeck,* probably spoke first. This reserved the second part of the presentation to the attorney general's staff, when the controversy with the Treasury Department would be heard.

Eames immediately addressed the points that he insisted would uphold the District Court's decree. He carefully reviewed the proceedings there. As his first point, he explained that the *Grey Jacket* and its cargo were properties of persons or entities, however they were owned, who were within the designation of enemies. Therefore, the property was capturable as enemy property. His second point was that the vessel and cargo were capturable for running the blockade. His third reason to uphold the District Court was that independent of running the blockade, the vessel and cargo were confiscable because of illicit trading with the enemy.

Next Eames argued that the request for further proof at the District Court level was properly denied, because the testimony submitted by Meaher to support the request was in direct and irreconcilable conflict with preliminary proofs and papers relied upon by the court. Meaher's assertion in his first affidavit that he was the owner of the cargo conflicted with his agreement with the Confederate government found in the ship's papers. Furthermore, Eames alleged, the affidavit carefully avoided any statement that Meaher did not intend to return to Alabama as set forth in his agreement with the Confederate government. Eames then reiterated and emphasized that when the original proof and papers accepted by the court so clearly set out the actual facts, the well-established principles and practice of the District Court, acting as a Prize Court, would not permit further explanations of those transactions by further proof. Eames concluded by submitting that absolutely no error had been committed by the District Court, and its decree of condemnation of the *Grey Jacket* and cargo should be upheld.

At this point, Ashton took over for the United States. He made reference to the petition submitted by Meaher as an additional answer to the Supreme Court, saying that Meaher was relying upon this petition to overturn the District Court. However, even if the court accepted the additional answer for filing, Meaher's case was still not conclusive and strong enough to overturn the existing decree.

Ashton stated that the offered answer consisted of two parts. The first consisted of the affidavit given by Meaher that recited the vessel and cargo's ownership and the vessel's destination when it was captured. These were the facts stressed by Butler in his argument on behalf of Meaher. The second was that subsequent to the decree being entered by the District Court, the secretary of the Treasury, by warrant under his hand and office, had remitted to Meaher all of the right, claim, and demand of the United States to the *Grey Jacket* and cargo. This was done under the terms of the act passed by Congress on July 13, 1861.

The first part of the offered additional answer was in the nature of further proof, Ashton argued, so the claimant was not entitled to submit further proof. If this additional answer was accepted by the court, and the court further accepted Meaher's statements that he was transporting his cotton from Alabama to a port of a loyal state, this in itself was a violation of the law. It violated the prohibition, then in force, against commercial intercourse between states of the Confederacy and states that remained loyal to the United States. Meaher should not be able to use a violation of the law as a basis for regaining his property.

Ashton then tackled the question concerning the remission by the secretary of the Treasury. He told the court that this remission was totally irresponsive and irrelevant to this case. The condemnation was done pursuant to the public law of war, an international law, and the powers of the secretary of the Treasury were derived from an internal public law that could not overturn the decrees of a Prize Court. Even if the law of July 13, 1861, applied to these facts, it still would not apply to the *Grey Jacket,* because, by the very words of the law, it applied only to merchandise in transit between the revolted states and the rest of the United States. Ashton pointed out that all the facts before the court indicated that the *Grey Jacket* was destined to Havana when captured.

He closed his argument by making a point that he thought was obvious to all parties: A capture and condemnation of property as a prize of war determines the ownership of the property concerned. There could be no intervening property rights based upon domestic law, because these rights were superseded by actions of the Prize Court.

Speaking for the office of the attorney general of the United States and the members of the crew of the *Kennebeck,* Ashton requested the court to affirm the decree of the District Court condemning the *Grey Jacket* and cargo.

Caleb Cushing, former U.S. Attorney General, appearing somewhat above all the turmoil, presented the arguments of the Treasury Department. In a very short and concise argument, Cushing approached the court on the basis that it was inconceivable that there could be any other view to the matter before the court except that of the Treasury Department. It was the department's firm belief that the *Grey Jacket* and cargo could only be condemned under the July 13, 1861, act. Further, that act was the primary law not only throughout the United States, but also in the Confederacy, because of the nature of the conflict as an insurrection. Cushing mentioned other Federal proclamations, laws, and legal cases where it was assumed, by the departments of the government administering them, that they applied throughout the constitutional limits of the United States, which included the Confederacy. He stated that these laws, including the law of July 13, 1861, were primary and of a paramount force over all laws in the United States, including the decisions of the Prize Courts. This law gave the secretary of the Treasury the power to remit property as was done on behalf of Meaher. Each secretary of the Treasury since the law was passed had assumed that this power was superior to that of the prize of war condemnations.

Additionally, Cushing stated that a prize of war belongs, of right, to the sovereign. As such, its distribution to the claimants or the captors was purely an act of grace, completely at the discretion of the sovereign government, the United States. All these very obvious points made it clear that the property should be remitted to Timothy Meaher pursuant to the warrant of the secretary of the Treasury.

With that, the arguments on behalf of all the parties came to a close.

The Opinion of the Court

Justice Noah H. Swayne gave the opinion of the court on May 6, 1867.[9] A progressive Republican, Swayne was a former U.S. attorney in Ohio who was vehement in his opposition to slavery and was probably more firmly based in the practical aspects of the law, and its application to people, than any of the other justices of the court.

Swayne began his opinion by carefully reciting the facts of the case. He stated that there were three questions to be decided by the court. The first was the effect of the Amnesty Proclamation of December 8, 1863, in connection with the oath taken by Timothy Meaher; the second was whether an order for further proof should be entered by the Supreme Court; and the third was to decide whether the remission by the secretary of the Treasury entitled Meaher to regain the ownership of the *Grey Jacket* and cargo.

First, Swayne indicated that the status of Meaher because of the oath taken by him as set forth in the president's proclamation of December 8, 1863, had not been argued by counsel, but that it was appropriate for the court to consider what effect the oath had on this case. The Justice stated that the president's proclamation had its basis in the Act of Congress of July 17, 1862, and that neither the statute nor the proclamation specifically stated that it applied to maritime captures. Therefore, Swayne held that neither had any application to cases such as that of the *Grey Jacket*. The justice also desired to make it clear that there was no possibility that an oath taken pursuant to the mentioned proclamation could be held to extinguish the liability of a vessel and cargo apprehended running the blockade. It would, indeed, be a strange result if a subsequent oath of a claimant, such as Meaher, were allowed to establish his innocence and compel the return of his property.

Second, Swayne held that the *Grey Jacket* was not a proper case for an order of further proof. Such an order should always be made with extreme caution, and only where the ends of justice clearly require it. Meaher forfeited all right to ask for such an order by his attempted concealment of the true facts as to the ownership of the *Grey Jacket* and cargo and the vessel's destination in his first affidavit. The granting of an order for further proof would hold out a strange temptation for future claimants to commit perjury, then ask for an order for further proof. The court was fully satisfied with the testimony and proofs in the case, and that a correct decision could be drawn from them. If Meaher's statements in his second affidavit were true, he had postponed his effort to escape too long. Swayne indicated that the law did not tolerate such delay. The motion in the form of a petition for further proof was thereupon denied.

As to the third question, which considered the effect of the remission of the vessel and cargo to Meaher by the secretary of the Treasury, Swayne held that the remission was limited in its terms to the rights of the United States arising under the act of July 13, 1861. Under that act, property was to be forfeited to the United States if the property, including the vessel or vehicle conveying the property, came from a state in rebellion into other parts of the United States. The act did apply to property arriving by water as well as land. The secretary of the Treasury, by another part of the act, could remit the property to its original owner if that original owner could prove that he had been loyal to the United States.

Swayne held that the act did not apply to vessels and cargoes traveling from a Rebel port to a neutral port. The *Grey Jacket* was not headed for a port in a loyal state. Meaher filed a second affidavit alleging this only after he became aware of the law. This contradicted his first affidavit. The second affidavit could not remove the fact that Meaher swore under oath in his first affidavit that the *Grey Jacket*'s final destination was Havana. Meaher did state, originally, that he might remove the cotton to a better market, but that would not satisfy the provisions of the act. The secretary of the Treasury had no power to remit property captured as a maritime prize of war, and the secretary could not extend his power to this area.

In addition, Swayne held that the property came from enemy country and therefore could be legally captured regardless of the innocence or loyalty of its owner. The prime exception to this rule was that a citizen loyal to the United States could escape with his property from the Confederacy shortly after the outbreak of hostilities. Provided the objective of this loyal citizen was to remove his property from the dominion of the Confederacy, he could maintain ownership. Meaher did not qualify under this exception, and therefore he had no justification for running the blockade.

Swayne held that the case of the *Grey Jacket* had "no redeeming feature," and that the vessel and cargo were properly condemned as enemy property for breaching the blockade. The decree of the District Court was thereupon affirmed.

>─┤─◆▸─O─◂◆┤─◄

The three cases set out in this chapter give a good representation of the problems citizens faced trying to deal with the blockade. Legal cases arising from the blockade were the most numerous of all Civil War cases reaching the U.S. Supreme Court. Though most of them were routine, many of them, as illustrated here, had unusual fact situations and were at the cutting edge of establishing or extending doctrines in the field of international law.

Chapter Three

Sea Engagements

Not all the legal cases arising from the sea involved the blockade. Other cases with interesting fact situations arising from sea engagements reached the Supreme Court as well. This chapter examines two of these cases.

THE CASE OF THE *ATLANTA*

As the conflict began and the opposing navies were called upon to initiate their operations, the South had many of the same problems as the North. The Confederate States had a dearth of seagoing vessels, making it very difficult to engage the blockading ships of the North, even though many of the North's vessels were also unfit for serious military operations. Initially, the South possessed neither the shipyards nor the raw materials to build new vessels to fill the gap, so the Confederacy turned to its European friends for assistance.

To initiate this policy, the new secretary of the Confederate navy, Stephen R. Mallory, appointed naval agents to several European countries. One of these was Cmdr. James D. Bulloch, who was sent to England. Bulloch wasted no time, and in just a few months he had contracted with shipbuilders in Liverpool to build several vessels for the Confederacy, two of which became the cruisers *Florida* and *Alabama*.

The *Bermuda* was under construction in Liverpool when Commander Bulloch arrived there. When completed, the *Bermuda* undertook her first voyage, laden with weapons and other merchandise badly needed by the Confederacy. Bulloch was aware of her success in running the blockade in Savannah.

Encouraged by this success, Bulloch purchased the iron screw steamer *Fingal* two months prior to the *Bermuda*'s triumphal return to Liverpool. The *Fingal* had the approximate dimensions of Fingal's Cave in the Hebrides, which was 227 feet in length and 40 feet wide, but there is no record of any connection. The *Fingal*'s displacement approached 1,000 tons.

Commander Bulloch loaded the *Fingal* with war materials and sailed her to Savannah, successfully running the blockade and arriving there in November 1861. Reportedly, this was the largest shipment of munitions ever to run the blockade.

Bulloch intended to reload the *Fingal* with cotton and take her back to Liverpool, but he was delayed while trying to acquire the cotton. By the time the cotton was available, the blockade had so intensified at Savannah that he decided not to risk the loss of the vessel. He arranged for the Confederacy to acquire the *Fingal* as a naval vessel, and it was reconstructed as the ironclad *Atlanta.*

Using the technology developed in the planning and construction of other ironclads, such as the *Merrimac,* the *Atlanta* was meant to be an unstoppable force when on the offensive and an impenetrable fortress when on defense. She had a long, low deck of 191 feet, 2 inches. Her extreme beam was 40 feet, 2 inches. The depth of the hold to the top of the beam measured 13 feet, 1/2 inch. Including the thickness of the new deck, she weighed just over 1,075 tons.

The *Atlanta*'s casemate, or housing, was a little in excess of 100 feet in length. Its width covered the entire deck except at the bow and stern, where there was open deck of about 45 feet on each side of the casemate. The casemate sides all around sloped at 29 degrees. It had three ports on each side with heavy port stoppers. The *Atlanta* mounted four Brooke's rifled ordnance guns. Two 7-inch guns, which threw balls weighing 150 pounds, were mounted on pivots in the front and back of the casemate. The other two guns were mounted one on each side of the casemate. These were 6-inch guns that threw balls weighing 100 pounds. With the forward and aft guns mounted on pivots, three guns could be used in a broadside.

More impressive was the thickness of the *Atlanta*'s sides. She was covered by two layers of iron plating, one horizontal and one vertical, each 2 inches thick. Where the casemate attached to the hull, the sides were 6 feet thick of solid wood. The deck was 2 feet, 1 inch thick, with plank under the iron covering. The sides of the casemate had 36 inches of solid wood under the 4 inches of iron. The pilot house was located slightly higher and toward the front of the casemate. It was similarly enforced and covered.

The vessel had a novel, powerful ram of solid wood strapped with iron bands above the water. Part of the ram was a torpedo held at the end of a jointed crane. The crane could raise the torpedo in the air or lower it into the water 20 feet in front of the bow. The torpedo was armed with 50 pounds of powder that would explode on contact.

The people of Savannah watched excitedly as the *Fingal* was converted into the *Atlanta,* which they believed would be the world's strongest naval fighting vessel. Word of the conversion of the *Fingal* also reached the North. Apprehensive that the *Atlanta* could cause massive destruction of the wooden blockading vessels, Adm. Samuel F. Du Pont assigned two monitors to stop the *Atlanta* from leaving Savannah.

The monitors were the *Weehawken,* commanded by Capt. John Rodgers, and the *Nahant,* commanded by Capt. John Downes. Rodgers was the senior and commanding officer. These vessels were twins, roughly following the plan of their prototype, the *Monitor.* They were each of 844 tons displacement, with low decks just above the waterline. Each had one revolving turret with two smoothbore Dahlgren guns, one of 15-inch caliber, more powerful than the guns on the *Monitor,* and one of 11-inch caliber. The 15-inch gun delivered a solid shot of 440 pounds or a hollow-core missile of 400 pounds. The 11-inch gun threw a solid shot of 168 pounds. The vessels were heavily armored, and their turrets, following the plan of the *Monitor,* were built of 1-inch iron plate, eight layers thick, with an extra inch around the gun ports.

These vessels joined the blockader *Cimmerone,* a wooden vessel, outside of Wassau Sound. Here they hovered, expecting the *Atlanta* to enter the sound by the Wilmington River when she was ready to display her prowess.

When the *Atlanta* was completed, she became the flagship of Flag Officer Josiah Tattnall, and her crew numbered 143. The vessel apparently took shake-down sojourns in the tidewater rivers about Savannah. In 1863, she was placed under the command of Lt. William Webb. The Confederate officers and most of the citizens of Savannah knew of the presence of the *Weehawken* and the *Nahant* at Wassau Sound.

In June 1863, the *Atlanta* set out to destroy the two monitors. It was thought that this would be a good breaking-in exercise for the crew. So confident were the Confederate officials that the *Atlanta* would have no difficulty quickly disposing of the monitors, that they allowed her to be accompanied by several steamers with passengers aboard to be spectators. Two of the steamers were armed and part of the Confederate navy. They were wooden vessels, however, and had orders to take no part in any action.

At first light on June 17, 1863, the watches of the *Weehawken* and *Nahant* observed the *Atlanta* steaming down into Wassau Sound. Captain Rodgers reacted quickly, ordering the *Weehawken*'s crew to slip cable and the *Nahant* to follow in his wake farther down the sound. He also ordered the wooden *Cimmerone* to avoid battle unless the wooden Confederate vessels got involved, then it should engage them.

The *Weehawken,* with the *Nahant* in her wake, steamed down the sound while their crews made ready for battle. When ready, the vessels turned sharply and headed directly toward the *Atlanta.* Just as they turned, the *Atlanta* fired upon the *Nahant.* The shot missed its target. The *Atlanta* stopped and was laid partly across the channel, apparently having some sort of difficulty with the channel sands.

When the *Weehawken* came within 400 yards of the *Atlanta,* she slowed and fired her 15-inch gun. Within 200 yards, she fired both guns simultaneously. The 15-inch guns had been installed in the *Weehawken* and the *Nahant* because the 11-inch guns of the *Monitor* had failed to penetrate the casemate of the *Merrimac.* The first 15-inch shot fired from the *Weehawken* was the first iron shot of that size ever recorded in naval warfare.

The shot struck the casemate of the *Atlanta,* knocking a hole in it but not penetrating. It ripped the interior woodwork of the casemate three feet wide along its entire length and caused solid balls in racks, as well as wood and iron splinters, to fly with intense velocity. Forty of the *Atlanta*'s crew were pros-trated and wounded or stunned, and the entire crew was demoralized. The sec-ond shot destroyed the pilot house, wounding the pilots and helmsman. Not realizing that the *Atlanta* had hauled down its colors and run up a white flag of surrender, the *Weehawken* fired each gun a second time.

The *Nahant* did not engage the *Atlanta*. Captain Downes intended to fire at the *Atlanta* only from close quarters. The *Atlanta* was just getting close enough to engage when the crew of the *Nahant* observed the surrender, so they with-held their fire. The *Cimmerone,* following orders, watched the engagement from afar but remained within signal distance.

The surrender was totally unexpected. Lt. William Webb of the *Atlanta* went aboard the *Weehawken* and surrendered his sword to Captain Rodgers, while Captain Downes of the *Nahant* went aboard the *Atlanta* and took posses-sion of her. Her crew members were taken into custody and became prisoners of war. They were ultimately incarcerated in Fort Warren in the Boston Harbor.

The *Atlanta* was libeled as a prize of war in the U.S. District Court for the District of Massachusetts. However, the *Atlanta* was never brought into the court's jurisdiction for adjudication. She was taken by the U.S. secretary of the navy and pressed into service. Her appraised value, a figure in excess of $350,000, was deposited in her place with the U.S. Treasury Department.

At this stage, the case was simply entitled *The* Atlanta and was listed as being filed by the officers and the crews of the U.S. monitors *Weehawken* and *Nahant* and the steamer *Cimmerone.* These men filed the case because they

The encounter on June 17, 1863, between the USS Weehawken, *right, and the CSS* Atlanta, *left. The USS* Nahant *can be seen in the distance.*

were entitled to a share of the deposited funds under the prize statutes. This became the most important case interpreting these statutes during the Civil War. The following consideration of the case reveals an insight into how these statutes were applied in actual war situations.

The officers and crews of the vessels filed this case through an agent named Hodge from the District of Columbia. This was necessary because these men remained on active duty and were dispersed according to their navy assignments, especially true with the crew of the *Weehawken*. In December 1863, the *Weehawken* sank at anchor outside of the Charleston Harbor as a result of an accident caused by the excessive weight of her ammunition, and her crew was reassigned to other vessels or port duties. Hodge was made an attorney-in-fact so that he could commit the officers and crew members, and actually execute required documents on their behalf. He submitted a written argument on behalf of the officers and crew, referred to in the case as the "captors." They were also represented by an attorney by the name of C. P. Curtis, Jr., who appeared primarily for the purpose of making an oral argument.

The U.S. attorney for Massachusetts, Richard H. Dana, Jr., represented the United States. This is the same man who appeared on behalf of the United States in the Prize Cases. He gave a very capable argument there, but here he was somewhat out of character. Dana had authored *Two Years before the Mast* nearly twenty-four years earlier. He was respected for his fights to uphold the rights of the deprived, such as slaves who were captured under the Fugitive Slave Act, and hard-pressed seamen. In this case, representing the government, he was forced to argue against the captors in the manner set forth below. It is possible that he appeared solely because this was part of his job and a Federal act was being interpreted by the court. At any rate, he did not take a vigorous stand on the government's behalf.

The case was heard in the U.S. District Court for the District of Massachusetts before Judge Peleg Sprague.[1] Sprague graduated from Harvard in 1812 and from Litchfield Law School shortly thereafter. As a former member of the U.S. House and Senate, he had practiced law in Maine. At the time of this case, he had served as a district judge for twenty-three years. He was respected for his expertise in admiralty law, and his legal decisions in this field had been separately published.

Because of the nature of the capture of the *Atlanta*, there was no question that she should be condemned, and this was done summarily following the filing of the libel. Thereafter, Sprague considered the depositions and arguments and gave his opinion concerning the remaining issues in January 1864.

He opened his opinion by stating that the only issues remaining concerned the distribution of the funds held in trust by the secretary of the Treasury, and how and to whom they should be distributed. Sprague quoted from the existing statute that if the captured vessel was of equal or superior force to that of the captors, the entire value of the captured vessel went to the captors. On the other hand, if the captured vessel was of an inferior force to that of the captors, the value of the captured vessel was divided between the United States and the officers and men who made the capture. As to who should be included in the distribution, Sprague read the law as stating that it should be distributed to the crews and officers of the vessels directly involved in the capture and of those within signal distance of the capture.

The judge went on to explain that the two issues were quite different. The vessel or vessels that made the capture would determine the percentage to be distributed. However, when considering to whom the sums were to be distributed, the officers and crews of the vessels within signal distance were to be included as well as the captors.

Sprague reviewed the facts concerning the construction of the vessels and the battle itself. He did not have the benefit of testimony from the officers of the *Atlanta,* because they had refused to testify. Nevertheless, he could still get a clear picture of the battle, which he characterized as the most significant naval battle of the time, except for that of the *Monitor* and the *Merrimac.*

The issue narrowed itself, Sprague said, when considering who should be classified as the captors—whether the *Weehawken* should be considered alone because the *Nahant* had not fired a shot, or if the two vessels should be considered in conjunction as captors. If only considering the *Weehawken,* the crews of the vessels would receive 100 percent of the sums in escrow, because the *Weehawken* alone would be of less force than the *Atlanta.* If both vessels were considered captors, however, the amounts distributed would equal only half of the values, because the two vessels together were of greater force than the *Atlanta.*

In considering the law established by previous cases, British cases were of no help, because the English law did not make a distinction in distribution based upon the relative strengths of those engaged in the battle. English law gave the entire prize in all cases to the captors. Sprague then recited his own holding in the case of the *Cherokee,* made in December 1863, where he held that there were two classes of vessels in the situation. In the first class were the vessels making the capture. In the second class were the vessels not involved in the capture but within signal distance of the capturing vessels. Being within signal distance, able and ready to give aid if required, does not bring a vessel within the first class. Therefore, he had no difficulty in excluding the *Cimmerone* and the wooden gunboats following the *Atlanta* in determining the relative force of the captors and the *Atlanta.*

Sprague then reviewed the comparative strength of the combatants. Following this, he cited the written argument that Hodge had submitted on behalf of the officers and crews, which pointed out that it was the shots from the *Weehawken* alone that disabled the *Atlanta* and forced her to surrender. The *Nahant,* according to Hodge, did her best to aid in the battle but should only be considered as a vessel within signal distance, similar to the *Cimmerone.* Hodge had pointed out in his argument that the statute was so constructed in order to stimulate and encourage vessels to attack equal or superior vessels at once and alone, and this policy should not be discouraged.

The judge stated that the government would doubtless desire that the court make a decision favorable to the men who had put their lives in peril and attained a success that had attracted the attention of the world. But despite this overwhelming feeling, his duty was limited to construing the statute. He observed, "I cannot make a gratuity of the public property, however meritorious the object."

He held that the *Nahant* must be considered in comparing the relative force of the two combatants. The *Atlanta* had come down the sound to attack both monitors. He could not speculate whether the *Atlanta* would have taken the same battle plan if she were confronted by just the *Weehawken*. Each monitor took part in the battle under one command. It was the *Nahant* that the *Atlanta* first fired upon, and drawing this fire had aided her consort. In addition, the *Atlanta* was aware that the *Nahant* was coming upon her at full speed, preparing to fire at close range. Sprague then mentioned in more detail the joint operations and close cooperation of the monitors.

Judge Sprague entered a decree holding that because the *Weehawken* and the *Nahant* constituted a force superior to the *Atlanta,* half of the proceeds from the trust should go to the government and half to the officers and crews of the *Weehawken,* the *Nahant,* and the *Cimmerone.* The officers and men who filed the case were obviously disappointed in the court's determination. Working through their agent and attorneys, they appealed the case to the U.S. Supreme Court.

In the Supreme Court, the case became known as *The Officers and Crew of the United States Ironclad* Weehawken, *John Rogers Commanding, Appts., v. The Steamer* Atlanta.[2] Note that the spelling of Rogers was changed from the District Court spelling of Rodgers. This changed spelling was used throughout the Supreme Court case. The abbreviation "Appts." stands for "Appellants," referring to the parties who take an appeal from a lower court to one of superior jurisdiction. The letter "v." designates "versus."

The Arguments before the Court

The case was argued before the court on March 27, 1866. The officers and men retained Reverdy Johnson to represent them.

Johnson opened the arguments by reviewing the facts for the justices. He made the point that the facts were undisputed, and the only issue before the court was whether the *Atlanta* was captured by an equal, inferior, or superior force. Because the justices had not considered many cases of this type, Johnson reminded the court that if the capture had been made by an equal or inferior force, the entire value of the prize would go to the officers and members of the crews involved. If the capturing force had been superior, only half of the prize, represented in the trust fund, would go to the men and half to the United States, in this case to the navy pension fund.

He then launched into an argument to convince the court that the capturing force should be defined to include only the vessels that took an active part in the capture. The *Cimmerone* had not been allowed to come into combat at all because she was a wooden vessel unfit to engage an ironclad. The *Weehawken* compelled the *Atlanta* to surrender before the *Nahant* could get into the action or even fire a gun. Therefore, the *Weehawken* was the capturing force unaided by the other two vessels. If the other two vessels had been absent, the result of the battle would have been precisely the same. Johnson then pointed out that Judge Sprague in the District Court had ruled that the *Cimmerone* was not part of the capturing force. In so doing, the court had conceded the entire principle of his argument.

Johnson concluded his argument by posing this question: If the *Cimmerone,* having taken no part in the action, was not considered part of the capturing force, why should the *Nahant,* which likewise took no part in the fight, be counted in the capturing force, when the *Nahant* did not contribute to the result any more than did the *Cimmerone*?

The government continued its otherwise unexpressed sympathy for the men who filed the case. No counsel appeared on behalf of the U.S. attorney general's office.

The Opinion of the Court

Justice Stephen J. Field gave the opinion of the court on April 3, 1866. Field was the tenth member of the court when he was appointed by President Lincoln, but since the death of Justice John Catron in May 1865, the court had reassumed its membership of nine.

Justice Field agreed with Reverdy Johnson that there was no dispute as to the facts of the case. In addition, he acknowledge that these facts were stated with accuracy and clearness by Judge Sprague in the District Court. After briefly reviewing those facts, Field stated that the main point to be decided by the court was whether the *Nahant* should be regarded as one of the capturing vessels within the meaning of the Act of Congress, cited by Judge Sprague in his District Court opinion. He again explained the importance of the issue for the record.

Field made the point that the fact that the only shots fired by the captors were by the *Weehawken* was not decisive of the case. Other factors must be considered, such as the entire operation of the *Nahant.* The fact that the *Nahant* was advancing upon the *Atlanta* at full speed, readying itself to fire another 400-pounder into the *Atlanta* after the devastating blow of the first shell of this size, may have hastened her surrender. The captain of the *Atlanta* could easily have suspected that another shot of that size at close range would have sunk his vessel and destroyed his entire crew.

The justice acknowledged everyone's appreciation and admiration of the arduous service of the officers and crews of the ironclad monitors. However, considerations of this character could not influence the court's decision. "However much we might feel disposed to do so," said Field, the court was not at liberty to award "the gallant officers and men" of the *Weehawken* and the *Nahant* the entire proceeds of the prize. The duty of the court was to announce and apply the law, and "there our power ends."

Field affirmed the decision of the District Court, which meant that the officers and members of the crews of the *Weehawken,* the *Nahant,* and the *Cimmerone* received half of the prize proceeds and the United States received half. Possibly the men ultimately shared some of the half awarded to the United States, as this portion was placed into the seamen's pension fund. The men who filed the case still did quite well. Alvah Hunter, first-class cabin boy on the *Nahant,* received $176.16 from the awarded funds. This equaled fourteen months of his pay.

THE CASE OF THE *GEORGIA*

The *Atlanta* case is rare because it arose directly from a sea battle. The second case for consideration is more interesting in some respects. It did not find its basis in a sea battle, though it concerned an incident that took place on the high seas. This is the case of the Confederate raider *Georgia.*

Raiding Union shipping was one of the more successful operations of the war conducted by the Confederate navy. The Confederate raiders *Alabama* and *Florida,* and men such as Cmdr. Raphael Semmes, raised so much havoc with Union shipping that ocean commerce under the flag of the United States came to a near standstill. Though not as successful as the *Alabama* or *Florida,* the *Georgia* was one of these raiders.

From April 1863 to May 1864, she roamed the seas from the Cape of Good Hope northward, preying upon Union vessels wherever they could be found. The *Georgia* was built at Greenock on the Clyde, in late 1862 and early 1863. The ship was purchased in March 1863 by the world's leading oceanographer, Matthew Fontaine Maury, who was a commander in the Confederate navy. During construction, the ship was named the *Japan.* At launching, it was renamed the *Virginia.* The vessel was an iron-hulled screw steamer of 600 tons capable of a speed of fourteen knots.

On April 2, 1863, the *Virginia* departed from Greenock with a token crew avowedly destined for Singapore. However, off the coast of France, she sojourned with a tug from Liverpool. The tug carried armament and munitions that were for the purpose of converting the merchantman to an armed raider. On April 9, 1863, Confederate commander William L. Maury, a distant relative of Matthew Fontaine Maury, assumed command of the vessel, which became the *Georgia.* Fully armed but understaffed for a sea raider, the vessel emerged from the French coastal waters and sailed south. Off the Canary Islands, she captured and burned her first Union vessel.[3]

Maury filled the vacancies in his crew by recruiting several crewmen of the doomed Union vessel into the Confederate navy. Thereafter, the *Georgia* sailed with a full complement of men. After successfully taking eight prizes, the vessel's iron-hauled bottom was hopelessly fouled with sea grass, and she was dry-docked at Cherbourg. Her suitability for further service as a raider was

The CSS Georgia *anchored off the coast of Cherbourg, France, in 1863.*

questionable. She was ordered to Morocco, where her armaments were to be transferred to another would-be raider while she was repaired, but the replacement vessel never arrived.

While the crew waited off the coast of Morocco, one of the shore parties of the *Georgia* was attacked by a unit of Moors. The *Georgia* shelled the Moors to protect her men. This exchange has been reported as the only foreign war engaged in by the Confederacy.[4]

Always cautious and taking measures to avoid Union vessels, the *Georgia* sailed to Liverpool, arriving on May 2, 1864. With the Union vessels *Kearsarge, Niagara,* and *Sacramento* cruising the waters around England searching for Confederate raiders, it soon became obvious that the *Georgia* could not safely exit from the Port of Liverpool.

Hoping to develop a solution to a growing problem, Cmdr. James D. Bulloch, the Confederate agent at Liverpool, decided to sell the *Georgia,* complete with her armament, at a private sale. Then at least the Confederacy could recoup the value of the vessel. The attempted sale was not successful, so Bulloch retained a broker named Curry, and he advertised the vessel's sale to the public.

Edward Bates, in the business of owning, operating, and leasing merchant vessels, indicated that he would be interested in purchasing the vessel if the armaments were removed. Bates had full knowledge of the history of the *Georgia,* and he was relieved when he was assured by the collector of customs at Liverpool that no objection would be made to registering the vessel at customs. Bates believed that since the sale was public, officers of the United States would have challenged the sale if they had any objections to it. The armaments were removed from the vessel, and Bates consummated the purchase of the vessel on June 13, 1864.

After completing the vessel's conversion to a merchantman, Bates chartered her to the government of Portugal. While cruising off the coast of Portugal under auspices of that government but under the flag of England, the *Georgia* was captured on the morning of August 15, 1864, by the U.S. ship of war *Niagara,* commanded by Comdr. Thomas Craven. The capture was made on the basis that the *Georgia* was a former naval vessel of the Confederacy that had committed depredations upon merchant vessels that flew the flag of the United States.

The prize crew put in charge of the vessel crossed the Atlantic and put into port at New Bedford, Massachusetts. A libel was filed against the vessel in the U.S. District Court for the District of Massachusetts. Edward Bates wasted no time in entering the case and filing a claim as owner of the vessel. At this stage, the case was simply referred to as *The* Georgia.

Most of the depositions and interrogatories in the case were taken in Liverpool and other overseas locations. This took a considerable amount of time, and the case was not heard before the District Court until September 1866.

The case was heard by Judge John Lowell.[5] Born in Boston in 1824, he graduated from Harvard in 1843 and was admitted to the bar in 1846. Successful in practicing law in Boston, he was appointed to the position of Federal district judge on March 11, 1865. He was a descendant of the John Lowell who, as a member of the Massachusetts constitutional convention in 1780, was instrumental in securing a clause in the new constitution that had effectively abolished slavery in Massachusetts. The senior John Lowell had also become a district judge, serving from 1789 to 1801.

Richard H. Dana, Jr., appeared as the U.S. attorney representing the United States and the captors. A. J. Loring represented Edward Bates.

The issue before the court was whether Bates's purchase of the *Georgia* and her conversion to a merchantman had legally changed her status. If yes, the vessel would be returned to Bates. If no, the crew of the *Niagara* would share the prize money with the United States.

Dana's argument was devoted to showing that the claimant had knowledge of the *Georgia*'s past history. As evidence, he used Bates's deposition and the diplomatic correspondence between the American minister to England, Charles F. Adams, and Lord Earl Russell, the English foreign secretary at the time the *Georgia* put into Liverpool. The *Georgia* was dismantled and sold for the express purpose of avoiding imminent capture. These conditions placed this case under the rule of law enunciated by Sir William Scott in the case of the *Minerva* in 1807.[6] In that case, Scott held that the purchase of a ship of war from a participant in the conflict was invalid while the vessel was in a neutral port where it had fled for refuge.

Dana also cited the case of the *United States v. the Etta.*[7] This case was decided in the District Court in an opinion given by Judge Richard S. Field. It enforced the doctrine of the *Minerva* case but was not appealed to the U.S. Supreme Court. Dana closed his argument by requesting the court to condemn the *Georgia* as a Confederate raider.

Arguing for Edward Bates, A. J. Loring stated that the entire case of the United States and the captors was based upon the case of the *Minerva.* However, that case could be easily distinguished from the case of the *Georgia,* and the facts of the *Minerva* did not apply to the facts before the court. The *Minerva* had been captured near enemy coastline, manned by an enemy crew, still armed. In the case of the *Georgia,* a sale of a merchant vessel was a valid sale even if made in an enemy port. Loring asked the court to enter a decree returning the vessel to Edward Bates.

Judge Lowell weighed the arguments with the depositions. He also admitted further proof in the form of diplomatic exchanges between the United States and England that also appeared in deposition form. These diplomatic exchanges were those mentioned by Dana in his argument before the court. These exchanges had been initiated by Adams, the U.S. minister to England, on June 7, 1864, wherein he informed Lord Russell that the United States would not recognize the validity of a sale of the *Georgia* in the port of Liverpool. Further, he stated that the United States would claim the right of seizing the vessel wherever it might be found on the high seas. This letter was sent six days prior to the sale of the vessel to Bates. Following the dispatch of this letter, the deposition further revealed that Adams then sent a communication to Commander Craven of the *Niagara* advising him to seize the *Georgia* if he had the opportunity. The history of the *Georgia* was so well known that the ship was the subject of a debate in Parliament on May 12, 1864.

Prior to getting to the substance of his opinion, Lowell explained that he was fully satisfied that the sale to Bates was a legitimate sale, a sale not made as a subterfuge to cover a continuing ownership on the part of the Confederacy.

Lowell stated that the only question of importance in the case was whether the American minister to England properly understood the law applicable to the facts before the court. Regarding the *Minerva* case, he said that it was the only case decided prior to the Civil War based upon similar facts, and that the text writers had determined that it settled the law in Great Britain that such a sale was invalid. In France, the doctrine was even more strict. The prohibition of sale applied also to purely merchant vessels. This was also the law in Russia. All of the countries where this fact situation was considered had held that the sale was illegal. Therefore, it was entirely appropriate in this case to determine that the sale to Bates was not a valid sale.

The judge stated that there were additional reasons to declare the sale invalid. In reply to Adams's letter of June 7, 1864, Lord Russell had stated that thereafter no ship of war, of either belligerent, would be allowed to enter any of Her Majesty's ports for the purpose of being dismantled and sold. Lowell held this to be an admission of the illegality of the *Georgia*'s sale to Bates.

In the case of the *Etta,* an opinion by Judge Field held that such a sale was invalid in an "able and learned judgment." The judgment rendered in the *Etta* case had been acquiesced to and affirmed by representatives of the British government. This was consistent with international law; it was the duty of a neutral to give no aid to either belligerent.

Lowell regretted that Bates, an innocent purchaser, should suffer, but the court must hold that his title was bad. If Bates had relied upon the proper government officials, he would not have found himself in such a predicament. The judge was sure that Great Britain, as a "right-minded" government, would indemnify Bates for his losses.

However, Bates was not in the mood to go through the machinations of the English bureaucracy in an attempt to get indemnification. He apparently had more confidence in the American court system. With the advice of his attorneys, he determined to get Judge Lowell's decision overturned and appealed to the U.S. Supreme Court.

The Appeal to the Supreme Court

At the Supreme Court level, the case assumed the name *The Steamship* Georgia, *Her Tackle, etc., Edward Bates, Claimant, Appt., v. The United States.*[8]

Bates changed attorneys for the appeal, retaining William Marvin and Augustin F. Smith. Attorney General W. M. Evarts and Assistant Attorney General J. Hubley Ashton represented the United States. C. Crowley represented the crew of the *Niagara.*

The parties went through the appeal procedures, filing the required documents, which always included a record of the lower case, in this instance the District Court case before Judge Lowell and the briefs setting forth their respective arguments. The case, however, was not argued before the court until January 13, 1869.

The Arguments before the Court

Marvin and Smith first argued on behalf of Bates. Their first point was that international law did not operate in a home neutral port. Therefore, a neutral in its home port could buy and sell every species of property to any person. Their second point was that there had been no previous decision in the American or British courts covering this fact situation. They insisted that the case cited by Judge Lowell in the District Court, the *Minerva,* was completely unlike the case before the court and should not be relied on as authority. Bates's attorneys then argued that Bates did not buy a man-of-war, as was the case with the *Minerva,* but a vessel completely disarmed, intended to be used for commercial purposes only.

The attorneys also pointed out the vast difference between the captures of the two vessels. In the case of the *Minerva,* the vessel was captured near the enemy coast, with an enemy crew and armament on board. The *Georgia* was captured as a merchant vessel under charter to a neutral government.

They closed by stating that such a purchase as Bates's had been recognized by prize courts in the past, citing three British cases. Based upon these arguments, they requested the court to overrule the judgment entered by Judge Lowell.

The attorneys for the United States opened their argument by stating unequivocally that the sale of the vessel to Bates was illegal. In support of this, they cited the French cases that had become the leading cases on the continent. They admitted, though, that the general rule of prize law as administered by the English courts accepted such a sale as valid where it was a bona fide sale and the enemy was divested of all future interest in the vessel. One of three exceptions to the rule, however, was that a sale of any type of enemy ship of war to a neutral in the neutral's port was illegal, and the sale was invalid. The U.S. attorneys were careful to demonstrate to the court that this was the precise fact situation of the sale of the *Georgia*.

Evarts and Ashton closed their argument by stating that Lord Stowell, the judge in the *Minerva* case, clearly meant to establish the above doctrine even though the sale itself was not tainted by fraud or collusion. The U.S. attorneys requested the court to uphold Judge Lowell's decision in the District Court.

The Opinion of the Court

Justice Samuel Nelson gave the opinion of the court on February 15, 1869. Nelson had given eloquent dissents in the support of the application of international law to prize cases in the *Hiawatha* case in 1863 and the *Circassian* case in 1865. Those who expected him to continue this support were not disappointed.

Nelson acknowledged that proofs in the case at the trial level had been introduced from more than the documentary evidence aboard the *Georgia* and from the interrogatories in preparatorio. This was a serious variance from Prize Court procedures unless there was a court order for further proof. Justice Lowell did not enter such a court order. The additional evidence submitted was extensive in the form of depositions and interrogatories bearing upon the capture's legality.

The attorneys for Bates had made a motion before the Supreme Court to exclude all of the evidence in the form of further proof because no court order could be found permitting its introduction. Nelson stated that this objection had come too late. Such a motion should have been made before Lowell at the trial level. Both parties had introduced this additional evidence; therefore, either the evidence had been introduced by mutual consent of the parties, or Lowell had given an order from the bench approving its admission that had not become part of the record.

Nelson then announced that the court was fully satisfied, based upon the proofs, that Bates had purchased the *Georgia* without any purpose of permitting the vessel to be armed and equipped for war service. However, Bates had been fully aware of the history of the *Georgia* and had been concerned that he might have difficulty registering the vessel at customs. When Bates was told by customs that they would register the vessel, he inquired no further from government officials with more authority.

If Bates had so inquired, said Nelson, he would have learned that the U.S. minister to England had called the attention of Lord Russell, the English foreign secretary, to the international law as it applied in England that forbade such a purchase. Bates also would have become aware of Adams's communication with the commander of the *Niagara* that the *Georgia* could be a lawful prize after such a purchase by Bates, regardless of what flag she was under.

Nelson referred favorably to the case argued by counsel that the applicable international law was based upon the opinion of Sir William Scott in the case of the *Minerva* in 1807. He quoted from the case that the "purchase of a ship of war from an enemy, whilst lying in a neutral port to which it had fled for refuge, is invalid." Nelson admitted that the facts of the *Minerva* case were different, but the decision was based mainly and distinctly upon the illegality of the purchase. He cited the "learned and most valuable commentaries" on international law by Sir Robert Phillimore, the judge of the High Court of Admiralty of England, which clearly supported the holding in the case of the *Minerva,* as well as other works in international law that supported the *Minerva* doctrine.

Concerning the argument that the purchase of the *Georgia* should be upheld because she was a merchant vessel at the time of capture, the justice pointed out that if such a conversion could take the vessel out from under the rule, it would always be within the power of a belligerent to avoid the rule and render futile the reasons on which it was founded. The removal of armament in a vessel such as the *Georgia* could just as easily be replaced, as the main framework of a war vessel remained after the conversion to a merchantman. Nelson quoted from Bates's testimony that the conversion of the *Georgia* cost 3,000 pounds. Probably an equal sum would have converted her back to a man-of-war.

The rule invalidating the purchase of the *Georgia* was based upon reason and justice, said Nelson. It prevented the abuse of the status of a neutral that could permit a man-of-war to find its way back into the service of the enemy.

Nelson referred to Lord Russell's advisement to Adams on the day the *Georgia* departed from Liverpool under charter to the Portuguese government: No ship of a belligerent would be allowed to be brought into any of Her Majesty's ports for the purpose of being dismantled and sold.

With that statement, Justice Nelson decreed, on behalf of the court, that Judge Lowell's opinion in the Prize Court was affirmed. The vote of the court was unanimous. The crew of the *Niagara* under Commander Craven would share in the prize money.

More important from a legal point of view, a clear doctrine was more firmly established in international law that was perpetuated far into the ensuing years following the close of the war.

Chapter Four

Political Radicalism

A t the initiation of combat, and indeed, throughout the war, vast numbers of citizens within the states that remained loyal to the Federal government objected to how the war was being conducted, and a large number to the war itself. The Confederacy had similar problems, though probably not to the extent that they occurred in the North.

People in the North objected to how the draft was run. They thought, with sound reasons, that it was unfair to the average citizen. Farmers and laborers on both sides of the battle lines worried about how the impending freedom of the slaves would affect their jobs. Many of the recent immigrants in the North had left their former homes to avoid armed conflict and had difficulty understanding why their new homes were now being torn apart by war. And though there were those who adamantly supported the war for moral reasons, citizens generally were appalled by the bloodshed, and nearly everyone on both sides had his or her own private reservations concerning the conflict. Most people quietly suffered and reluctantly did what was expected of them to get the war over with and get on with their lives. On both sides, however, especially in the North, there were those who vociferously expressed their opinions and engaged in conduct dictated by their consciences, but which clearly impeded the war effort.

In both the Union and the Confederacy, the governments took steps to control these objectors. Early on, President Lincoln suspended the right to have a writ of habeas corpus responded to in the normal manner, making these writs ineffective. This was later followed with the passage by Congress of the Habeas Corpus Act of 1863. Congress also passed laws making it illegal to conspire to overthrow the government, to levy war against the United States, and to perform acts that impeded Federal officials from performing their jobs. The conscription laws incorporated provisions making it illegal to resist or impede the draft. Additional laws interpreted what constituted treasonous activity and gave immunity to officials who might be sued for malicious prosecution for their arrest of citizens who were accused of violating these and other laws meant to control the objectors.

Despite the laws passed that were meant to control the activities of people who went beyond the normal standard of political debate, politicians emerged who attempted to mold the objections to the war held by the common people into a political movement. They hoped to then use this movement as a base to stop the war and bring peace to the nation.

One of these politicians was Clement L. Vallandigham.[1] Born in New Lisbon, Ohio, on July 29, 1820, he spent his early years in that community. He attended Jefferson College at Canonsburg, Pennsylvania, became an attorney, and practiced law in New Lisbon and Dayton, Ohio. He was very charismatic and fought hard for the civil rights of the citizens of Ohio. He became an antiwar, antiabolitionist "Peace Democrat." Accumulating a large following of voters who were concerned about where the political fights in Washington were taking the nation, he was elected to the U.S. House of Representatives. He took his seat in 1858 in a disputed election settled by the House itself. He again won a seat in the House by 134 votes in 1860 while campaigning vigorously for Stephen A. Douglas for president. The theme of many of his speeches was that Northern fanaticism was the curse of the nation and that secession advocated by many in the South was a reaction to this attitude. He repeatedly proclaimed from the floor of the House and in his public speeches that he would not vote one penny in appropriations for arms to coerce the South to remain in the Union.

Vallandigham was a member of the emergency session of the 37th Congress called by Lincoln to meet on July 4, 1861. During this session, he vigorously opposed the war measures passed by the short term. A good parliamentarian, he attempted to block the legislation passed during that session, going to the lengths of opposing the seating of certain members. He introduced seven resolutions that censured Lincoln for his alleged unconstitutional acts of having citizens arrested by the military and suppressing the freedoms of speech and the press. All of the resolutions were tabled by the House of Representatives.

He continued his tactics into the final session of the 37th Congress. On December 22, 1862, Vallandigham introduced a resolution that proposed an immediate cessation of hostilities. In a moving speech given in the House in January 1863, Vallandigham came to be recognized as the leader of the peace movement. As this growing movement's leader, he was asked to speak at peace rallies throughout the North. He often combined his activities at these rallies with political campaigning for peace candidates.

Later in the spring of 1863, Major General Burnside was appointed commander of the Department of the Ohio following his removal as commander of the Army of the Potomac. This department included the states of Kentucky, Ohio, Indiana, Illinois, and Michigan. Establishing his headquarters in Cincinnati, Burnside was appalled by the widespread criticism of the government and of the progress of the war. Burnside believed that this incessant carping and faultfinding was undermining confidence in the government, and that it was adversely affecting the war effort. He came to the conclusion that these activities verged on treason.

Once he reached that conclusion, it did not take Burnside long to act. On April 13, 1863, he issued General Order No. 38. This order first described many acts that, if committed by individuals within the Union lines, could result with the perpetrators being arrested and convicted as spies or traitors with the penalty of death. It went on to state: "The habit of declaring sympathies for the enemy will not be allowed in this department. Persons committing such offenses will be at once arrested, with a view to being tried as above stated, or sent beyond our lines into the lines of their friends. It must be distinctly understood, that treason, express or implied, will not be tolerated in this department."

Eight days later, Burnside followed with Special Order No. 135. This order appointed a military commission composed of seven individuals, one of whom was Maj. James L. Van Buren, a Democrat and relative of former president Martin Van Buren. Brig. Gen. Robert B. Potter was appointed the presiding officer of the commission, and Capt. James M. Cutts served as the judge advocate. The purpose of the commission was to try any individuals who were arrested for violating General Order No. 38.

In the meantime, Vallandigham was giving speeches throughout Ohio in connection with the spring elections and at other political rallies. In these speeches, often before very large crowds, he spared no words in his castigation of Lincoln's policies and the methods used by Burnside to carry them out. Reports of these fiery speeches reached Burnside, who rapidly reached the point where he could no longer put up with Vallandigham's obvious intent to violate his order.

When Burnside heard that Vallandigham was to address a large rally at Mount Vernon, Ohio, on the first day of May 1863, he assigned two aides, Capt. Harrington R. Hill and Capt. John A. Means, to go to Mount Vernon and take notes on what the congressman said there. It is reported that Vallandigham became aware that these aides were to be present, and when he gave his speech, this caused him to be even more vehemently critical of Lincoln and Burnside than he had been in the past.

Vallandigham appeared before a sympathetic crowd estimated to number close to 20,000, many of whom goaded him to new heights of exhortation. His tie askew, his arms moving like an orchestra leader's in time with the beats of his powerful voice, the speaker's stand reverberated as he emphatically proclaimed his beliefs:

> that the present war was a wicked, cruel and unnecessary war, one not waged for the preservation of the Union, but for the purpose of crushing out liberty and to erect a despotism; a war for the freedom of the blacks, and the enslavement of the whites; and that if the administration had not wished otherwise, that the war could have been honorably terminated long ago; that peace might have been honorably made by listening to the proposed intermediation of France; that propositions by which the Southern States could be won back and the South

guaranteed their rights under the Constitution, had been rejected the day before the late battle of Fredericksburg, by Lincoln and his minions.[2]

He also charged that the government of the United States was about to appoint military marshals in every district to restrict the people's liberties and deprive them of their rights. He characterized Burnside's General Order No. 38 as a base usurpation of arbitrary authority, inviting his hearers to resist such regulation by informing their government that they would not submit to such restrictions upon their liberties. Vallandigham added that he was resolved to do what he could to defeat the attempts to build a monarchy "on the ruins of free government." He reiterated, in closing, that the men in power were attempting to establish a despotism more cruel and oppressive than had ever existed before.

On May 5, 1863, after being briefed by the aides who had listened carefully and taken notes on Vallandigham's speech, Burnside dispatched a detachment of soldiers from Cincinnati to Dayton under orders to arrest the congressman. At his home, Vallandigham refused to allow them entrance, and the troops battered down the doors. By this time, Vallandigham's friends had gotten word of what was taking place and hurried to his home to try to rescue him. Unsuccessful, they rioted, and several hours later they set the *Dayton Journal* building on fire and cut the telegraph wires. The event of Vallandigham's arrest was accurately reported, sketched, and commented upon by the news media. The troops returned to Cincinnati with Vallandigham the same day as his arrest. While imprisoned in Cincinnati, he wrote a moving letter, "To the Democracy of Ohio," portraying himself as a martyr defending the rights and freedom of the people. This letter was given nationwide circulation by the press.

THE TRIAL BEFORE THE MILITARY COMMISSION
On the following day, Vallandigham was arraigned before the Military Commission under a specification that detailed charges of his having expressed sympathies for those in arms against the government of the United States and having uttered in the Mount Vernon speech disloyal sentiments and opinions with the object of weakening the government in its efforts to suppress the Rebellion.

At his arraignment, Vallandigham denied the jurisdiction of the Military Commission and refused to plead. After consultation, the members of the commission directed the judge advocate to enter a plea of not guilty and to proceed to trial. Vallandigham was given the right to have witnesses present to combat the evidence that would be introduced against him. The trial began on the same day as the arraignment and continued to a second day.

The congressman was tried under the rules of military law. The case against him was established by the testimony of Burnside's aides who had witnessed and heard the speech. Vallandigham was informed that he had the right to have his counsel cross-examine the witnesses who appeared against him, but he declined. Because he felt that the presence of his counsel would somehow validate the proceedings, he chose to represent himself. Vallandigham was also allowed to call witnesses in his behalf. Three "gentlemen" of his choice attended the trial, but the record indicates that the three did not testify but remained in an adjoining room. Near the end of the proceeding, when Vallandigham was told to bring his evidence to a close, he introduced the Honorable S. S. Cox, a member of the House of Representatives from Ohio. Cox testified that Vallandigham did not advocate resistance to military orders or attack conscription, but that he counseled resistance to the Lincoln administration by means of the ballot and free discussion. Concerned about the three gentlemen in the adjoining room, the judge advocate entered into the record a stipulation that had the three testified, their testimony would have been the same as that of Cox.

Vallandigham closed his defense by reading to the commission a lengthy statement that was inserted into the trial record. This statement challenged his arrest, the jurisdiction of the Military Commission, and the trial itself. He stated that his arrest was not valid because he was arrested without due process and without a warrant issued from a judicial body. He stated that the Military Commission did not have jurisdiction over him because he was not in the military, his alleged offenses were not known to the Constitution or any law, and further, that his words were spoken to a legal gathering in a spirit of legitimate criticism. Vallandigham further challenged the trial because he was entitled to be tried on an indictment or a grand jury presentment, neither of which was present. He also challenged the legitimacy of the trial on the grounds that he was entitled to a public trial before a jury; he was entitled to confront witnesses who accused him; he was entitled to compulsory process for witnesses; his counsel was entitled to be present; and he had the right to submit evidence and argue his case according to the common law and rules of procedure in use in the regular judicial courts.

The judge advocate closed the trial by arguing that as far as the jurisdiction of the commission was concerned, that had been settled by the authority convening and ordering the trial. He pointed out that Vallandigham had the right to counsel and the right to compel the attendance of witnesses. As far as the charges were concerned, he stated that they were determined by the evidence. The judge advocate closed his argument by maintaining that Vallandigham's criminality was something peculiarly for the commission. He then rested his case.

The Military Commission took the matter under consideration and decided that Vallandigham was guilty of the majority of the charges listed in the specification. The commission sentenced Vallandigham to be kept in close confinement in some fortress of the United States for the duration of the war.

THE HEARING FOR A WRIT OF HABEAS CORPUS
Two days after the Military Commission made its decision, George E. Pugh, a former U.S. Senator, acting as Vallandigham's attorney, moved for a writ of

habeas corpus on behalf of Vallandigham in the U.S. Circuit Court for the Southern District of Ohio.[3] There the case was titled *Ex Parte Vallandigham,* and it became a rallying point for members of the peace movement.

A *writ* is a court order requiring the performance of a specified act or giving authority to have an act performed. *Habeas corpus* refers to a person having a body in detention. Thus, one applying to a court for a writ of habeas corpus has asked the court to issue an order to the person, or persons, holding an individual in custody to produce that individual in court and explain the basis for the prisoner's detention. The court will hold a hearing in the prisoner's presence as to whether the prisoner's rights had been violated. In the event such a violation took place, the court would issue a further order releasing the prisoner. This hearing would not determine the case on its merits, but only determine whether the prisoner was being held pursuant to due process.

The writ of habeas corpus has been an integral part of English law and has been regarded for hundreds of years as the most celebrated writ in that body of law. It came to the United States as part of English common law and found its way into the U.S. Constitution in Article I, Section 9, Clause 2, which states that "the Privilege of the Writ of Habeas Corpus shall not be suspended, unless when in Cases of Rebellion or Invasion the public safety may require it."

Early on, the writ of habeas corpus was granted as a matter of right. That is, when an application was made to the court, the court would grant the writ without a hearing or even notifying the other party or parties until they received the writ itself in the form of a court order to produce the prisoner. Then a hearing would take place to decide if the prisoner was being properly held. At the time of the Vallandigham case, the American courts were moving away from this procedure and requiring the applicant to at least make a prima facie case that the granting of the writ was warranted by the production of good evidence that the confinement was improper, prior to the issuance of the order to produce the prisoner. For the writ to be effective, the court in question must have personal jurisdiction over the prisoner and the individuals holding the prisoner in confinement. This can be accomplished if these individuals are within the geographical jurisdiction of the court.

This was the status of the law when Pugh petitioned the court for a writ of habeas corpus on behalf of Vallandigham. When the petition was received by the Circuit Court, the court followed its policy that a prima facie case had to be shown before it would issue the writ. The court, rather than issuing the writ to Burnside, notified the general that a hearing would take place to determine whether the writ should issue. The hearing was promptly held, probably beginning on May 11, 1863, and ending with the court's opinion five days later.

This hearing was held before Judge Humphrey Howe Leavitt, who was a district judge for the Southern District of Ohio but was presiding alone over the Circuit Court on the days of the hearing. Normally, a district judge and a justice of the U.S. Supreme Court would occupy the bench of a District Court. It was consistent with the court rules, however, for either the judge or the justice to conduct the court in the absence of the other. Leavitt could easily identify with Vallandigham. He had begun his law practice in a small Ohio town and was elected to three terms in Congress. He did not complete his last term because he was appointed a district judge in Ohio in 1834.

The hearing began with a brief review of what had taken place before the Military Commission. The judge recited the petition, General Order No. 38, the charge and specifications against Vallandigham, and the congressman's statements before the commission.

Then the court entered Burnside's reply to the notice of hearing into the record. Burnside's statement was not a legal document. Rather, Burnside stressed patriotism and the necessity to maintain the morale of the army. He said that if he, or other officers and soldiers, engaged in wholesale criticisms of government policies, it would demoralize the army under his command, and every good citizen would call these activities traitorous. The general said that it was his duty to avoid saying anything that would weaken the army by deterring a single recruit from joining. If a representative from the enemy demoralized the troops by speeches, he said, he would have him arrested and hung. Burnside thought that all citizens would support him in this. Then he posed the question that if we would treat an enemy in that fashion, why should such speeches by our own people be allowed?

Burnside continued his statement by stressing the existence of the war. He said that this dissident activity could be treated much more expeditiously by military law rather than civil. He said that the thousands of listeners had no understanding of the effect that dissident speech had upon members of the army, because they had not been in the field and faced the enemy. He insisted that all should support the government, and if they did not approve of the government's policies, they should discuss these policies in the proper tone.

The general then called for all of the family members, friends, and neighbors of the soldiers in the field to stop intemperate discussions that discouraged the armies, weakened the government, and strengthened the enemy. He closed his statement with a moving exclamation that if the suppression of the Rebellion failed, "the dread horrors of a ruined and distracted nation would fall alike on all, whether patriots or traitors."

George E. Pugh then gave a long, protracted argument to the court on behalf of Vallandigham. The argument was a classic dissertation on the rights of Americans. It was given extemporaneously, and it incorporated the points of constitutional liberties of Americans that he must have argued on behalf of his clients over many years of law practice before state and Federal courts.

Pugh first engaged in an exchange with Judge Leavitt. He politely explained to the judge that Burnside's statement was in the nature of a return to the writ as though it had been issued. Pugh stated that Burnside's statement acknowledged the truth of all the allegations in his petition; however, the body of the petitioner not being in court, the execution of the sentence could not be delayed without the issuance of the writ compelling Burnside to stay the execution.

Judge Leavitt then observed from the bench that it was the settled practice of the court to give notice to the defendant in cases of military arrest before issuing the writ. He explained that Justice Noah Swayne had established this policy of the court during the previous term.

Pugh responded by saying that such a policy should apply to the future. Since the new rule had not been argued before the bar, he wished to be heard in opposition to the court's establishing such a rule. He proceeded to argue that there were no English or American precedents for the new rule. He mentioned that an appeal based upon the merits of the writ would be impossible if the writ were not granted by the court. Pugh then reminded the judge that he had issued a writ of habeas corpus on behalf of one of his clients under the old rule in his chambers less than two years before.

The judge then stated that, at any rate, the granting or refusing of the writ was a matter of judicial discretion. Pugh agreed, but stated that the discretion must be guided by principles of law, not by "convenience or favor." Leavitt agreed, and the hearing continued.

The writ should be granted as a matter of right, Pugh argued, citing the English precedents establishing the doctrine and the English policy that this right could be suspended only by Parliament. As further support, Pugh quoted from famed British jurist Sir William Blackstone, and then from the Judiciary Act of 1789. He cited the Habeas Corpus Act of 1863 as stating that the writ could be suspended during the Rebellion by the president. But he pointed out that the president had not suspended the writ in Ohio. He now challenged the court, arguing that it did not possess the right to establish the practice of not issuing the writ as a matter of right when it was so at variance with the English and American practice. This completed Pugh's argument pertaining to the procedural practices of the court.

Next, Pugh stated that the only real question before the court was whether Vallandigham was lawfully or unlawfully imprisoned. In further answer to Burnside's statement to the court, Pugh argued that members of the military were subject to very strict rules under the Articles of War. These rules prevented military people from making criticisms of their officers and commander-in-chief in public and in private. When one joined the military, he left his rights as a citizen behind and attested to follow the military codes. Vallandigham, however, was not a member of the active military and thus retained his rights as a private citizen. As a private citizen, Pugh argued, the military did not have the jurisdiction to apply the strict military code to Vallandigham and therefore did not have the power to arbitrarily and violently arrest him.

All citizens would sustain the general "in the darkest hour of his despondency," said Pugh. The citizens would sustain the war effort by all their means, counsel, and lives, but not their liberties. Stating that "eternal vigilance is the price of liberty," Pugh argued that citizens' liberties should not be entrusted to anyone upon the promise that when he shall have conquered an enemy, or put down a Rebellion, he will give them back.

Pugh's argument then turned to a definition of treason. He questioned whether the country had reached the stage where it was treason for a citizen to propose the cessation of war. He argued that Vallandigham had said many of the things contained in his Mount Vernon speech in his speeches in the House of Representatives. He asked the court whether it was treason when these thoughts were expressed in the House. Pugh then read the resolutions passed by the Ohio General Assembly that denounced President Polk for his prosecution of the war against Mexico. The language of the Ohio resolutions was similar to the language used by Vallandigham in his Mount Vernon speech. If the Ohio resolutions were not treasonous, how could Vallandigham's statements be treason?

In answer to his own question, Pugh stated that treason requires an overt act. He cited English cases and statutes that held that words alone were not sufficient to be classified as treason. He read the provisions of Article 3, Section 3 of the U.S. Constitution and the cases interpreting this section, which hold that overt acts were required for there to be treason. As far as the effect of Vallandigham's words upon members of the army, Pugh said that soldiers were very critical and were not the "tender plants" that Burnside imagined. He insisted that Burnside's statement that the habit of declaring sympathy for the enemy was treason would not survive any legal test.

Pugh then cited the rights of a citizen under the Constitution, particularly the Bill of Rights, and brought to the court's attention that no one should be forced to answer to a capital crime unless it was based upon an indictment from a grand jury and the trial was before a jury. He closed his long argument by stating that the civilian courts were open in Ohio at the time Vallandigham was tried before the Military Commission. Therefore, the penalties administered by this military tribunal were illegal, as long as the civilian courts were operating.

When Pugh closed his argument, Aaron F. Perry presented an argument to the court on behalf of General Burnside. Perry was a distinguished attorney of the Cincinnati bar who had apparently been requested by the court to represent Burnside.

Perry opened his argument by stating that Burnside desired that the issues be discussed on the "broad basis of their merits." He established the point that if the application for the writ showed the arrest to be legal, the court should go no further, and the application should be refused by the court.

Ohio was a war zone, Perry argued. He indicated that the protection of the state's railroads and the navigation on Lake Erie were most important to the war effort. He reminded the court that just recently the court records had been removed to protect them, and that the embankments and forts thrown up around the city, and the fact that the streets of the city were patrolled by military guards, made the city a military garrison. Being in a war zone, he said, the laws of war applied. He quoted Vattel's *The Law of Nations* extensively throughout his argument. Perry emphasized that one of the objects of war was to take life.

He argued that the greater included the less, and thus the right to take life implied the right to take everything.

Perry continued his argument by stating that habeas corpus did not meddle with arrests legally made. Circumstances could stand in the place of a warrant for arrest, he argued, and war was such a circumstance; an order sending an army to make war was all the warrant needed to initiate every act of war. Perry then insisted that the writ of habeas corpus was not suspended, but it was respected and enforced; however, Vallandigham was arrested pursuant to the laws of war.

The Constitution must be considered as a whole document, Perry said, including its war measures. He argued that the rights of war were as sacredly guaranteed in that document as the right of trial by jury and other rights, and that the rights of the individual must yield in cases of extreme necessity. This did not suspend the Constitution, but rather enforced it. Perry then applied this analysis to individuals imprisoned by the military.

Next, he brought the attention of the court to instances in history where the writ of habeas corpus had no effect, such as the Whiskey Rebellion during Washington's administration and other instances during the administrations of Jefferson and Jackson. He then posed a question to the court. He asked whether an interference by the court with the duties of a military command would not disturb the harmony between different branches of the government at a time when this harmony was most especially desired. With this question, Perry closed his argument requesting the court to refuse to grant the writ of habeas corpus.

The next to speak was U.S. Attorney Flamen Ball. Ball had spent most of his professional life as the law partner of Salmon P. Chase. He argued in defense of Burnside, but his primary role was to represent the United States.

Ball first backed Judge Leavitt by stating that the writ of habeas corpus should not be treated as a writ of right. He cited cases upholding the rule that a prima facie case must be established supporting the writ before the writ would be issued. Ball recognized the importance of the writ of habeas corpus in English and American law. However, he insisted, the very existence of our country was in jeopardy. Though it was true that the individual had rights, the country had rights also, and among those was the right of self-preservation. This, said Ball, was a paramount right.

Burnside had been given charge of a large department of five states, Ball explained, one of which was being invaded and three of which were threatened. The general was responsible for clothing, feeding, and supplying medicine, munitions, and habitation to members of this large army. The power of this army should not be weakened by falsehoods spread within its lines by Rebel emissaries and sympathizers, Ball said. The only way to deter this was by means of a rigorous police system. Ball went on to argue that military power was above, beneath, and under the Constitution. The supreme law of the land was that of national self-preservation.

Ball closed his argument by addressing Leavitt directly, in a voice trembling with emotion: "I feel sure, also, that there is no judge now on the bench of the courts of the United States whose patriotic heart does not fill with indignation at the wrongs inflicted on our country by the armed traitors now levying war upon the constitution and laws, and by unarmed, but quite as dangerous, enemies, who sympathize with and encourage domestic treason."

Thus the long, involved, in some ways even classic arguments before the court were completed.

Judge Leavitt took the case under consideration and gave a decision on May 16, 1863, the same day that Burnside approved and confirmed Vallandigham's sentence levied by the Military Commission.

Leavitt began his decision by carefully setting out the progress and the facts of the case, including the charges against Vallandigham. The judge was still not aware of the decision of the Military Commission. He then repeated the statement he had made to Pugh when the attorney filed the application for the writ. He stated that the writ was not grantable as a matter of course and would be granted only on a sufficient showing that it ought to issue. Leavitt held that, despite the detailed and moving arguments of Vallandigham's attorney, he was entirely satisfied with the correctness of that course. In support of this holding, Leavitt cited Chief Justice Marshall of the U.S. Supreme Court[4] and Chief Justice Lemuel Shaw of the Supreme Court of Massachusetts.[5] The judge also held that there was no doubt that the court had the power to issue the writ under the Judiciary Act of 1789, but the cited authorities justified the refusal to issue the writ until a showing was made at a hearing concerning the application that the granting of the writ would result in the release of the petitioner.

Leavitt then recited the notification given to Burnside of the pendency of the hearing on the petition. He stated that Burnside had presented a respectful communication to the court, and able counsel had represented him. The judge acknowledged that the case had been argued "at great length and with great ability."

He then referred to a case that was determined by the court in the October term of 1862.[6] In an oral opinion, which had not been reported, Justice Noah Swayne held that it must be shown that there was a probability that the prisoner would be released if the writ were granted, and further, that this court would not grant a writ of habeas corpus when the detention or imprisonment of the petitioner was under military authority.

Swayne was the representative on the Circuit Court from the U.S. Supreme Court, and therefore the Circuit Court's presiding judge. Leavitt stated that under the circumstances, he could not make a decision contrary to Swayne's opinion, because he, sitting alone on the Circuit Court, could not overrule the presiding judge. Further, Leavitt stated, the facts of the case from the October 1862 term were identical to this case, except for the fact that the petitioner in that case was an unknown, and Vallandigham was famous as a politician and statesman. Leavitt held that he would not allow this difference to influence his decision.

Leavitt acknowledged that Vallandigham's counsel did not base his case on this point alone. Pugh had argued a wide latitude of issues very forcibly. The judge said that he was greatly interested in them, but after hearing the long arguments, he had not the physical strength to discuss all of the issues at length. Leavitt then concluded that the essence of Vallandigham's argument rested upon the assumption that he was not liable to arrest by a military power because he was not in the military or naval service of the government. Therefore, he was not subject to the rules and articles of war, but he possessed all of the constitutional rights of a citizen.

The judge then questioned, "Are there not other considerations of a controlling character applicable?" He went on to explain that the court was imperatively bound to regard the present state of the country and whether the court's interference with the military at that time would be expeditious. The court, said Leavitt, could not shut its eyes to the grave fact that a war existed and the life of the republic was imperiled. The judge repeated the phrase that Ball had used in his argument and nearly made it a doctrine of the court: "Self-preservation is a paramount law."

At this point, it was clear how Leavitt was going to hold. However, apparently feeling that the war emergency holding may not survive on appeal, the judge proceeded to weave a very detailed constitutional analysis that the separation of powers in the government would, in itself, preclude the court from granting the writ.

He began this analysis by pointing out that in time of war, the president derived his authority and power expressly from the Constitution's provisions that he should be the commander-in-chief of the army and navy. This, the judge added, invested the president with very high powers that were not defined in the Constitution or by legislation. A memorable instance of the exercise of these powers was the Emancipation Proclamation. The president must use his own judgment in the exercise of these powers. The only control was that an abuse of these powers made the president amenable to impeachment.

These powers, the judge continued, undoubtedly incorporated the right to arrest people who, by their acts of disloyalty, impeded the military operations of government. The president could not discharge these duties in person, but the power of this type of an arrest must be assigned to the officer in charge of a military department. He then held that it was not necessary that martial law exist for a general in command to perform the duties assigned to him. Leavitt indicated that the officer in question, General Burnside, had the total confidence of the president and the American people. When "artful men" disguised their latent treason and contrived to interfere with the enforcement of the absolutely necessary conscription law in the Ohio Department, Burnside clearly had not transgressed his authority in arresting Vallandigham. This arrest, the judge held, was the act of the executive department under the power vested in the president by the Constitution. Leavitt went on to say that he was unable to perceive on what principle a judicial tribunal could annul or reverse this act of the executive department. If General Burnside had abused his powers, he was subject to discipline by the executive department.

Leavitt then stated as the final holding of the court that he could not judicially pronounce the arrest of Vallandigham a nullity. Finally, he held that no sufficient ground had been exhibited for the granting of the writ applied for. The issuance of the writ of habeas corpus was therefore denied.

When the findings and sentence of the Military Commission were approved and confirmed by Burnside on May 16, 1863, Burnside designated Fort Warren as the location of Vallandigham's imprisonment.

At this point, President Lincoln had very little knowledge of Burnside's activities in relationship to Vallandigham. When he was fully briefed on what had taken place, he had deep concerns. One of these concerns was that he realized that the imprisonment of Vallandigham could make him a martyr to the members of the various peace movements, and he could become a symbol around whom the dissident could rally. The president was also of the opinion that to reverse Burnside's decisions would undoubtedly undermine his authority, a thing that he could not allow to take place at that time. Examining Burnside's General Order No. 38, the president noted the alternative penalty that a person committing the offenses listed could be "sent beyond our lines into the lines of their friends." It seemed to Lincoln that this was the appropriated solution. On May 19, Lincoln commuted Vallandigham's sentence and directed Burnside to send him to Gen. William S. Rosencrans for removal beyond the military lines of the North to the Confederacy.

This order was understandably difficult to execute; nevertheless, after a wait of two or three days, possibly to be sure that the president was serious, Burnside arranged for Union military officers to escort Vallandigham to the Confederate lines, where he was turned over to the officers of Confederate general Braxton Bragg. Each step of the turnover was reported by the press, as a newsman of the *Cincinnati Gazette* accompanied the escorts all the way to the Confederate lines.

It did not take long for Vallandigham to be interviewed by several Confederate officials and the Southern press. During his stay in the South, his critics in the North accused him of treasonous activities, such as encouraging the Confederate advance northward. His supporters, however, insisted that he conducted himself as a man loyal to the Union. These matters were not uppermost on Vallandigham's mind, however. He became convinced that with all of the publicity accompanying his arrest and banishment, he could run for and win the 1863 race for the governorship of Ohio. He realized that if he were to actually undertake this task, it would be necessary to place himself in a geographical location where he could at least oversee a campaign. He certainly could not run for governor of Ohio from behind the Confederate lines.

With the help and cooperation of his Southern hosts, Vallandigham made his way to North Carolina, where he managed to board a British steamer at Wilmington. The steamer departed for Bermuda around June 17, 1863. After

LIBRARY OF CONGRESS

Clement L. Vallandigham being turned over to the officers of Gen. Braxton Bragg pursuant to President Lincoln's May 19, 1863, commutation of his sentence and direction to remove him beyond the military lines of the North to the Confederacy.

several harrowing moments running the blockade, the steamer arrived there on June 20. It took Vallandigham ten days to obtain passage on another British steamer to Halifax, Nova Scotia. This steamer, too, had several trying moments avoiding the blockading vessels. Aided by several rolling fog banks, the vessel arrived safely in Halifax on July 5. Vallandigham pushed on through Quebec and Montreal, where he received public welcomes, to Windsor, where he rented an apartment. This apartment was close enough to Ohio to enable him to meet with his political supporters. This was important, because by the time Vallandigham became settled in the Windsor apartment, the Peace Democrats had nominated him for governor to oppose John Brough, who had been nominated by the War Democrats and the Republicans. Prior to election day, Union victories had turned the tide of the war, and the peace advocates lost much of their support. Vallandigham lost the election.

While Vallandigham was leading this exciting life, his attorney, George E. Pugh, filed a petition for a writ of certiorari with the U.S. Supreme Court. If the court granted this petition, an order would have been served upon the judge advocate general of the army requiring that the complete record of Vallandigham's trial before the Military Commission be sent to the Supreme Court for review as to whether any errors had been committed in that hearing, or indeed, if that commission even had jurisdiction to hear the case.

Pugh did not appeal the denial of the petition for a writ of habeas corpus by the Circuit Court. A successful appeal of that case would have resulted in an order from the Supreme Court requiring the officers who had custody of Vallandigham to produce him in the Circuit Court for a hearing on whether he was validly in custody. Since these officers no longer had custody of Vallandigham, Pugh correctly surmised that such an appeal would have been dismissed because the case would have been moot. The only way that Pugh could get the U.S. Supreme Court to aid Vallandigham, therefore, was to request that the court review the proceedings that took place before the Military Commission and point out the errors based upon violations of Vallandigham's constitutional rights and that the commission did not have jurisdiction of the case in the first place.

THE APPEAL TO THE SUPREME COURT

The hearing before the Supreme Court was titled *Ex Parte in the Matter of Clement L. Vallandigham, Petitioner.*[7] The petition application was argued before the court on January 22, 1864.

In his presentation to the court, Pugh presented a short, concise, and logical argument in contrast to his lengthy argument before the Circuit Court. Citing extensively from the Constitution, statutes, and cases he thought were applicable, he attempted to establish several points to the court. First he made the point that a Military Commission was a court of regular authority under the law, but with limited jurisdiction. Next he argued that the jurisdiction of a Military Commission did not extend to an individual not on active duty with one of the branches of the military. Therefore, he argued, the Military Commission in Vallandigham's case administered a sentence in excess of its jurisdiction.

Pugh then made the point that General Burnside had no authority to enlarge the jurisdiction of the Military Commission, especially by an order such as General Order No. 38. He explained that the court had authority to issue a writ of certiorari, and that it was appropriate to issue such a writ to inquire whether a tribunal had exceeded its jurisdiction.

Certiorari was a writ of right, Pugh argued. It was not subject to court discretion and could be issued in cases such as Vallandigham's after sentencing, because there was no other remedy. He pointed out to the justices that the record of the Military Commission had been sent to the office of the judge advocate general in Washington, and it was therefore appropriate to serve that officer with the writ. Pugh concluded his arguments, which were carefully woven together and, on the surface at least, seemed impenetrable.

The task of responding to Pugh's arguments fell to the judge advocate general of the army himself, Joseph Holt. Technically, Holt's response was at the direction of the secretary of war, Edwin M. Stanton.

Holt's argument was simple. He insisted that the Supreme Court did not have the right to review the decision of the Military Commission under either its original or appellate powers. Although Military Commissions acted under color of authority of the United States, they did not exercise judicial power. Further, Holt argued, military power in time of war inhered to the military commander to the exclusion of the civil courts. If the Supreme Court had the authority to review military acts in time of war, the Supreme Court could, with as much propriety, be called upon to enjoin the proceedings of Congress or otherwise revise all proceedings and punishments of military authorities. In time of war, Holt insisted, these acts were done in conformance with the usages of civilized nations, and the Supreme Court had no authority to interfere. Holt concluded his argument, and the issues were clearly drawn.

The Opinion of the Court

The court rendered its decision on February 15, 1864. The decision was written by Associate Justice James M. Wayne. Wayne was appointed to the court in 1835 by President Jackson, and on the date of this decision, he had been on the court one year longer than the then Chief Justice Roger Brooke Taney. Taney did not take part in this case because of illness.

Following a detailed review of the facts of the case and a summary of the arguments made before the court, Justice Wayne began his opinion proper by citing with apparent approval several instructions for the governance of the armies of the United States published by the secretary of war on April 24, 1863. These instructions stated that military jurisdiction was of two kinds. The first was that granted by statutes, and the second was that derived from the common law of war. Military offenses under statutes, the justice continued, had to be tried as the statutes required; however, offenses not under statutes had to be tried by military commissions. Wayne held that these instructions were as applicable to a rebellion as to a war with a foreign power.

The justice then stated that as far as issuing a writ of certiorari was concerned, there was no analogy whatsoever between the procedure used in the United States and that used in England. He found that although the purposes were the same, there was no similitude in the origin of the powers. In England, the Court of King's Bench had a superintendence over all courts of inferior criminal jurisdiction and could have any criminal action removed and brought before it. The courts of the United States, however, derived this authority solely from the Constitution or legislation pursuant to the Constitution. Wayne then expressed the view of the court that neither the original jurisdiction granted to the court by the Constitution nor the letter or spirit of the laws interpreting its appellate jurisdiction gave the court this authority.

It was clear, said Wayne, that a military commission was not a court within the meaning of the then current law, the Judiciary Act of 1789. That act established the district and circuit courts of the United States, and the 14th Section thereof declared that "all of the before-mentioned courts" of the United States had the power to issue certain writs, "and all other writs not specially provided for by statute, which may be necessary for the exercise of their respective jurisdictions, agreeably to the principles and usages of law." Wayne held that "the before-mentioned courts" could only have had reference to the courts as were established in the act, and further, the term excluded the idea that a military commission could be one of them. Vallandigham's petition could not, therefore, have basis in the original jurisdiction of the court or in its appellate powers. The justice also agreed with Hale that, all else aside, the powers of the Military Commission were not of a judicial nature.

The court, through Associate Justice Wayne, then denied the petition for certiorari. Vallandigham thus lost his last resort to appeal the decision of the Military Commission.

This loss did not cause Vallandigham to diminish his activities. In June 1864, he prepared a careful disguise for himself and reentered Ohio at Hamilton just in time to be chosen as a delegate to the Democratic National Convention from Ohio's Third Congressional District. As a leader of the peace movement at the convention, he was instrumental in getting the infamous "peace plank" accepted into the platform in August 1864. Vallandigham also renewed giving speeches in Ohio and elsewhere, which were reputed to be more radical than the speech that originally caused his arrest.

Following the war, Vallandigham continued his colorful life. He remained active in politics and was very successful in the practice of law as a criminal defense attorney. Defending a client accused of murder, Vallandigham's defense was that the slain man had shot himself. While demonstrating how the slain man had accomplished this, Vallandigham shot himself. He died from this wound on June 17, 1871, at the age of fifty-one.

Chapter Five

Combating Insurrection

While the Vallandigham case was winding down, another Peace Democrat, Lambdin P. Milligan, came into conflict with the military in Indiana. Unlike Vallandigham, who was considered a political radical solely because of his speech and writing, Milligan engaged in activities that could classify him as a legitimate insurrectionist. A lawyer and teacher, Milligan was a respected citizen of Huntington, Indiana. Like Vallandigham, he was severely critical of the Lincoln administration's lack of adherence to individual rights. His concern was so extreme that it took him to the point of joining hands with the Sons of Liberty, a secret order that supported the Confederacy. This support manifested itself in resisting the draft in the North and smuggling supplies to the Confederate forces.

There was evidence that Milligan participated in plans of the Sons of Liberty that included the seizure of state and Federal arsenals and using the arms gained there to assist the Confederate forces in invading Kentucky and Missouri. When Maj. Gen. Alvin P. Hovey, the military commander of the District of Indiana, became aware of these activities, he issued orders to arrest Milligan and several other leaders of the peace movement. These arrests were made on October 5, 1864.

Like Vallandigham, Milligan and the others arrested were tried by a military commission while the civilian courts were open and operating. The Military Commission tried Milligan and the others on charges that they conspired against the government of the United States, they afforded aid and comfort to the Rebellion, they incited insurrection, they engaged in disloyal practices, and they violated the laws of war. Also like Vallandigham, Milligan and the other defendants claimed that the Military Commission did not have jurisdiction over them. They pleaded that they were not in the military forces; that they were citizens of Indiana, where neither war nor insurrection existed; and that the state and Federal courts were open and functioning. Therefore, the defendants claimed, they were entitled to all of the constitutional guarantees that would have been afforded them in the civil courts.

The Military Commission disagreed and on October 21, 1864, found the defendants, including Milligan, guilty. The commission sentenced Milligan and two of the other defendants to death by hanging. The date of the execution was set for May 19, 1865.

When the death sentence was brought to Lincoln's attention for approval, he was leaning toward clemency, possibly merely holding Milligan and the other defendants for the duration of the war. However, Lincoln was assassinated on April 15, 1865, before this policy could be initiated. President Andrew Johnson believed that treason was a most serious crime and would not interfere with the defendants' planned executions. When the president was overwhelmed with requests and demands that Milligan's execution be commuted, the president postponed the execution date to June 1.

In the meantime, Milligan filed for a writ of habeas corpus on May 10, before the U.S. Circuit Court for the District of Indiana. The two judges of that court, one being Justice David Davis of the U.S. Supreme Court, could not agree. They therefore certified three questions to the Supreme Court: First, ought a writ of habeas corpus be issued? Second, ought Lambdin P. Milligan be discharged from custody? And third, did the Military Commission have jurisdiction to try and sentence Milligan?

THE SUPREME COURT HEARING

The case before the Supreme Court was known as *Ex Parte in the Matter of Lambdin P. Milligan, Petitioner.*[1] The United States was represented by Attorney General James Speed and deputies from his office, Henry Stanberg and Benjamin F. Butler. The cases of the other two individuals tried and sentenced to death at the same time as Milligan were argued at the same time under the names of *Ex Parte Bowles* and *Ex Parte Horsey.*[2] Representing the defendants were Jeremiah S. Black, Joseph E. McDonald, James A. Garfield, David Dudley Field, A. L. Roache, and John R. Coffuth.

This was Garfield's first appearance before the U.S. Supreme Court. David Dudley Field was the older brother of Stephen J. Field, one of the justices on the Supreme Court hearing the case. Stephen J. Field had studied law in the office of his older brother. No mention was made of any possibility of a conflict of interest in the report of the case.

The arguments to the court were made from March 5 through March 13, 1866.

The government presented its argument first. Though the attorney general argued orally to the court, the main argument of the government, as it appeared in the reports, was taken from the brief submitted to the court prepared by both James Speed and Benjamin F. Butler.

Speed and Butler first brought to the court's attention the rule confirmed in the Vallandigham case pertaining to writs of habeas corpus: that if it appeared from the facts of the case that Milligan would not be discharged upon the return of the writ, then the writ should not issue. This, they stated, brought two issues before the court: whether the Military Commission had the jurisdiction to hear the case, and if not, whether the military had the right to detain Milligan as a military prisoner for the duration of the war, then turn him over to the civilian courts for prosecution.

Once again relying upon the Vallandigham case, the attorney general and Butler insisted that the legal issues of the case could be determined only under the legal tenets of martial law. The decisions made by the officer in charge became the law under martial law, and that officer had the right to assign whether the laws had been violated to military commissions. They mentioned that Gen. George Washington had used military commissions in the Revolutionary War and that Gen. Winfield Scott had used them in the war with Mexico.

They then argued that there was a legal and constitutional basis in the fact situation of the case to establish martial law, and that the writ of habeas corpus had been suspended, citing a proclamation of the president to that effect and the legislative Act of March 3, 1863.[3] Even though Milligan's crimes were committed in Indiana, they said, it was not necessary for him to be in an area of hostilities to be subject to military arrest, because the president had the power to punish anyone who cooperated with the enemy no matter where they lived.

Speed and Butler insisted that there did not exist any legislation depriving military tribunals of their jurisdiction over military offenses. They claimed that Milligan was as much a prisoner of war as if he were taken in battle. Under these circumstances, civil authority was subordinate to military power. The constitutional provisions against searches and seizures and the rights of persons in trials were all "peace" amendments and did not apply in times of war.

They closed their arguments with the assertion that if the court should hold that the Military Commission did not have jurisdiction to try Milligan, the military certainly had jurisdiction to hold him in custody as a prisoner of war pending the termination of the war, at which time Milligan would be turned over to the civilian authorities. This was not a request for the court to hold that the military would have the authority to continue to confine Milligan, but rather a statement of what the military intended to do if the court should hold against the government. This statement was meant to inform the court of this intent so that if the court disagreed, it could incorporate the appropriate instructions in the final decree.

David Dudley Field then gave an oral argument on behalf of Milligan. He began by explaining that his statements divided into two parts similar to the two issues discussed in the brief of Speed and Butler. The first was a rephrasing of the question of whether the Military Commission had the jurisdiction to try Milligan. In the second part of his argument, Field specifically addressed whether the military would have the right to continue the confinement of Milligan until the termination of the war, if the court found that the Military Commission was not a competent tribunal to try Milligan. Field concentrated this second part of his argument into the question of whether Milligan could be released by the Circuit Court under a writ of habeas corpus, or some other procedure, assuming the court found that the Military Commission proceeding was invalid.

Regarding the first issue, Field stressed to the court that Milligan could have been tried for the alleged offenses in civilian courts. These tribunals, he argued, have always been open and operating. The war had not ever interrupted them. Field then quoted from the specifications pursuant to which Milligan was tried. These specifications stated that the alleged crimes were committed during the armed rebellion at or near Indianapolis, within the military lines of the U.S. Army. Field then revealed his complete frustration with the U.S. attorney general's office by stating to the court that this allegation was a "gross perversion of the facts." He pointed out to the court that Indiana was not within military lines as they are normally envisioned, and reminded the court that Milligan was a simple citizen, not belonging to the army or navy, and was not in any official position.

Field then challenged the creation of the Military Commission and its assigned duties. He argued that there being no act of Congress establishing such a commission, the only basis for its creation must have been executive acts of the president. He insisted that there was no basis in the constitutional vestments of executive powers for establishing a military commission to try civilians. The constitutional provisions setting out the rights of the person were meant to apply at all times, even times of war, not just in peacetime as argued by the attorney general.

If there was any basis for the establishment of military commissions, Field said, it rested in the area of martial law. He then went into a lengthy discussion taking the court back hundreds of years into English law, explaining that in England there was no form of military or martial law that could try civilians. Only military persons could be subject to military law. This was the law, Field argued, when the colonies were created, and the colonists clung to this law and their personal right with "immovable tenacity." When those personal rights were being abolished, one of the grievances enumerated in the Declaration of Independence was that the king had made the military independent of and superior to civil power. Field wound up this phase of his argument by stating that considering the hundreds of years of history, military commissions trying civilians were entirely new, and he was incredulous that they should ever have received the "smallest countenance."

Field then went on to argue that under the existing law, the writ of habeas corpus was appropriate to release Milligan. Further, he argued that if the president did not have the power to apply martial law to civilians, he also did not have the power to suspend the writ of habeas corpus, that power being given to Congress. The additional basis for his argument, Field explained, was the longstanding rule in England that only Parliament could suspend the writ. Field concluded by stating that even if the president's suspension of the writ was considered valid, it was no longer applicable to Milligan, because under Sections 2 and 3 of the Act of March 3, 1863, the suspension of the writ lapsed by its own provisions, and Milligan was entitled to a release by its terms.

Joseph E. McDonald and A. L. Roache continued the argument on behalf of Milligan. They first argued that the personal rights of citizens set forth in the Constitution could not be affected by a suspension of the writ of habeas corpus. They pointed out to the court that no unwritten criminal code existed in the United States. Therefore, they argued, a citizen could be tried only for crimes created by acts of Congress. All trials of these crimes must have been in accordance with the constitutional guarantees of personal rights.

Turning to the court system, McDonald and Roache maintained that Congress had created civil courts where Federal laws were administered according to common law, and military courts in which military law was applied according to its rules. They then argued that no person could be legally tried for any offense against the United States unless he was tried by one or the other of these courts and the defendant's constitutional rights were observed. A military commission was not a court under either of the two categories created by Congress. They then pointed out in an elaborate argument, point by point, that the president's proclamation of September 4, 1862,[4] did not legally give General Hovey the right to create a military commission that had the jurisdiction to try civilians.

McDonald and Roache closed their argument by telling the court that the only law relating to the case was the Act of Congress of March 3, 1863. Under its provisions, Milligan should have been discharged because, although it sanctioned military arrests, it restored the writ of habeas corpus to those who were not indicted by a grand jury. Milligan had not been so indicted. Therefore, he was entitled to the issuance of the writ, and the facts would show that he must have been discharged.

Jeremiah S. Black and James A. Garfield then argued on behalf of Milligan. Black was a former chief justice of the Supreme Court of Pennsylvania. He also had been attorney general of the United States and secretary of state during the Buchanan administration. President Buchanan had nominated Black to fill a vacancy of the Supreme Court during his administration, but he had been rejected by the Senate. From 1861 to 1864, Black acted in a very capable manner as the Supreme Court reporter. Black had the reputation of an attorney and counselor without peer.

According to John Niven in *Salmon P. Chase: A Biography,* Black's presentation in the Milligan case was impressively eloquent, citing the ancient Greeks, the Bible, Shakespeare, and British and French precedents. He was reported to have argued for the larger part of two days without notes and quoting from his sources by memory. Strangely, the *U.S. Supreme Court Reports, Lawyers' Edition,* condenses the arguments of both Black and Garfield into six paragraphs, together with a list of authorities cited.

Black and Garfield insisted that the proceedings of the Military Commission were null and void from the beginning. They argued that the Constitution gave every person accused of committing a crime the right to be tried before an ordained court and an impartial jury. No power existed in any department of the government to take away this right or otherwise suspend the Constitution and substitute some form of martial law in its place.

If Milligan and the other two defendants were charged with any crime understood in the law, Black and Garfield explained, it was the crime of conspiracy under a law passed in 1861. They argued that the very terms of that law indicated that the defendants could not be punished without first being convicted in a Federal district or circuit court.

They then argued that even the law of March 3, 1863, suspending the writ of habeas corpus declared that defendants, in the identical situation as these defendants, must be handed over to civil courts for trial, or be discharged, if no indictment was found against them by a grand jury.

Black and Garfield then maintained that martial law could be enforced only at a place where war was "actually blazing," where the courts had been closed because of the conflict. Martial law also could not be tolerated in a place that was peaceful because the courts were closed by war activities in another place. Such an institution of martial law in a peaceful area would be a fictitious necessity, and that was the situation in Indiana at the time of the Milligan arrest. They closed their argument by insisting that the only just alternative for the court would be to order the release of Milligan and his fellow defendants.

The Decision of the Court

On April 3, 1866, Chief Justice Salmon P. Chase announced the decision of the court. Chase held that a writ of habeas corpus should be issued, and that Milligan and the other two defendants should be discharged under the terms of the congressional Act of March 3, 1863. Chase further held that the Military Commission had no jurisdiction to legally try and sentence Milligan and the other defendants. He ordered that the decision be certified to the Circuit Court. The chief justice then announced that the formal opinion of the court together with any dissents would be read at the next court term.

The formal opinion of the court was given at the opening of the following term on December 17, 1866.[5] The vote of the court was unanimous. The actual decision of the court remained as the holdings expressed by Chief Justice Chase on April 3, 1866. Justice David Davis explained the bases of that decision by writing the opinion of the majority of the court represented by himself, Justice Samuel Nelson, Justice Robert C. Grier, Justice Nathan Clifford, and Justice Stephen J. Field. Chief Justice Chase wrote a concurring opinion in which he was joined by Justice James M. Wayne, Justice Noah Swayne, and Justice Samuel Miller.

Justice Davis first recited the facts of the case, then reviewed the three questions certified to the Supreme Court by the Circuit Court: Ought a habeas corpus issue, ought Milligan be discharged, and did the Military Commission have jurisdiction?

Prior to getting into the body of the opinion, Davis emphasized the momentousness of the case by stating that the importance of the questions to be determined by the court could not be overstated, because they involved the very framework of government and the fundamental principles of American liberty. With the Vallandigham case in mind, Davis acknowledged that during the Rebellion, the temper of the times did not produce an atmosphere that would permit a careful and calculated answer to the questions then before the court. Now, he said, these questions could be determined without the passion that was involved during the Rebellion. Davis then briefly held that the Supreme Court had jurisdiction of the case, and that the Circuit Court had proper jurisdiction to certify the three questions to the Supreme Court.

The justice now got to the crux of the matter. The controlling question before the court, he said, was whether the Military Commission had jurisdiction to try and sentence Milligan. Davis stated that if a law existed to support the military trial, the Supreme Court would not interfere; however, if no law existed, it was the duty of the Supreme Court to nullify the whole proceeding. Wayne in the *Vallandigham* case had taken the opposite approach, holding that if no law established the military commissions as courts, the Supreme Court could not touch them, because it was obvious that the Supreme Court had no jurisdiction over them. The ultimate determination of the question, Davis said, did not depend upon judicial precedents or arguments of experts, but had to be based upon the U.S. Constitution and the laws passed under it.

Davis then indicated that the constitutional guarantees pertaining to all trials of crimes, such as the restrictions of searches and seizures, the application of a grand jury, and trial by jury, all applied to Milligan's military trial. These guarantees were laws that applied to rulers and people, in war and peace, and covered all classes of men with a shield of protection at all times and under all circumstances. None of these provisions could, at any time, have been suspended by agents of the government.

He then posed a question: From what source did the Military Commission derive its authority to try Milligan? Davis indicated that no judicial authority was assigned to a military commission by the Constitution or by any law. He further answered his question by stating that neither the president nor some type of unwritten criminal code could have conveyed jurisdiction to the Military Commission.

The justice then held that jurisdiction could not be conveyed to the Military Commission that tried Milligan under laws and usages of war. Such jurisdiction could never be applied to citizens of states where the courts are open and unobstructed. In such states, Congress did not even have the power to grant such jurisdiction to a military commission.

The writ of habeas corpus could be suspended anywhere in a dire emergency, Davis stated; however, this did not mean that the accused forfeited his right to be tried by civil courts.

Turning to martial law, Davis stated that it might be instituted in areas where conflicts had closed the courts, but it could not be instituted where an invasion was merely threatened. In addition, the fact that courts were closed somewhere in the country, such as in Virginia, would not be a basis for martial law in Indiana.

The justice then answered the third question certified by the Circuit Court by holding that the Military Commission did not have jurisdiction to try Milligan. As to the remaining questions, because the trial before the Military Commission was contrary to law, Milligan was entitled to be discharged, and the writ of habeas corpus should have issued as a matter of course by the Circuit Court. When a return of the writ was made to the court, Milligan should have been released.

Just to clear the record, Davis added that Milligan was not a prisoner of war. He was not engaged in legal act of hostility against the government, so he could not plead the rights of war. If he was not entitled to so plead, he certainly could not enjoy the immunities of a prisoner of war.

Davis then reminded everyone that the decision of the court in the Milligan case, and in the two related cases, had been made by Chief Justice Chase in the preceding term of the court. The justice indicated that the orders entered at that time were proper, and no additional entry was required.

At this point, Chase indicated that it was necessary for him to submit a concurring opinion on behalf of himself and Justices Wayne, Swayne, and Miller, because although they agreed with the final decision of the court, they had different reasons as a basis for the court's decision.

Chase then reviewed the congressional Act of March 3, 1863. He repeated the understanding of the court that the first section of that law authorized the president to suspend the writ of habeas corpus during the Rebellion. That section was twofold. The first part required the authorities involved to supply the judges of the Federal District and Circuit Courts a list of all prisoners held under the act, not prisoners of war. The second part of the second section provided that if the grand jury meeting at the time of the arrest of an individual should adjourn without indicting that prisoner, then that prisoner should be discharged. The third section of the act provided that any citizen might obtain a court order releasing a prisoner following the adjournment of a grand jury that had failed to indict that prisoner. That section also provided for the eventuality that if no list of prisoners was provided to the courts, any citizen could still obtain an order releasing a prisoner twenty days after the failure to produce the list and the grand jury failed to indict. It was under this third clause, Chase indicated, that Milligan had sought his release, because no list of prisoners had been furnished to the courts, and the grand jury had closed without indicting Milligan.

Under these provisions, Chase pointed out, it was clear that Milligan should have been heard pursuant to his petition for a writ of habeas corpus, and further, he should have been discharged. This discharge, however, would have been from military custody only. Milligan still could have been tried by the civilian courts because they were open and operating.

The first and second questions certified to the Supreme Court having been answered in the affirmative, Chase went on to the third question of whether the

Military Commission had jurisdiction to try Milligan. The answer was negative, he said, because of the affirmative answers to the first two questions.

Then Chase revealed the true concern of the concurring justices and their need for a concurring opinion. They believed that the majority went too far in holding that Congress did not have the authority to authorize military commissions, and indemnify their members, in areas where the civilian courts were still operating. Congress always had this power, he said, but he agreed that Congress had not used this power to set up military commissions in Indiana prior to the *Milligan* trial.

In support of this stand, Chase stated that Congress, having the power under the Constitution to declare war, therefore had the power to enact legislation designed to prosecute a war to success. He insisted that the constitutional guarantees to individuals did not apply where Congress had used these powers. However, where peace existed, the laws of peace applied. It was up to Congress, said Chase, to decide whether peace or war existed.

Chase then reiterated the views of the concurring justices that Congress had the power to authorize and install military commissions in Indiana even though the civilian courts were operating. The civilian courts, said Chase, could be incompetent to handle threatened war dangers, and the majority opinion could cripple the constitutional powers of the government in times of invasion or rebellion. The *Milligan* case thus came to a close.

With the passage of time, the *Milligan* case has become recognized as an important one in the constitutional history of the United States. One of the more interesting aspects of the case is that neither of the opinions rendered made reference to or discussed the *Vallandigham* case. Since these cases, on the surface at least, are opposite decisions, one would expect the justices to have stated that the *Vallandigham* case was overruled or to otherwise reconcile the decisions. To explain why this was not done would be mere speculation.

Two conservative judges were lost to the court between the two cases. Chief Justice Roger Brooke Taney left the court on October 12, 1864, and died two months later. Chief Justice Salmon P. Chase took the oath of office as his replacement just three days later. On May 30, 1865, Justice John Catron died. The court was composed of ten members at Justice Catron's death. He was not replaced, and the court undertook the *Milligan* case with nine members. Both of these justices were very conservative members, both Democrats in their pre-court days, and both supported the Vallandigham decision. Their loss could have contributed to the change in the court's approach to the issues confronted by the two cases.

Though it was true, as Justice Davis explained in the majority opinion in the *Milligan* case, that the decision in that case could be arrived at without the pressures of war imposing itself upon the justices, it was also true that the war pressure was replaced by political pressures nearly as great. The case became the center of a Reconstruction dispute between the radical Republicans and the Democrats. The Republicans had a deep concern for the safety of the former

slaves in the South. They had come to the conclusion that the only way to effi-
ciently enforce the law against those who committed violence against the former slaves was to use military commissions as courts. The Democrats were
violently opposed. This dispute was carried on at all levels of government and
in the media.

All the justices of the court had to do to experience the pressures of this
dispute was to look down from the bench and observe that Milligan, an average
professional man from a small Indiana town, was represented by a legal team
composed of the very best trial lawyers in the country, who served without
compensation. At the prosecutor's table sat James Speed, the attorney general
who had rendered an exhaustive legal opinion stating that it was constitutional
for the Lincoln conspirators to be tried by a military commission, not by the
civilian courts.

How do the Vallandigham and Milligan cases relate to each other today?
One observation may be safely made in the event a similar fact situation is
faced by the court. If the country is in dire peril of its very existence, the court
likely will follow Vallandigham. On the other hand, if comparative peace
reigns, it is more likely to follow Milligan. Of course, the pressures created by
constantly changing domestic and international situations will qualify the
approach of the events.

Chapter Six

Prisoner Retaliation

Though both the *Vallandigham* and *Milligan* cases attracted national attention in newspapers and magazines throughout the country, there were thousands of arrests for alleged treasonous activities in both the North and the
South. Most of the people arrested were not known beyond small circles of
friends or beyond the membership of groups composed of similar-minded people. These former prisoners always felt strongly that their activities resulted
from legitimate beliefs, and that they had the welfare of their nations uppermost. Their stories would be lost except for the records of many legal cases that
were generated from physical or mental injuries that the prisoners suffered
because of or during their arrests, together with the fact that their constitutional
rights were not granted them during their confinement. Very few of these cases
reached the U.S. Supreme Court.

As the war wound down and finally came to an end, many of these former
prisoners could not erase how they were treated from their minds. In the post-
war societies, they craved vindication. Many of the former prisoners understood
the law well enough to realize that anyone in public office who abused the powers of that office could be liable for the results of that abuse on either a criminal
or civil basis. Many had strong opinions that their arrests and trials, if indeed
they had trials, had deprived them of their legal rights, and that this led to their
injuries. This, they reasoned, would be an abuse of the powers of a public
office. Therefore, the only way they could retaliate and eventually win vindication was to sue the individuals who had arrested them for malicious prosecution
or other abuses of public powers.

This chapter considers three of these cases, all in different settings, and
examines the interesting ramifications of the prisoner retaliation suits.

THE *JAMES HICKMAN* CASE
One of the more interesting cases concerned a citizen of the Confederacy
named James Hickman. The case itself did not reach the U.S. Supreme Court
until 1869; however, the facts that gave rise to the case took place in the

Confederacy during the war. The case reached the court under the title *James Hickman, Plff. in Err.* (Plaintiff in Error), *v. William G. Jones, Edward C. Betts, Thomas McCalley, et al.*[1]

James Hickman was a resident of northern Alabama. When the Southern states formed their own government, Hickman, living in that area, became a citizen of the Confederacy. He actively supported the Rebellion; however, when the U.S. troops first entered northern Alabama, he was accused by his fellow citizens of possibly changing his allegiance.

When the Confederacy was organized, it continued the court system as it existed under the United States. In northern Alabama, there was established a court known as the District Court of the Confederate States of America for the Northern District of Alabama. Shortly following its organization, a grand jury for this district was assembled, and it considered facts and testimony that seemed to indicate that Hickman had indeed aided the Union troops as they invaded that part of the country. After considering all the evidence, the grand jury issued an indictment against Hickman alleging that he had committed treason against the Confederate States.

The indictment was lengthy. In part, it stated that the troops of the United States were in the Northern District of Alabama engaged in a hostile enterprise against the Confederate States, and that Hickman "did traitorously" with the force of arms array and dispose himself with the said troops and did levy war against the said Confederate States. A warrant was issued for the arrest of Hickman, and he was duly arrested and imprisoned.

Hickman applied to Judge William G. Jones of the court to post bail. Bail was denied, and Hickman remained in jail. In due course, but with the lapse of some time, during which Hickman remained imprisoned in very callous conditions, he was tried, acquitted, and discharged.

When the war came to a close and the judicial system of the United States was reinstated, Hickman still remembered vividly his suffering as a prisoner in the Confederate jail. The fact that he was acquitted did not ease his pain or salve his conscience. He reasoned that if the Confederate government had never been recognized by the United States or any other nation as a true government, then the court system created by that government could not possibly have been a valid court system. That being the case, his arrest and imprisonment were without foundation, and the individuals who participated in his arrest and imprisonment were guilty of committing malicious acts toward him.

Hickman acted upon his beliefs and filed suit in the District Court of the United States for the Northern District of Alabama. He sued William G. Jones, the judge of the Confederate court; Moore, the clerk of the court; Regan, the district attorney who prosecuted his case; Robert W. Coltart, the deputy marshal; and the members of the Confederate grand jury who indicted him. He also sued a man named J. W. Clay, who was the editor and publisher of a newspaper called the *Huntsville Confederate*. Hickman alleged that Clay had incited his prosecution by means of malicious attacks upon him.

The case came to trial, but the published opinions of the District Court where it was held do not contain any reference to the trial. However, what took place at the trial can be deciphered from the Supreme Court opinion. The trial court was concerned with whether Hickman actually participated in the Rebellion on the side of the Confederacy. Evidence apparently was introduced at the trial that seemed to indicate that Hickman was a genuine Confederate sympathizer. The judge at the trial instructed the jury that if the acts of Hickman that reflected his complicity with the Confederacy were performed because he honestly believed that if he did not perform them his life and property would be in danger, and further, if other credible evidence revealed that Hickman was always at heart truly loyal to the Union, the jury should find for Hickman. If the jury suspected anything short of this, however, the jury should find for the defendants. The judge also instructed the jury that it was their duty to acquit two of the defendants, one of whom was Clay, the newspaper editor and publisher. Following these instructions, the jury found for all of the defendants. Upset with the trial court's judgment, Hickman then appealed to the U.S. Supreme Court.

The Arguments before the Court

The case was not argued before the court until November 22, 1869. Hickman retained Reverdy Johnson to represent him. The defendants retained three attorneys, Richard W. Walker, George A. Gordon, and W. W. Boyce.

On behalf of Hickman, Johnson argued that there were facts in dispute at the trial, and it was improper for the judge to deprive the jury of its right to determine those facts. Therefore, the charge to the jury to dismiss the case against two of the defendants was improper. Second, Johnson argued that Hickman's loyalty or disloyalty to the Union had nothing to do with the allegations made by Hickman. Even if he had been disloyal to the Union, that disloyalty would not erase the fact of his imprisonment caused by the defendants. Johnson closed by requesting the court to overrule the District Court and give Hickman a new trial.

The defendants' attorneys steadfastly maintained, citing the Prize Cases, other cases, and several international law treatises, that the controversy was not a mere insurrection, but a territorial civil war to which the rules applicable to foreign wars justly applied. Therefore, they argued, the Confederate government was a government in fact to which citizens living under the Confederacy owed allegiance. Under international law, the Confederacy had the right to impose a government on its inhabitants and establish courts and punish offenses. The acts of the defendants, they maintained, were done under the auspices of a legitimate court, and therefore they were immune from a suit such as that filed by Hickman.

Further, the defendants' attorneys pointed out to the court that Hickman was a Rebel and the evidence showed that he actively supported the Confederacy. They insisted, again citing several authorities, that Hickman could not collect from these defendants for an alleged wrong, "however grievous," unless he himself was free of blame; "no polluted hand shall touch the pure fountain of justice," they quoted from the ancient laws of equity. Maintaining that in such a situation the law should leave the parties where it found them, they asked the court to affirm and uphold the District Court opinion.

The Opinion of the Court

The opinion of the court was given by Justice Noah H. Swayne on January 24, 1870. The court consisted of eight justices at that time, no replacement having been made for Justice James M. Wayne, who died on July 5, 1867. Under the Judiciary Act of 1866, the size of the court was to be reduced to seven by attrition. The Judiciary Act of 1869, however, established the number of justices at nine. Also it is interesting to note that the court's opinion was rendered just one week prior to the resignation of Justice Robert C. Grier. The extent of his participation in formulating the decision is not clear.

Justice Swayne began the opinion by taking the attorneys to task. He was clearly upset with them because they did not follow the court's rule that the materials filed with the court from the trial court should contain only the evidence supporting the points presented for the court's consideration. In the appeal file, Swayne complained, the attorneys had included all of the evidence on both sides and the entire charge of the court. When this was done, he pointed out to the attorneys, the labors of the court were unnecessarily increased, and the true issues of the case could be obscured by all of the extraneous materials.

Having gotten that off his mind, Swayne began the formal part of his opinion by reminding the attorneys that the Rebellion was without legal sanction. "In the eye of the law," the Rebellion was the same as if it had been an insurrection of a county or city against the state in which it was located. The size or duration of the struggle did not affect its legal character. Swayne then held that there was no Rebel government *de facto* such as to give legal efficacy to its acts. The Confederacy had not been recognized as a legal government by any other governmental entity. He did admit, however, that for the "sake of humanity," certain belligerent rights were conceded to the insurgents, but this recognition for military purposes did not extend to the "pretended" government of the Confederacy. Here the justice was referring to the rules of international law that controlled military activities and the treatment of prisoners and civilians.

Swayne then held that the very act of the Confederate Congress in creating the court that had tried Hickman was void; therefore, the court was a nullity and could exercise no jurisdiction over anyone or anything. The people who acted under the auspices of the court, which included most of the defendants, therefore had no immunity protecting them from the consequences of their acts.

The justice next considered the rulings of the trial court. As for the court's instruction to the jury to acquit Clay, the newspaper editor, and Coltart, the deputy marshal of the Confederate court, Swayne held that the learned trial judge had "mingled" the duty of the court and jury. Whenever there existed any evidence pertaining to the issues before a trial court, it was the jury's right to pass upon them, and it was improper for the court to wrest this part of the case from the jury. It was as much within the province of the jury to determine questions of fact before them as it was within the court's jurisdiction to decide questions of law. There being facts for the jury to determine, Swayne held that the trial judge had improperly given this instruction to the jury.

Swayne then turned to the second instruction the trial judge gave to the jury, that if Hickman had been a traitor to the United States, he could not rightfully recover against those who arrested, imprisoned, and tried him for treason committed against the Confederacy. The justice reiterated that Hickman's alleged treason consisted of aiding and abetting the troops of the United States while they were engaged in suppressing the Rebellion. He held as a matter of law that there was no connection between Hickman being a traitor to the Union, if indeed he was, and the facts of his arrest and imprisonment as an alleged traitor to the Confederacy. Giving aid to the troops of the United States was a lawful and meritorious act, the justice observed. Any subsequent complicity by Hickman with those engaged in the Rebellion might reflect on his character, but this could not take away his legal rights. Any evidence of Hickman's treasonous activity against the United States was completely alien to the issue before the trial court. To admit this type of evidence, Swayne held, was to put Hickman on trial as well as the defendants. Even if he were subject to this type of trial, his guilt could in no way affect the legal liability of the defendants. Swayne then held that all evidence of Hickman's traitorous activity against the United States was incompetent and should have been excluded from the trial. Therefore, the second instruction given by the trial judge to the jury was also erroneous.

On behalf of a unanimous court, Swayne reversed the judgment of the trial court and ordered that the court conduct a new trial of Hickman's allegations against the defendants. However, no opinion of that new trial ever appeared in the published reports of the District Court.

THE *ROBERT MURRAY AND WILLIAM BUCKLEY* CASE

There were thousands of arrests in the North similar to Hickman's arrest in the Confederacy. The policy in the Union, however, was different in that the goal was not to try and convict those arrested, but simply to put them out of circulation so that their activities that interfered with the war effort would cease. With the suspension of the rights under the writs of habeas corpus and the use of martial law, this was easy to accomplish. Those arrested were merely held in jail without indictments, arraignments, or trial dates, and when the time was appropriate, they were released.

To protect the marshals, sheriffs, and deputies making these arrests from civil suits for malicious prosecution or imprisonment, Congress incorporated a provision in the Habeas Corpus Act of 1863 that stated that any arrest made under an order of the president during the Rebellion would be a defense in all courts to any action initiated for an unlawful arrest, imprisonment, or similar type action. This immunity also applied to an arrest or imprisonment under color of any law of Congress. Since all of the arrests for engaging in the type of activity discussed here were technically made under either an order of the president or a law of Congress, this gave a blanket immunity to those individuals carrying out the arrests or imprisonments.

Toward the end of the war and after, suits of this type nevertheless were filed. They were normally filed in state courts because they did not qualify for Federal jurisdiction. The state courts were much closer to the people and reflected the extreme consternation and general upset that the people had with their loss of individual rights in this area of the law. Juries in the state courts often found the marshals and others who caused these arrests liable for damages for malicious prosecutions and imprisonments despite the immunity provisions in the Federal law.

This possible separation and disagreement between the state and Federal courts had been foreseen by Congress. Another section of the Habeas Corpus Act of 1863 provided that any such suit commenced in a state court could be removed to the Federal Circuit Court of the United States in that area, either before or after judgment. It was not necessary that these transfers qualify under the normal Federal jurisdiction requirements. In the case of such a removal after judgment, the Circuit Court "shall thereupon proceed to try and determine the facts and the law in such action, in the same manner as if the same had been there originally commenced, the judgment in such case notwithstanding." It was this clause that caused interminable problems to the Federal courts.

The *Robert Murray and William Buckley* case is an interesting one that reflects both the difficulties confronted by the litigants and the problems created in the court system when the above statutes were attempted to be applied to specific life situations. The case has been referred to as *The Justices v. Murray,* but the formal name of the case is *The Justices of the Supreme Court of the State of New York for the Third Judicial District and for the County of Greene, and the County Clerk of said County, Plffs. in Err., v. The United States ex rel. Robert Murray and William Buckley.*[2]

This case was originally filed as *Albert W. Patrie v. Robert Murray and William Buckley in the Supreme Court of the State of New York for the County of Greene.* Patrie alleged that between the dates of August 27 and September 3, 1862, he was falsely arrested and imprisoned, and further, that he was assaulted and battered by Murray and Buckley. Murray was the marshal of the Southern District of New York at the time of Patrie's arrest. Buckley was the deputy who actually made the arrest.

The case was heard before a jury. Murray and Buckley defended themselves by alleging that the arrest and imprisonment were made pursuant to an order of the president of the United States. Apparently the men were not able to present evidence of the president's order sufficient to satisfy the jury, or the court simply refused to apply the Federal law in its instructions to the jury. The jury found for Patrie on June 8, 1864, and awarded him a judgment of $9,343.34.

Murray and Buckley then sued out a writ of error under the Habeas Corpus Act of 1863, which provided for the transfer of such cases to the Federal circuit courts. The writ of error was in the form of an order issued out of the Circuit Court of the United States for the Southern District of New York, directed to the New York court to transfer the case, including its records, to the Federal court. Such a writ was granted as a matter of course without a hearing. With the Federal statute providing for such a transfer, the transfer itself would normally be routine. This writ was issued in December 1864.

The Supreme Court in New York refused to comply with the order, however, claiming that the section of the Habeas Corpus Act of 1863 that provided for a retrial of the facts already determined by a jury was in violation of Amendment 7 of the U.S. Constitution. Part of this amendment provided that no fact tried by a jury could be reexamined by any court of the United States except in accordance with the common law. The phrase pertaining to the common law applied to new trials granted by an appeals court or by the court in which the original trial was held. In these two instances the facts would be reconsidered by a new jury, which would have no application to this case.

The more basic reason that the New York court refused to comply with the writ of error was probably that it resented the interference of the Federal courts in a case that it felt was of purely local concern. The justices of the New York court also were of the opinion that the Federal court would demonstrate an obvious bias in favor of Murray and Buckley, who were carrying out orders of the president.

When the New York court failed to comply with the writ of error issued by the Federal Circuit Court, the latter court had no alternative but to hold a hearing as to whether an order, in the form of an alternative mandamus, should issue forcing the clerk of the New York court to transfer the case to the Circuit Court. This case, under the title of *Murray et al. v. Patrie,* was heard before the Circuit Court on July 17, 1866. Murray and Buckley, the plaintiffs in error in this case, were represented by Samuel Blatchford and Clarence Seward. Blatchford, at age forty-six, was an attorney of distinction. The following year, he was appointed as a district judge in New York, and in 1882, he was appointed and confirmed as a justice of the U.S. Supreme Court. Patrie, the defendant in error, was represented by Amasa J. Parker.

The justices of the Supreme Court rode the circuit and presided over the Circuit Courts within their jurisdiction. The U.S. Circuit Court for the Southern District of New York was in Justice Samuel Nelson's jurisdiction. Nelson was seventy-three years old at the time of this hearing and was entering the final years of a distinguished judicial career.

The arguments of the attorneys centered upon the constitutional issues. Amasa J. Parker, arguing for Patrie, insisted that the mandamus should not issue because the applicable sections of the Habeas Corpus Act of 1863 were clearly unconstitutional. The attorneys for Murray and Buckley argued that these laws were constitutional, and further, that this was not the time to raise the issues of constitutionality. This should be done at the trial proper, not at a mandamus hearing.

Circuit Justice Nelson gave a short and concise opinion. He first repeated the laws as set forth above, then recited that the basis of these laws rested upon an act passed March 3, 1815. He then cited two cases that discussed the removal of cases from state courts to the circuit courts of the United States and determined that these authorities set forth ample basis for the transfer in this case.[3]

As to the constitutional issues, Nelson stated that he was not inclined to rule as to whether the constitutional issues would deprive the Circuit Court of jurisdiction; these issues should be argued at the trial of the case. He then entered an order requiring the clerk of the Supreme Court of New York for the County of Greene to make the return to the writ of error already issued by the court.

Again the New York court held its ground. It refused to transfer the case and merely made a return to the Circuit Court that set forth the facts of the suit, trial, and judgment. To this return, the attorneys for Murray and Buckley filed a common-law pleading called a demurrer. This pleading said, in effect, that although the facts in the return of the New York court may have been true, Murray and Buckley were still entitled to the remedy sought, the transfer of the case to the Circuit Court.

The Circuit Court considered the demurrer and, without further hearing, issued an order sustaining it. This order resulted in a peremptory mandamus again ordering the New York court to transfer the case under the cloud of severe penalties if the court did not comply. This order for a peremptory mandamus was then appealed to the U.S. Supreme Court. This appeal was also done by a writ of error entered by the Supreme Court to the Federal Circuit Court. Murray and Buckley consented to the two orders for mandamus so that the issues raised in the dispute between the New York court and the Federal Circuit Court could be settled by the Supreme Court.

This was one of the only times in U.S. history where a division between the state courts and the Federal courts posed a serious threat to the smooth functioning of the court system. All eyes looked to the Supreme Court to settle the dispute.

The Arguments before the Court

The case was argued before the court two times. The second argument did not take place until February 16, 1870. The justices of the New York court became the appealing parties, replacing Patrie. Amasa J. Parker, who had represented Patrie in the lower court proceedings, now argued on the justices' behalf. The interests of the justices and Patrie were identical: Patrie desired to preserve his judgment, and the justices also wanted to preserve Patrie's judgment as part of the larger objective of maintaining the integrity of the New York court, as well as all state courts that found themselves in a similar position.

Parker's argument was very forceful and concise. He referred to the holding of the New York court given when it refused to comply with the writ of error: that Amendment 7 would not permit a fact once determined by a jury to be reviewed by another court. He argued that in that holding, the New York court carefully followed an opinion by Chief Justice Parker of the Massachusetts Supreme Court,[4] which gave the reasons for Amendment 7. In that case, the chief justice indicated that after a jury in a state court found the facts in a given case, it would be totally improper to have those facts redetermined in a Federal court. The witnesses in the state court proceeding would almost always be composed of local people. Because the Federal courts covered large geographical areas, the locations of the courts could be miles removed from these witnesses. Considering the difficulties of travel, it would be difficult, at times impossible, for those witnesses to travel the distance necessary to testify a second time in the Federal court.

This view was fully substantiated by the founding fathers, Parker argued, maintaining that the prohibition against having a fact determined by a jury reviewed by another court was broad and comprehensive, and that there was no exception for a case tried in a state court.

Parker closed his argument with a question to the court: "How can the court make an exception which the framers of the constitution did not make?"

Because of the constitutional issue, the argument in opposition to the justices was taken over by the United States. The arguments for Murray and Buckley were therefore first made by the attorney general, William M. Evarts. Shortly thereafter, Evarts resigned as attorney general. Evarts had been one of President Andrew Johnson's counselors in the impeachment proceedings. Following his success there, he became the president's attorney general, but he only served until March 1869. Later Evarts became the secretary of state in President Rutherford Hayes's cabinet and eventually a U.S. senator. The new attorney general, E. R. Hoar, made the second argument with his assistant, W. A. Field. Whether or not the resignation of Evarts caused the reargument of the case is not clear from the court's opinion.

Hoar and Field also concentrated their argument on Amendment 7. Their first point was that the section of the Habeas Corpus Act of 1863 that provided for a transfer of cases to the Federal court before trial was constitutional. Therefore, they argued, the only issue before the court was the constitutionality of the provision of the law that provided for the transfer of the case to the Federal court after judgment with a retrial of the facts before a new jury.

They then quoted the first part of Amendment 7, which stated that where the value of a controversy exceeded twenty dollars, the right to a jury trial should be preserved. They pointed out to the court that this part of the amendment applied only to Federal courts. Therefore, the second part of Amendment 7, which provided that no fact tried by a jury should be reexamined in any court of the United States, must be read in connection with the first part of the amendment and thus also applied solely to Federal cases and not to a case transferred from a state court.

Because the two parts of Amendment 7 could not be separated, Hoar and Field concluded, there was absolutely no doubt that this amendment would not prevent the consideration of a Federal constitutional issue by a jury in Federal court, even if that issue had been once determined by a jury in a state court. It was obvious that Hoar and Field were confident that their interpretation of Amendment 7 gave the only logical meaning to that amendment, and that it was the only interpretation consistent with the intentions of the founding fathers.

The Opinion of the Court

Justice Samuel Nelson gave the opinion of a unanimous U.S. Supreme Court on March 14, 1870. This is another example of a justice of the Supreme Court sitting in judgment of himself as a judge of the Circuit Court, as it was Nelson sitting as circuit justice who wrote the opinion of the Circuit Court that here was being reviewed. In the Supreme Court, however, he had the aid of the other justices, and it was only reasonable that they turned to him for guidance and to write the opinion because of his familiarity with the case.

Nelson began his opinion by reciting that the case had been argued before the court on two occasions by counsel, each time with "ability and care." He then assured the parties and their counsel that the case had received the "most deliberate consideration" by the court.

The justice then stated that the argument was essentially confined to two issues: whether that part of the law that provided for a transfer of the case after judgment by a state court to the Federal Circuit Court for a new trial was constitutional; and whether the provision of Amendment 7 of the U.S. Constitution, which declared that no fact tried by a jury should be reexamined by any court of the United States except according to the rules of common law, applied to the facts tried by a jury in a cause in a state court.

Instead of analyzing the arguments before the court and leading up to a decision to climax his opinion, Nelson cut to the chase and stated that since the court had arrived at the conclusion that Amendment 7 applied to a cause tried by a jury in a state court, it would not be necessary to consider the first issue, because an affirmative answer to the second issue disposed of the case.

Nelson then explained the reasoning of the court. He restated Amendment 7, whose wording has not been changed since this case: "In suits at common law, where the value in controversy shall exceed twenty dollars, the right of trial by jury shall be preserved: and no fact tried by a jury shall be otherwise reexamined in any court of the United States than according to the common law."

The justice then indicated that it was without dispute that the first part of the amendment applied to cases in Federal courts. He admitted that there would be some logic to conclude that the second part of the amendment would also apply to Federal courts, thus construing the two phrases together. This, however, was not how the Supreme Court had interpreted this amendment. In a previous case that considered this matter, Justice Joseph Story had held that the second part of the amendment should be read as a substantial and independent clause.[5]

The ten amendments first adopted as part of the constitution were limitations upon the Federal government, not upon the states. However, said Nelson, this did not apply to whether Amendment 7 prevented a Federal court from retrying a case from a state court; the amendment itself was silent on this question. Nelson then stated that the only reasonable, if not necessary, interpretation was that the amendment must apply to all cases wherein a Federal question was to be decided without regard as to whether they were of Federal or state origin.

Nelson referred to Alexander Hamilton's discourse on the subject in *The Federalist Papers* for further support of the court's holding.[6] He also cited the Judiciary Act of 1789 as even further intent that the amendment should be interpreted in the manner that the court was setting forth. Additionally, Nelson observed, one of the basic reasons that Amendment 7 had been drafted and accepted was due to the apprehension and alarm that the people generally held concerning Federal review of not only Federal, but also state cases. To interpret the amendment differently would betray this concern.

The justice then held that so much of the Habeas Corpus Act of 1863, which provided for the removal of a judgment from a state court in which the cause was tried by a jury to the Circuit Court of the United States for a retrial of the facts and law, violated Amendment 7 of the U.S. Constitution that it was therefore void.

Nelson went on to hold that the judgment of the Circuit Court, which had been made by him, was reversed, and that the writ of error and the proceedings under it issued by the Circuit Court, ordering the case transferred to the Circuit Court from the Supreme Court of the State of New York for the County of Greene, were dismissed.

Thus the dispute between the state and Federal courts was determined by the U.S. Supreme Court in a decision that held the state court to be in the right. Justice Nelson, in effect, overruled his own decision made in the Circuit Court, and Albert W. Patrie kept his judgment of $9,343.34 plus interest that accumulated during the battle of the courts. This case is still cited today as a guide to the courts and attorneys in interpreting Amendment 7.

THE *PHILIP BOWYER* CASE
Very few of the cases filed by former prisoners reached the U.S. Supreme Court, however. Unless a case qualified for Federal jurisdiction at the outset, such as the Hickman case, all of the cases were filed in state courts. To appeal from a state court to the U.S. Supreme Court, it had to be shown that a Federal issue was involved. The court applied a very narrow interpretation to what constituted a Federal issue. In addition, it was popularly thought by the former prisoners that they would be treated much better by the state courts. The vast majority of the arrests made were by Federal officials under authority of presidential proclamations and Federal law. The former prisoners believed that the Federal courts would be more prone to lean toward their Federal brethren.

An excellent case illustrating the problems involved in appeals of this type is a case called *Allen T. Caperton, Plff. in Err., v. Philip Bowyer.*[7] This case arose on June 29, 1862, when Caperton forcibly seized Bowyer and imprisoned him. The official opinion of the case does not say where this arrest took place

or what activities of Bowyer prompted the arrest. Other evidence indicates that
the arrest took place in Monroe County, Virginia, when this county was part of
the Confederacy. There was a great deal of civil unrest in this area at that time,
prompted by citizens who desired to separate Monroe County and join the proposed new state of West Virginia. It is possible that Bowyer engaged in some of
these activities and this brought about his arrest. Monroe County became part
of the new state of West Virginia when it entered the Union on June 20, 1863.

Four years after his arrest, Bowyer sued Caperton in Monroe County, West
Virginia, for false imprisonment in the Circuit Court there. He alleged that his
arrest by Caperton was with force and arms, and that he was imprisoned in a
dungeon for twenty-four days. Bowyer claimed that his separation from his
home and family, combined with the hardships and dangers he was subjected
to, seriously impaired his health and forced him to endure great pain and distress to both his body and mind.

Caperton defended himself by stating that even if everything claimed
against him in the pleadings filed with the court were true, Bowyer still did not
have a case. He further claimed that Bowyer filed his case after the statute of
limitations had run out, that the arrest was made when he was a provost marshal
under military orders of the state and therefore had the rights of a belligerent,
and that the president had given him a full pardon on September 7, 1865.

Bowyer responded that even if Caperton's defenses were true as alleged,
they still were not sufficient to disallow his claims. He additionally alleged that
the statute of limitations did not disallow his claims; then he "tendered an issue
to the country" on each of his responses. This was an ancient method of
requesting that these issues be submitted to a jury.

The Monroe County Circuit Court determined all of the legal issues in
Bowyer's favor. In addition, the court threw out Caperton's claim of belligerent
rights and refused to admit his pardon into evidence. The issues of fact were
submitted to the jury, who decided them in favor of Bowyer and awarded him
damages against Caperton in the amount of $833. The court entered a judgment
in favor of Bowyer in that amount. Caperton excepted to the judgment and
removed the case on appeal into the Supreme Court of Appeals of West Virginia. That court could find no wrong in the findings of the trial court and
affirmed the judgment.

Caperton then obtained a writ of error to bring the case to the U.S.
Supreme Court for review. The basis of the requested appeal was the special
jurisdiction granted to the U.S. Supreme Court by Section 25 of the Judiciary
Act of 1789. That section provided, in part, that if a statute of a state was challenged to be in violation of the U.S. Constitution, and the state court ruled on
the validity of that statute, the case was eligible to be appealed to the U.S.
Supreme Court under a writ of error, where the statute could be reexamined and
the state court could be reversed or affirmed. In addition, the section provided
that if an act exercised under the authority of the United States was declared
invalid by the state court, a similar appeal could be undertaken.

The case was appealable, Caperton claimed, because a state statute tolling the statute of limitations during the war years was in violation of the Federal constitution, and the state court had erred in denying his defense of belligerent rights and in not allowing his presidential pardon to be admitted into evidence.

Attached to the judgment of the state court of appeals was a certificate, signed by the clerk of the court and certified to by the presiding justice, stating that the constitutionality of the act of the state pertaining to the statute of limitations had been brought into question, and that it was the decision of the highest court in the state that the statute was constitutional.

The Arguments before the Court

Arguments were made to the court on April 11, 1872. Caperton was repre sented by Conway Robinson, Simeon Nash, and R. T. Merrick, and Bowyer by R. Stanton and J. H. Ashton. The details of these arguments are not set forth in the official opinion of the case. From the nature of the case, however, the arguments were undoubtedly restricted to the history of the cases before the West Virginia courts and whether this history revealed a Federal issue sufficient to give the Supreme Court jurisdiction of the case under Section 25 of the Judiciary Act of 1789.

The Opinion of the Court

Justice Nathan Clifford gave the unanimous opinion of the court on May 6, 1872. The complexion of the court had changed prior to this opinion. Justice Robert C. Grier, who had been appointed to the court by President James Polk, retired from the court on January 31, 1870, at age seventy-six, after twenty-three years of service. He was replaced by Justice William Strong of Pennsylvania, who took the oath of office on March 14, 1870, at age sixty-one. The nine-member court was completed with the appointment of Justice Joseph P. Bradley of New Jersey, who took his oath of office on March 23, 1870.

Clifford began his opinion by stating that the special jurisdiction given to the Supreme Court to review cases of a state court by writ of error was very narrow in scope. Two things were required. First, at least one of the questions specified in the Judiciary Act should have arisen, and second, the question that arose should have been decided by the state court in such a way as to give jurisdiction to the Supreme Court to reexamine the question.

Following a discussion of the facts of the case and its history in the state courts, Clifford acknowledged that the legislature of the state of West Virginia had passed two acts, both of which tolled the statute of limitations—that is, provided that it would not run, or be counted—during the war years and up to the time of the passage of the second act on February 26, 1866.

Generally, a statute of limitations prescribed that no suit within a specified cause of action should be maintained unless it was brought within a designated period of time after the right accrued. Bowyer was arrested on June 29, 1862. There was probably a two-year statute of limitations on Bowyer's right of action for false imprisonment. This meant that Bowyer would be required to file his case prior to June 29, 1864. However, since the war was being fought at that time and many of the courts were closed, the new legislation prescribed that the war years up to the time of the passage of the act should not be considered when computing the statute of limitations. This meant that in Bowyer's case, the statute of limitations did not even start to run until February 26, 1866. Bowyer filed his case in 1866, well within the new statute of limitations, but four years after his right to file would have accrued on a normal basis. This was what Caperton claimed to be unfair and unconstitutional. Caperton had asked the state Circuit Court to rule on this issue, but it had refused to do so. Caperton excepted to his refusal at the state Supreme Court of Appeals level. Justice Clifford indicated that this exception was not sufficient to show that the case qualified for appeal to the U.S. Supreme Court under the provisions of the Judiciary Act of 1789.

Clifford then held that the certificate certified by the presiding judge of the West Virginia Supreme Court of Appeals, reciting that the constitutionality of the West Virginia legislation was drawn into question, also was not sufficient to comply with the requirements of the Judiciary Act. This was because the only matter before that court was the exception, which did not state a basis for the constitutional challenge. Clifford reminded the parties to the suit that the Supreme Court itself already had held that the period when the courts were closed in West Virginia by reason of the insurrection and rebellion should not be considered when computing a statute of limitations. He then referred to other court cases where similar acts of Congress were held to be constitutional.

The justice then made reference to the universal rule that enemy creditors could not prosecute claims subsequent to the initiation of hostilities, because they were disqualified from maintaining actions in tribunal of the other belligerent. This was by the law of nations. The restoration of peace removed this disability and opened the doors of the courts.

Tested by all these considerations, Clifford stated, it was likely that the judge of the state trial court followed the precedent of these cases in the instructions he gave his jury, and that he did not express any opinion as to the constitutionality of the state laws. Therefore, the Federal issue did not arise in the case in a manner that would give the Supreme Court jurisdiction of the case under a writ of error to the state Supreme Court of Appeals.

As to Caperton's argument of belligerent rights, Clifford held that it was obvious that the Supreme Court of Appeals did not decide this issue. The justice indicated that it was "plain law" that questions not put in issue in the court of last resort of the state did not give jurisdiction to the Supreme Court to consider that issue under the Judiciary Act.

Clifford then discussed the state court's refusal to consider Caperton's presidential pardon. Caperton had offered the pardon in mitigation of damages and in justification of the alleged wrongful acts. Bowyer had objected to its submission, and the courts agreed and refused to have the pardon considered.

Nothing appeared in the record showing why the state trial court refused to have the pardon considered, or that the state Supreme Court of Appeals had ruled specifically on the issue. Clifford held that questions not considered in the state court because they were not raised by the complaining party would not be reexamined in the Supreme Court on a writ of error under Section 25 of the Judiciary Act of 1789.

Justice Clifford then ordered the writ of error dismissed for a lack of jurisdiction. The Supreme Court thereby refused to consider the case on appeal, and the judgment awarded to Bowyer was upheld.

Chapter Seven

Financing the War: Legal Tender Cases

The objectives that individuals in the North affixed to the war were as diversified as the people themselves. A businessman, a member of the military, a teacher, a farm housewife, and a politician in government all could very easily have had differing aspirations as to what the war efforts should achieve. However, one thing rested upon all alike: The war had to be paid for, and this expense fell upon the shoulders of everyone in some fashion.

Prior to the war, the income of the Federal government came from customs collections, the sales of public lands, and a gaggle of other diverse, but smaller, sources. All things were purchased by the people and the government with the understanding that they would be paid for, directly or indirectly, with specie—that is, silver or gold coin, or other coin that had intrinsic value—or with bank notes redeemable in specie. These bank notes were issued by an estimated 1,600 state banks and were of several thousand varieties. The worth of these notes was correlated to specie and could not be legal tender, as mandated by the Federal constitution. This financial system, bred from an essentially agricultural economy, was not equipped to finance anything of the magnitude of the war that was about to beset the nation.

When Salmon P. Chase was confirmed by the Senate on March 5, 1861, as the new secretary of the Treasury, the government of the United States was essentially insolvent. With the costs of the war rising rapidly in amounts previously unheard of, Chase attempted to meet these expenses with proceeds raised from short-term loans and quickly assembled bond issues. The inadequacy of these measures caused turmoil in the financial markets, and the national and international financial institutions were either unable or unwilling to cope with the resulting economic chaos. The financial stress was so overwhelming that all of the nation's banks suspended specie payments by December 30, 1861.

It was urgent that the nation's financial problems be addressed. In this regard, Congress was apparently a step or two ahead of the secretary of the Treasury. Several members of Congress were convinced that the only solution available was to provide for Federal paper money. A bill was introduced in the

A $1 greenback issued in 1862 with a portrait of Salmon P. Chase. Congress made greenbacks legal tender to pay all debts.

House, and after heated arguments, those favoring paper money prevailed primarily because no viable alternative was seen. The bill passed both the House and Senate as a war measure, and it became effective on February 25, 1862. The new legislation contained several provisions that were termed the Legal Tender Acts. It provided for the issuance of $150 million in "United States Notes," which would be legal tender to pay all debts, with minor exceptions related to the government itself. The first paper money ever issued by the United States, these notes were promptly labeled "greenbacks."

Slow to support the pending legislation, Chase, after evaluating the situation, determined that there was no other solution to the nation's economic problems. He soon became an active supporter and was instrumental in conveying that support to the members of the Senate and House of Representatives. It is interesting to note that his likeness adorned the one-dollar bill when this unit was authorized for issuance. Further issuances of the greenbacks were provided for in the ensuing months, until a total of $450 million was authorized. Never on a true par with gold or silver, the value of the greenbacks varied not only in relationship to these metals, but also relative to the successes or failures of the Union army in battle. This variance in value of the greenbacks was a source of litigation in the state courts. One of these cases, from the state of New York, *Roosevelt v. Meyer*,[1] reached the court during the war in 1863. However, with the greenbacks carrying the burden of financing the war at that time, the court deemed it not appropriate to consider the constitutionality of the Legal Tender Acts at that time and dismissed the appeal under a very questionable interpretation of Section 25 of the Judiciary Act of 1789. The court had a full complement of ten judges at that time.

The court did not consider the constitutionality of the Legal Tender Acts until the war itself came to a close. This was done in the famous Legal Tender Cases. Though they were considered by the court after the war, the facts giving rise to the cases were generated during the conflict and were typical of the problems in which people found themselves.

THE *HEPBURN* CASE

The first of the Legal Tender Cases was originally filed in the state courts of Kentucky. It challenged the constitutionality of the greenbacks law as it applied as legal tender to pay debts created prior to the passage of the act. The very nature of the case ultimately placed the constitutionality of the entire legislation creating the United States notes into question.

The case involved a couple, Susan P. and Henry H. P. Hepburn, and a man named Henry A. Griswold. On June 20, 1860, the Hepburns gave Griswold a promissory note with a due date of February 20, 1862. Following the passage of the act of February 25, 1862, which made greenbacks legal tender for the payments of all debts, the Hepburns tried to give Griswold greenbacks in the face amount of the debt to pay the note in full. This greatly upset Griswold, because when he made the loan to the Hepburns, he expected to be paid in specie. If he accepted greenbacks in payment, he would have substantially discounted his note from its face value. Griswold refused to accept the greenbacks in payment and sued the Hepburns for payment in specie. The case was filed in the Louisville Chancery Court in Kentucky.

The Hepburns argued that the February 25, 1862, legislation made greenbacks legal tender for all existing debts, which even included debts incurred prior to the time that the legislation became effective. The Hepburns deposited an amount of greenbacks equal to the face amount of the note, plus interest and costs, with the court, and they asked the court to force Griswold to accept them in full payment of the note. The chancellor of the court, reading the new legislation literally, felt that he had no alternative but to order a decree entered that Griswold must accept the greenbacks deposited with the court as full payment. He therefore issued a court order declaring that the note was paid in full.

Griswold stubbornly refused to accept the trial court's decision and appealed to the Court of Appeals of the State of Kentucky. There he argued that the debt was not fully satisfied, because the greenbacks were not equal in value to coin, which was the only legal tender at the time the note was made. Griswold argued that the act was unconstitutional insofar as it applied to debts and contracts made prior to its passage. The Court of Appeals took a different approach from the lower court. Agreeing with Griswold, it reversed the Louisville Chancery Court and held that the greenbacks could not be used to pay a debt that was entered into prior to the passage of the act making greenbacks legal tender.

The Hepburns were just as stubborn as Griswold. They appealed to the U.S. Supreme Court by a writ of error. The case came to the court under the title of *Susan P. Hepburn and Henry H. P. Hepburn, Plffs. in Err., v. Henry A. Griswold.*[2] The U.S. government was vitally interested in upholding the acts of February 25, 1862, in all of their facets. However, the government did not petition to become a party to the case. The attorney general, William M. Evarts, took the more expeditious approach of associating himself with the Hepburns' attorney, W. Preston, as co-counsel. Griswold was represented by Clarkson N. Potter. Griswold associated himself with Potter as co-counsel.

The Arguments before the Court

The arguments to the court were not made until December 10, 1869. The Hepburns' attorneys were the first to present their case. It appears that their attorneys, Evarts and Preston, were not very well coordinated in their presentations. Their arguments were convoluted and at times difficult to follow. Points were repeated, at times the same point being presented in different ways.

Their first point was that what constitutes money and its measurement, and what constitutes legal tender, was a proper function of government. Addressing themselves to the disparity in values between greenbacks and specie, they argued that no theory based upon liberty or personal rights of individuals could possibly withdraw this function from government. However, they were careful to point out to the court that this function of government was not a substantive power of government, but rather it was a correlative function of some substantive power of government. Therefore, whether or not this function was constitutional had to be considered in terms of how it related to and furthered the power to which it was adjunct. In doing this, the only question to be answered was whether the use of the money and legal tender powers in this fashion were within the realm of the legislative power of Congress. These powers would be within the legislative realm of Congress, they argued, unless it could be shown that the whole power of determining legal tender was assigned to the states, or that the exercise of the power was otherwise in excess of its Federal authority.

The Hepburns' attorneys then pointed out to the court that the act of Congress in question was not an encroachment upon the jurisdiction of the states, because legal tender was so closely associated with the regulation of money, and this power was assigned to the Federal government under Article I, Section 8 of the U.S. Constitution. Similarly, the power to coin money and emit bills of credit were denied the states in Section 10 of the same article.

Evarts and Preston had greater difficulty in dealing with another part of Section 10, which said that no state could make anything except gold or silver a tender in the payment of debts. Although they admitted that this passage seemed to indicate that states had some authority to deal with legal tender, using an unusual approach, they cited the Connecticut delegates to the Constitutional Convention as explaining at that time that this language in Section 10 was placed there as a necessity to ensure security to commerce. The intent of the constitutional language, taken all together, they maintained, showed a clear indication that the control of money and legal tender was assigned to the Federal government. Therefore, they concluded, the Federal government, in passing the acts of February 25, 1862, did not infringe upon powers held by the states, because all the powers of money and legal tender were held by the Federal government.

The next point in their argument was that the Federal government had not exceeded these powers by passing the acts. They began by pointing out to the court that there were no constitutional limitations placed upon the Federal government pertaining to legal tender, currency, or financial arrangements made to raise funds. This, combined with the fact that the Constitution granted the powers to coin money to the Federal government and restricted this power from the states, as previously argued, demonstrated that the founding fathers meant that the Federal government should possess these powers, the attorneys insisted. The founding fathers were careful to construct the Constitution in such a way that the problems that people would encounter, such as the problem of legal tender, could be met, not avoided. Any conclusion differing from that which determined that the Federal government had the power to issue paper money and to make it legal tender was intolerable and irrational, they asserted.

Evarts and Preston then argued that the total responsibility to conduct war descended upon the Federal government. Under Article VI of the Constitution, laws made in pursuance of the Constitution were the supreme law of the land. Congress had the choice of allowing the government to fall under the stress of war or treating the problem. They asserted that the condition of war compelled the nation, however opulent, to substitute "coined credit," and fix it as legal tender, to solve the inadequacy of coined money.

As a concluding point clinching their argument, the Hepburns' attorneys maintained that under Section 4 of the new Fourteenth Amendment to the Constitution, the validity of the public debt could not be questioned. Therefore, they stated that any challenge to paper money was out of line and should be suppressed. At this point the arguments on behalf of the Hepburns came to a close.

Potter and Griswold's argument was directed at proving that insofar as the greenbacks law applied to the payment of debts prior to its passage, it was unconstitutional. Much of this argument, if accepted by the court, brought into question the constitutionality of the entire law.

They began by characterizing many of the arguments of supporters of the law as purely political. They insisted that these arguments started "in the clouds" and developed "misty notions" as to the role of government by muddling up and confusing a government of unlimited sovereignty with a constitutional government. Potter and Griswold then reminded the court that those who insisted that a statute was constitutional bore the burden of proof, and they would test the constitutionality of the law on the basis of the letter and spirit of the Constitution, not on what a political party thought the Constitution said.

It was not a proper constitutional interpretation, they argued, to say that if a power was not prohibited to the Federal government, it therefore existed. On the contrary, the Federal government was a government of enumerated powers that were delegated; all powers not delegated did not exist. The Federal government had certain specified war powers, as delegated in Article I, Section 8 of the Constitution. However, they maintained, the Constitution was the same in peace and war.

Continuing this line of argument, Potter and Griswold pointed out that the only part of the Constitution that mentioned tender was set forth in Article I, Section 10, which forbade states from making anything other than gold and silver legal tender. This was all the proof needed to show that the power to fix legal tender was delegated to the states, they argued; if it were not so delegated, there would be no basis for this prohibition to appear.

The only grant of power over money to the Federal government in the Constitution was contained in Article I, Section 8, they said, which gave the Federal government the power to coin money and regulate its value. This provision, Potter and Griswold insisted, referred only to metallic coin; to consider Treasury notes as coin under this provision was absurd. They went on to argue that if Treasury notes were considered coin, then foreign coin, which Congress could regulate and allow to circulate, could consist of notes of the Bank of England or Turkish "shinplasters" or other "worthless rubbish."

Potter and Griswold then told the court that it bothered them that greenbacks were merely evidence of debt, like promissory notes. If a creditor accepted them in payment of a debt, he had simply substituted the government as payer in place of the debtor. This was not payment, they argued, as true payment occurred only when a debt was paid with coin.

They next argued that the greenbacks law interfered with the terms of existing contracts, and this was not a proper application of law. Using greenbacks to pay debts that were incurred prior to the passage of the law enabled a debtor to be released from his contract without full performance, they explained, and this deprived the creditor of his property without full compensation. This, they argued, improperly gave the Federal government the power to annihilate all debts.

The counsel continued with Griswold's case by arguing that the making of greenbacks legal tender for all debts was an independent, substantive power analogous to taxation. However, as a tax it was invalid, because it was not uniform and the money that was deprived from creditors did not revert to the government, but rather to debtors.

Referring back to war powers, Potter and Griswold, as they had argued in the lower courts, reasserted that the Constitution provided the means of raising funds to conduct the war in Article I, Section 8: taxation and the borrowing of money. These means, they insisted, must be used regardless of the emergency before the country. And, they added, issuing paper money was not within the power to borrow money.

Griswold and Potter closed their reasonably concise and well-reasoned argument by asking the court to declare unconstitutional that part of the Legal Tender Acts that made greenbacks legal tender to pay debts incurred prior to the enactment of the law.

The Opinion of the Court
The justices took the case under consideration and rendered their decision on February 7, 1870. The opinion was written by Chief Justice Salmon P. Chase.

This was one of the more unusual opinions of the court, in that it rambled and intertwined Chase's strong personal opinions with the law and the legal findings of the lower courts. Chase was secretary of the Treasury when the Legal Tender Acts were passed on February 25, 1862. Though slow to support the "greenbacks law," he did so vigorously when he became convinced that no alternative existed to solving the nation's financial dilemma.

Chase had been appointed to the court by President Lincoln on December 15, 1864, replacing Roger Brooke Taney as chief justice. It can be assumed that Chase believed that there was a constitutional basis supporting the statute when he advocated its passage as secretary of the Treasury. The Hepburn case placed him in a position where he was forced to consider that constitutionality as chief justice of the Supreme Court. Six justices remained on the court in addition to Chase when the decision was made, Robert C. Grier having retired from the court just six days prior to the court's decision. They were Nathan Clifford, Samuel Nelson, Noah Swayne, Samuel F. Miller, Stephen J. Field, and David Davis.

The chief justice began the court's opinion by stating that the question to be determined by the court was whether the payee or assignee of a note made prior to February 25, 1862, was obliged by law to accept United States notes at face value in full payment of the note. In order to make this determination, Chase said, the constitutionality of that part of the statute fixing the United States notes as legal tender would have to be determined insofar as the statute applied to that fact situation.

Chase then included in its entirety that part of the law that declared United States notes to be legal tender in the payment of debts, public and private, within the United States. The law stated certain exceptions, and three cases previously considered by the court set out additional exceptions. The exceptions in the law were that the notes would not be legal tender to pay duties on imports, claims against the United States, or interest on government bonds and notes. Chase himself had written the opinions in the three cases creating additional exceptions. In *The County of Lane v. Oregon,*[3] decided February 8, 1869, it was held that the Legal Tender Acts had no application to the payment of state taxes; in *Bronson v. Rodes,*[4] decided February 15, 1869, it was determined that contracts that expressly called for payment in coin could not be paid with United States notes; and in *Butler v. Horwitz,*[5] decided on March 1, 1869, the court held that damages incurring in Bronson-type contracts should be paid with coin. Chase stated that none of these exceptions applied to the fact situation in the *Hepburn* case.

The chief justice then set out the established rule for the interpretation of statutes: that they must be interpreted in a manner consistent with justice and equity to the exclusion of another interpretation, unless the meaning of a statute was otherwise clearly ascertained. Then the court must give effect to the clearly ascertained legislative intent of the law as long as that intent was not repugnant to the Constitution. Applying this rule, Chase indicated that strong reasoning supported the clear intent of the statute that it was meant to apply to debts contracted subsequent to the law's passage.

It was clear that the United States notes were not equal in value to the money, gold and silver, that the parties had contracted for in debts incurred prior to the passage of the law, Chase said. He cited that at one time it took $2.85 in greenbacks to equal $1.00 in gold, and even at the greenbacks' high point during the course of the case, it still took $1.20 in greenbacks to equal $1.00 in gold.

Chase then stated that there was no doubt that the Legal Tender Acts also were meant to cover debts incurred prior to the passage of the statutes. This meant that a holder of a note was forced to accept an amount substantially less than his contract called for. This arbitrarily altered the terms of the contract, Chase observed, and this was contrary to justice and equity. This interpretation of the law was not to be favored if any other intent of the legislature could be found. He posed the question as to whether it would be a fair and reasonable construction of the acts to say that the debts referred to applied only to debts following their passage. Chase answered the question, after reviewing several aspects of the law itself, that the term debts, as well as the legal tender clause, applied to contracts made before the passage of the acts as well as to contracts made after. That being the case, the chief justice repeated that the prime question to be determined by the court was whether Congress had the power to make United States notes legal tender to pay debts contracted prior to the passage of the Legal Tender Acts, when it was understood by the parties involved that these debts were to be paid in gold and silver coin when they were contracted.

The opinion continued to ramble. However, it was apparent that Chase would answer the prime issue before the court by considering three questions: whether the Constitution granted Congress the express or implied power to make United States notes legal tender outside of its war powers; whether Congress had the ability to legislate legal tender under its war powers; and whether provisions of the Fifth Amendment prohibited Congress from establishing legal tender in the manner provided for in the greenbacks law.

Chase began his analysis of the first question by observing that Congress had only the legislative powers granted by the Constitution, and had no powers not granted as set out in Amendment X. The exception to this was that Congress had incidental, or implied, powers to carry out purposes of the express powers. The chief justice noted that the majority of governmental functions were carried out by Congress under the provisions of implied powers.

It was obvious, he said, that there was no express grant in the Constitution that allowed Congress to make a credit currency legal tender to pay debts. The true question was whether or not there was an implied power. Chase indicated that the rule defining implied powers was set forth in detail by the former Chief Justice John Marshall in the famous case of *McCulloch v. Maryland*,[6] decided in 1819. In that case, Marshall stated that if the end was legitimate and within the scope of the Constitution, all means adopted to achieve that end, if they were not otherwise prohibited and were consistent with the letter and spirit of the Constitution, were constitutional.

Chase then said that there was no doubt that the power to establish a standard of value and to determine lawful money and legal tender was a governmental power arising out of the congressional power to coin money. However, the power to issue notes as currency and make them legal tender to pay debts incurred prior to the passage of the Legal Tender Acts was not the same as coining money. He observed that the whole history of the country refuted the action that the power to issue bills and notes incorporated the power to make them legal tender.

The chief justice emphasized this point further by saying that the states had the power to authorize and regulate the issue of bills for circulation by banks, but they were prohibited from making anything other than gold or silver legal tender under the provisions of Article I, Section 10 of the Constitution. Chase declared that this was decisive on the point that the power to issue notes and the power to make them legal tender were not the same. He then repeated that as far as the normal congressional powers were concerned, he could not find that Congress had the power to make the United States notes legal tender.

Chase then turned to the question of whether this power could be found within the powers of Congress to conduct war, regulate commerce, and borrow money under Article I, Section 8 of the Constitution. He began by posing the question of whether the making of United States notes legal tender was an appropriate means of carrying on the war. The main argument in support of this, he said, was to permit the government to pay the debts generated by its war activities. If this argument were valid, according to Chase, Congress could justify doing anything, because the exercise of any power involved the use of money. This argument proved too much because it would create a government of unlimited powers. These same considerations were equally valid when applied to the powers to regulate commerce and to borrow money.

The chief justice then considered the consequences of legal tender as applied to all debts under the provisions of the Fifth Amendment to the Constitution. The Fifth Amendment provided that a citizen should not be deprived of his property without due process of law, nor should private property be taken for public use without just compensation. Chase carefully explained that individuals who were paid in notes for debts incurred after the passage of the act did not suffer. People in this position would not contract to be paid in notes for more than they were worth; the price of the commodity would rise in ratio to the notes' depreciation. But those whose debts were incurred before the passage of the act did not have the opportunity of experiencing this price adjustment. These people would clearly lose part of their property, in violation of the Fifth Amendment. Also, said Chase, this would impair contracts, which would be a violation of the spirit of the Constitution.

For all the reasons stated, the chief justice then held that the judgment of the Court of Appeals of Kentucky was affirmed, holding on behalf of the court that debts incurred prior to the passage of the Legal Tender Acts could not be paid with United States notes.

The vote of the court was four to three. Justice Samuel F. Miller wrote a dissenting opinion in which Justices Noah Swayne and David Davis joined. In contrast to the majority opinion by Chief Justice Chase, the dissenting opinion was concise and well reasoned.

Justice Miller began his opinion by agreeing with Chase that the issue before the court was whether Congress had the express or implied power to make United States notes legal tender. Miller indicated that this power was specifically denied to the states and was not forbidden to Congress, though it was not made an express power that Congress could exercise. The specific powers granted to Congress in the Constitution were that Congress was authorized to coin money and regulate its value, to declare war, to suppress insurrection, to raise and support armies, to provide and maintain a navy, to borrow money, to provide for defense, and to provide for the general welfare, all under Article I, Section 8 of the Constitution. The power to make notes legal tender may not stand alone, Miller said, but it could exist as an implied power to carry out any one of the enumerated express powers.

The justice then considered the general constitutional clause that closed the specific enumeration of the powers granted to Congress in Article I, Section 8: that Congress should have the power to make all laws that should be necessary and proper for carrying out the purposes of the express powers. When an act of Congress was brought to the test of this clause, Miller said, its necessity must be absolute and its adoption to the conceded purpose unquestionable.

Miller also quoted Chief Justice John Marshall in *McCulloch v. Maryland* that this constitutional provision must remain flexible, for it was intended to endure for the ages and be adoptable to various crises in human affairs. The rules interpreting this clause, Marshall said, must not be immutable, because this would make the Constitution nothing more than a legal code. Miller continued expressing Marshall's views that Congress must be allowed to operate within rules that would allow it to accommodate legislation to circumstances.

These statements of the venerable Chief Justice Marshall, said Miller, applied to the situation where Congress had made United States notes legal tender as a means of prosecuting a war. Without legal tender, the war could have ended disastrously. Large armies in the field would have remained unpaid, and the then current expenditures of over $1 million a day could not have been met. Prior to legal tender, said Miller, the credit of the government was exhausted, and taxation resources were inadequate to pay even the interest on the public debt. Legal tender provided an instant means of paying soldiers in the field and permitted the filling of the coffers of the commissaries and quartermasters. By also furnishing a medium for the payment of private debts, it restored confidence in the public. Legal tender, according to Miller, enabled the government to borrow double the amount of money that existed in the entire country. It gave money perpetual value because it could discharge debts; without legal tender, the value of money would have become worthless.

Commenting upon congressional acts that impaired contracts, Miller stated that the government had long had this power through its express powers to legislate in the field of bankruptcy under Article I, Section 8 of the Constitution. The argument that private property could not be taken for public use was too vague and dangerous, he said, for a declaration of war in itself reduced the value of many citizens' properties, such as ships used for ocean transport.

Miller closed the dissenting opinion by stating that where there was a choice of means to obtain the objectives of express powers, the selection of the means was with Congress, not with the courts. He believed that Congress had acted properly, and that the Court of Appeals of Kentucky should have been overruled.

The court's decision in the *Hepburn* case greatly disappointed those who backed and had come to rely upon the paper money system—people in various government departments, farmers, small businessmen, and many others who found themselves constantly in debt. These people were worried that the indebtedness they incurred with greenbacks would have to be repaid with gold. Those who delighted in the *Hepburn* decision were the bankers, creditors, and advocates of so-called "hard" money.

Further disturbing to many people was the fact that the opinion of Chief Justice Chase not only determined the issue in that case that greenbacks could not be used to pay debts incurred prior to the passage of the Legal Tender Acts, but also seemed to question the constitutionality of the entire acts. Most of the public was left with the feeling that the court must further clarify the application of the acts, while the justices who participated in the majority opinion of the court took the stand that the issues had been irretrievably settled.

However, this was not the last to be heard on the subject. The justices who were in the minority in the *Hepburn* decision put pressure on the court to somehow have the case reviewed. Meanwhile, the membership of the court changed. Justice James M. Wayne had died in July 1867, and Justice Robert C. Grier resigned on February 1, 1870. These two vacancies, combined with new legislation passed by Congress in 1869 raising the number of justices on the court to nine, gave President Ulysses S. Grant an opportunity to fill these two positions. Indeed, on the same day that the decision was rendered in the *Hepburn* case, February 7, 1870, Grant appointed William Strong and Joseph P. Bradley to the court. They were both confirmed by the Senate the following month.

As a jurist on the Pennsylvania Supreme Court, William Strong had participated in a state court decision that upheld the Legal Tender Acts. Strong was a stalwart Christian and part of a group that advocated the amendment of the Constitution making Jesus Christ the supreme authority. Joseph P. Bradley's law practice had consisted primarily of railroad clients. Once on the court, however, he was a hard-headed advocate of his concept of Christian standards.

THE *KNOX* AND *PARKER* CASES

Two more Legal Tender Cases arrived at the Supreme Court in 1869 and 1870 and were argued concurrently. Back in March 1863 in the state of Texas, the

Confederacy confiscated and sold 608 sheep owned by Phoebe G. and Hugh Lee as property of an alien enemy, because Texans claimed that the Lees had remained loyal to the Union. This was done under terms of a Confederate law that set aside the proceeds of such a sale as an indemnity for like confiscations that were taking place in the North. William B. Knox purchased the sheep at the sale.

When the war came to a close, the Lees sued Knox to recover the value of the confiscated sheep. The case was filed in the reconstituted Circuit Court of the United States for the Western District of Texas. At the trial, the court held for the Lees, holding that the Confederate government was not capable of conveying good title to the sheep to Knox. Before the Lees closed their case, however, they offered to prove to the court the difference in value between specie, gold and silver, and greenbacks. The purpose of this was to show the court that the sheep had greater value in specie, and thus their damages should be paid in gold and silver, a matter that the Legal Tender Acts and the *Butler* case did not clearly answer.

Knox objected to this offer of proof on the basis that greenbacks were made legal tender by law, and legally there was no difference in value between the two. The court sustained the objection and excluded the offered evidence. It then held that no good title could be conferred by the Confederate government and therefore entered a decree in favor of the Lees. The court also held that whatever amount the jury awarded to the Lees could be paid in legal tender United States notes, greenbacks. Knox appealed to the U.S. Supreme Court on the judgment itself by writ of error. This brought the issue of the Circuit Court's denial of the Lees' offer of proof of the difference in value between greenbacks and gold and silver before the Supreme Court.

A second case arrived to the court concurrently with the *Knox* case. Within the commonwealth of Massachusetts and prior to the passage of the Legal Tender Acts, George Davis had entered into a contract to purchase a woodland from Thomas H. Parker. The contract was basic and simple. It stated that when Davis put together the amount of money called for in the contract and tendered it to Parker, Parker would execute and deliver a deed conveying the property to Davis.

Upon the passage of the Legal Tender Acts, Davis raised the amount of money called for in the contract in greenbacks and tendered the amount to Parker. Parker refused to accept the greenbacks and to execute the deed to the woodland. Davis then filed suit in Massachusetts, which culminated with the Supreme Judicial Court of the Commonwealth of Massachusetts decreeing an order of specific performance in favor of Davis against Parker. This order was entered in February 1867 and stated that Davis should pay the agreed amount of money into the court, and Parker should thereupon execute the deed to Davis conveying the woodland to him. Pursuant to the decree, Davis paid the sum ordered by the court in greenbacks into the court. Parker again refused to execute the deed, still insisting that he was entitled to have the sum paid into court in coin, and that a payment in greenbacks did not comply with the court's order.

At this stage, the Massachusetts court ordered a further hearing. Listening to the arguments of counsel, the court then ordered Parker to execute a deed to Davis when Davis deposited with the court the contractual amount in Treasury notes of the United States. "Treasury notes" did not always include greenbacks; however, one thing that was clear was that Davis was not required to deposit coin under terms of the court order. Totally exasperated at this point, Parker appealed this order to the U.S. Supreme Court.

Although the situations leading to the *Hepburn, Knox,* and *Parker* cases all occurred in the midst of the Civil War, the court strove mightily to avoid making a decision on the constitutionality of the greenbacks during the conflict. Following the close of the war, it seemed apparent to nearly everyone who had thought about it that a modern nation moving into the industrial age could not survive without paper money as its financial base.

The *Hepburn* decision was restricted to the facts before the court, yet the reasoning used in the court's opinion threatened the legality of all paper money. When the court was presented with the *Knox* and *Parker* cases in 1869 and 1870, seven and eight years after the fact situations had occurred, the court still tried to avoid them as though the consideration of the constitutionality of legal tender was like coming into contact with a communicable, fatal disease.

Finally the *Knox* case was set on the docket for argument on November 17, 1869. It was ordered reargued on February 23, 1871, in conjunction with the *Parker* case.[7]

The First Arguments before the Court

William B. Knox was represented by George W. Paschal and George W. Paschal, Jr. Their arguments were concentrated upon whether the Confederate government could convey a good title to the sheep. It was easy to argue that every act of the Confederate government was void from the beginning, they said, yet the Confederate government operated with a strong arm of power, and it was in actuality a *de facto* governmental entity. Knox's counsel quoted texts and Justice Miller in supporting the view that the acts of a *de facto* government should be accepted as valid. As to the offer of the Lees to prove the difference in value between specie and greenbacks, the Paschals argued that the finding was in error and it was a basis for a new trial.

The Lees were represented by attorney J. A. Wills. He argued, on behalf of the Lees, that the Paschals' claim that laws passed by a *de facto* government were valid, if carried to its logical consequences, would validate all of the acts of the Rebel government. Wills then quoted Chief Justice Chase in the case of *Texas v. White* that the acts of the Rebel government that were necessary to further peace and good order among the citizens, if valid if decreed by a lawful government, could be accepted as valid. However, the acts of a *de facto* government in aid of the Rebellion would be invalid and void. Therefore, Wills argued, the conveyance of the sheep to Knox by the Confederate government in aid of the Rebellion did not convey good title.

The balance of Wills's argument was spent on damages. He indicated that the Lees had suffered $8,106.66 $2/3$ in damages, saying nothing about the difference in value computed by specie against greenbacks. The arguments in *Knox v. Lee* thus came to a close.

With no interruption, the court then heard the arguments in the case of *Parker v. Davis*.[8] Benjamin F. Thomas represented Thomas H. Parker. Thomas's argument was short and concise. He argued that the Legal Tender Acts made greenbacks legal tender to pay debts. However, his client's contract with Davis was a conditional contract, and no debt existed until Davis had tendered coin. Coin was required because the entire arrangement had been entered into prior to the passage of the Legal Tender Acts. Since this was not accomplished by Davis, Thomas concluded, Parker had no duty to execute a deed on the woodland and convey the property to Davis.

Four attorneys represented Davis: Benjamin F. Butler, George S. Boutwell, D. S. Richardson, and George F. Richardson. Butler, their spokesman, submitted to the court that under the contract between the parties, no amount was due Parker from Davis until the judgment of the trial court created a debt. This was done in 1867, substantially after the passage of the Legal Tender Acts. Butler then argued that the trial court's decree, given in equity, was a totally competent thing for the trial court to do. This was not reviewable by the Supreme Court, Butler argued, because no Federal issue was involved. Further, he insisted that there was no issue before the Supreme Court as to whether the Legal Tender Acts applied to debts before their passage, because the debt was created after passage. With this, the arguments in both cases came to a close.

At this point, the cases, except for the delays, were more or less routine. Counsel had treated the *Knox* case in such a manner that legal tender was not the main issue in the case. In the *Parker* case, legal tender was involved, but only to the extent as to determine whether the debt was incurred before or after the date the Legal Tender Acts were passed. Based upon how the parties had handled the cases, the court could have decided them easily and proceeded to other business.

However, at the end of the oral arguments, Clarkson N. Potter, the attorney for Henry A. Griswold in the case of *Hepburn v. Griswold,* stood and approached the lectern. Being recognized by the chief justice, Potter requested of the court that he be heard on the constitutional question that the Knox and Parker cases presented. Although it was somewhat of a stretch, that question was the constitutionality of the Legal Tender Acts. That request being made, President Grant's new attorney general from Georgia, Amos T. Akerman, stood and expressed a desire to also be heard on the issues if the court should grant permission to Clarkson N. Potter to be heard on the constitutionality of the acts.

What took place here was a most unusual, if not unheard of, procedure. There was nothing in the rules of the Supreme Court that covered an attorney requesting to be heard in a case where he was not listed as a counsel to one of the parties before the court. This situation was probably a reflection of the great animosity that had been generated among the justices of the court when they considered the *Hepburn* case in conference. This animosity grew in intensity as pressures arose within and without the court to reconsider the *Hepburn* decision. The *Hepburn* case held that greenbacks were not legal tender to pay debts that were incurred prior to the passage of the Legal Tender Acts. It was apparent, however, that the justices constituting the majority in that case, Chase, Clifford, Nelson, and Field, would have had the entire acts declared unconstitutional if they were given a chance to do so. The minority justices, Miller, Swayne, and Davis, believed the majority decision to be an aberration and wanted the issue brought back before the court as soon as possible.

When President Grant appointed Strong and Bradley to the court, the justices realized that the minority in the *Hepburn* case had, in all likelihood, become a majority. The former majority justices retreated to defending the *Hepburn* decision, insisting that the decision had been irrevocably made and could not, under any circumstances, be reconsidered.

There must have been an informal and unofficial communication between the court, possibly by means of the court's clerk, and Clarkson N. Potter, informing him that the court may reconsider the *Hepburn* case, and that from the briefs previously submitted, the issues had not been adequately covered. The attorney general must have been aware that Potter was going to make his request to be heard, for there was no other reason for him to have been present. The true facts are obscured. It is known that after the requests to be heard were made, they were considered by the court in conference and agreed to in a short order given by Justice Nathan Clifford. The justice ordered that Potter and the attorney general be heard on April 12, 1871, on the questions of whether the Legal Tender Acts were constitutional as to contracts made before their passage, and whether the acts were valid when applied to transactions since their passage.

Though he gave the order, Clifford then dissented from the order, especially from the first question, stating that the first question had been conclusively settled by the *Hepburn* case. Justices Nelson and Field joined him in the dissent.

On April 12, 1871, Justice Clifford delayed the hearing yet another time because of the illness of Justice Nelson. At this time, Justice Swayne gave an informal opinion reciting the history of the two cases and prodding the justices of the court to hear the cases just as quickly as feasible, that such a long delay as had been experienced with these cases involved a denial of justice. For the sake of the court as well as the public, said Swayne, both cases, and the important questions they presented, should be decided and put to rest as speedily as could be done with propriety. Nelson recovered sufficiently by April 18, 1871, and the cases proceeded to argument in their second phase on that date.[9]

The Second Arguments before the Court
Clarkson Potter argued first. He gave a much longer and more involved argument than his presentation on behalf of Henry A. Griswold in the *Hepburn*

case. He opened by lecturing the court concerning Federal powers. It was an analysis that most of the justices of the court had heard several times by this stage of the cases. Nevertheless, Potter deemed it fundamental and important, and he went through it yet again. The Federal government had no powers except those expressly delegated to it by the Constitution. It also possessed the powers necessary to execute the delegated powers. If the end was legitimate and within the scope of the letter and spirit of the Constitution, Potter conceded, all appropriate means not otherwise prohibited could be used to carry out the specifically delegated powers.

Potter then posed the question that since there was no express delegation of the power to make Treasury notes legal tender, could the delegated powers to coin money and regulate its value, to borrow money, to regulate commerce, and to raise and support an army and navy and the other war powers be sufficient to allow the Federal government to make Treasury notes legal tender?

Certainly, Potter argued, the power did not arise from the right to coin money. This power, he added, was not a grant to create money, but only to coin money. The founders of the Constitution clearly meant these words as a power to strike metallic coin. The power to regulate money was only a power to regulate its value. Treasury notes, according to Potter, had no intrinsic value. Their only value was the promise to pay, and creating promises to pay clearly did not fall within the power to coin money.

Potter went on to argue that the powers of Congress to regulate value throughout the nation's history had been to regulate the values of coined money only. He gave several illustrations from U.S. history to show that Congress had always sought to conform the stamped value of a coin to its true intrinsic value, and that Congress had made a coin legal tender only in that instance. At times, other aspects of a coin, such as convenience and portability, caused a coin to circulate at a struck value higher than its intrinsic value, but this was rare. Potter argued that debasements of the currency in the past had been to equalize intrinsic values. The first coinage in 1792 established gold and silver in the relative value of 15 to 1. In 1823, when the intrinsic values adjusted to 16 to 1, Congress followed with legislation making that ratio legal. When the California gold rush reduced the value of gold, Congress provided for the minting of silver 3-cent pieces at a depreciated value, later reducing silver 6 percent in value.

Throughout these times, Potter argued, Congress did nothing to impair the rights of creditors or to impair contracts. The debasements, when made, were always based upon intrinsic values and were too trifling to be regarded. Congress never assumed that it had the power to strike coined metals with false or arbitrary values, and therefore, he argued, there certainly did not exist the power to print mere promises to pay and make these promises legal tender.

Congress had no right to assume this power in the time of danger such as the war, Potter asserted. The financial crises caused by the war could have been adequately handled by the congressional powers to borrow money and regulate commerce. Potter argued further that no necessity had existed to issue the notes.

He asserted that times were prosperous in 1862, and the panic of 1857 had already led to a general liquidation. The entire business of the country was being handled by unredeemable bank paper, which was not legal tender and had not suffered any great depreciation. Potter asserted that there was no danger of a general insolvency of the country; specie payments had been suspended in 1837, 1857, and 1861 without the country experiencing financial ruin. In addition, Potter queried, if the Legal Tender Acts were passed because of necessity, how could the acts prevail when the necessity had passed?

In a most unusual argument, Potter indicated that Treasury notes had been in circulation in the Confederacy since 1861. The notes were not legal tender, and they were accepted to pay all debts. Potter did acknowledge, however, that the Confederate notes fluctuated in value according to the success, or lack of success, of the Confederate armed forces.

Potter then explained to the court that the power of legal tender was not a right to be assumed as an inherent right of sovereignty. He cited William Blackstone, the noted British jurist, that sovereignty did not extend to debasing or enhancing the value of coin below or above its sterling value. The tender power, argued Potter, was forbidden to the states and never delegated to the Federal government. The tender power was reserved to the people and was never intended to be granted to the Federal government. Potter repeated his earlier arguments that the founders of the country had clearly indicated this. As further support, he quoted Daniel Webster from *Webster's Works* that there never could be any other legal tender but gold and silver.

Legal tender power could never be properly exercised under the commerce power or under the power to fix weights and measures, Potter asserted. As to the latter, Congress could not reduce a pound to eight ounces or a foot to six inches.

Potter then maintained that the Legal Tender Acts impaired the obligations of contracts; those who argued that Congress had the power to do so failed to recognize that Congress had such powers only where such powers were specifically delegated, as in the field of bankruptcy.

Advocating the gradual return to a specie dollar as the only feasible alternative to the country's currency problems, Potter concluded his argument by adding that Congress should not have had the power to authorize notes as legal tender, especially to pay debts incurred prior to the passage of the acts. This was one of the few times in Potter's entire argument where he emphasized the payment of debts incurred prior to the acts' passage. Potter emotionally pleaded with the court to enter a judgment consistent with his arguments, and said that such a decision would roll back the wave of centralization and "rescue that system of localized and limited government, in which alone true liberty can be found."

Amos T. Akerman, the attorney general of the United States, then gave a very short and concise argument that the Legal Tender Acts were constitutional when applied to the payment of debts incurred both before and after the passage of the acts.

First Akerman referred to the *Hepburn* opinion and the reasons stated by Chief Justice Chase as to why the Legal Tender Acts were unconstitutional when applied to the payment of debts incurred prior to the acts' passage. Akerman severely criticized the *Hepburn* decision by questioning whether the court should have had any role whatsoever in the legal tender issue. He argued that where the object contemplated by Congress was lawful, and if the power selected to put that object into being was constitutional, the means selected, whatever may be the opinion of the court as to the practical wisdom of the means, was a political and administrative question, not a judicial one. The only role of the court was to determine whether the means adopted, if not prohibited by the Constitution, had the design of executing the constitutional power. It was not the court's role to ascertain whether, in the opinion of the justices, the means had proved practical and successful.

Akerman was attempting to get the justices to think in terms of basic concepts of the role of the court, rather than about the details of various aspects of the law, such as whether contracts had been affected and whether certain people had been improperly deprived of their property. He was trying to persuade them to think along the lines that if the congressional object, such as fighting an insurrection, was lawful, and the means used to fight the insurrection, such as the making of Treasury notes legal tender, was not unconstitutional in its own right and furthered the objective, the means used was within the province of Congress, not the courts, because no judicial issue was involved. And certainly, Akerman added, the court had no right to consider the means used on the basis of its practicability or success; these clearly were not judicial issues.

He then argued that Congress had the undoubted power to carry on war; to provide for the raising, equipping, and supporting of armies and navies; to borrow money to pay the debts of the United States; and to issue bills of credit in time of war. During the Rebellion, these activities took sums of money greatly exceeding all of the gold and silver coin in the United States. Is it to be held, Akerman asked, that it was not within the constitutional powers of Congress to declare that bills of credit carrying the pledge of the government to pay were of the same value as coined money? He asserted that it was incompetent for any court to determine and declare that these bills were of less value.

The attorney general posed a fact situation: Suppose, he asserted, that A was paying a debt to B with gold. During military operations, it was perfectly legal for the government to confiscate the gold from B and give B a certificate of indebtedness. What was the difference, Akerman asked, if the gold were confiscated in this fashion or a certificate of indebtedness were given A to transfer to B?

Akerman then posed a question: "Can any citizen rightfully say or ask this court to decide that the promise of the government does not import and possess the full value of that which it promises, in any case in which he is invoking the aid of the government to enforce his rights?"

He concluded his argument by reminding the justices that the power to determine what should be legal tender was a proper function of government, it was not reserved to the people, and it was denied to states. Nowhere was it explicitly prohibited to the national government. Furthermore, Akerman argued, this power was used by the governments of every civilized nation. Could this power be denied the United States by a judicial decision?

The attorney general filed as part of his argument the brief prepared by then Attorney General William M. Evarts, in *Hepburn v. Griswold.*

The Opinion of the Court

The majority opinion of the court was written by Justice William Strong, one of the two new appointees to the court. The opinion was handed down by the court on May 1, 1871. Strong had participated in upholding the Legal Tender Acts while a judge on the Pennsylvania Supreme Court.

The justice opened his opinion by stating that the issue before the court consisted of whether the Legal Tender Acts were constitutional when applied to contracts before their passage and when applied to debts contracted since they were passed. Strong acknowledged that these issues had been elaborately argued, and he stated that the court had given them the consideration that their great importance demanded. He emphasized that this decision would affect the entire business of the country and possibly determine the continued existence of the national government. Every sovereign country had the power to determine legal tender, he said, and if it should be held that the United States did not possess that power, the national government would be without the means of self-preservation. In addition, such a decision would cause great business derangement, widespread distress, and the rankest injustice. The justice acknowledged that men throughout the country, relying on the legal tender of Treasury notes, had bought, sold, borrowed, lent, and assumed a large variety of obligations. Indeed, he said, legal tender Treasury notes had become the universal measure of value. If the decision of the court was that these debts could be discharged only by gold coin, the government would become an instrument of the grossest injustice, and the demand for gold would create ruinous sacrifices, distress, and bankruptcy. These consequences were too obvious to admit of question. When considering the constitutionality of the Legal Tender Acts, Strong held, there was in actuality no difference between considering the acts' application to debts before and after their passage. To hold the Legal Tender Acts unconstitutional, he said, that unconstitutionality would have to have been plainly obvious. A decent respect for a coordinate branch of the government demanded that the judiciary should presume the acts to be constitutional unless the violation of the Constitution was so manifest as to leave no room for reasonable doubt.

Following a lengthy discussion of the theory and nature of constitutional government, Strong stated that it would have been a most unreasonable interpretation of the Constitution to deny the government the right to have freely employed every means, not prohibited, necessary for its preservation and the fulfillment of its duties. This right was guaranteed by the last clause of Article

I, Section 8, and this section, together with other aspects of the Constitution, tended to plainly show that powers existed with the national government that were neither expressly specified nor deducible in that document, but grew out of the aggregate powers attributed to the government.

The justice cited many examples of instances where the national government exercised powers not specifically granted by the Constitution. Among these were the rights to sue, make contracts, build a capitol or a presidential mansion, and pass a penal code that was much more expansive than specifically provided in the Constitution. The court's past approval of these powers demonstrated, said the justice, the undisclosed governmental powers that existed as aids to the execution of expressed powers.

He went on to state that the whole history of legislation illustrated that the government possessed a very wide discretion, in times of emergency or peace, in the selection of a necessary or proper means of putting into effect its many express powers, and the court had sanctioned the use of these powers. The justice followed this statement with another elaboration of where these powers had been exercised in the past. Then he cited Chief Justice John Marshall that the government must be empowered to have a choice of means to put into force a power granted by the Constitution. Marshall had made a specific reference to the government's ability to use the means most eligible to effect the payment of its debts. Strong again quoted the famous statement of Marshall that if the end were legitimate, all means, not prohibited, consistent with the letter and spirit of the Constitution, may be used to effectuate that end.[10]

Strong then held as a matter of law that before the court could hold the Legal Tender Acts unconstitutional, the court must be convinced that the acts were not an appropriate means conducive to the execution of any of the powers of Congress. To ascertain this, a consideration of the time and circumstances existing when the law was passed must be examined.

The justice stated that he did not propose to "dilate at length" upon these circumstances because they were of such recent occurrence that to enlarge upon them would not be justified. He stated that at the time of the passage of the Legal Tender Acts, a civil war was raging that threatened the overthrow of the government and the destruction of the Constitution. To conduct the war, large armies and navies were required, which demanded money to an extent beyond the capacity of the ordinary sources of supply; the Treasury was nearly empty, and the credit of the government was exhausted. No more resources could be expected from financial institutions, because specie payments had been suspended, and the amount raised by taxation was so inadequate it could not even pay the interest on the debt already incurred. The army was unpaid. The soldiers in the field were owed nearly a score of millions of dollars. Regular expenditures exceeded $1 million a day. Strong then stated that the entire amount of coin in the country, including that in private hands and with banking institutions, if all applied to government expenditures, was not sufficient to supply the needs of the government for more than three months.

It was in such circumstances, Strong said, that Congress was called upon to devise means to secure the large amount of money required to preserve the government created by the Constitution. Congress passed the Legal Tender Acts as the means of solving the financial problem. If it were certain, Strong posed, that nothing else could have supplied the solution and saved the government and Constitution from destruction, could anyone be bold enough to assert that Congress had transgressed its powers? Could anyone maintain that this was not a legitimate end for the use of the legal tender power? To insist that some other procedure, such as Treasury notes without legal tender, might have solved the problem would not have made any difference, said the justice, because this was just conjecture. In addition, if other means were available, Congress still had the right to choose what means it thought suitable. If the court held that one means was more appropriate than another, it would have entered the legislative area. Despite this statement, Strong then made the observation that notes without legal tender would not have accomplished the goal. He then concluded and held on behalf of the court that making Treasury notes legal tender was not an inappropriate means for carrying into execution legitimate powers of the government.

Next the justice considered whether the Legal Tender Acts were forbidden by the letter and spirit of the Constitution. He acknowledged that those arguing against the constitutionality of the acts relied most heavily upon this argument. This approach hinged upon the constitutional grant to Congress of the power "to coin money, regulate the value thereof, and of foreign coin," and the firm belief that this language restricted congressional power only to declaring precious metal as legal money. Strong disposed of this argument by stating that if this point of view meant that because certain powers over currency were expressly granted to Congress, all other powers relating to currency were implicitly forbidden, this was not a proper interpretation of the Constitution. The justice then gave many examples where it had been ruled that power over a particular subject might be exercised as auxiliary to an express power, though there existed another express power, less comprehensive, relating to the same subject.

The next issue considered by Strong was whether the Legal Tender Acts impaired the obligation of contracts. This argument, he explained, applied only to contracts made prior to the passage of the acts on February 25, 1862, and not to contracts consummated after that date. Strong held that neither of the two assumptions that the acts impaired contracts or that Congress was prohibited from taking any action that impaired contracts could be accepted by the court as true. He explained that every contract calling for the payment of money was necessarily subject to the constitutional power of the government over currency. The contracts in question called for the payment of lawful money of the United States, and Congress was empowered to regulate money. It was not sound, said the justice, to maintain that the Legal Tender Acts impaired the obligation of contracts. However, if the acts in fact impaired contracts, they would not be unconstitutional, because all property was subject to the demands of the sovereign, and all contracts were always made in reference to the possible exercise of the rightful authority of government. No contractual obligation, said Strong, could defeat legitimate government authority.

Furthermore, he continued, the argument that the Legal Tender Acts were prohibited by the Fifth Amendment, which forbade the taking of private property for public use without just compensation or due process of law, had never been applied to consequential injuries resulting from the exercise of lawful powers. Strong made reference to a new tariff or a war that could bring an individual great losses, but nobody had ever assumed that the new tariff could not be passed or war declared because of the Fifth Amendment.

At this point, the justice was exhausted and inclined to stop; however, he was sorely pressed to note the argument that a unit of money must possess intrinsic value. He noted that this argument emanated from the assimilation of the constitutional provision pertaining to the standard of weights and measures with the power to coin money and regulate its value. He acknowledged the argument that there could be no standard of weights without weight, or a measure without length or space. Strong said that the court had been asked how anything could be made a uniform standard of value that has no value in itself. This question, he said, was foreign to the subject before the court. The Legal Tender Acts did not attempt to make paper a standard of value, but rather the paper constituted a promise to pay the equivalent value in coinage. The dollar contained gold and silver, but it was in no sense the standard of a dollar, but rather a representation of it. Strong then mentioned that the pound sterling, coined in 1815, was almost immediately debased, yet it was the unit of British currency for many generations.

Strong concluded the court's opinion holding that the Legal Tender Acts were constitutional as applied to contracts made both before or after passage of the acts. The case of *Hepburn v. Griswold,* said the justice, was specifically overruled. He went on to mention that the *Hepburn* decision was by a divided court having fewer justices than the law provided for. The cases then present before the court, he said, were considered by a full court, and the issues received the court's most careful consideration. These issues were of the utmost national importance and should not have been heard in the *Hepburn* case in the absence of a full court. Strong went on to state that any previous case decided by the court should not be overruled inconsiderately. In considering and deciding the issues of such far-reaching consequences, the court was thoroughly convinced that Congress had not transgressed its powers, and it regarded it as its duty to affirm both judgments in the cases before it.

The judgments in each case were affirmed. A concurring opinion was rendered on the same day by the second new justice appointed to the court, Joseph P. Bradley. Justice Bradley made a few introductory remarks stating that but for the great importance of the subject of the cases, he would feel out of place adding anything to the opinion just rendered. The new justice indicated that it was his feeling that where there existed such important constitutional issues, no member of the court should hesitate to express his views. Bradley then indicated that he did not intend to explore the subject at large, but only to make such additional observations as appeared to be proper under the circumstances.

Bradley opened the main part of his opinion by doing what he had just indicated he would not do: He explored at large the constitutional makeup of the national government. Bradley covered the constitutional character of the government from its organization to the then current understanding of its constitutional powers. The justice mentioned that the issuance of bills of credit had been the practice of governments in the area since the commencement of the eighteenth century. The independence of the colonies had been achieved in great degree, he said, by bills issued by the Continental Congress that were similar to the bills issued in the cases before the court. Prior to the Revolution, these bills were generally legal tender, until legal tender was prohibited by the English Parliament in 1751 in the New England colonies and in 1763 in all of the colonies. This was one of the causes of discontent that led to the Revolution.

The justice went on to explain that when the Revolutionary War began, the Continental Congress issued bills of credit that financed the war without other resources for nearly four years. We owe our national independence to the use of these bills of credit, he said. The justice then quoted Dr. Benjamin Franklin as stating that the public debt was proportionately diminished by the depreciation that took place in these bills of credit issued by the Continental Congress, and further, that the currency as then managed was a "wonderful machine" because it clothed the troops and provided food and ammunition. In 1777, the Continental Congress passed resolutions encouraging the states to make these bills legal tender and tying their value to the Spanish dollar. The Congress also recommended to the states that they pass laws that anyone refusing to accept the continental bills should be deemed an enemy to the liberties of the United States.

Bradley had gone through this short analysis, he said, to show that when the Constitution was adopted, bills of credit were deemed a legitimate means of meeting the obligations of government, and legal tender was a quality entirely discretionary with the legislative branch of government. He then stated that the founders imposed no restriction upon the general government in this regard, and the conclusion could not be resisted that the founders intended that the power of legal tender remain with the national government in case the solution of future problems required its use.

No one had ever seriously doubted that the government had the power to emit bills, the justice stated. This power had been exercised by the government without its being questioned for a large part of its history. Giving such bills the quality of legal tender followed as a matter of course.

It was the prerogative of every government, not otherwise restrained by its Constitution, to issue bills of credit, Bradley held. Whether or not these bills of credit should be legal tender was an incidental matter to be determined at the discretion of the government. Further, this power was distinct and separate from that of coining money and regulating value. Bradley held that this power was embraced within the powers to make auxiliary laws and to borrow money.

Another basis for the power to issue Treasury notes, said the justice, was the providing of a proper currency for the country. Currency was a national necessity; the operations of government and of private transactions were wholly dependent upon it. The justice then spent another large portion of his opinion reviewing and adding to the various arguments supporting the Legal Tender Acts.

Bradley took a minority position pertaining to contracts specifically payable in specie. The court had held in the case of *Bronson v. Rodes*[11] that because these contracts were specifically payable in specie by their terms, the creditors in these contracts had the right to demand payment in gold or silver. Bradley differed; he stated that these contracts should also be payable in Treasury bills because, in essence, they were no different from other contracts payable in money.

The justice then held that the power of legal tender was a power not to be resorted to except in extraordinary and pressing occasions, such as war or other public exigencies of great gravity and importance, and it should be exerted no longer than all of the circumstances demanded. When to assert the power and how long it should prevail, stated Bradley, was for the legislative department to determine.

With a touch of humor, Bradley reviewed the legal tender situation in England, where, with all of its emergencies, it never made its exchequer bills legal tender. The justice indicated that this was a "eulogium" on British conservatism in relation to contracts which that nation could "hardly regard as flattering." The situation in England was such that the people and government were forced to regard notes as legal tender or suffer bankruptcy, he said. Bradley mentioned a man who brought a case in an English court to collect specie under the terms of his contract. He was so badly treated by the court, said Bradley, that he was the very last man to ever show himself in an English court on that issue. Bradley acknowledged that since 1833, Bank of England notes had been made legal tender.

The justice then referred to the fact that nearly every nation in Europe had found it necessary to resort to making their currency legal tender in order to carry on their operations or defend themselves from aggression. Foreign powers and creditors would rejoice, he said, if the United States were deprived of the power to make its Treasury notes legal tender.

Bradley closed his opinion with a statement pertaining to national sovereignty: "It is absolutely essential to independent national existence that government should have a firm hold on the two great sovereign instruments of the sword and the purse, and the right to wield them without restriction on occasions of national peril." He concurred in the overruling of *Hepburn v. Griswold* and closed his opinion by stating that the cases before the court should be affirmed.

Chief Justice Salmon P. Chase, as could be expected, wrote an extensive dissent.[12] Chase's health had been deteriorating through this period. He had previously suffered a slight heart attack, and he had high blood pressure and touches of malaria and diabetes. Since his majority opinion in the *Hepburn* case, he had suffered a stroke that had partially paralyzed him. The stroke seemed to affect his reasoning and writing ability. Nevertheless, Chase expressed his opinion that the overruling of *Hepburn* and the holding of the Legal Tender Acts as constitutional was a reversal unprecedented in the history of the court.

In his majority opinion in the *Hepburn* case, Chase had declared the Legal Tender Acts unconstitutional when applied to contracts consummated prior to the passage of the acts because there was no express grant of Congress giving that body the power to declare greenbacks legal tender; neither did Congress possess an implied power to do so under the war powers or any other express power. Further, Chase had held that the Fifth Amendment, where it provided that a citizen should not be deprived of this property without due process of law, and that private property should not be taken for public use without just compensation, prohibited the application of the Legal Tender Acts to contracts consummated prior to the acts' passage. In addition, Chase had held that making greenbacks legal tender would impair contracts in violation of the "spirit" of the Constitution.

The chief justice indicated that none of the justices who were in the majority in the *Hepburn* case had changed their opinion, and these justices were more convinced than ever as to the soundness on the constitutional doctrines enunciated in *Hepburn* and in their importance to the country. After reasserting the holdings in the *Hepburn* case, Chase indicated that he would not add to those holdings in this minority opinion.

Chase then attempted to answer the many questions raised as to his backing of the Legal Tender Acts when they were before Congress and he was secretary of the Treasury. He indicated that he had backed the passage of the law because it was so necessary to the welfare of the country. The actual passage of the acts, he explained, was in jeopardy because of the arguments in committee pertaining to legal tender. Chase said that he had testified before the Ways and Means Committee that legal tender was necessary because his testimony in that manner shook the law loose, brought it to the floor of Congress, and aided its passage. He apparently felt at that time that the passage of the law itself was more important than its parts. Now, upon reflection, he had decided that opinion was erroneous, and he was convinced that greenbacks would have performed the tasks set out for them just as well without the attribute of legal tender. Chase then engaged in a long dissertation in support of this view. He concluded that legitimate notes in circulation would be hurt, not helped, by legal tender, and that the legal tender quality was valuable only for "purposes of dishonesty." He then declared, on behalf of the minority justices, that it was their conviction that making the notes legal tender was not a necessary or proper means of carrying on the war or to the exercise of any express power of government. Chase then reiterated the view of the minority that Congress had no specific or implied power to make notes legal tender under the power to coin money.

The chief justice ended the minority opinion by stating that his brothers Clifford and Field concurred in the views expressed in the opinion but would render their own dissenting opinions, and that Justice Nelson dissented without a separate opinion.

It is interesting to note that in the *U.S. Supreme Court Reports, Lawyers' Edition,* the three dissenting opinions exceeded in length everything that had gone before in the cases. Clifford's opinion consisted primarily of a seventy-year historical review of money and currency in the United States, designed to show that Congress had never made paper money legal tender.[13] This was interspersed with several arguments that were already expressed against the constitutionality of making the greenbacks legal tender.

Justice Field insisted that the *Hepburn* decision, having been argued by eminent counsel, with every point raised having been the subject of extended deliberation, was more fully argued and more maturely considered than any case that had been before the court since its organization. A judgment so reached, said Field, should not be lightly disturbed.[14]

He then reviewed at length the previous times in history when the government had issued notes under its power to borrow, and he pointed out how these notes differed from those authorized in the Legal Tender Acts. Field indicated that the greenbacks did not bear interest or bear on their face a period of payment. There was no objection to this, Field maintained, but only to that part of the acts declaring the new notes legal tender. There was no constitutional or implied power as a basis for legal tender, he said, and the status of legal tender given to these notes was a clear interference with contracts. Furthermore, said Field, the true value of the legal tender notes fluctuated with the failures or successes of the armed forces, and the legislature could not alter this fact "one jot or tittle."

The justice repeated at length the arguments already made to the court several times and intertwined them with historical accounts. In fact, he quoted the Old Testament story about when Abraham bought the field of Machpelah, mentioning that it was done with silver over four thousand years ago, metal always being the standard of money from that time to the present.

Field concluded his dissent by stating that in his judgment, the Legal Tender Acts were unconstitutional and void. He then followed his conclusion with a statement that reflected a situation that greatly bothered him on a personal basis. There had been times during the discussions of legal tender, he said, when there existed "covert intimation" that opposition to legal tender was an expression reflecting an unfavorable attitude toward the war effort of the Union. "All such intimations I repel with all the energy I can express," he asserted. Field then spoke of his honor and reverence toward the "noble and patriotic men who were in the councils of the nation during the terrible struggle with the Rebellion." He attributed to these men the "greatest of all glories" in having saved the Union and having emancipated a race. The justice said that he could not give blind approval to everything that was supposed to support the war effort because of his obedience to the Constitution and the laws clearly made in pursuance of it. It is only by this obedience that affection and reverence could be shown to a superior having a right to command. "So thought our great Master," said Field, "when he said to his disciples: 'if ye love me, keep my commandments.'"

So ended one of the great legal battles, not only of the Civil War, but in the history of the nation. Paper money with the attributes of legal tender has been part of the life of our nation and our people since these times.

Chapter Eight

Financing the War: Taxation Cases

In both the North and South, the war was financed by paper money, taxation, and loans. Of these three methods, the least important was taxation. Apparently the reason for this was that people considered tax laws to be permanent, and nearly everyone at the beginning stages of the war expected a short conflict.

Nevertheless, both sides experimented with such laws. One of the most unusual laws was the country's first income tax, passed by Congress in Washington on August 5, 1861. The tax was meant to be temporary and began at 3 percent on incomes of $800 per year after an exemption of $800. The rates and amounts changed with subsequent amendments.

Since time immemorial, people have searched for ways to reduce their taxes, and the Civil War era was no different. One of the loopholes taxpayers quickly discovered was that if they could claim their income in specie, they could make out their return in terms of specie, then pay the tax with greenbacks. As the greenbacks were worth less than specie, a taxpayer doing this would receive a reduction in his taxes equal to the difference in actual value between specie and greenbacks. Congress took steps to rectify this loophole on July 13, 1866, when it passed a very involved amendment to the Income Tax Law requiring a taxpayer to state whether his return was in terms of specie or legal tender currency. If the return was in specie, the government assessor receiving the return was to convert the income to legal tender currency, and the tax was required to be paid on the new amount in greenbacks.

THE *PACIFIC INSURANCE COMPANY* CASE

The interpretation and validity of this provision were addressed in a case before the court in 1869. In addition, the issues of the case expanded to incorporate the first test of the constitutionality of the Income Tax Law itself. An additional and very strange aspect of this case is that it seems to have been lost to historians and political scientists, for it is set forth in most texts on the subject that the constitutionality of the income tax was not brought into question before the court until 1881. The case came before the court under the title of *The Pacific Insurance Company, Plff., v. Frank Soule, Collector of Internal Revenue.*[1]

The facts of the case were simple. The income to the insurance company was in specie, gold and silver. The company computed its tax on that basis as $5,836 and attempted to pay this amount in greenbacks. The Internal Revenue assessor, however, converted the listed income of the insurance company from specie to legal tender currency. On that basis, the tax amounted to $7,365. After some unfruitful negotiations, the insurance company paid the larger amount under protest. Later the insurance company filed suit in the Federal courts in California seeking a refund, and the case appeared before the Circuit Court of the United States for the District of California. The judges could not reach a decision and, pursuant to the applicable Federal court rules, certified seven questions to the U.S. Supreme Court.

When the case appeared before the Supreme Court, the justices concluded it could be determined by answering just two of the seven questions.[2] The first question concerned the interpretation of the legal tender conversion statute. The second would answer the question of whether the income tax was a direct tax, thereby determining whether the Income Tax Law was constitutional. Article I, Section 9 of the U.S. Constitution provided that "no capitation, or other direct, tax shall be laid, unless in Proportion to the census or Enumeration herein before directed to be taken." The Income Tax Law as passed was not in proportion to the census. If the law was classified as a direct tax, not being so proportioned, the law would be declared unconstitutional.

The Arguments before the Court

The parties argued these issues before the court on January 14, 1869. The Pacific Insurance Company was represented by John A. Wills and W. O. Bartlett. Wills had successfully represented the Lees in the *Knox v. Lee* case. So convinced were these counsel that the income tax was a direct tax, and therefore unconstitutional, that they did not argue the first issue concerning the interpretation of the statute. Wills filed with the court an abstract of an argument on the constitutionality of the income tax written by Bartlett. The oral argument given by Wills and Bartlett was based upon this abstract.

Bartlett first argued that the income tax was a poll, or capitation, tax. He quoted Dr. Adam Smith, "no higher authority on this subject," as stating that the income tax, however it was termed, was a direct tax.[3] He then cited one of the major works on taxation of the time, by J. R. McCulloch.[4] McCulloch, Bartlett pointed out, divided his work into two parts, "Direct Taxes" and "Indirect Taxes." McCulloch placed his discussion of the income tax under the heading of "Direct Taxes." John Mill, Bartlett continued, also defined income taxes as direct taxes, as did a man by the name of Dr. Francis Lieber, who wrote an article on the subject in volume 7 of *Encyclopedia Americana.*[5]

Next Bartlett argued that the framers of the Constitution considered a tax on land and a general assessment on property to be direct taxes. He then constructed an argument that if a tax on land were a direct tax, certainly Congress could not get around this interpretation by taxing income from the land and calling it an indirect tax, for it, too, would be classified as a direct tax. Bartlett then cited the "celebrated carriage case," the 1796 case of *Hylton v. U.S.*,[6] stating that the attorney Alexander Hamilton had appeared there on behalf of the government and termed a capitation tax, taxes on land, and general assessments as direct taxes.

Bartlett closed his argument by mentioning to the court that the reasoning used by John Marshall, Gov. Edmund Randolph, James Monroe, James Madison, and Patrick Henry, as revealed in the debates in the Virginia Convention called to ratify the Constitution, would classify land taxes, and income taxes by inference, as direct taxes. Wills and Bartlett requested the court to hold the income tax unconstitutional and to so inform the Circuit Court in California.

William M. Evarts represented Frank Soule, the collector of Internal Revenue. Evarts was the losing attorney in the *Hepburn v. Griswold* case.

Evarts's argument was notable for its brevity. He claimed that the only question presented to the court was whether a legally assessed tax against the insurance company of $7,365 could be satisfied by the payment of $5,836. Evarts argued that it was obvious that the Income Tax Law did not confer such a right on the insurance company.

The insurance company had been assessed according to law, said Evarts, provided that the law was constitutional. Evarts pointed out to the court that a tax on incomes was not a direct tax within the meaning of the Constitution, and therefore it was not subject to apportionment. He argued that the case cited by the insurance company's attorney, *Hylton v. U.S.*, where the court determined that a tax on carriages was not a direct tax, was conclusive on that point.

In closing, Evarts requested the court to hold that, according to the wording of the Income Tax Law, the insurance company must report its income and pay its tax in legal tender currency, and that the Income Tax Law, as written, was constitutional.

The Opinion of the Court

The opinion of the court was presented on February 1, 1869. At that time, the court was composed of eight justices: Nathan Clifford, Samuel Nelson, Robert C. Grier, Salmon P. Chase, Noah Swayne, Samuel F. Miller, Stephen J. Field, and David Davis. Justice Noah Swayne delivered the opinion of a unanimous court.

The judges of the Circuit Court had divided on the issues of how the new amendment to the Income Tax Law should be interpreted and whether the income tax was a direct tax. Under the rules of the Supreme Court and the Circuit Court at that time, in such a division, the judges of the Circuit Court could stay the proceedings before them and certify the questions that were the source of their division to the U.S. Supreme Court for determination. Following this procedure, the judges of the Circuit Court had certified seven questions to the

Supreme Court. Under the rules of both courts, the questions, when submitted under these rules, had to be specific questions of law of gravity and importance that were actual questions that arose in the case, and their answers would determine the merits of the controversy. The answers of the Supreme Court were binding upon the Circuit Court; therefore, the effect of the Supreme Court's decision was the same as if the case had been a formal appeal.

Justice Swayne opened his opinion by acknowledging the facts of the case, and that the record of the case reflected that seven questions had been submitted to the Supreme Court by the judges of the Circuit Court. He then indicated that the view that the Supreme Court took of the case was that it would be sufficient to answer just two of the questions, for these answers would cover the entire controversy, and their determination would be conclusive of the case.

Swayne reiterated the first question: Must that part of the amendment concerning the type of income, and how the tax must be paid, be interpreted as an accounting rule only governing the currency in which the returns were to be stated, or was it a hard and fast rule that stated that if a payer reported income in specie, he must add the difference in value between specie and currency to his income and pay the tax on the new total amount?

Swayne began the court's answer to this question by stating that the meaning of the statute was so clear that argument or illustration was unnecessary. To allow the insurance company to compute its income in specie and pay its tax in currency, whereas others paid their taxes based upon income computed in currency, was "subversive of the plainest principles of reason and justice." Stating that "equality is equity," the justice held that the insurance company's income should have been computed in currency and the tax paid on that amount.

The court then considered the second question: whether the Income Tax Law passed by Congress was a direct tax that, according to the Constitution, should have been apportioned among the states and territories according to the last census. Swayne adverted to several provisions of the Constitution in Article I pertaining to the tax powers of the Federal government. He then mentioned that the Federal government was of limited jurisdiction and had no faculties except what the Constitution had given it. He stated that the taxing powers of the Federal government were unfettered except for the limitations placed upon it in Article I. These limitations were that direct taxes, including the capitation tax, must be apportioned; that duties, imposts, and excises should be uniform; and that no duties should be imposed upon articles exported from any state.

If the income tax was a direct tax, said Swayne, it was clear that it had not been apportioned as required by the Constitution, and it was therefore an unconstitutional tax. The justice then referred to the 1796 case of *Hylton v. U.S.*, mentioning that one of the justices on the court at that time, James Wilson, had been a distinguished member of the convention that had framed the Constitution. Wilson and the other justices of the court had unanimously held in the *Hylton* case that a tax upon privately owned carriages was not a direct tax.

It was stated in that case that the only direct taxes were the capitation, or poll, tax and a tax upon land. If a tax on carriages was not a direct tax, said Swayne, he could see no basis upon which a tax on the business of an insurance company could be a direct tax.

Swayne closed the court's opinion with an illustration that it was not practical to apportion an income tax on corporations, pointing out that where corporations were numerous, the tax would be light; where there were no corporations, the tax could not be collected; and where there were just a few corporations, the tax would fall upon them with such "weight as to involve annihilation." The justice followed his illustration by stating, "The consequences are fatal to the proposition."

The court held that the income tax was not a direct tax, but rather it was a duty or excise tax, therefore constitutional. This holding, together with the court's interpretation of the statute in the first question considered by the court, required the plaintiff insurance company to pay the Federal government not the $5,836 paid by the company, but the $7,365 assessed by the Federal assessor.

The Circuit Court was so informed, and a decree incorporating these holdings was entered by that court.

Although the court's decision strictly applied to the income tax as it taxed the income of corporations, the arguments to the court and the opinion of the court applied to the Income Tax Law generally. In the event that the court had found the law unconstitutional as it applied to corporations, this would have invalidated the law as it applied to everyone. This would have been a serious blow to the government in Washington. Not only would this have further impaired the Federal government's ability to pay its wartime indebtedness, but the government would have been faced with the repayment of the tax collected since 1861 to the citizens of the North.

THE *VEAZIE BANK* CASE

Not all tax laws passed by Congress during the war were for the strict purpose of raising revenue to finance the war. The tax that is the subject of the next case was not passed to raise war funds, though it did enable the enforcement of a second law that raised funds to assist in the wartime financing.

The Legal Tender Acts initiated the first Federal paper money, the greenbacks. As this currency came into use, a very large number of state banks and some other institutions continued to support the circulation of their own currencies. The value of these currencies fluctuated wildly. Everyone was forced to be aware of the true value of these currencies and their value relative to each other, and to greenbacks, to conduct business or merely to maintain their daily existence. Unfortunately, many of these currencies were on the level of scams, and many people were hurt by them.

In an attempt to bring order out of this mass of confusion, Salmon P. Chase, while he was still secretary of the Treasury, actively promoted the creation of a national bank system. Congress considered this, and a law wound itself through the congressional machinations. A statute establishing a national banking system was finally passed on June 3, 1864.

This act provided for the granting of national charters to banking associations, which became national banks supervised by the Treasury Department. To qualify for a charter, each of the new banks was required to have capital in the amount of $50,000, of which $30,000 must have been invested in U.S. Treasury securities. Another part of the act created a new currency called national bank notes, which were circulated through the national banks.

Nearly everyone expected that the state banks would afford themselves of the advantages offered by the new act and quickly apply for the national charters. The state banks, however, enjoyed their freedom from Federal control and, finding their business profitable, were greatly resistant to converting. This defeated the objectives of the new law to create order out of the morass of circulating currencies, and Congress was forced to cope with the problem once again.

Congress had previously passed a small tax on the outstanding amounts of state bank currencies, initially in the amount of 1 percent. This tax accomplished the objective of setting up a method of keeping track of the total amount of state bank currencies in circulation, the tax being too low to raise much revenue beyond paying the costs of its administration. Congress seized on this opportunity to overcome the reluctance of the state banks to convert to national charters by raising the tax to a confiscatory 10 percent.

The state banks, and indeed, the state governments themselves, were aghast at this Federal move. The tax amounted to an ultimatum that the state banks convert or go out of business. The new tax accomplished its goal when the state banks began to apply for national bank charters as a matter of survival. However, many state banks still refused to convert; they paid the tax, intending to go to court and prove that the tax was an unconstitutional taking of property.

Such was the situation with the Veazie Bank, a state bank corporation chartered by the state of Maine. This charter gave authority to the Veazie Bank to issue currency, and this currency was subject to the 10 percent tax. The president and the board of directors of the bank paid the tax under protest, then sued Jeremiah Fenno, the collector of Internal Revenue, to recover the tax. The case was filed in the Circuit Court of the United States for the District of Maine under an agreed statement of facts, which was permitted by the court rules. However, when it came time for the court to grant a motion for instructions to the jury, the two judges were opposed in opinion, and they certified three questions concerning whether the 10 percent tax was valid and constitutional for determination by the U.S. Supreme Court. The case reached the Supreme Court under the title of *The President, Directors and Company of the Veazie Bank, Plffs., v. Jeremiah Fenno, Collector of Internal Revenue.*[7] The case was argued to the court on October 18, 1869.

The Arguments before the Court

The bank was represented by Caleb Cushing, Reverdy Johnson, and W. W. Boyce. Cushing was a colorful and well-known lawyer of the time. In 1834, he had been elected to Congress as a Whig. He later switched to the Democrat Party and in 1861 to the Republican Party. He served as attorney general under President Franklin Pierce. On January 9, 1874, President Ulysses Grant nominated Cushing as chief justice of the Supreme Court to replace Chief Justice Salmon P. Chase. The Senate refused to confirm him.

Jeremiah Fenno was represented by the U.S. attorney general, Ebenezer Rockwood Hoar. Just two days after the decision was rendered in this case, Hoar was nominated to the Supreme Court by President Grant. His nomination was turned down by the Senate. This case was distinctive in that two of the counsel appearing for the parties were later nominated to the Supreme Court and rejected by the Senate.

Caleb Cushing and Reverdy Johnson opened the arguments on behalf of the bank. They first insisted that the 10 percent tax on circulating bank notes was a direct tax and therefore must be apportioned among the states. Since the tax was not apportioned, Cushing and Johnson told the court, it was unconstitutional. They were critical of the *Hylton* carriage case, stating that "what are direct taxes, was very crudely considered in that case."

If the tax was not a direct tax, Cushing and Johnson continued, then it was a duty. A duty, they argued, must be uniform, and the tax could not be uniform unless it was extended to the circulation of national banks. The tax did not apply to national banks, and therefore it was unconstitutional for that reason.

Then Cushing and Johnson got to the crux of their argument. They argued that the 10 percent tax was imposed not for the sake of raising revenue, but solely for the purpose of destroying the state banks. If it could be determined, said Cushing and Johnson, that Congress could destroy the state banks, Congress could just as easily destroy the railroad system. If the 10 percent tax was sustained, it would be an indication that the taxing power of Congress would be unlimited and beyond inquiry by the court. If this were allowed to be true, the powers of Congress would be supreme, and the body could do anything without limitations as long as it was done in the form of levying a tax.

The bank's attorneys then argued that Congress did not have the power to pass a law abolishing the state banks. It was a maxim of the law, they argued, that Congress could not do indirectly what it could not do directly. In this regard, this was the confiscation of private property for public use without compensation.

Cushing and Johnson closed their presentation by pursuing an argument that pointed out to the court that the Veazie Bank was franchised, or chartered, by the state of Maine, and the Federal government could not tax agencies of the state governments. The bank's attorneys rested.

The attorney general of the United States, Ebenezer Rockwood Hoar, responded to the bank's arguments with several well-organized and precise statements. The first statement of his argument was that the 10 percent tax was not a direct tax, citing the *Pacific Insurance* case reviewed earlier in this chapter. Hoar told the court that, at any rate, the 10 percent tax was not capable of being apportioned. The 10 percent tax was an excise tax or a duty, he explained, and it satisfied the requirement of uniformity in that it was applied uniformly to all businesses of the same character.

The attorney general then argued that Congress did have the right to prohibit the state bank currencies. Therefore, he maintained, what Congress could prohibit, it could regulate or permit upon a condition. In certain areas of business, Hoar maintained, Congress could even be destructive. He then stressed that the degree of taxation was solely within the discretion of Congress, and the motives of Congress were not within the jurisdictional inquiry of the court.

To conclude his argument, Hoar reemphasized the need that the tax be uniform. He stressed again that the 10 percent tax did not violate the necessity for uniformity by the national bank exception, because the exception itself was uniform throughout all of the states.

The Opinion of the Court

The court took the arguments of the counsel under consideration, and Chief Justice Salmon P. Chase gave the opinion of the court on December 13, 1869. The vote of the court was six to two. No replacements had been made to the court since the deaths of Justices Catron and Wayne. This was in conformity with the Judiciary Act of 1866, which had required that the size of the court be reduced by attrition from ten to seven justices. The Judiciary Act of 1869 reestablished the number of justices to nine, but it had not yet been acted upon.

As secretary of the Treasury, Chase had pushed hard for the passage of the National Bank Law. He had been appointed chief justice of the court by President Lincoln on December 12, 1864, just six months after the final passage of the act. This case gave Chase the opportunity to rule on the constitutionality of the tax aspects of the act as a member of the Supreme Court.

Chief Justice Chase began the court's opinion with a brief history of money circulation in the North. At the beginning of the war, the circulating medium had consisted almost entirely of state bank notes. At that time, transactions of the Federal government were conducted in coin, and there was no national currency in circulation.

On July 17, 1861, the first Federal act authorizing a kind of quasicurrency authorized the Treasury Department to issue Treasury notes. These notes had due dates and carried interest, but they were also convertible on demand into coin. This legislation did not help the economy, and on December 31, 1861, the financial condition of the country was so bad that the state banks suspended specie payment. Chase pointed out that a completely new national financial policy became necessary. This resulted in the legislation that created the United States notes, which was passed on February 25, 1862. These notes, known as greenbacks, were legal tender and convertible into certain Federal bonds at par. The greenbacks were the first authentic Federal currency.

The chief justice then covered the history of the act authorizing the national banking associations. He stated that it was originally passed by Congress on February 25, 1863, and finalized by the Act of June 3, 1864. This act acknowledged and recited the purpose of the 1 percent and 2 percent taxes on the currency circulation of state banks. This was followed by the Act of March 3, 1865, reenacted on July 13, 1866, which raised the tax on note circulation of state banks to 10 percent. Chase observed that originally in this legislation, Congress had discriminated in favor of the state banks; however, with the issuance of the United States notes and the national bank notes, the discrimination had turned, "and very decidedly turned," against the state banks.

The chief justice stated that the question before the court, as presented by the Circuit Court of the United States for the District of Maine, was whether the 10 percent tax imposed by the legislation of July 13, 1866, upon the circulation of state banks was valid and constitutional.

Chase acknowledged the arguments of Cushing and Johnson that the tax was unconstitutional, reciting what he regarded as their two main points: first, that the tax was an unapportioned direct tax; and second, that the tax was illegal because it impaired a franchise granted by the state. He stated that these points were argued with "much force and earnestness."

Regarding the first point, Chase stated that the early Confederation relied on revenue being received only from the states. This proved unsatisfactory, resulting in the Confederation being reduced to impotency. One of the leading objects of the Constitution, said Chase, was to give the government power to raise revenue by the taxation of persons and property to pay for the common defense and general welfare of the country. He recited again that if Congress imposed a capitation or other direct tax, it was required to be apportioned among the states according to the census. If Congress imposed a tax on duties, imposts, or excises, the tax was required to be uniform. Chase indicated that the taxing power was comprehensive, and the limits he just discussed did not limit the power, but only prescribed the mode in which it should be exercised. The comprehensiveness of this power, Chase speculated, might have been the reason for the absence of debate in the Constitutional Convention concerning the terms of the tax grant to Congress.

Much diversity of opinion existed as to just what a direct tax was, Chase acknowledged. Attempts to identify a direct tax by reference to the definitions given it by political economists were not satisfactory. A review of the history of direct taxation, beginning with the first direct tax passed in 1798, showed that personal property, contracts, and occupations had never been the proper subjects of a direct tax, Chase explained.

The chief justice then said that the argument made by some that the tax treatment of slaves as a direct tax, when slaves were classified as personal property, was a basis to treat the taxation of personal property as a direct tax was not sound. The states taxed slaves not as personal property, but as a capitation tax or as real estate, both direct taxes.

Chase concluded that direct taxes, under a practical interpretation of the Constitution, had been limited to taxes on land and its appurtenances, and on poll or capitation taxes. He pointed out that this interpretation was consistent with the treatment of the subject by the delegates to the Constitutional Convention and by the court in the *Hylton* case.

The chief justice held as a decision of the court that a tax on the circulation of bank currency was not a direct tax.

Chase then turned to the second point: whether the tax under consideration was a tax upon a franchise granted by a state. He explained that if the franchise was created under the state's reserved powers—that is, the employment of all necessary agencies by a state for the legitimate purposes of state government— the franchise would not be taxable by the Federal government. In this case, he pointed out, the object of the tax was not the franchise creating the bank, but the property created, or the contracts made and issued under the franchise, such as the use of the power to issue currency. Chase then drew a corollary to railroads. He indicated that a railroad was a franchise from the state, but its freight receipts, bills of lading, and passenger tickets were all subject to Federal taxation. This was similar, he said, to taxing the currency circulated by a state bank, though the bank itself was a franchise from the state. Both types of contracts were means of profit to the corporations issuing them. The taxation of this means, or of the profit itself, was therefore not a tax upon a franchise granted by a state.

Next Chase treated Cushing and Johnson's argument that the tax was so excessive as to destroy the bank franchise granted by the state, and that it was therefore beyond the constitutional powers of Congress. He answered this argument by stating that the judiciary could not prescribe to the legislative department of government limitations upon the exercise of the legislature's acknowledged powers. The responsibility of Congress was not to the courts, he said, but to the people who elected the members of Congress. If a tax were unduly repressive, the courts could not, for that reason only, declare the tax unconstitutional.

The chief justice then stressed another reason for validating the tax, which probably reflected his background in the Treasury Department. He stated that the Constitution gave Congress the power to provide for the circulation of coin. This included currency, said Chase. Congress had undertaken to provide a currency for the entire country, and Congress had the power to secure the benefit of that currency to the people by any means it deemed appropriate. Congress therefore could restrain the circulation of money not issued by its authority, and without this power, said the chief justice, attempts to create a sound and uniform currency throughout the country would be futile.

Chase then held on behalf of the court that the 10 percent tax was constitutional and the Circuit Court of the United States for the District of Maine would be so informed.

Following Chase's majority decision, Justice Samuel Nelson announced that he was unable to concur in the opinion of the majority of the court, and he submitted a dissenting opinion.

Nelson began his opinion by quoting the Tenth Amendment to the Constitution, that the powers not delegated to the Federal government, nor prohibited to the states, were reserved to the states or to the people. He followed with the statement that the power to create banks was not expressly granted to the Federal government, nor was this power prohibited to the states. The question in the past, the justice explained, was not whether the state banks were constitutional, but whether the Federal government had an ancillary power to create national banks. As to the state banks, the Federal government had not legislated against them, or in any other way interfered with them by acts of Congress, from 1787 to 1864. Nelson reminded the court that in *Briscoe v. The Bank of the Commonwealth of Kentucky,*[8] the Supreme Court had held that the states possessed the power to grant charters to state banks, and that the banks' issuance of currency was legal.

He then recited the Federal taxes that had been placed upon state banks, including the 10 percent tax in question, plus the 5 percent tax on dividends granted to shareholders of state banks and the 1 percent tax upon deposits and capital of the banks. The justice said that this amounted to a 16 percent annual tax upon state banks. Nelson pointed out that the true question in this case was whether these taxes, including the 10 percent tax, were constitutional in the face of the incontrovertible authority that the states possessed to create state banks.

The justice then took an unusual approach to the question. He indicated that the 10 percent tax was not a tax on properties of the banks, but a tax upon debts of the banks. The reason for this, according to Nelson, was that the outstanding currencies of the banks were obligations of the banks and appeared on the debit side of their balance sheets. Certainly, stated the justice, no government had yet "made the discovery" of taxing both assets and liabilities of anyone or thing as property. The imposition upon the state banks of the 10 percent tax could not be upheld as a tax upon property, he insisted, for it was nothing more than a mode to annihilate the powers of the states to charter state banks. Although this Federal tax struck at only the powers of the state to create state banks, he continued, this Federal tax power could just as well apply to other corporations, such as railroads, turnpikes, and manufacturing companies.

The 10 percent tax was clearly a tax upon the powers and faculties of the states to create state banks, said Nelson, and this detracted from the sovereignty of the states. These powers were state functions, and they should have been totally exempt from Federal taxation.

For all these reasons, Justice Nelson expressed his opinion that the 10 percent tax was clearly unconstitutional. He indicated that Justice David Davis concurred in this dissent.

THE *BENNETT* CASE

The next case involved a tax whose purpose was to raise revenue to assist in the financing of the war, but whose method of levy and of collection were already obsolete at the time of its passage. The tax was passed by Congress on August 5, 1861. It was designed to raise $20 million by a direct tax upon the land of the entire nation. In accordance with Article I, Section 9 of the U.S. Constitution, being a direct tax, it was apportioned among all of the states in proportion to the census. For the purposes of this discussion, the amount of the tax apportioned to the state of Virginia was $937,550.66.

The tax law provided that if any state had seceded from the Union and the tax therefore could not be collected, the president should take the necessary steps to collect the tax as the authority of the United States was reestablished in the area. Congress helped clarify this part of the law by passing a second tax law, complementing the first, which set out provisions on how the tax would be collected in the insurgent states where Union troops had reestablished control. This act passed on June 7, 1862.

In loyal states, this tax was to be collected and paid by the states, but in the reclaimed areas of the insurgent states, the tax law was to be administered by agents of the Federal government. The law provided that after the Federal authorities took control of an area in an insurgent state, the land involved would have the tax assessed by the Federal agents. Payment of the tax was then required in sixty days. If the payment was not forthcoming in that period, a penalty of 50 percent, plus interest, was assessed in addition to the tax. Further provisions of the law stated that the land was then forfeited to the United States and would then be subject to a public sale. If the owner paid the tax, plus the penalty and interest, prior to the public sale, the sale would be canceled.

When the state of Virginia seceded from the Union, some parts of the state remained loyal to the Union. One of these was the old county of Alexandria. Under the provisions of the tax law, Federal agents began collecting the tax in this area just as though the area had been reestablished to the Union by force. The land that is the subject of this case was a beautiful parcel in this county. It was owned by B. W. Hunter, who had a life estate in the land, the remainder being owned by his son, Alexander. Owning a remainder meant that Alexander Hunter would own the property with no strings attached following the death of his father. The father, however, would have complete rights to the property during his life.

When the war got under way in earnest, Alexander Hunter left Alexandria County and joined the Confederate army. His father, B. W. Hunter, remained on the land. As the Federal agents moved through the county, assessing the land tax on its properties, the Hunter property was duly assessed. During 1864, however, the father died, and ownership of the property became vested in Alexander Hunter, who still fought as an officer in the Confederate army. Because of this, the tax was not paid within the allotted sixty days. The Federal agents assessed the property the penalty of 50 percent, plus interest and costs, and in addition, declared that the property was forfeited to the United States. The Federal agents, now termed tax commissioners, set a date for the sale of the property. Someone, it is not known who, tendered the total amount owing to the tax commissioners prior to the public sale; however, the commissioners refused to accept the money, because they interpreted the law as requiring the owner of the property, and no one else, to personally pay the tax.

At the public sale, the property was sold to an individual who appeared at the sale through Henry M. Bennett, who, in addition to representing the purchaser at the sale, became his tenant and took possession of the land. Bennett continued to represent the purchaser, whose name was not disclosed in the reports of the case. As far as the Federal government and Bennett were concerned, this settled the tax issue forever, and the tax commissioners moved on and continued their collection activities.

The war came to a close, and Alexander Hunter returned from the Confederate army to what he thought was his home, only to discover that Henry M. Bennett had possession of his property. Some discussion likely took place between Hunter and Bennett. However, Bennett was not about to give up possession of the property, and Hunter determined that his only recourse was to file a lawsuit against Bennett. He filed the case in the Circuit Court of Alexandria County, alleging that he was entitled to have the land returned to him. He claimed, as set out in his pleadings, that the total amount owing was tendered to the commissioners prior to the tax sale, and that they had no right to refuse it just because it was not tendered by the owner. In addition, Hunter alleged that the tax law had as its sole purpose the raising of revenue, and the sale of just a small portion of the property would have raised enough funds to pay the tax, penalties, interest, and costs. Under those conditions, Hunter alleged, it was improper to sell the entire property.

The Circuit Court in Alexandria County agreed with Hunter and entered a decree that returned the property to him. Henry M. Bennett, still acting for his landlord, disagreed with the court's judgment and appealed to the Supreme Court of Appeals of the Commonwealth of Virginia. This court also agreed with Hunter and affirmed the decision of the Circuit Court. Bennett then appealed to the U.S. Supreme Court. The case came to the Supreme Court under the title of *Henry M. Bennett, Plff. in Err., v. Alexander Hunter.*[9] The arguments to the court were made on February 23, 1870.

The Arguments before the Court
Each party was represented before the Supreme Court by a staff of attorneys. Bennett's personal attorneys were W. Willoughby, L. E. Chittenden, and A. G. Riddle. In the past, Riddle had been a close political ally of Chief Justice Salmon P. Chase. The Federal government had a great interest in upholding the tax law and moved the court for permission to appear on behalf of the government. This motion was granted, and the government was represented by Attorney General Ebenezer Rockwood Hoar and his assistant, W. A. Field.

Alexander Hunter was represented by James A. Garfield, Jeremiah Sullivan Black, George W. Brent, and S. Ferguson Beach. James A. Garfield later became president of the United States. Jeremiah S. Black had a long and colorful history. He was the U.S. attorney general for a while under President James Buchanan. In 1861, Buchanan nominated Black to the Supreme Court, but he was rejected by the Senate. From 1861 to 1864, Black was the very respected

Supreme Court reporter. Previously, Garfield and Black had appeared before the court in their successful representation of Lambdin P. Milligan in the *Milligan* case.

The attorneys representing Henry M. Bennett and the government opened with arguments based upon a brief filed by Attorney General Hoar and W. A. Field.

Their arguments began with a summary of both the August 5, 1861, and the June 7, 1862, acts, with the additional statement that the first of the two acts had been wholly inadequate to accomplish the goals of the laws. The prime issue before the court, the counsel said, was the constitutionality of the provisions contained in the June 7, 1862, act.

The counsel stressed that the only defense under the terms of the act, once the property had been sold, was to show the court that the property was not subject to the tax, that the tax had been paid prior to the public sale, or that the property had been redeemed according to that section of the law. He stressed that payment of the taxes prior to the public sale must have been paid by the owner in person to cancel the sale.

The attorney general insisted that the acts could not be unconstitutional because of any inequality of their operation. He pointed out to the court that the laws applied to any and all states and territories, nor was there any inequality as to persons, because all landowners, loyal and disloyal, were subject to the law's provisions.

Bennett's attorneys and the attorney general then argued that the claims made by Hunter in the Virginia courts that the title to the land did not pass to the United States because the Federal government did not have the constitutional power to forfeit land for the nonpayment of taxes was a total misapprehension of the origin and extent of the powers of taxation. These powers were essential to the existence of all governments, they argued, be they Federal or state.

They then pointed out to the court that the justices had held in the past that a statute ought not be declared unconstitutional unless its "nullity and validity are placed beyond all reasonable doubt." The attorneys then carefully illustrated the terms of the acts, that when the tax was not paid in sixty days, the title was forfeited, and at the tax sale, the title passed to the purchaser from the government, not the owner. Only the owner paying the amounts owing in person was able to save the land from forfeiture or public sale.

The counsel repeated their argument that there was nothing in the law that would make it unconstitutional. They also insisted that it was wholly within the powers of the legislature to make a deed from the government evidence of title and therefore prima facie evidence of the regularity of the proceedings. The attorneys then commented on the provisions of the laws, stating that only the owner in person could pay the tax, and that it was "trifling" to argue that some other person could do it just as well.

The attorney general and Bennett's personal attorneys closed with the statement "Ita lex scripta est." This was not translated in the report of the case, because it was a common phrase of the time used by attorneys, judges, and law enforcement people. It meant "so the law is written," conveying the idea that the law must be obeyed notwithstanding the rigor of its application.

At this point, James A. Garfield and S. Ferguson Beach argued on behalf of Alexander Hunter. They concentrated not on a claimed unconstitutionality of the tax acts, but rather on explaining to the court that a strict reading of the laws, accepting the most reasonable interpretation of their meaning, would result with the land being ordered returned to Hunter.

Garfield and Beach argued that the object of the tax acts were to collect the tax, and here the amount of the tax plus interest, penalties, and costs was offered to the tax commissioners prior to the tax sale. The provisions in the tax laws providing for a sale were not "merely for the sake of having a sale," they said. The sale was to accomplish the objective of collecting the tax. When the tax was offered to be paid prior to the sale, there was no need for the sale. The attorneys then argued what was on the minds of all those who were sympathetic with Hunter: that the sale as administered in this case was to get the land, not to collect the tax.

They then explained to the court that the tax laws permitted the stripping of the property from Hunter for failure to pay a tax without notice to him. No notice of any sort had been given Hunter, not of the amount to be paid, the time when it was to be paid, or the place where it was to be paid. True, they argued, Hunter was an officer in the Confederate army; but was it fair to take his property for failure to pay the tax while keeping him in utter ignorance of the fact that any tax was payable?

Garfield and Beach then posed this question to the court: What was the penalty for the failure to pay the tax? They quoted from the law that the penalty was an additional charge of 50 percent of the tax. How absurd, they argued, to tack on a 50 percent penalty if the loss of the entire property was the penalty.

The counsel for Hunter pointed out another inconsistency in the law. The law stated that the government possessed a lien against the property for the unpaid tax. This was totally at odds with the forfeiture of the property to the government for the nonpayment of the tax, they argued. If interpreted as it was written, and the land was forfeited for the nonpayment of the tax, the payment of the tax prior to the public sale would simply compound the loss. The owner of the land would lose the amount of the tax as well as the land.

Next they argued the issues set forth in the Virginia courts that the entire land should not have been sold for such a small tax, and that reliance upon a certificate of sale from the government stating that the sale was valid was a meaningless and self-serving document. The counsel for Hunter closed their case by citing an Illinois case where the judge referred to a similar fact situation as "nothing less than a moral fraud."[10]

Garfield and Beach respectfully requested the justices of the court to affirm the decision of the Supreme Court of Appeals of the Commonwealth of Virginia.

The Opinion of the Court

Chief Justice Salmon P. Chase gave the decision of the court on March 21, 1870. He first reviewed the facts leading to the case, as well as the history of the case itself. He concluded that to dispose of the case, it was necessary to consider and determine one point only, that being whether the tax commissioners could make a sale for taxes notwithstanding the fact that there was a previous tender of the amount due prior to the sale.

The answer to this question, stated the chief justice, was entirely dependent upon the construction to be given to the 4th Section of the Act of 1862. Chase then reviewed that section. It provided that land for which the tax had not been paid became forfeited to the United States and was thereafter sold at a public sale. At the sale, the land became either vested in the United States or the purchasers at the sale. The purchasers' titles were free of all encumbrances.

Chase then explained that the purpose of the law was to raise revenue, and the assessment of the tax merely created a lien against the land that was discharged when the taxes were paid. It was an unreasonable interpretation of the act, he said, considering that it was a revenue measure, to give it a construction that would defeat the right of the owner to pay the amount assessed against his land and remove the lien. Therefore, it would be unreasonable to interpret "forfeiture" in the act as an actual transfer of the land to the United States.

The chief justice continued his opinion by going into a short history of forfeiture and how the court had treated the term in the past. Under the forfeiture provisions of any statute, he explained, the court had consistently required a hearing and a written record before a citizen's property could be transferred to the national government. Therefore, the drafters of the act under consideration must have meant "forfeiture" to state the grounds of forfeiture, that is, the nonpayment of the taxes. The land then could be acquired by the United States or another purchaser at a public sale, the sale itself constituting a record.

Chase then discounted the argument that the right to pay the tax expired in sixty days. It was more reasonable, he said, to assume that the tax could be paid as long as title to the land remained with the owner; that would be until the public sale. This was verified by other parts of the act, which said that proof of payment prior to the public sale invalidated any certificate of conveyance.

Then the chief justice raised the question that had perturbed the court during the arguments: Who had the right to make the payment prior to the public sale? The act clearly stated that the owner of the land should pay the tax; however, said Chase, it was a "familiar law" that acts done by one on behalf of another were valid if ratified either expressly or by implication, and such ratification would be presumed in this case in the interests of justice. The chief justice held on behalf of the court that the payment of the taxes need not have been made solely by the owner, and that it was the tax commissioners' duty to accept the amounts owed when they were tendered by the third party prior to the public sale.

Chief Justice Chase then held for the court that the application of the principles he discussed in his opinion determined that the land should be returned to Alexander Hunter, and the decree of the Court of Appeals of Virginia was affirmed.

The vote of the court was unanimous. Justice Grier had retired from the court on January 31, 1870. Justice Strong was formally admitted to the court on March 14, 1870, after the arguments in the case had already taken place, and probably did not participate in the decision. Justice Bradley did not join the court until two days after the decision. The vote of the court was therefore seven to zero.

Chapter Nine

Financing the War: Bond Cases

The Confederate States of America was formed at a convention composed of representatives from six Southern states, which convened in Montgomery, Alabama, on February 4, 1861. While completing the drafting of a constitution and electing a president and vice president, the body also acted as a provisional legislature. The first bond issue of the Confederacy was authorized on February 28, 1861. It was in the amount of $15 million, and its sale was accomplished within the year of its passage. The sale of these bonds was primarily to banks and bankers.

THE *PADELFORD* CASE

One of these bankers was Edward Padelford, who purchased a substantial quantity of the bonds. Padelford lived in Savannah, Georgia, and was an officer and one of the larger shareholders in the Marine Bank of the city of Savannah. The bank was owned by Northern shareholders, and Padelford acted as their representative in Savannah. The Marine Bank purchased $100,000 worth of the bond issue.

The methods used in selling these bonds were revealed in a case concerning an entirely different dispute, but in determining the outcome of the dispute, the courts found it necessary to review the circumstances of the sales of the bonds to Padelford and the Marine Bank.

As a banker in Savannah, Padelford had many business opportunities available to him. He took advantage of one of these opportunities by entering into a business arrangement with Randolph L. Mott to jointly buy and sell cotton. The two of them carried on this activity throughout most of the war until December 21, 1864, when Savannah was captured by the Northern forces under Gen. William T. Sherman. Just one month later, Padelford took and subscribed to the amnesty oath prescribed by the president's Proclamation of December 3, 1863. It was clear that Padelford was not within the disqualifying exceptions named in the proclamation, and that he was careful to comply with the requirements and conditions named in the proclamation after he took the oath.

A bond issued by the Confederate States of America carrying the likeness of Thomas Bragg, the attorney general.

After Padelford took the oath, the Northern forces took possession of Mott and Padelford's cotton, which consisted of 1,293 bales. The cotton was turned over to a U.S. Treasury agent and was sold under the provisions of the Abandoned and Captured Property Act of March 12, 1863. The proceeds, $246,277.77, were paid into the Treasury of the United States.

The provisions of the Abandoned and Captured Property Act permitted Mott and Padelford to claim that they rightfully owned the cotton and were entitled to the proceeds of the sale. Such claims were required to be filed in the U.S. Court of Claims. This was done, and the Court of Claims permitted Mott and Padelford to sever their claim; each of them then sued separately for half of the proceeds of the sale.

To prevail in the Court of Claims, Padelford was required to prove to the court his ownership of the cotton, its capture by the Union army, the receipt of the proceeds of the sale of the cotton by the U.S. Treasury, and that he had remained loyal to the United States. All of these matters were easy for Padelford's attorneys to establish except the requirement that he had remained loyal to the United States during the war. The government, which would be entitled to the funds if he did not successfully establish his claim, challenged Padelford, asserting that he had not remained loyal to the United States because of the fact that Padelford, and his Marine Bank, had given aid and comfort to the Rebellion by investing in Confederate bonds. In addition, the government introduced evidence that Padelford, as a banker, had become the surety on the official bonds of several of his friends, which permitted them to become officers in the Confederate government.

To overcome these charges of disloyalty, Padelford introduced testimony concerning the methods used to sell the bonds. After the war began in April 1861, the people of Savannah were so moved and excited with war fervor that they would not tolerate anyone not investing in the Confederate bonds. When extreme pressure was put upon Padelford, his life even being threatened, he purchased $5,000 worth of the bonds personally.

The banks in Savannah purchased the maximum amounts permitted by their capitalization, even if they had to increase their capital. However, the Marine Bank refused to buy the bonds; this subjected the bank and its officers to public odium, and the people of Savannah began to refer to the bank as the "Yankee Bank." When public excitement was at its highest in Savannah, a crowd of citizens gathered in front of the bank and loudly communicated to the bank's officers and directors that if the bank did not invest liberally in the Confederate bonds, they would pull the bank down piece by piece. Under these conditions, the Marine Bank invested $100,000 in the bonds. Padelford opposed this loan to the Confederacy and thereafter refused to attend most of the meetings of the directors, claiming that the governance of the bank was controlled by outside pressure.

These facts were proven to the satisfaction of the Court of Claims, which held that Padelford's actions in investing in the bonds, personally and through the bank, and in acting as surety on his friend's bonds, did not constitute the giving of aid or comfort to the Rebellion, or to persons engaged in the Rebellion. The court entered a judgment in Padelford's favor. The court's decree held that the government had no right to retain the funds from the sale, and that half of the proceeds from the sale, $123,138.88, should be paid to Padelford.

The government did not agree with this judgment and appealed the decision to the U.S. Supreme Court. The case reached the Supreme Court under the title of *United States, Appt., v. Edward Padelford.*[1]

The Arguments before the Court

The case was argued before the Supreme Court on April 21, 1870. Representing the government in this appeal were the attorney general, Ebenezer Rockwood Hoar, and Robert S. Hale, special counsel. Padelford retained three attorneys: James Mandeville Carlisle, who was considered to be the flower of the Washington, D.C., bar; J. D. McPherson; and T. W. Barkley.

Robert S. Hale spoke first on behalf of the attorney general and the government. He opened by challenging the interpretation of the findings of the Court of Claims. He pointed out that the laws regulating the Court of Claims in cases interpreting the Abandoned and Captured Property Act, as well as the act itself, required that Padelford prove to that court that he had in no way voluntarily aided, abetted, or given comfort or encouragement to the Rebellion. The language in the act itself, explained Hale, did not include the word *voluntarily*. The correct interpretation of those findings should have concluded that Padelford had not proven his case, he argued. Hale then maintained that Padelford had obviously aided, abetted, and given comfort to the Rebellion, and the threat of destruction of property would not excuse these acts. Only a threat to Padelford's life and the likelihood that the threat would be executed would be sufficient excuse for his activities.

Further, Padelford's cotton was effectively captured when the Union forces captured Savannah; therefore, the amnesty oath had no effect, because it was taken after the capture of the cotton. In addition, argued Hale, the statutes being interpreted by the court were not penal statutes, so the amnesty oath would not apply.

The attorney general and Hale closed by asking the court to overrule the decision of the Court of Claims and allow the government to retain the proceeds of the sale of Padelford's cotton.

J. D. McPherson then argued to the court on behalf of Padelford. McPherson's argument was short and concise. He stated that the question presented to the court was whether the loaning of money to the Confederacy by the purchase of the bonds, and becoming surety on the bonds of officers of the Confederacy, constituted aid and comfort to the Rebellion. McPherson indicated to the court that these acts had been committed by Padelford without intent to aid the Rebellion. Without intent, McPherson argued, they were not acts of aid and comfort.

Furthermore, the legal date of seizure of the cotton was not when General Sherman captured Savannah, but rather when the cotton was physically seized by the Union army. That date was after Padelford took the amnesty oath, McPherson then pointed out to the court that all offenses, if any, committed by Padelford were "obliterated to every legal intent" by the amnesty oath. Not only this, but it was clearly illegal for the government to seize Padelford's cotton after he took the oath of amnesty. Citing the case of the *Venice*,[2] McPherson insisted that the property of an individual who took the oath was protected from seizure as much as was the property of a loyal citizen in the North.

McPherson closed the argument on Padelford's behalf by stating that it was most important to Federal policy that the terms of the amnesty oath proclamation be respected. It was also highly important that the court diligently follow its own earlier decisions that had interpreted the effects of taking the oath, which held that the government could not seize an individual's property after he took the oath.

Padelford's attorneys requested that the court affirm the decision of the Court of Claims. With that request, Padelford's argument came to a close.

The Opinion of the Court

The opinion of the court was given by Chief Justice Salmon P. Chase on April 30, 1870, just nine days after the oral arguments. A court of nine justices participated in a unanimous decision.

Chief Justice Chase opened the court's opinion by stating that the case consisted of an appeal under the terms of the Abandoned and Captured Property Act of March 12, 1863. He acknowledged that the court had decided several cases under the act during that term of the court. The cases, especially the case of *United States v. Anderson,*[3] held that the act was remedial in nature and required a very liberal construction to give effect to the beneficent intention of Congress.

The chief justice indicated that the first issue of the case to be determined was whether Padelford had given aid and comfort to the Rebellion by the purchase of Confederate bonds. He followed with the statement that it would violate the "soundest maxims" of interpretation if the act were construed to deprive claimants of the benefits afforded by the act because of aid and comfort to the Rebellion not voluntarily given. Chase was clear that as far as the court was concerned, this statement determined and disposed of this issue.

The chief justice then acknowledged that Padelford had acted as surety on three bonds, two of commissaries and one of a quartermaster in the Confederate army. These acts, said Chase, were not made under compulsion, but were voluntary because the individuals were Padelford's friends, and without a doubt, they constituted aid and comfort to the enemy. Despite the will of Congress to have the act liberally construed, said Chase, this did not warrant a relaxing of the requirements set forth by Congress by a "forced interpretation." However, the issues created by Padelford's actions as a surety were, in the opinion of the court, not necessary to determine.

Chase then undertook an explanation as to why the surety issue need not be determined by the court. He stated that the rights to private property, as opposed to public property, are not disturbed by a military capture of the area in which the property is located. Private property is captured only on the date of actual seizure.

Agreeing totally with the arguments made on Padelford's behalf by J. D. McPherson, the chief justice cited the case of the *Venice* and held that Padelford's cotton was not subject to seizure following the capture of Savannah. This holding went even further than McPherson's argument that Padelford's cotton was not subject to seizure following the capture of Savannah and his taking of the amnesty oath. The taking of the oath, said Chase, only reinforced Padelford's right not to have his property seized because it further showed his loyalty at the time the cotton was seized.

The argument that under the provisions of the Abandoned and Captured Property Act, Padelford must have affirmatively proven that he gave no aid or comfort to the enemy, and that involuntariness or intent had nothing to do with it, Chase said, was "ingenious" but not sound. The chief justice went even further by suggesting that the proof of a pardon was a complete substitute for the proof that he gave no aid or comfort to the Rebellion. A different interpretation of the amnesty and oath, held Chase, would defeat the "manifest intent" of the amnesty and oath proclamation.

Under the proclamation and the act, held the chief justice, the government was a trustee of the funds generated by the sale of the cotton. The government being fully reimbursed for its expenses incurred, it had nothing to lose by awarding Padelford the proceeds of the sale, which "simply awards to the petitioner what is his own."

The court thereupon affirmed the judgment of the Court of Claims, which had awarded Padelford his half of the proceeds of the sale of the cotton, $123,138.88 less expenses.

THE CASE OF *TEXAS V. WHITE*

In another case, a state in the Confederacy had actually sold United States bonds to finance its war obligations. This was one of the longer and more hard-fought cases of the Civil War. It was one of the more important cases of the Reconstruction period, and it has had a continuing long-term effect as a result of its definition of both the legal status of a state and the legal aspects of how all states are related to each other within the Union. It was also one of the more important Civil War–related legal opinions rendered by Chief Justice Salmon P. Chase. An unusual combination of politics and facts came together to form the basis of the claims that led to the court dispute.

The rough and abrasive politics prevalent in Texas in 1861 gave birth to the facts of the case. It was just one year after Texas had observed its twenty-fifth anniversary as the twenty-eighth state in the Union, and its governor, Sam Houston, had celebrated his sixty-eighth birthday. In that year, a convention whose delegates were Texas citizens adopted an ordinance that dissolved the ties between the state of Texas and the other states of the Union. Concerned about the authenticity of the convention, Gov. Sam Houston called the Texas Legislature into extra session on January 22, 1861. At this session, the legislature endorsed the acts of the convention by ratifying the selection of delegates to the convention. Later, the ordinance of secession itself was submitted to the vote of the citizens of Texas, where it was ratified by a three-to-one margin.

Following this vote, the convention passed a resolution that required the officers of the state government to take an oath to support and defend the Confederate States of America. If an officer refused to take the oath, his office would be declared vacant, and it would then be filled with someone loyal to Texas and the Confederacy. Gov. Sam Houston, who had waged the last campaign of his life against secession, refused to subscribe to the oath, and he was replaced by the lieutenant governor, Edward Clark.

A new legislature was then formed. On January 11, 1862, the new legislature formed a Military Board to oversee the transition of the state from the Union to the Confederacy. That same day, the new legislature, frantically searching for ways to finance the war, instructed the Military Board to sell any bonds owned by the state that were in the state treasury. The Military Board found that $5 million worth of United States indemnity bonds were part of the treasury and available for sale. These were bearer bonds and part of a $10 million issue by the United States to the state of Texas as compensation for the settlement of a boundary dispute at the time Texas entered the Union. The bonds were dated January 1, 1851. They carried interest at 5 percent per annum, were in $1,000 units, and were redeemable at par after December 31, 1864. They were authorized by the Compromise Act of 1850, and their receipt had been authorized by the loyal Texas Legislature. When received, the bonds were placed into the school fund of the state, and the legislature had passed an act stating that no bond could be available for transfer into the hands of a holder until the bonds were endorsed by the governor of Texas. The insurgent legislature repealed that requirement when it instructed the Military Board to sell the bonds.

The Military Board sold 136 of these bonds to a Texas commission house owned by George W. White and John Chiles. The sale was probably made shortly after the legislature gave instructions to sell the bonds, but it was not confirmed in writing until January 12, 1865. At that time, White and Chiles resold the bonds in varying amounts directly or through the open market to John A. Hardenburg, Samuel Wolf, George W. Stewart, the Branch of the Commercial Bank of Kentucky, Weston F. Birch, Byron Murray, Jr., and a man by the name of Shaw. (Shaw's given name does not appear in the published reports of the case.) All of the bonds were sold after their due date, and the facts appear to reflect that one or more of these individuals had submitted the bonds to the Federal government for payment and had received some payments in gold.

A strange shadow hung over these sales. White and Chiles had initially paid for the bonds with an inventory of cotton cards and medicines; however, the state of Texas did not receive this consideration. While the cotton cards and medicines were en route from Mexico to Austin, Texas, robbers raided the shipment and seized the entire inventory. Apparently the state of Texas never recovered any items in the shipment.

As the war in the West turned against the Texans and the Confederate army of the Trans-Mississippi Department surrendered, the governor, secretary of state, and treasurer of Texas fled to Mexico. To cope with the anarchy that this created, President Andrew Johnson issued an executive proclamation appointing a provisional governor of Texas, a man by the name of Andrew J. Hamilton. Another part of the same proclamation directed the people of Texas to draft a new constitution and form a state government. The people of Texas proceeded to do this, and among their organizational activities, they elected a governor, J. W. Throckmorton. At this point, it appears that the affairs in Texas became intertwined in Washington politics, and the military commandant of that area, Gen. Philip H. Sheridan, appointed the "actual" governor of Texas, Elisha M. Pease. Each of these three governors exercised executive functions and represented the state in its executive department. As far as the facts of the case reveal, their terms actually overlapped to a great extent.

The agents of the U.S. Treasury Department were aware of the situation in Texas and became reluctant to pay off the bonds resold by White and Chiles. As the buyers of the bonds began to push harder for payment, the officers of the new loyal state of Texas came to the realization that the bonds were no longer in the state treasury. Reacting quickly, the financial officers of the state, believing that the bonds had been sold illicitly and the proceeds used to aid and abet the Rebellion, determined to file suit against the bonds' owners and regain the bonds for the state of Texas. The signatures of all three governors of the state, evidencing approval of the legal action, were obtained, and a suit against the bond owners was filed directly as an original suit in the U.S. Supreme Court. This was done under Article III, Section 2 of the U.S. Constitution, which stated that the Supreme Court had original jurisdiction in all cases "in which a State shall be a Party." The suit appeared on the docket of the court as *The State of Texas, Compt., v. George W. White, John Chiles, John A. Hardenburg, Samuel Wolf, George W. Stewart, the Branch of the Commercial Bank of Kentucky, Weston F. Birch, Byron Murray, Jr., and Shaw.*[4]

The Arguments before the Court
The state of Texas was represented by George W. Paschal, J. R. Brent, R. T. Merrick, George Taylor, and B. H. Epperson. John Chiles retained Albert Pike, Robert W. Johnson, and James Hughes to defend him against the charges filed by the state of Texas. James M. Carlisle represented John A. Hardenburg. George W. White retained P. Phillips to present his case. Weston F. Birch, Byron Murray, Jr., and the others hired S. S. Cox and J. W. Moore to represent them.

A total of twelve attorneys took three full days to present their cases to the Supreme Court on February 5, 8, and 9, 1869. Since the court had original jurisdiction of the suit, it was conceivable that the court could have conducted a regular trial; however, it appears from the printed reports that reflect the arguments of counsel and the opinion of the court that the evidence of the case was brought before the court by means of the answers of the defendants, unchallenged documents, interrogatories, and affidavits.

The attorneys for the state of Texas presented their case first. The state of Texas had initiated the suit by filing a bill, which amounted to a complaint, on February 15, 1867, alleging that the bonds were owned by the state of Texas. The bill further requested that an injunction be issued by the court that would restrain the defendants from cashing the bonds and would require the defendants to surrender the bonds to the state.

The Texas attorneys explained to the court that the defendants had based their case entirely upon the alleged validity of the possession of the bonds by the defendants White and Chiles. The validity of that possession was founded upon the session laws of the Confederate Texas Legislature, which authorized the sale of the bonds to finance the war against the United States. This, combined with the heretofore unmentioned fact that the bonds were to be replaced by Confederate bonds, clearly showed the illegal purpose of the sale, argued the attorneys. Not only that, but the original bonds were for school purposes, and the legislation of the Confederate Texas Legislature could not change this specially dedicated purpose.

In addition, the attorneys for Texas posed the question of whether the revolutionary government of Texas legally acquired ownership of the bonds. They went on to explain that the attorneys for the defendants had insisted that all of the acts of the Confederate Texas Legislature were valid, because if the acts performed by that legislature were illicit, all of the marriages solemnized and the decisions, civil and criminal, of the courts would be null and void. This, of course, was not true, argued the Texas attorneys, because whatever was done by the Confederate Texas Legislature to preserve the social community from anarchy and to maintain order should be accepted as lawful acts. These acts would remain valid and effective even after the Confederate Legislature was dismantled. However, those acts passed by the Confederate Texas Legislature designed to promote the Confederacy or that were in violation of the U.S. Constitution were illegal, they argued. Therefore, they explained to the court, the sales of the bonds, the proceeds from which were meant to finance the Confederate war effort, were illegal.

These rules not only applied to the transfer of the bonds to White and Chiles, they said, but also to those who took transfer of the bonds from them, because they could be in no better position than White and Chiles. It was a sound legal principal of long standing that those who purchased bonds after their maturity date took the bonds subject to all equities between the original parties, in this case to the claims of ownership by the state of Texas. Therefore, the attorneys asserted, the purchasers of the bonds who claim to be bona fide purchasers of the bonds without notice, completely ignorant on any defects in their title, still could not, under any theory, obtain a title better than that of White and Chiles. Their title was not a good title, and the title of all the defendants therefore failed, they stated. Hardenburg and the other defendants had a claim against White and Chiles for the defect in the bonds, but they had no right to claim a valid title to the bonds themselves. In conclusion, these attorneys told the court, any of the bondholders who had actually received payment from the U.S. government as bona fide purchasers were subject to a personal judgment against them for the amounts they had received. With this statement, the attorneys for the state of Texas concluded their argument.

Albert Pike, Robert W. Johnson, and James Hughes then presented the case of John Chiles. These attorneys first stressed an argument that the attorneys for the state of Texas had not even mentioned. They made reference to the constitutional provision that gave the parties original jurisdiction in the Supreme Court if one of the parties was a state. This case did not qualify, and the jurisdiction of the court failed, they asserted, because Texas was not a state as contemplated by the constitutional provision; it was a territory governed by the other states as a conquered province. Chiles's attorneys pointed out that Texas had no representatives in Congress, nor was it permitted to participate in the election of the president and vice president. The citizens of the state, they argued, had no constitutional rights and were governed by military authorities.

If the court should hold that Texas was a state, they said, then it was necessary to examine whether the contract that the Confederate state of Texas made with White and Chiles was valid. It had been asserted, said Chiles's attorneys, that all of the acts done by the Confederate state of Texas that conflicted with the Federal constitution were void. However, the sale of the bonds subject to the suit in consideration of cotton cards and medicines did not violate the Constitution. Such acts as selling these bonds by a revolutionary government were never void, the attorneys asserted. They were done for the benefit of the people of the state, and just because the government changed, the people could not subsequently repudiate the sales.

If, on the other hand, the contract was illegal, posed the counsel, then the general principle, "for which we need not cite authorities," was that neither party could have a remedy against the other in a court of justice, law, or equity. The counsel for Chiles then ended their presentation by arguing that the people of a state were that state. To assert that the people of a state were somehow different from the state itself was a legal and practical fiction. The people performed acts through their representatives, and those acts, counsel insisted, were valid regardless of who those representatives were. Therefore, if Texas was a valid state, said Chiles's counsel, the sale of the bonds was legal and the state of Texas could not recover them.

At this point, the brilliant James Mandeville Carlisle took over, representing John A. Hardenburg. Carlisle's argument was very short and relied upon the fact that Hardenburg's situation was wholly unconnected with that of any of the other defendants, except that all of Hardenburg's bonds but one had also been owned at one time by White and Chiles.

Carlisle explained to the court that Hardenburg had purchased the bonds in the open market in New York City in November 1866. He had purchased the bonds in good faith for full market value from reputable brokers in the regular course of business. Not only did he have no knowledge of any infirmity in the title of the bonds, but he was totally without any suspicion that there was anything untoward with the bonds.

It was a "misnomer and a confusion of ideas," Carlisle asserted, to call the government of Texas something less than the true government of Texas at the time of the contract with White and Chiles. Even if one called the government of Texas at that time a "revolutionary" government, the attorney argued, there was no question but that the contract was binding upon the state at the time of the contract and also upon the later restored government. Carlisle adamantly stated that it would be a "vain parade of learning to cite authorities for a proposition so universally admitted in the public law of nations."

Carlisle then took notice that the state of Texas also asserted that it had not received consideration for the bonds from White and Chiles. He acknowledged that having purchased the bonds after their due date, Hardenburg was subject to defenses that could be asserted by the state of Texas against White and Chiles; however, the attorney argued, the lack of consideration for the bonds was not one of those defenses. With that statement, Carlisle brought his argument on behalf of Hardenburg to a close.

George W. White's attorney, P. Phillips, then stepped in and presented his client's stand on the issues. His first argument was a repeat of the stand taken by the attorneys for John Chiles that Texas was not a state within the meaning of the constitutional provision that if one of the parties to a suit was a state, the Supreme Court had original jurisdiction of the case. Phillips cited the case of *Hepburn v. Ellzey*,[5] in which Chief Justice John Marshall had held that only a political body entitled to representation in the Senate and House of Representatives, and that had the authority to appoint electors, qualified as a state under that constitutional provision. Since the state of Texas was in actuality controlled by the military, and the state was denied the right of representation in Congress, argued Phillips, it did not qualify as a state under Marshall's definition.

Phillips then turned his argument to the legality of the contract between the state of Texas and White and Chiles. He stated that there were, in essence, two contracts. One provided for the delivery of the bonds; the second was for the delivery of certain commodities as consideration. These commitments were not dependent on each other, Phillips insisted; the failure of one did not alter the validity of the commitment of the other. Therefore, the failure of the delivery of the commodities by White and Chiles did not change the obligation of the state of Texas to deliver the bonds.

Another issue pertaining to the contract, said White's attorney, was the allegation that the contract was for illegal purposes. He cleverly asserted that for a contract to be illegal because of illicit purposes, both parties must be involved in the illegality. Here the contract was not illegal, asserted Phillips, because White had no idea what the state of Texas was intending to do with the cotton cards and medicine. Further, if both parties were involved in an illegality, "in pari delicto, melior est conditio possidentis," where each party was equally at fault, the law favored the party that was actually in possession. Phillips insisted that this was a maxim of public policy equally respected in courts of law and equity.

White and his attorney then tackled the argument that there was no authority in Texas competent to enter into an agreement during the Rebellion. If this were true, said Phillips, the Texas Confederate government had no power of legislation, no executive or judiciary, and all that had been done during the four years of the Confederate government was null and void. The "shocking consequences" of such a doctrine were themselves the best refutation, he said. "The civilized government recognizes the necessity of government at all times."

Phillips closed White's argument by pointing out the ramifications of the state of Texas entering into an illegal contract to make war against the United States. If this were true, insisted Phillips, the state of Texas had no right to resort to aid from the Supreme Court.

The attorneys for Weston F. Birch, Byron Murray, Jr., and the other defendants were of the opinion that all of the points favoring the defendants had been adequately covered and waived the right to additional arguments.

Thus the arguments were concluded, and not only the parties involved, but also the judges of the lower Federal courts and the state courts, as well as a goodly portion of the American people, anxiously awaited the decision of the court.

The Opinion of the Court

Chief Justice Salmon P. Chase gave the opinion of the court on April 12, 1869. The chief justice began his opinion by relating the nature of the suit in one very long sentence. He stated that it was an original suit in which the state of Texas claimed certain United States bonds as state property. In connection with this claim, the suit requested the court to issue an injunction restraining the defendants from receiving payments from redeeming the bonds from the Federal government, and to compel them to surrender the bonds to the state of Texas.

After reviewing the facts of the case, Chase turned the court's attention to the two issues raised by John Chiles. The first, an issue that Chiles's attorneys raised but did not argue before the court, was that sufficient authority to prosecute the case on behalf of the state of Texas was not shown the court. The second issue, argued extensively, was that Texas was not a state qualified to file an original suit with the court as set out in the Constitution.

The chief justice disposed of the first issue promptly by making reference to the evidence of the case, which revealed that all three of the governors of Texas had, in one way or another, approved and authorized the suit. He held that as long as Texas was a state in the Union at the time, the approval of one or more of the governors was all that was needed to validate the authority to file the suit.

The second issue, that Texas was not a state such as was envisioned by the Constitution as qualified to file an original suit in the Supreme Court, was a matter of basic jurisdiction, said the chief justice. If this allegation were true, the court clearly had the obligation to dismiss the suit. Chase then digressed to comment upon the importance of the issue and the interest it had excited among the people. He further observed that the issue was impossible to dispose of in such a way as to satisfy the conflicting judgments of men "equally enlightened, equally upright and equally patriotic." Nevertheless, he said, the court would meet the issue and use its best judgment under the sole guidance of the Constitution.

The chief justice then indicated that an important aid to understanding the true sense of the Constitution was to consider the idea of a state separate and apart from the concept of a state within the Union. Following a review of the many concepts of a state, he concluded that a state under the Constitution was a political community of free citizens who occupied a territory of defined boundaries and had a government under the terms of a written constitution established by the consent of the governed. It was a union of such states that constituted the United States and made the people and states into one people and one country. It should also be noted, added the chief justice, that there were provisions in the Constitution that clearly distinguished the state itself from the government of the state.

Chase then began to apply the concept of a state that he had just defined to the state of Texas by reviewing the history of Texas and its separation from the United States. He detailed the steps of this separation and the fact that Texas had joined the war of the Rebellion. The chief justice then posed a question: Did these facts cause Texas to cease being a state, or if Texas remained a state, did that state remain a member of the Union?

The chief justice began his analysis of the answer to those questions by stating that the Union of the states was never an artificial or arbitrary relation. It was a very real relationship growing out of the attempts to solve the problems of the colonies, and it was consummated in the Articles of Confederation. Those articles, said Chase, solemnly proclaimed that the relationship created among the states was perpetual. When these same states created the Constitution, the relationship was meant to be a more perfect union. The reading of those two documents together, observed the chief justice, the first declaring the Union to be perpetual, the second declaring it to be more perfect, clearly conveyed the idea of an indissoluble union. "What can be indissoluble if a perpetual Union, made more perfect, is not?" he asked. Therefore, under the Constitution, the Union was indestructible, and it was composed of indestructible states.

The process that brought Texas into the Union was something more than a compact, he said; it was the incorporation of a new member into the political body, and this was an indissoluble relationship and it was final. The chief justice then held on behalf of the court that the Texas Ordinance of Secession, and all of the acts of the Texas Legislature intended to give effect to that ordinance, were absolutely null and void and without operation in the law. The obligations of the state as a member of the Union, and of the citizens of the state as citizens of the United States, remained "perfect and unimpaired," he held. It was therefore the conclusion of the court that the state of Texas never ceased being a state within the Union.

That did not mean, however, that the rights of Texas as a state and the rights of her citizenry were not suspended during the war. This suspension created duties upon the United States to suppress the Rebellion and reestablish the broken relations with the Union. These duties were found in the Constitution under the powers to suppress insurrection and the obligation of the United States to guarantee every state a republican form of government. The national government undertook measures as fulfillment of these duties and successfully reorganized the government of Texas following the cessation of hostilities. After reviewing these measures briefly, the chief justice held that the Supreme Court had jurisdiction to hear the case, because Texas was a state under the constitutional provisions that defined the court's jurisdiction. The question of the court's jurisdiction being thus determined, the chief justice continued on to consider the merits of the issues raised by the purported sales of the bonds.

The first issue to be answered in this regard, said Chase, was whether the bonds were actually conveyed by Texas to White and Chiles by the contract with the Military Board. There was no question that the state of Texas owned the bonds at the time of this contract, said the chief justice; this ownership was not denied and therefore not an issue. However, the bonds were conveyed to White and Chiles without the endorsement of the governor as required by the Texas Legislature in 1861. The Confederate Texas Legislature repealed this provision in 1862, and the question was raised whether this repeal was valid. The chief justice then held that acts of the Confederate Texas Legislature necessary to the peace and good order of society, such as the sanctioning and protection of marriage, governing descents, and similar laws, were valid; however, acts in furtherance or support of the Rebellion or to defeat the rights of citizens were invalid and void.

The Military Board had as its purpose the levying of war against the United States, the chief justice stated, and the activities of the board furthering this objective were invalid. Chase refused to consider the argument of White and Chiles that the sale of the bonds was merely to obtain cotton cards and medicine. The sale, he held, was in furtherance of the war effort and therefore void. It followed that title to the bonds always remained with the state of Texas.

The chief justice then turned his attention to the claims of several of the defendants that they were innocent purchasers of the bonds without notice of any defects in the title that was held by White and Chiles. These defendants had cited *Murray v. Lardner,*[6] which held that such purchasers held good title to the securities regardless of the want of good title in the seller. This rule, said Chase, was still good law; however, the rule had never been applied to securities purchased after their maturity. In such cases, he explained, the purchasers took nothing but the actual right and title of the vendors. In this case, the bonds had matured on December 31, 1864, and the defendants purchased the bonds from White and Chiles after that date. Therefore, the defendants acquired only the title owned by White and Chiles. Since that title was defective, held the chief justice, the defendants acquired nothing by the purchase.

Chase then held on behalf of the court that the state of Texas was entitled to the relief sought by the filed bill and ordered a decree entered reflecting this holding. Because this was an original action in the Supreme Court, a decree that would normally be entered by a trial court was entered by the Supreme Court. Before the decree was entered, however, Justice Robert C. Grier carefully rendered a dissenting opinion.

Justice Grier began his dissent by stating that he regretted that he disagreed with the majority of the court "on all points raised and decided" in the case. The first of these points was the matter of jurisdiction of the court to hear the case at all. The justice stated that whether Texas was a state when the bill was filed should be decided "as a political fact, not as a legal fiction." He thought it was unnecessary to listen to the astute arguments of counsel when the subject had been treated in a clear and commonsense manner by Chief Justice John Marshall in the case of *Hepburn v. Ellzey.* That case held that a state was an entity that had representatives and senators in Washington and was entitled to have electors participate in the election of the president. Grier pointed out that not only did Texas not have these representatives in Congress, but it was occupied and governed by the U.S. military. He insisted that in this regard, the state of Texas was no different from a territory or an Indian nation, and these organizations did not qualify as states.

Grier determined that this was a matter under the jurisdiction of Congress, and he was "not disposed to join in any essay to prove Texas to be a State of the Union when Congress have decided that she is not." This was a simple question of fact, he said. The fact was that Texas was not a state, and whether this was right or wrong was not a question before the court.

Obviously very moved by the questions posed by the case, the justice continued on to the second issue, which was whether the conveyance made by the Confederate state of Texas to White and Chiles could be invalidated. He opened his discussion of this issue by stating that Texas, having relied upon one fiction that she was a state of the Union, now wanted to rely on a second fiction "that she was not a state at all during the five years that she was in the rebellion." Grier insisted that Texas had set up "the plea of insanity" and had asked the court to invalidate all her acts "made during the disease." Texas could not act like a chameleon and assume the color of the object to which she adhered, he said, and then ask this court to involve itself in the contradictory positions.

In his opinion, stated Grier, the state of Texas was stopped from denying its own identity in disputes with its own citizens. He indicated further that if these citizens had not fulfilled their contracts, Texas could seek a remedy in its own courts. Furthermore, to aid the state of Texas in invalidating Hardenburg's purchase of the bonds in the open market was to place the court in the position of assisting Texas in perpetrating a great wrong.

Grier concluded by stating that neither his reason nor his conscience could give assent to the court's decision. "I am justly convicted by my brethren of an erroneous use of both," he said, "but I hope I may say without offense, that I am not convinced of it."

Justice Noah Swayne then stated that he agreed with Grier as to the incapacity of Texas to maintain an original suit in the Supreme Court, but he agreed with the majority of the court on the merits of the case. Swayne added that Justice Samuel F. Miller agreed with his views. This made the vote of the court five to three.

There followed an entry of the decree of the court, which held that the contract selling the bonds to White and Chiles dated January 12, 1865, was null, void, and of no effect. White, Chiles, their agents and attorneys, and all others claiming to act on their behalf were perpetually enjoined from asserting any rights or claims under the contract. The decree then ordered that the state of Texas was entitled to receive the bonds and coupons and proceeds received from them. All of the defendants were then perpetually enjoined from asserting any rights or title to any of the bonds or coupons.

The decree then recited that three of the defendants, Birch, Murray, and Hardenburg, had received payments from the redemption of certain of the bonds from the U.S. Treasury Department prior to the filing of the case. These defendants had requested a further hearing because they could not turn over the bonds as the court ordered. The court granted this request and set a hearing date of the first Friday in October 1869. It also indicated that all of the parties were at liberty to check with the court for further directions.

The court closed by affixing the final shackle upon the defendants in the form of an order requiring them to pay all of the costs of the state of Texas.

Hardenburg, Birch, and Murray did appear again before the court. The court affirmed that Hardenburg was liable to turn over the proceeds that he had received from the redemption of the bonds. Birch and Murray, however, did not have to turn over the proceeds received from the sale of four bonds, because the state of Texas had failed to request this specific remedy in the filed bill.

Stewart also requested the court that four bonds he had cashed before being served with the bill be exempt from the decree. This the court denied.

THE *PASCHAL* CASE

The collection of the bonds and the funds from their redemption was overseen by the attorney for the state of Texas, George W. Paschal, who had been retained by all three governors of Texas to file the suit in 1865. There was no specific agreement as to his fee, but by the standards prevalent at that time, it was understood that the fee charged would be consistent with his responsibility, the expense entailed, and the time, skill, and service rendered.

Paschal was a sincere, honest attorney who took his responsibility very seriously. Finding it difficult to conduct a case in Washington, D.C., from Texas, he left his home and a very profitable law practice in Texas and moved to Washington, where he would be on the spot to conduct the case and to work with the Treasury Department. The third of the governors, Elisha M. Pease, visited Paschal in Washington. Impressed with Paschal's work, Pease retained him to recover additional bonds from the same issue that were in the hands of other individuals or brokerage firms who claimed to own them. They agreed on a more specific fee for this work on a contingent basis of 25 percent, and in some cases 20 percent, of what Paschal succeeded in recovering.

The attorney appeared to be doing an excellent job; everything pertaining to the cases was moving smoothly. But Texas politics were in a turmoil caused by the continuing squabbles and serious fights among the radicals, conservatives, carpetbaggers, and the old Confederates who wanted to regain power. Paschal tended toward being a conservative Republican, reflecting the views of the three governors who had retained him. In an admitted perverted election of 1869, the radical Edmund J. Davis was elected governor, replacing Elisha M. Pease. On January 27, 1870, Davis sent a telegram to Paschal informing him that he was dismissed as the attorney for the state of Texas, and that a cohort of the new governor, Thomas J. Durant, had been retained to replace him.

Paschal, who was working hard at collecting the bonds and some gold under the terms of the decree he had obtained in the prime case, and was negotiating settlements on the other bond cases that Governor Pease had retained him to handle, was shocked. He refused to give up his post and continued to handle the cases. More serious, he refused to turn over to Durant the sum of $47,325 in gold that he had received under terms of the court decree. As far as carrying out the terms of the decree in Washington was concerned, the situation was at an impasse.

Durant, the new attorney, finally filed two motions with the court.[7] In the first, he asked the court to order Paschal to turn over the gold to the clerk of the court for the benefit of the state of Texas. In the second, Durant requested the court for an order changing the docket of the court, striking Paschal as counsel for the state of Texas and substituting the name of Durant. Incorporated in the second motion was a request for an order forbidding Paschal from interfering with the cases.

The motions were handled as regular cases before the court. They were argued for two days, December 10 and 19, 1870. Justice Joseph P. Bradley gave the opinion of the court on January 23, 1871. After reviewing the law applicable to attorneys' liens, the justice held that Paschal had the right to withhold the gold and apply it to the costs of the cases and his fees. Bradley also indicated that the merits of the amounts withheld could be heard in a court of competent jurisdiction if Durant saw fit to file it in such a court. As to the second motion, Bradley held that the state of Texas had the right to dismiss Paschal through its governor. The second motion was granted.

Chapter Ten

Confederate Currency

Except for its lack of recognition by the members of the international community, the Confederate States of America was a sovereign nation in all respects. Even the United States conceded the rights and obligations of a belligerent to the Confederacy shortly following the initiation of the war. A good case could be made that the Confederacy was a true state under Chief Justice Chase's definition in his opinion in *Texas v. White* that a state was a "political community of free citizens occupying a territory of defined boundaries, and organized under a government sanctioned and limited by a written constitution, and established by the consent of the governed."

As such a state, the Confederacy possessed all of the attributes of nationhood, including its own system of currency. Not having in place an organized system of Federal taxation, and lacking other resources available to the North, a system of paper currency was vitally essential to the Confederacy to pay for the equipment and other essentials necessary to carry on the war. The paper currency created by the Confederacy, the so-called "graybacks" or "bluebacks," was issued in various denominations ranging from a $1 bill to a $100 bill. Paper was also issued for fractional parts of a dollar. These bills were called "shinplasters" in the North, and this derogatory term found its way to the South.

The amount of paper currency issued by the Confederacy exceeded $1.5 billion, which gave the Confederacy the means of paying more than half of its wartime indebtedness. This currency, called treasury notes, was the equivalent of the greenbacks of the North; however, this money was never made legal tender. It was assumed by the Confederate Congress that the people of the South would accept their paper money as legal tender even though it was not designated as such by law. In this regard, the Congress was correct; the patriotism of the people of the South would not permit a citizen to refuse to accept Confederate treasury notes to pay a debt or purchase a product. Other entities—states, banks, and even cities—also issued currency. An interesting aspect of the Confederate currency was that it was easily counterfeited, and counterfeiters, some of the largest and most expert being in the North, had a field day. Rather than spend time and money tracking down the counterfeiters, the Confederate government simply accepted most of the expert counterfeit currency as legitimate.

The Confederate notes were to be redeemable in gold or silver two years after independence was achieved. As the fortunes of war turned against the South, and it became doubtful that this redemption date would ever be reached, the value of the currency plummeted. When the war ended, the Confederate currency had value only to the world's numismatists.

During the course of the war, the economy of the Confederate States was probably a normal economy for a nation at war. The people bought and sold items that were necessary to their subsistence. They purchased or sold homes and made investments in things such as land or cotton. Many of these transactions took place pursuant to the terms of written contracts. As might be expected, when the war ended, many of these transactions were not completed and balances were owing. Since the initial payments in these transactions had been made in Confederate currency, and the parties to the transactions expected Confederate currency to be used to pay any balances due at the time the agreements were entered into, could the debtors pay the balances owing in Confederate currency after the war ended? Creditors in the South were aghast at the thought of accepting Confederate money as payment of these debts. Confusion reigned in this area, and thousands of creditors and debtors waited for the courts to clarify the situation.

THE *THORINGTON* CASE

One of the first cases to reach the U.S. Supreme Court consisted of an appeal from the District Court of the United States for the Middle District of Alabama. The situation that led to the case took place in November 1864, when two men,

A $500 bill issued by the Confederate States of America featured Gen. Stonewall Jackson. These "graybacks" or "bluebacks" were issued in higher denominations following the first minting of this paper money. They were redeemable in gold or silver two years after the Confederacy gained its independence; however, they were not legal tender.

William B. Smith and John H. Hartley, purchased land from a third, Jack Thorington. The land was in or very close to the city of Montgomery. The agreed price was $45,000, of which $35,000 was paid in Confederate currency, the only currency available to the parties. A note was given by Smith and Hartley to Thorington for the balance of $10,000. At the time the note was given, it was expected that it would be paid in Confederate currency.

Toward the end of the war, when Confederate currency had very little or no value, Smith and Hartley tendered Confederate money to Thorington to pay the note. Thorington refused to accept Confederate currency and insisted that he be paid in something of value—gold, silver, or United States dollars. Smith and Hartley refused, insisting that although the note itself did not specify payment in Confederate dollars, there was an oral agreement to that effect. Thorington argued that this was the same as not paying the note at all. He therefore filed suit for the $10,000 and asked the court to grant him a vendor's lien against the land. He further asked the court for an order executing his vendor's lien by selling the land and applying the proceeds from the sale to pay his note. Smith and Hartley defended the action by stating that the United States did not recognize the Confederate States as a legal entity, and therefore the court could not even enforce a contract calling for the payment of Confederate money. The District Court agreed fully with the argument presented by Smith and Hartley and dismissed Thorington's suit. With that decision, Thorington would receive nothing for his note, and Smith and Hartley would keep the land. When Thorington appealed to the Circuit Court, that court, in a routine decision without a written opinion, affirmed the District Court.

Thorington then appealed to the U.S. Supreme Court. The case came up to the Supreme Court under the name of *Jack Thorington, Appt., v. William B. Smith and John H. Hartley.*[1]

The Arguments before the Court

The case was argued twice, on March 18 and on October 6, 1868. Two attorneys appeared on behalf of Thorington: W. P. Chilton and P. Phillips. No counsel appeared for Smith and Hartley. This lack of representation was probably not a reflection of their confidence of victory, but rather of their lack of financial resources.

Thorington's attorneys gave a very short and concise argument. They informed the court that the note was to be paid in dollars. Since the only dollars of value at the time Smith and Hartley attempted payment were United States dollars, this was the currency that should have been used to pay the note. To introduce oral statements as evidence to prove that the note was to be paid in Confederate dollars, they pointed out, in effect changed the contract. They went on to argue that it was accepted in all Anglo-American courts that parol, or word-of-mouth, evidence of an oral agreement that altered a written contract was never accepted as evidence. Further, the attorneys assured the court, the contract between the parties was neither immoral nor illegal. Therefore, it was enforceable and payable in United States dollars.

The Opinion of the Court

Chief Justice Salmon P. Chase gave the decision of the court in an opinion given on November 1, 1869. The chief justice first related the facts of the case. He indicated that there was no dispute that Smith and Hartley had purchased the land from Thorington, and that a note had been given for the balance owing. If this were all before the court, he explained, there would be no doubt that Thorington would be entitled to a decree in the amount of the note, and the land would be ordered sold to satisfy the debt. However, the case was compounded in its difficulty because the purchase of the land took place in the Confederate States and Confederate currency had been used in the transaction. Because of this, the chief justice mentioned, Smith and Hartley had defended the case by claiming that the U.S. courts did not have the authority to enforce a contract payable in Confederate currency. He indicated that this claim was the basis for the case's dismissal in the District Court of the United States.

Chase understood the importance of the case to the thousands of people in similar positions. He obviously believed that a simple affirmance or reversal of the trial court with nothing more would leave the people who had engaged in these contracts in a state of confusion. It was very apparent that the court had undertaken a full review of the subject when the chief justice defined the issues of the case. The first issue that the court would determine was whether a contract made during the Rebellion in the Confederacy, payable in Confederate notes, could be enforced in the courts of the United States. The second issue was whether evidence could be received by the court that a contract payable in dollars could be paid in currency other than that of the United States. The third issue was whether the evidence in the record of the case established that the agreement of the parties was that the note was to be paid in Confederate currency.

The chief justice then referred to the first question as a difficult one. Contracts made in an attempt to overthrow the government of the United States could not be enforced in the courts of the United States, he said, and the issuance of Confederate treasury notes was for the purpose of overthrowing the U.S. government. But was the contract of the parties one of that character?

Chase recited the formation of the Confederacy, step by step, and acknowledged that the Confederate government was the actual government in all of the insurgent areas under its control. It was a true *de facto* government. The highest degree of such a government, acknowledged the chief justice, assumed the character closely resembling that of a lawful government. He then pointed out that the distinguishing characteristic of such a government was that its participants in war against the actual, or *de jure,* government did not incur the penalty of treason. In addition, certain obligations undertaken by the *de facto* government would be honored and respected by the *de jure* government when it was restored.

The chief justice cited England under the commonwealth as an example of this. That government had incurred obligations that the government of England assumed after the Restoration. However, the Confederate government never enjoyed the status and recognition enjoyed by the English government at the time of the commonwealth.

There was another, possibly more appropriate, *de facto* government, he said. This was a government maintained by military power, and while it existed, it had to be obeyed by the citizens who occupied the territory over which it maintained jurisdiction. One example of this type of *de facto* government was that which existed in Castine, Maine, when it was occupied by the British during the War of 1812. From September 1, 1814, to the ratification of the Treaty of Peace in 1815, the British government exercised all civil and military authority over Castine, and the laws of the United States could not be enforced there. The citizens of Castine were forced to follow the laws of England and were not subject to the laws of the United States until the Treaty of Peace was signed.

Another example of this type of *de facto* government was the occupation of Tampico and the entire state of Tamaulipas by U.S. forces during the Mexican War. During that occupation, Chase pointed out, the citizens of Mexico living in the area were forced to follow U.S. law, and other nations acknowledged the territory as being governed by the United States.

The central government of the Confederacy was not unlike the temporary governments that existed at Castine and Tampico, explained Chase, no matter that it was unlawfully achieved. The chief justice observed that the power of the insurgent government within its military lines could not be questioned. It was this government that had issued the Confederate treasury notes, and these notes had been the exclusive currency in the insurgent states. Chase then observed that although the notes were redeemable only if the Confederacy won the war, nevertheless, during the war, they had a contingent value and were used as money in the business transactions of millions of people. Therefore, he held, this currency must be considered in the same light as if it had been issued by a foreign government temporarily occupying part of the territory of the United States. Contracts stipulating for payment in Confederate currency could not be considered as made in aid of the Rebellion for this reason only. The chief justice then held on behalf of the court that these contracts could be enforced in the courts of the United States to the extent of their obligations after the restoration of peace. Thus the first issue posed to the court received an affirmative answer.

Considering the second issue before the court, whether testimony, in this instance oral testimony, could be accepted by the court to prove that Thorington's contract was to be paid in Confederate dollars, the chief justice indicated that the admission of such evidence in this case did not alter the terms of the contract, but explained an ambiguity. Under the rules of evidence, an ambiguity could be clarified by parol evidence, he stated. Chase once again referred to the Confederacy as the same as a foreign power, and said that contracts consummated under Confederate jurisdiction must be interpreted and enforced with the understanding that Confederate currency was the only measure of value at the time the contract was consummated, and that the use of the Confederate money was a matter of necessity. He added that it was "hardly less than absurd" to say that these dollars should have been regarded as identical in value with United States dollars, obviously a statement directed at Thorington's argument that the final payment of his contract should have been made in that currency. The chief justice then held that evidence should have been received by the trial court indicating that the payment should have been made in Confederate currency. Chase added that Thorington could recover the actual value of the Confederate dollars paid to him in United States dollars at the time and place of the final payment, a holding that did not give Thorington much comfort.

The chief justice then held that it was not necessary for the Supreme Court to closely examine the evidence in the record to answer the third issue before the court. Weighing all of the evidence, he said that it was obvious that Thorington's final payment was to be made in Confederate dollars.

A unanimous Supreme Court overruled the Circuit Court and sent the case back to the District Court to be reheard in conformity with Chief Justice Chase's opinion.

An interesting footnote to the case took place in the court on this same day in the form of a similar case, but one in which the creditor used a different and somewhat novel approach to the problem. Chase gave the opinion in four short paragraphs, making reference to the *Thorington* case as controlling. In the footnote case, a man by the name of Lecil W. Dean had conveyed land by deed to W. H. Younell. The transaction took place in Georgia during the war, and Confederate currency was the medium of exchange. When Younell approached Dean to make his final payment in Confederate dollars after the war came to an end, Dean refused to accept them. Younell subsequently died, but Dean sued his estate to cancel the deed to the land based upon inadequate consideration and fraud. A dismissal of the case was affirmed in the Circuit Court of the United States for the Northern District of Georgia, and Dean appealed to the U.S. Supreme Court. The title of the case was *Lecil W. Dean, Appt., v. Robert D. Harvey, Administrator of W. H. Younell, Deceased.*[2] Both parties were adequately represented. The case was argued on October 21, 1869. Chief Justice Chase gave the opinion of the court following his opinion in the *Thorington* case on November 1, 1869.

As to the alleged inadequacy of the consideration, the chief justice cited his opinion just given in the *Thorington* case holding that courts in the United States could enforce contracts even though the consideration involved in the contracts was Confederate currency.

Considering the allegations of fraud, the chief justice indicated that the sole basis for the alleged fraud was that the land was sold for Confederate money. Chase then held that because Dean could not prove that he was induced to accept the Confederate notes by fraudulent misrepresentations, the allegations of fraud could not be sustained.

On behalf of a unanimous court, Chief Justice Chase affirmed the Circuit Court, and the case was dismissed.

The results of these two cases were that the courts of the United States possessed the authority to enforce contracts where the consideration for the contracts was Confederate currency, and further, that allegations of inadequate consideration or fraud would not carry the day to defeat court orders requiring the creditors to accept Confederate currency.

THE *BETHELL* CASE

The U.S. Supreme Court sent a clear message to the people in the *Thorington* case that contracts and agreements expected to be consummated in Confederate currency would be enforced by the courts. The decision did not apply to contracts whose purpose was to aid the Rebellion or to contracts clearly opposed to public policy, such as the purchase and sale of slaves. Contracts in these two categories were considered to be null and void when consummated.

However, the question soon presented itself again to the court in a different form. As the Southern states reorganized themselves to reenter the Union, it became a common practice for them to include a provision in their new constitutions stating that all agreements based upon Confederate currency were null and void. The new legislatures of these states followed with the passage of laws detailing the enforcement of these constitutional provisions. Notwithstanding the *Thorington* decision, the citizens involved in these contracts again were concerned as to how the courts would treat the issue. The solution was not as easy as it might appear, because issues involving public policy and constitutionality soon inserted themselves.

The reorganized state of Louisiana was one of the states that included in its constitution a provision making all agreements based upon Confederate currency null and void. The reorganized Louisiana Legislature followed with the passage of laws that were added to its state code, implementing the constitutional provision. Two cases made their way through the judicial system and eventually arrived before the U.S. Supreme Court, which interpreted these provisions.

The first of these cases was generated on April 2, 1862, when Joseph T. Hawkins and an associate borrowed $15,000 in Confederate currency from Pinckney C. Bethell. The borrowers gave Bethell two notes of $7,500 each. These notes were secured by a mortgage upon certain premises and were due in two and three years following the date of their execution.

Even though it was understood by the parties when the loan was made that the notes would be paid in Confederate dollars, Bethell refused to accept them when Hawkins offered them to pay the notes, as the Confederate dollars had declined in value. Then, claiming that he had not been paid on a timely basis, Bethell filed suit against the borrowers in the Louisiana District Court. Hawkins died prior to the initiation of the court proceedings, and his place was assumed by his widow, Elizabeth A. Demaret. Bethell was successful in obtaining a judgment against Demaret-Hawkins at the trial level, and the court ordered that the mortgaged premises be sold and the proceeds applied to the judgment.

At this stage of the suit, Demaret-Hawkins appealed to the Supreme Court of Louisiana. That court reversed the trial court on the basis that under the laws and constitution of Louisiana, Confederate money was not valid consideration at the time the loan was made, and therefore the notes and mortgage were null and void. The state Supreme Court based its decision on several previous cases of the court that established a strong public policy in this area.

Bethell then appealed the case to the U.S. Supreme Court. The case appears in the court records as *Pinckney C. Bethell, Plff. in Err., v. Elizabeth A.*

Demaret, Widow of Joseph T. Hawkins, Deceased, et al.[3] Bethell was represented by an attorney named Miles Taylor. Demaret-Hawkins appeared through J. A. Campbell. Campbell carefully analyzed the case and came to the conclusion that there was no basis for Federal jurisdiction. He therefore filed a motion to dismiss the case, submitting it to the court on January 20, 1871. The court determined the motion by considering the briefs submitted by the parties.

The Arguments before the Court

The argument submitted by J. A. Campbell on behalf of Demaret-Hawkins was brief and concise. He argued that the U.S. Supreme Court could consider the case based only upon the record of the case as it was formulated by the two Louisiana state courts. That record, Campbell argued, did not disclose that any Federal constitutional, statutory, or treaty issue was determined by the state courts. Neither did those courts determine any state constitutional or statutory issues that raised a Federal question. The sole issues before the state courts, Campbell claimed, were matters of fact. These issues, he argued, did not form a basis for an appeal to the U.S. Supreme Court. He therefore requested the court to forthwith dismiss the case and allow the decision of the Supreme Court of Louisiana to be the final decision of the case.

Miles Taylor, on behalf of Bethell, agreed that the Supreme Court of Louisiana determined the case only upon the facts of the case. However, he argued, when those facts revealed that the decision itself violated a section of the U.S. Constitution, there was ample basis to support an appeal to the U.S. Supreme Court. Taylor went on to point out to the court that the contract entered into by the parties on April 2, 1862, was valid under the laws of Louisiana when it was entered into. Therefore, no action by the Louisiana Legislature or judiciary could impair that contract under the U.S. Constitution, Article I, Section 10, Clause 1, which stated that no state should pass a law impairing the obligation of contracts. When the constitution of Louisiana was passed containing the provision that all agreements that had Confederate currency as consideration were null and void, the agreement of the parties before the court was impaired, he argued. This was "too plain to require argument."

Taylor claimed that this case came under the provisions of Section 25 of the Judiciary Act of 1789 as being clearly appealable to the U.S. Supreme Court. Under that act, he argued, any decision rendered by a state court that was repugnant to the U.S. Constitution was open to reexamination before the Supreme Court. It made no difference, he insisted, whether the unconstitutional allegations were made and the applicable constitutional sections were cited in the records of the lower courts.

Taylor requested the court to deny the motion to dismiss the case and consider the case on its merits.

The Opinion of the Court

Justice Samuel Nelson gave a written opinion of a unanimous court on January 30, 1871. First Nelson reviewed the facts of the case and its history in the

Louisiana courts. He observed that the decision of the Supreme Court of Louisiana was placed upon the ground that Confederate money did not constitute valid consideration of the two notes and mortgage at the time they were executed. The justice indicated that the Louisiana court based its decision on past cases it had decided and the public policy of the state, not upon the laws or the constitution of the state.

He then stated that the record of the case indicated that no Federal question was presented in the Louisiana courts by Bethell, nor was any statute of the state brought into question. Without any statute being considered by the court, said the justice, Section 25 of the Judiciary Act of 1789 was not applicable. Neither could it be considered that the mere decision of a court in a state would create a basis for appeal to the U.S. Supreme Court absent the consideration of the applicable constitutional or statutory laws in the record of the case.

Justice Nelson closed his opinion by stating that since no Federal question appeared in the record of the case, the motion to dismiss filed by Demaret-Hawkins must be granted.

This case was consistent with the long-standing rules of appeals courts in the Anglo-American system of law. The role of an appeals court was to review the record of the case in the lower courts; matters not in the record would never be considered. This is easy to understand; if the appeals courts allowed the introduction of new materials at the appeals level, they would not be appeals courts, but trial courts. In such instances, they would be forced to rule upon the authenticity of new materials, which they were not equipped to do from their very nature.

However, Justice Nelson left the door open. He stressed that the Bethell case could not proceed to full review because no Federal question had been introduced at the trial level. No state statute or constitutional provision had been challenged at that level. If such a challenge had been made, the decision could very well have been different.

THE *DELMAS* CASE

In another case from Louisiana, the facts were more complicated, but the issue that ultimately came before the Supreme Court concerned whether the use of Confederate currency could invalidate a contract. The difference between this case and *Bethell v. Demaret* is that the constitutional issue that Bethell tried to bring before the court, and failed, became the central issue of the case.

This second case had its beginning when Bressole Gilbert and his wife sued Joseph Menard in the 5th District Court of New Orleans. The basis of the suit did not appear in the reports, but the Gilberts' claim was successful. In addition, the Gilberts obtained an order from the court that ordered the sale of certain real property owned by Menard. The proceeds of the sale were ordered to be applied to the judgment of the Gilberts. The sheriff conducted the sale and sold the property to John Henderson on July 1, 1867, for the sum of $5,635.

Following Louisiana law, Henderson paid the sheriff the amount of the Gilberts' judgment plus costs, other charges, and taxes. The sheriff paid this amount to the Gilberts, and they were out of the case. Henderson then retained the balance of $3,499.07, which, under the laws of Louisiana, he held in trust to pay other creditors of Menard who held liens against the property.

Either Henderson was not aware of the number of claimants who had liens against the property he had purchased, or if aware of the number, he did not have knowledge of the amounts of the claims or how strongly the creditors felt about them. Just one month after Henderson purchased the property at the sheriff's sale, the Merchants' Mutual Insurance Company filed suit against him, claiming all of the money that Henderson held in trust for the creditors and, in addition, claiming that the property purchased by Henderson should be sold again by the sheriff and the proceeds of this sale applied to its claim. The total claim of the insurance company was $5,000. The basis for the claim was a note that Menard had executed to the insurance company prior to the original suit by the Gilberts.

In the meantime, the money held in trust by Henderson was seized by John T. Delmas, who was executing a judgment he had received in the 2nd District Court of New Orleans against Menard. The basis of this suit was a note for $4,500 that Menard had failed to pay, which was secured by a mortgage on the property.

At this point, Henderson felt that he was getting hit from all sides and that the situation was getting out of hand. He defended himself by filing a case in the 5th District Court of New Orleans, in which he requested that the court assist him in properly apportioning the money he was holding in escrow to the creditors of Menard. This kind of case was called an action of interpleader. He in effect told the court: "I have this money that is claimed by these people and these companies. I do not know who is entitled to the funds. Please render a decision as to who is entitled to receive the money." Henderson also requested that the court enjoin the claimants from further activity in seizing the funds that he held until the rights of the parties were determined by the court.

The dispute in the case soon settled down to a contest between Delmas and the insurance company. Delmas claimed he had rights to the funds that were prior to Merchants'. He also claimed that the note and mortgage claimed by Merchants' were null and void under the legal theory that the insurance company had failed to pursue its rights for such an extended period of time that it had effectively waived its rights. Merchants' denied all of Delmas's assertions and alleged that its claim was prior to the mortgage held by Delmas. In a further answer, Merchants' created the prime issue of the case by alleging that the judgment Delmas had obtained against Menard was invalid because the consideration for the note and mortgage sued upon by Delmas was Confederate currency.

The trial was held in the 5th District Court in New Orleans on May 9, 1868. That court agreed with Merchants' that the constitution of the state of Louisiana clearly stated that contracts that had Confederate currency as consideration were null and void and could not be enforced by the courts of Louisiana. Therefore, the note and mortgage that Delmas had used to obtain a judgment in the 2nd District Court of New Orleans were invalid, and the judgment failed and would be set aside. Delmas argued that this judgment could not be collaterally attacked, to no avail. He then appealed to the Supreme Court of Louisiana. That court agreed fully with the results in the trial court and affirmed the judgment. Delmas then appealed to the U.S. Supreme Court.

The Arguments before the Court

The case was argued before the court on November 12, 1872, under the title of *John T. Delmas, Plff. in Err., v. Merchants' Mutual Insurance Company, John H. Henderson, et al.*[4] Delmas was represented by Thomas J. Durant. A. G. Riddle argued on behalf of Merchants'. The argument essentially repeated the cases as they were presented at the trial level. Durant, on behalf of Delmas, pushed the issue that the Louisiana constitutional provision invalidating contracts founded upon Confederate currency, in the case where the contract was valid when entered into, violated the Federal constitutional provisions prohibiting the states from passing any law impairing the obligation of contracts. A. G. Riddle, on behalf of Merchants', pressed the contention that past Louisiana cases, and now the *Bethell* case, invalidating contracts the consideration of which was Confederate currency were valid on the basis of a long-standing public policy of the state. These presentations clearly defined the issues of the case.

The Opinion of the Court

Justice Samuel F. Miller gave the opinion of the unanimous court on November 25, 1872. Miller first defined Henderson's position under Louisiana law. He stated that Henderson was responsible under provisions of that law to pay the creditors of Menard who held liens against the property purchased by Henderson from the escrow funds he held. However, Henderson could not do this because the claims of the creditors who claimed to have liens amounted to more money than the amount in escrow. Plus, Delmas and Merchants' both claimed that their own lien had the highest priority. Unable to reconcile the disputes, related the justice, Henderson filed an equitable bill of interpleader with the state court. This transferred the responsibility of determining who was entitled to the funds to the court. By this proceeding, Miller explained, Henderson relieved himself of liability; he would simply pay the creditors pursuant to the court order.

Miller then pointed out that the dispute narrowed to a contest between Merchants' and Delmas in the interpleader proceeding. The Supreme Court of Louisiana had determined that Merchants' had a superior claim because the Louisiana constitution invalidated Delmas's claim, as the note and mortgage given Delmas by Menard were based upon Confederate currency.

The justice acknowledged that it was held in the *Thorington* case that Confederate currency could be valid consideration for a contract as long as that currency was circulating as money at the time the contract was entered into. He attempted to reconcile the differences between the *Thorington* and *Bethell* cases by saying that when a state court held that Confederate currency was not valid consideration for a contract based upon a long-standing public policy of the state, thereby holding that such a contract was invalid at its inception, the decision was not reviewable by the Federal courts because no Federal question had been raised in the record. Miller referred to the *Bethell* case as one in this category.

Miller then distinguished the case before him from the *Bethell* case. The state court held the note and mortgage given to Delmas invalid squarely upon the provision in the Louisiana constitution stating that "all agreements, the consideration of which was Confederate money, notes or bonds, are null and void, and shall not be enforced by courts of this state." The application of this provision to the Delmas note and mortgage, which were valid at the time they were entered into, clearly violated Article I, Section 10 of the U.S. Constitution, said the justice, because it not only impaired the obligations, but destroyed them completely.

Furthermore, he continued, the U.S. Supreme Court, in cases such as this, always decided for itself whether a valid contract existed in any given case and would not rely upon the state court for this determination.

Miller then held on behalf of the court that the Supreme Court of Louisiana had committed error in holding that the note and mortgage of Delmas were void for the reason that Confederate notes were their consideration. He formally reversed the Louisiana Supreme Court and remanded the case to it for further proceeding in conformity with this opinion. The record of the case was returned to the Supreme Court of Louisiana. This court in turn returned the record to the 5th District Court in New Orleans, with instructions to retry the case but consider the Delmas note and mortgage valid, or amend the original judgment with the Delmas note and mortgage considered valid, if this could be done.

›—•—O—•—‹

Thousands of people found themselves in the same position as the parties in the cases considered in the chapter. Unless the parties themselves agreed that the balance of a contract would be paid in United States dollars, the court held that if the contract was valid and legal at the time it was entered into, it should close according to its understood terms—that is, with the payment of Confederate money. The one exception was that if a state treated such contracts as invalid at their inception based upon public policy, the Supreme Court would not interfere, because no Federal question was involved. If, however, a state declared such contracts invalid, even at their inception, because of a constitutional provision passed after the contract was entered into, the Supreme Court would force the state courts to accept the contract because of the Federal constitutional provision that no state could pass a law impairing contracts.

Through these cases concerning the use of Confederate currency, the U.S. Supreme Court endeavored to indicate to other citizens involved in such agreements what their rights were, and how they should conduct themselves to terminate those agreements.

Chapter Eleven

Procurement Problems

When the war began, the North was bound to a military tradition that dictated how ground troops were to be raised and equipped. There were the Regular army, the volunteer national army, and the state militias. The Regular army was composed of professional troops and was not large, possibly 16,000 men before the resignations of those who left to fight for the Confederacy.[1] The voluntary army consisted of men who had volunteered to be part of local units assembled by the states or under the auspices of the states. The militias had existed since the founding of the republic and also initially were state units. Lincoln's first call was for the expansion and reporting for duty of members of the militias.

Congress followed with provisions for the expansion of all three organizations, especially the volunteer army. Though Congress passed the laws, the actual expansion was under the supervision of the states. However, with some exceptions, particularly pertaining to the militias, the equipping of the men was expected to be accomplished by the Federal government. This became a problem; many military units waited months for their equipment, and many reported for duty with no, or inferior, equipment.

The states became impatient and soon took it upon themselves to attempt to equip the volunteer units, expecting the Federal government to reimburse them for their expenditures. Therefore, the states sent purchasing agents into the domestic and foreign arms markets to buy armaments of all types. These agents of the states bid against each other and also against similar Federal agents, much to the consternation of the Federal government. Considering that in the European arms markets, buying agents representing Confederate states and the Confederate government were also competing to buy the available arms, a chaotic sellers' market was created. Markets of this type attract middlemen and speculators hoping to cut in on large profits and politicians hoping to look good to the folks back home. These markets were no different. This situation was ripe for the unscrupulous to negotiate huge, unwarranted profits. Because these individuals had no true concern for the quality of the products, often inferior, even dangerous arms of all types were sold as efficient, safe, and genuine.

Many legal cases were generated by these conditions. One of the more interesting cases to reach the U.S. Supreme Court that clearly illustrated these problems represented a group of cases that involved a popular American of the time, John Charles Frémont. At age forty-eight, he was famous throughout the country for his exploits in connection with his western expeditions and as the new Republican party's first presidential candidate in 1856.

In 1861, Frémont was on private business in France. When notified that the war had begun, he dropped his private business efforts, made sure President Lincoln was aware that he was available for duty, and then set about buying arms for the North from European suppliers. He had no official authority to purchase arms; nevertheless, he not only did so, but he used his own credit.

Returning to the United States, he stepped into the middle of the efforts of Lt. Gen. Winfield Scott and President Lincoln to raise up younger leaders. Acknowledging Frémont's reputation and his popularity among the people, Scott and Lincoln appointed him as one of the first four major generals in the Northern army. At that time, the army was divided into Departments of the East and West. Considering Frémont's association with the West, Lincoln overlooked the fact that Frémont had never commanded a large number of men and appointed him commander of the Department of the West. This area included all of the territory between the Mississippi and the Rockies, Illinois, and parts of Tennessee and Kentucky. Frémont, after buying 23,000 guns in New York to be delivered to his headquarters in St. Louis, arrived at his headquarters with his wife on July 25, 1861.

Frémont entered a scene of complete disorganization. He commanded 30,000 troops who were spread throughout the entire area, most were inexperienced, the enlistments were expiring for many, it appeared that most were behind on their pay, and nearly all were inadequately equipped. There were Confederate forces in the area that seemed motivated to occupy all of Missouri, and they threatened the river towns. It was obvious to Frémont that he had to take immediate emergency measures to equip an army and create a river navy. But in this he was thwarted from Washington; since Bull Run, the War Department ordered that all available arms and equipment be delivered to the Department of the East. That order even applied to the guns that Frémont had personally purchased in New York prior to his departure to St. Louis. Frémont had no choice but to enter the arms market in the West and contract for the equipment he needed with local suppliers. He promptly did this through his quartermaster general, Maj. Justus McKinstry.

McKinstry was serving in the office of quartermaster general when Frémont arrived. A political appointee, McKinstry was already earning a reputation for meticulously rewarding those to whom he was indebted for his office. Nevertheless, Frémont undertook through McKinstry a frenzied negotiation of supply contracts. The contracts stressed the need for rapid delivery of the equipment, to the neglect of those portions that addressed the suppliers' profit. Soon reports of scandalous, even fraudulent, profits on many of Frémont's contracts began to reach Washington. The Congressional Subcommittee that had a continuing duty to investigate government contracts deemed it urgent to look into the situation. A very concerned chairman of the subcommittee reported to Congress that it was hard to conceive of the fraud, extravagance, and even robbery that was taking place under Frémont's command.

For this reason, and several others that are outside of the realm of this study, Frémont, after barely serving 100 days on the job, was replaced on October 14, 1861, by Gen. David Hunter. Frémont's dismissal was delivered to him in the field while he was successfully pushing the Confederates out of Missouri into Arkansas. He received the news very badly, and his troops were so upset that they were on the verge of revolt. The American people generally did not receive the news very well. But this history is secondary to the case examined here, which shows how contracts with alleged excessive and fraudulent profits were handled by the War Department and the Federal courts. This in itself is fascinating history that is not generally known.

THE *ADAMS* CASE

Prior to Frémont's dismissal, he entered into a contract with a man named Theodore Adams. This was a large contract, signed on August 24, 1861, calling for Adams's company to build thirty-eight mortar boats at $8,250 each. In September, Frémont contracted again with Adams for eight tugboats at $2,500 each and eight tugboat cabins at $1,800 each. The boats were also to include pilot houses, steering apparatuses, and windlasses. The contracts were consummated on behalf of the government by the infamous quartermaster general, Maj. Justus McKinstry.

Adams's company fulfilled the contracts with dispatch and delivered the equipment in November 1861. The equipment was received into the service of the government by orders of the secretary of war, Simon Cameron. However, by the time the equipment was delivered, but before Adams was paid, the alleged unethical profits and other irregularities engaged in by the suppliers of arms and equipment to Frémont caused President Lincoln to order Cameron to suspend all payments on the contracts executed within Frémont's department, pending an investigation of the many charges.

The secretary of war then appointed a Board of Commissioners to examine and report to him concerning all unsettled claims generated by the contracts. The men appointed to the board, David Davis, Joseph Holt, and Hugh Campbell, were men of the "highest intelligence and character." Davis was a close and respected friend of the president from Illinois. Lincoln appointed him to the Supreme Court the following year. Joseph Holt had been the secretary of war under President James Buchanan, and he would become the U.S. judge advocate general. Two years later, Holt presented the government's case against Clement L. Vallandigham when he was tried before the Military Commission convened for that purpose in Ohio. The charge to the Board of Commissioners was "to examine and report to the Secretary of War upon all unsettled claims against the military department of the west, that had originated prior to the 14th day of October, 1861, the day General Frémont had been superseded." In the meantime, McKinstry was dismissed as quartermaster general, and he was later dishonorably discharged.

The commissioners met promptly in the city of St. Louis, having first given notice to all persons with claims against the government to present them for examination with such supporting data as they desired to submit. Adams responded by submitting an outstanding bill of $183,500 on the mortar boat contract, acknowledging receipt of $130,000. In addition, he submitted an outstanding bill of $25,400 as remaining unpaid on the September contracts. Adams acknowledged that he had been paid $9,000 against these contracts. He attached copies of the contracts to the submitted bills.

The commissioners reviewed the Adams contracts and the balances owing. They deleted the amounts that they believed represented excessive and fraudulent profits but still awarded Adams $75,959.24 against the claimed balance of $183,500 and $20,196 against the claimed balance of $25,400. This reduced the mortar boat total contract by 34 percent and the September total contracts by 18 percent. The commissioners offered Adams government vouchers for the amounts they awarded if Adams would agree to execute a receipt that his contracts were paid in full. Adams agreed, but he noted on the receipt that he signed it "under protest." Then, in an unusual move, Congress passed the following joint resolution on March 11, 1862:

> Resolved by the Senate and House of Representatives of the United States of America, in Congress assembled, that all sums allowed to be due from the United States to individuals, companies or corporations by the Commissioners heretofore appointed by the Secretary of War (for the investigation of military claims against the Department of the West) composed of David Davis, Joseph Holt, and Hugh Campbell, now sitting at St. Louis, Missouri, shall be deemed to be due and payable, and shall be paid by the disbursing officer, either in St. Louis or Washington, in each case upon the presentation of the voucher with the Commissioners' certificate thereon, in any form plainly indicating the allowance of the claim, and to what amount. This Resolution shall apply only to claims and contracts for service, labor or materials, and for subsistence, clothing, transportation, arms, supplies and the purchase, hire and construction of vessels.

Following the passage of this resolution, Adams presented his vouchers and received payment of the amounts awarded by the commissioners. Nevertheless, he strongly believed that the commissioners not only were unwarranted in reducing the amounts he received under his contracts, but that they had seriously tarnished his reputation as well. When his attorneys advised him that new legislation passed by Congress would expand the jurisdiction of the U.S. Court of Claims and permit him to sue the government for the unpaid portions of his contracts, a course not available to him at the time he submitted his vouchers for payment, he instructed his attorneys to proceed and file a petition for his claim as permitted by the new legislation. The new legislation had amended the powers of the Court of Claims and changed it from a purely advisory body to a true court. It in effect added a new court to the Federal system. The new legislation went into effect on March 3, 1863, and shortly thereafter the attorneys for Adams filed a petition with the court demanding that he be granted a judgment against the government in the amount of the unpaid portions of his contracts.

With the petition, Adams filed copies of his contracts, evidence that the mortar boats and tugs had been delivered to and accepted by the government, and evidence showing the amounts that he had been paid. The government responded by detailing the unconscionable profits Adams would have received if he had been paid the full amounts called for under the terms of the original contracts. The government also set forth the findings of the Board of Commissioners and the fact that Adams had accepted payment according to the commissioners' findings and the joint resolution of Congress. The Court of Claims weighed the evidence and gave Adams a judgment against the government of $112,748.76, which, when considered with the amounts already paid to Adams, actually exceeded the amounts of the original contracts by $4.00.

The attorneys for the government had no choice but to challenge the judgment given to Adams. If the judgment were allowed to stand, everyone who contracted with Frémont could appeal to the Court of Claims and have the Board of Commissioners overruled. The unconscionable profits and fraud would then have court sanction, and all of the work of the commissioners and Congress would have been for naught. The government therefore filed an appeal with the U.S. Supreme Court.[2]

The Appeal to the Supreme Court

Filing the appeal for the United States was the attorney general, Ebenezer Rockwood Hoar. He was assisted by the assistant attorney general, T. L. Dickey, and an attorney named E. P. Norton. Adams was represented by a team of attorneys: B. R. Curtis, Matthew H. Carpenter, John A. Willis, Louis Janin, R. W. Corwine, and James Hughes.

The arguments were made to the court on March 31, 1869. The court at that time included eight justices, three of whom were veterans. Associate Justice Samuel Nelson was appointed to the court by President John Tyler in 1845. Associate Justice Robert C. Grier was appointed by President James Polk in 1846. President James Buchanan appointed Associate Justice Nathan Clifford in 1858. President Lincoln appointed the remaining five: Associate Justices Noah H. Swayne, Samuel F. Miller, and David Davis in 1862; Associate Justice Stephen J. Field in 1863; and Chief Justice Salmon P. Chase in 1864.

Davis was a member of the Board of Commissioners that had reviewed the Adams contracts and made the recommendations that the profits they found excessive be excluded from the payments to Adams. Chase was secretary of the Treasury and sat as a member of Lincoln's cabinet when the Frémont investigations were ordered. He undoubtedly shared in the embarrassment of the Lincoln administration when the Frémont scandals became public. Under modern standards of ethics and rules of the court, these two justices would have excused themselves from hearing the case because of their obvious conflicts of interest. This was not expected in 1869.

In addition, Field had expressed the entire court's intolerance to questionable payments connected with government contracts in the 1865 case of *The Providence Tool Company v. Samuel Norris.*[3] In that case, Justice Field, who wrote the opinion on behalf of the court, held that a finder's fee in connection with the procurement of a governmental contract was contrary to the most efficient and economical mode of meeting the public's wants and was against public policy and therefore illegal. The language used in Field's opinion could easily be applied to profits that were claimed to exceed those that were considered normal and reasonable. Thus, as the government began to present its case, it was obvious that Adams had a heavy burden to overcome to be victorious.

The Arguments before the Court
The attorneys of the attorney general's office first argued that the United States was not bound by the Frémont contracts because, from a legal point of view, the United States was never a party to them. The attorney general based this argument upon a statute passed on May 1, 1820, which stated that no contract could be made by heads of the departments of the government except under a law that authorized the contract or under an appropriation law that was adequate to pay the contract. The Frémont contracts with Adams, the attorneys argued, not only were made without lawful authority, but also were forbidden by statute. In addition, the acceptance of the mortar boats and tugboats by the secretary of war did not overcome the fact that there were no valid contracts between the parties.

They then argued that the proceedings before the Board of Commissioners were a true arbitration. Adams had not been forced to appear before the commissioners, but once he subjected himself and the contracts to the jurisdiction of the commissioners, they asserted, he was bound by the result. This was confirmed when Adams stipulated that he would accept the sums fixed by the commissioners in full payment of his claims, signing a receipt to that effect, and afterward accepting the actual cash pursuant to the resolution passed by Congress. This, they insisted, was good satisfaction in law of the whole claim. The attorneys concluded the government's case by requesting the court to overrule the Court of Claims.

The attorneys for Adams, operating under the realization that they were in a serious uphill legal battle, presented a thorough and strong case to the court. In answer to the attorney general's argument that the United States was not bound by the Frémont contracts because Frémont did not possess lawful authority to consummate them, Adam's attorneys argued that Frémont was invested by the law of war with the power necessary to consummate the legal contracts with Adams. Whether Frémont had this power could not be found in either the statutes of the United States or in the regulations of the army, neither of which set out the authority of a commander of a military department in time of war.

They explained to the court that Frémont's powers to contract could only be defined by the U.S. Constitution, which stated that in wartime, the war powers of the president and his subordinate commanding generals were unlimited except by the law of war itself. This power was defined by Adams's attorneys as that power that must be exercised to achieve a legitimate objective and was equal to and measured by the demands of the occasion. The person exercising the power, the attorneys argued, was the judge of the necessity and propriety of using the power.

Adams's attorneys then quoted Alexander Hamilton's reference to the law of war as stating that the means ought to be proportional to the end.[4] The persons from whom the attainment of the end was expected possessed the means to obtain that end. The attorneys followed with more support for this war powers view from Chief Justice John Marshall and Justice Joseph Story.[5] To reach the goals that had been set out by a river campaign on the Mississippi, they argued, it was obvious that Frémont needed the mortar boats and tugs; therefore, he possessed the powers to contract for them, and these contracts bound the United States.

If Frémont did not possess the powers to contract under the law of war, they added, he nevertheless possessed the power because it was an implied authority derived from the secretary of war. If there was doubt as to either of the argued theories, then certainly Frémont's negotiation of the Adams contracts was confirmed by the government when the secretary of war accepted the mortar boats and tugboats on behalf of the government.

The counsel for Adams then responded to the arguments of the attorney general that Adams was bound by the amounts found owing by the commissioners because he had agreed to the amounts when he executed the receipt as paid in full. The commissioners had no authority to settle any claims, the attorneys insisted, because they were not a judicial body; they constituted a board of investigation to report to the secretary of war concerning certain unsettled claims. The conduct of the commissioners in extorting a receipt in full as a condition of partial payment, then presenting it in a court of justice as evidence of full payment based upon a compromise freely and voluntarily made, was a clear and unequivocal usurpation of power, the attorneys argued. Furthermore, it was settled law in all jurisdictions that a receipt in full given for part payment was only prima facie evidence of full payment and could be explained that it was not given as a fair and deliberate compromise. They then cited a large number of texts and cases in support of this position.

The counsel for Adams then reviewed their arguments for the court's benefit and concluded by insisting that the Frémont contracts were made or ratified by competent legal authority, and that the government was bound to them as found by the Court of Claims. Further, the receipt given by Adams was no bar to the recovery of the balance owing, as shown by the many citations of texts and cases. Therefore, the attorneys for Adams asked the court to uphold and confirm the judgment of the Court of Claims.

The Opinion of the Court

Justice Samuel Nelson, the most senior of the justices on the court, gave the opinion of a unanimous court on April 12, 1869. Nelson began by reciting the history of the case in careful detail, during which the justice summarized the billing invoices submitted by Adams together with the amounts he had been previously paid and the sums he had collected based upon the findings of the commissioners. These figures revealed that the government had failed to pay Adams the sum of $112,744.76. This figure had been disallowed by the commissioners because they had determined that it represented excessive and irregular profits. This was the amount that Adams had sued for in the Court of Claims, the justice stated. The Court of Claims awarded Adams a judgment of $112,748.76. This was the judgment, said the justice, that this court had to review.

Nelson then acknowledged the "good deal of discussion between learned counsel" concerning the questions of whether Major General Frémont had the required power to negotiate valid contracts to build the boats, and whether the government had ratified the contracts when it accepted delivery of the boats. The justice stated that considering the view taken by the court of the case, it was not material how these questions were answered. However, he added, for purposes of this opinion, the competence of Frémont's power to negotiate such contracts would be admitted.

He went on to explain that the source of power to negotiate contracts rested with the secretary of war. If the secretary of war detected that frauds were being committed in connection with any contracts, he had not only the power, but the duty to adopt effectual measures to protect the government. Therefore, said Nelson, it was entirely justifiable for the secretary of war, in the situation before the court, to issue the order to suspend payments and to create the Board of Commissioners to meet at the place where the transactions occurred. The only alternative available to the parties was to resort to Congress or the Court of Claims as then constituted. Neither of these bodies had jurisdiction at that time to legally settle the claims. In addition, these bodies met in Washington, D.C., which was most inconvenient to the parties, who were situated in Missouri.

The Board of Commissioners had no authority to compel a hearing and to legally adjust the claims, the justice stated. That board was created for the "simple purpose" of affording claimants the right to have their claims promptly heard and decided without the delay and expense that would be incurred in traveling to Washington and using Congress or the then constituted Court of

Claims to reconcile the disputes. This was done for the convenience of the claimants. Therefore, said the justice, the criticisms made that the claimant's appearances before the board were mandatory were a misapprehension. The only compulsion facing a claimant was the realization that if he did not choose to have his claim heard by the board, his only alternative was to spend the time and money to travel to Washington and file a claim with the Court of Claims or try to influence Congress to pass an authorization to pay his claim. Nelson then observed that the Court of Claims at the time the Board of Commissioners was appointed did not have the authority to render a judgment, but only to recommend a solution to Congress. The Court of Claims was given judicial authority by the legislation of Congress on March 3, 1863. The creation of the Board of Commissioners simply added another tribunal to hear these claims. The choice of using the board afforded an additional advantage to the claimants in that if, after a hearing, a claimant was not satisfied with the results, he was free to seek redress in the other tribunals.

The justice then acknowledged the arguments of counsel pertaining to the effect that Adams's signature of the receipt had upon the results of the case. Again, he pushed this issue aside, as he had the others, and stated that it was not necessary for the court to settle this issue.

Nelson then got to the heart of the court's decision. He agreed with the arbitration argument submitted by the attorneys from the office of the attorney general by holding that Adams's voluntary submission of his claims to the board, his participation in the hearing, and his acceptance of payment as set out in the vouchers given him by the board barred any further legal demands against the government. The justice indicated that it was the government's duty to arrest the execution of fraudulent contracts, but resort to the courts was a remedy open only to individuals. The only course open to the government was to create such a body as the Board of Commissioners, and those who used this tribunal were bound by the results.

The Board of Commissioners was created as an act of kindness to the claimants, Nelson went on to state, but it could hardly have been supposed or believed by the claimants that the government would have gone to the expense of furnishing this tribunal if the board's purposes were merely to conduct a preliminary inquiry into the contracts and to make advances on them, leaving the residue for further litigation.

Nelson then stretched the court's holding to the limit by drawing an analogy between the Board of Commissioners and the Court of Claims before the latter had judicial powers. The justice said that in the case of a voluntary submission before the board, the court regarded the finding of the board, followed by an acceptance of payment, as conclusive upon the claim as if the claim had been before the Court of Claims. He then indicated that it would be an error for the current Court of Claims to overrule a finding of payment due by Congress or by the old Court of Claims. It would be a similar error for the Court of Claims to overrule the Board of Commissioners. Unless the claims of Adams were forever barred, he said, it would be difficult for the government to determine when there would be an end to claims against it, because there was no statute of limitations applicable to the claims before the court.

Justice Nelson concluded by holding that it was the judgment of the court that the Court of Claims decree must be reversed and the cause must be remanded to that court with directions that the petition filed by Adams be dismissed.

Further Related Decisions

Five additional cases involving the Frémont contracts appealed by the government from the Court of Claims were disposed of by Justice Nelson speaking for the court on the same day, April 12, 1869. Nelson did not render full opinions in these cases. He simply recited the facts in each case, then he reversed the Court of Claims in each case because the cases fell within the decision just rendered of *United States v. Adams*. The cases were *United States v. Mowry*,[6] which concerned contracts to build box and platform railroad cars; and *United States v. Morgan*,[7] *United States v. Burton*,[8] *United States v. Geffroy*,[9] and *United States v. Benjamin Higdon*,[10] all regarding contracts to purchase horses.

Another case involving Frémont contracts appeared before the Supreme Court on October 19, 1871: *United States v. Alonzo Child et al.*[11] In this case, Child insisted that the *Adams* case did not apply to him and the others involved in the suit because they did not voluntarily appear before the Board of Commissioners, their billing vouchers were never submitted to the board, and they accepted the settlement offered by the board solely to avoid bankruptcy.

Justice Samuel F. Miller rendered the decision of the court on October 30, 1871. The justice held that the fact that the claimants appeared before the board and accepted the settlement was sufficient to bring the case under the rules established by the *Adams* case, and the Court of Claims was again reversed, this time not by a unanimous court, but by a vote of seven to two. Justice Nathan Clifford and Chief Justice Salmon P. Chase dissented on the basis that the *Adams* case should not have controlled the decision.

The court had not heard the last from Theodore Adams. Taking an unusual step, Adams filed a motion with the court on November 25, 1869, to enter a stay of the mandate to the Court of Claims. He requested that the Supreme Court amend its decree to hold its judgment in abeyance in order to enable Adams to obtain a correction of the record and to hear his cause again under the amended record in the Court of Claims.

The ground for the motion was that the record in the Court of Claims, and thus the record used in the Supreme Court appeal, was erroneous in a material fact. That material fact, asserted Adams, was that the record set out that Adams had voluntarily submitted his claim to the Board of Commissioners. Adams insisted that this was not true. He alleged that Gen. Montgomery C. Meigs, who apparently was in charge of investigating the alleged frauds, had seized Adams's records, and that he was the one who had submitted Adams's case to the board. There it was heard without Adams's presence and without witnesses being heard in his defense.

Justice Nelson, his judicial countenance at its limit, gave the opinion of the court on February 14, 1870. The justice made short shrift of the motion. He indicated that Adams had been aware of this discrepancy in the record prior to the case being heard before the Supreme Court, but he did nothing to correct it because he thought that the discrepancy was immaterial. Nelson said that he had no doubt but that the belief of Adams was "honestly entertained," and that this motion was made in good faith. However, rules existed to correct mistakes in the record, and it was dictated by these rules that corrections be made in the record prior to the case being heard in the Supreme Court. Granting such a motion to correct the record at this point, after the hearing before the court, would create a precedent that would lead to great abuse and indeterminable delays in hearing cases. Such a precedent, said the justice, would work a greater injustice in its general use than any hardship incurred in denying a similar motion in any specific case.

Nelson then reviewed the case before the board, pointing out that although Adams did not participate in the hearing itself, he did have other contacts with the board and clearly had made himself a party to the proceedings. The court unanimously denied the motion.

The decision in the *Adams* case was clearly one where the court pushed aside the issues of the case, which clearly favored Adams, and decided for the government because it was the expedient thing to do. If the Supreme Court had affirmed the Court of Claims, thus holding for Adams, the Court of Claims would have been inundated with similar cases. Justice Nelson emphasized in his opinion that the government would have had no idea when there would be an end to such claims. It was conceivable that the attorneys for the government could have been tied up fighting those claims through the 1870s.

THE *GARRISON* CASE

The raising of volunteers was a task assigned to the states, as provided for in laws passed by Congress. The state governors supervised the recruitment of the men and commissioned the officers. On occasion, however, the president circumvented this procedure and commissioned men who had large citizen followings together with political influence. These men were authorized to raise a specified number of regiments and equip them to fight. Those so commissioned became known as "political generals."

Such a general was the colorful Maj. Gen. Benjamin Franklin Butler of Massachusetts. On September 1, 1861, shortly after Lincoln commissioned Butler, the president approved an order given by the secretary of war authorizing Butler to raise, organize, arm, uniform, and equip a force not exceeding six regiments in the New England states. His requisitions to the army were to be paid, provided that Butler's total cost did not exceed that of raising and equipping like troops "now and hereafter" entering the service of the United States.

One case that resulted from Butler's procurement activities and reached the Supreme Court reveals how this political general raised the arms to equip his men and how loosely the purchase contracts were handled.

When Butler undertook to arm the men in his six regiments, he entered into a contract with Cornelius K. Garrison, a dealer in guns, to supply 6,000 "Minie rifles by Liege pattern, with saber bayonets." The United States agreed to pay for each rifle that passed inspection the sum of $27, "or such less sum as the Ordnance Department may have paid for guns, like quality or description, or contracted to pay for, to said Garrison."

Shortly thereafter, at the suggestion of the chief of ordnance for the area, long Enfield rifles with triangular pattern bayonets were substituted for the Minie Liege rifles, "upon the value conditions as are herein specified." The change was noted on the original contract and signed by Butler.

Garrison delivered the rifles under terms of the contract as altered by Butler's notation. The rifles were accepted and approved. The government paid Garrison $27 per gun for 2,800 guns and $20 per gun for 3,200 guns, claiming that this lower price was the amount it had begun to pay for Enfield rifles following the payments for the first 2,800 rifles.

Insulted by the lower payment for the 3,200 rifles, Garrison claimed that he was entitled to $27 per rifle for all the rifles. The Enfield rifles were substituted for the same price that Butler had agreed to pay for the Minie Liege rifles, he said. This would be $27 per rifle, because the Minie Liege rifles had never been sold to the government at a lower price.

When Butler and Garrison could not reach an agreement, Garrison filed a petition in the Court of Claims asking for a judgment requiring the government to pay for all the rifles at the rate of $27 per rifle. The Court of Claims dismissed Garrison's petition. Garrison then appealed to the U.S. Supreme Court. The case came to the court under the title of *Cornelius K. Garrison, Appt., v. The United States.*[12]

The Arguments before the Court

The arguments were made to the court on April 7, 1869. Garrison was represented by T. J. D. Fuller. The United States was represented by the attorney general, Ebenezer Rockwood Hoar, and an attorney named T. H. Talbot.

Fuller began the arguments by insisting that the Court of Claims had misinterpreted the amendment written by Butler. The court, argued Fuller, not only allowed for the change in the rifles and bayonets, but also changed the amount of the payment, which was not provided for by the amendment. The amendment continued the same payment by its wording "upon the value conditions as are herein specified," maintained Fuller. Those value conditions, he insisted, were the amounts agreed to be paid for the Minie Liege rifles with saber bayonets. No question existed or was argued in the Court of Claims on the relative values of the two types of rifles. The agreement, therefore, was for the payment of $27 per gun for the entire 6,000 rifles.

The Court of Claims, according to Fuller, held that the wording of the amendment indicated that there was no fixed or agreed price. If that were true, the government, under the existing rule of law in such instances, should have paid what the arms were reasonably worth, not what the government was paying for similar rifles at the time of delivery. Fuller closed his argument by asking the court to reverse the Court of Claims, requiring it to accept Garrison's petition and entering a judgment in Garrison's behalf.

Talbot then argued for the United States. He pointed out that the Court of Claims interpreted the contract and amendment as stating that the government should pay $27 per gun or such less sum as the government paid for similar guns to other persons or to Garrison himself. Talbot maintained that the government found no other contracts involving Garrison selling Enfield rifles to the government; therefore, it paid Garrison the average of the amounts it had paid to other persons for those rifles, this being $23 per gun. Since this was the precise amount paid to Garrison, the Court of Claims was correct in dismissing Garrison's petition. He closed his argument by making reference to the September 1, 1861, order to Butler that set out the limits Butler could spend for raising and equipping his regiments. The government's case was consistent with keeping the costs of the contract within these limits, he said. Talbot then asked the court to sustain the dismissal of Garrison's petition by the Court of Claims.

The Opinion of the Court

The opinion of the court was given by Justice Samuel F. Miller on April 16, 1869. The justice first reviewed the facts of the case and the arguments submitted to the court. Then, referring to the amendment written on the contract, the justice confessed that the acceptance of Enfield rifles "upon the value conditions as are herein specified" was just not very clear. However, the court was inclined to agree with Garrison for the following reasons:

1. The amendment was drafted and signed by Butler, not by Garrison. Its doubtful expression should therefore, according to a well-known rule of law, be construed against the party who used the language.
2. The change in the contract was made by the government's ordnance officer. Therefore, it was an accommodation for the government.
3. The amendment was first acted upon by the government's ordnance officer, who paid $27 per gun for the first 2,800 rifles. That ordnance officer would have paid $27 per gun for the balance but for the intervention of the secretary of war, who insisted upon the lower figure of $20 per gun.
4. The $27 per gun was the price that the government had already agreed to pay Garrison on another Liege gun contract. Both the government and Garrison knew of this price and agreed to it. Butler may have been unaware of this price, but nevertheless, this reflected the real intention of the parties.

Acknowledging the government's argument that Butler's prices were limited by what the government had paid for similar arms, Miller indicated that the court did not understand this limit in the order to Butler. The limit was an aggregate limit, he said, not one that limited each contract. The aggregate limit was that set for the cost of raising and equipping like troops then or hereafter raised for service of the United States. Miller observed that this was merely directive to Butler, "for it could not have been supposed that he could contract with any person for arms, clothing, etc. at prices to be determined by what the government could buy them for afterwards." Butler had the discretion for contracting for each article he needed, the justice continued. He was within the rule of the order as long as the total of all his contracts did not exceed the expenses set out in the order.

Justice Miller, speaking for a unanimous court, then held that the judgment of the Court of Claims was reversed. Instructions were directed to that court to enter a judgment for Garrison for the difference between $20 and $27 for each of the 3,200 rifles subject to this dispute.

The urgent haste that characterized procurement activities created many such disputes. Fortunately, only a few of these disputes found their way into the courts, and only a very small percentage of those ended in the U.S. Supreme Court.

THE *JUSTICE* CASE

Another type of procurement problem surfaced when the soldiers in the field reported to their superiors that the arms they were using not only did not function as designed, but in some cases actually were dangerous to the user. Such was a case involving a gun supplier by the name of Philip S. Justice. In August 1861, Justice entered into a contract with the U.S. Ordnance Department to supply it with muskets. He apparently had a continuing contract with the government for this purpose. As part of this particular contract, Justice gave the government a sample musket and agreed that the muskets to be supplied in this order would be similar to the sample in all regards.

Justice supplied the muskets, and they were dispersed among the members of three regiments of Pennsylvania volunteers after they were compared with the sample and approved by subordinates of the officer who had negotiated the contract. However, it was not long before the men in the field who were using the muskets complained that they were at times inoperable and at other times dangerous to the user. When these complaints got back to the regiments' officers, an experience commissioned officer was dispatched to inspect the muskets and compare them with the sample furnished by Justice. This inspecting officer condemned the muskets as worthless and dangerous to those who used them.

The chief of the Ordnance Department withheld payment of the voucher covering the muskets and referred the matter to the War Department's Audit Commission in Washington. Justice defended himself at the hearing before the commission. Following this hearing, the commission held that Justice had not supplied serviceable arms and adjusted the amount owing to him. Justice accepted this amount, and the Treasury secretary on December 8, 1862, drew a warrant upon the U.S. Treasury in favor of Justice for the amount the commission found due. Justice acknowledge receipt of the amount, which was a draft for $2,301.25 and certificates of indebtedness of $6,000, but he gave no other receipt. Despite the fact that under the terms of the original contract, Justice still would have been owed $10,870, he outwardly accepted the amount fixed by the commission and went about his business. Then, nearly five years later, when knowledge of the judgments rendered by the Court of Claims in similar commission awards cases became general knowledge to government suppliers, Justice filed a petition in the Court of Claims for the balance of the contract.

The Court of Claims held that though the muskets were in fact unserviceable and even unsafe, and they did not fully conform to the sample submitted by Justice, the government had accepted the muskets following the inspection done when the muskets were delivered. Therefore, the Court of Claims awarded Justice a judgment for the $10,870. This judgment was of very great concern to the government, and it appealed to the U.S. Supreme Court. The case came to the court under the title of *United States, Appt., v. Philip S. Justice.*[13]

The Arguments before the Court

The arguments were made to the court on November 8, 1872. The United States was represented by the office of the attorney general, who at that time was George H. Williams, appointed by President Ulysses S. Grant on December 14, 1871. Williams had been chief justice of the Supreme Court of Oregon Territory and later a member of the U.S. Senate. During the year following this case, Grant nominated Williams to be chief justice of the U.S. Supreme Court. However, great criticism of the appointment was received from members of the eastern establishment, who believed that a frontier lawyer from Oregon would be ill suited to that position. Grant withdrew the nomination. Two attorneys from Williams's office, William McMichael and C. H. Hill, handled the case for the government. Justice was represented by J. Hubley Ashton.

The government attorneys argued that it was Justice's obligation, not to necessarily have his muskets pass an inspection, but to have them be of a certain caliber, quality, and standard. In this obligation, they said, Justice had failed. Justice had been fully aware of the defects in the muskets, they maintained, and he could not take advantage of a nominal inspection at the arsenal by subordinates when delivery was made to screen himself from the consequences of the later inspection by qualified officers.

Further, they argued, Justice had assented to the price fixed by the commission. Proof of this was that he did not file any complaint or object to the amount received for five years; Justice had fully agreed that the government could retain the defective arms at the price set by the commission because this was the true worth of the muskets. The attorneys closed by citing the *Adams* case as finally determinant that Justice was not entitled to any payment above that which he had already received.

Ashton then argued on behalf of Justice. His first point was that the muskets had passed the inspections provided for in the contract. Second, Ashton maintained that Justice never accepted the funds as full payment. Unlike the

Frémont cases, he had not given a receipt acknowledging payment in full. Therefore, the Frémont cases did not set a precedent that would tend to determine this case.

The attorney then repeated the argument often made in these cases that the acceptance of a lesser amount than a contract called for could never be interpreted as payment of the entire contract. Ashton claimed that there were no facts in the case that would indicate that Justice was not merely accepting what was paid as a partial payment of a liquidated amount set out in the voucher. The appearance of Justice before the commission could not prejudice him from receiving the full amount of his contract, insisted Ashton. Ashton closed his argument by requesting that the court affirm the decision of the Court of Claims.

The Opinion of the Court

Justice David Davis gave the opinion of the court on November 25, 1872. Davis began his opinion by referring to the record of the case in the Court of Claims. The Court of Claims, he pointed out, concluded that the evidence showed that the arms supplied by Justice were unserviceable and even unsafe for the troops to handle. Davis then mentioned that the first inspection of the guns, which was made when the arms were delivered, was negligently performed. The second inspection, made after the troops in the field complained about the arms, was a competent inspection. That inspection revealed that the arms were essentially worthless and dangerous.

The dispute was then given to the Audit Commission in Washington, said Davis, which determined that Justice had not fulfilled his obligation to sell "a serviceable arm." Justice accepted the amount fixed as owing by the commission and did not dispute it until five years later. The question before the court, explained Davis, was whether Justice could maintain this action under these conditions.

Davis then began the essence of the court's opinion. The government, he said, had always tried and should endeavor to be fair to the people with whom it deals. However, the government had to work through agents, and when these agents did not function in the expected manner, or the person with whom the government had dealt imposed upon the government, how should the government have reacted? If the government paid those who imposed upon it, Davis said, a bad example with "ruinous consequences" could have resulted. On the other hand, it would not have been appropriate to indefinitely hold up the payment to honest contractors, because this could create a hardship. "Common fairness," said Davis, dictated that some mode should be adopted to speedily adjust any differences. He then submitted that a commission of intelligent and disinterested persons hearing and determining these disputes was by far the most fair mode of handling these problems.

Several such commissions had been created, and one was sitting in Washington when this dispute arose. Davis reiterated that these commissions did not have judicial powers and could not require anyone to appear before them;

however, if someone did appear before them and accepted the findings of the commission by accepting the money award that the commission thought to be fair, this precluded that individual from further litigation. When a person appeared before the commission, he was not bound to accept the commission's finding; he could walk away and use other alternatives to try to collect the money he felt was owed him. But if a person appeared before the commission voluntarily and accepted the commission's finding, this amounted to a binding arbitration. Davis further held that the fact that Justice did nothing for five years was indicative that he had accepted the commission's findings, and that his filing of the suit with the Court of Claims was the result of an afterthought.

Davis then indicated that these holdings disposed of the case, and he stated further that the *Adams* and *Child* cases, although they contained some elements not applicable to this case, nevertheless were determinative of this case also. Justice Davis then held that the Court of Claims was reversed, and the case was ordered remanded with instructions to that court to dismiss the petition filed by Justice.

Chapter Twelve

Captured Property

One of the objectives of the tactics used by the military in the Civil War was to capture property of the enemy. By such captures, it was hoped not only to weaken the enemy, but also to penalize those who were guilty of treason. The laws pertaining to prize were well defined by international law; they were amended by national laws only to define procedures and who would share in the prize and to what extent. The law of prize has been with us for an extended period and is the most well known of the wartime property capture laws. In the Civil War years, both the U.S. and Confederate Congresses passed additional property confiscation laws that complemented the prize laws and had wide application during the war.

On August 6, 1861, the U.S. Congress passed an act providing for the seizure and confiscation of property used to aid, abet, and promote the Confederate cause.[1] Nothing was declared unlawful by the act, and no penalty was imposed; the act provided that the property itself was the guilty subject. Any property that had been used to aid, abet, or promote the insurrection was subject to capture. The act was intended to apply only to private property, and a judicial decree was required to divest the title of the owner.

A second confiscation act was passed on July 12, 1862.[2] It differed from the 1861 act in that it did not authorize the capture of property used in the insurrection, but it authorized the seizure of property owned by those hostile to the Federal government. One target of the law was Confederate officers who owned properties in the North. This was a punitive statute in that it was not directed at the property itself, but was designed to punish the owner for his insurrectional activities regardless of their nature. The outright seizure of the property was required before the courts had jurisdiction to enter a decree of forfeiture. Because the act was meant to punish only the offending owner of the property, where land was the property being confiscated, the interest forfeited was only a life estate. The offending owner lost all control over the property during his life, but when he died, the property was passed to the offender's heirs, and the rights of the purchaser of the property in the judicial sale ceased.

On March 12, 1863, a third act was passed.[3] Commonly called the Captured and Abandoned Property Act, it applied to properties seized in the Confederacy by the military forces of the United States. The act applied to properties engaged in aiding the Confederate cause. It made no difference whether the owner was classified as an enemy or had remained loyal to the North. It also made no difference whether the owner was present or absent, because the property was sold without the necessity of a judicial proceeding. The United States became trustee of the funds generated by the sale. Provisions were incorporated into the act that allowed an owner who claimed that he or she had remained loyal to the United States to file a petition in the Court of Claims to obtain the funds from the sale. If the petitioner-owner could prove loyalty, the funds were paid to the petitioner. On the other hand, if the government could show that the owner of the property had aided the Confederacy, the funds were forfeited to the government.

As might be expected, there was a good deal of litigation under the above acts. Most of the facts leading to the litigation were routine. Cotton, for example, was captured by Federal forces. It was then turned over to an agent of the U.S. Treasury. The cotton was sold under auspices of the U.S. District Court. The Southern owner of the cotton could claim that he or she had remained loyal to the Federal government and file a petition in the Court of Claims for the money received from the sale. The court would decide the loyalty question and order the funds from the sale either paid to the owner-petitioner or forfeited to the United States. However, the facts in several of the cases were not routine, and several of the decisions unexpectedly had wide application beyond the interpretation of the above statutes. The Confederate States of America had similar statutes and, it can be assumed, had similar problems to those that arose in the cases considered below.

THE *ALEXANDER* CASE

One interesting case concerned Elizabeth Alexander, a sixty-five-year-old woman of uncommon ability who owned a plantation along the Red River in Louisiana in the parish of Avoyelles. She had operated the plantation since 1835, and it was one of the better run and higher producers of all the plantations along the river. The plantation was close to a Confederate military installation called Fort De Russy. When Fort De Russy was constructed, Mrs. Alexander had assisted in the construction by lending the builders slaves and mules.

In March 1864, Maj. Gen. Nathaniel P. Banks initiated a Union offensive from the New Orleans area up the Red River toward Shreveport. The objectives of the offensive were to clear western Louisiana of Confederates and invade Texas. Obtaining a foothold in Texas was thought to be important by the Lincoln administration because of the French presence in Mexico. In addition, Banks was intrigued by the possibility of capturing cotton, which he thought he could start on its way east to the New England textile mills.

The Union forces moving up the Red River were accompanied by sixty navy transports and gunboats, with full crews and support personnel under Rear

Adm. David Porter. In addition, Gen. Ulysses Grant had ordered Maj. Gen. Frederick Steele, who led an army of 13,000 men in Arkansas, to join with Banks in Shreveport. The combined forces—army, navy, and marines—numbered an estimated 45,000 men. The diversity of commands made coordination among the groups very difficult.

The Confederate forces opposing Banks were under the command of Lt. Gen. E. Kirby Smith. Because they were hopelessly outnumbered, Smith ordered Maj. Gen. Richard Taylor, the son of former president Zachary Taylor, to use his forces to harass the Union men and then withdraw safely in front of the advance. Aware that one of the objectives of the Union advance was to capture cotton, Taylor ordered his men to burn all the cotton they encountered as they retreated.

Under these conditions, the Union forces advanced to a point halfway between the mouth of the Red River and Alexandria. They entered Avoyelles Parish and captured Fort De Russy. Consolidating the land surrounding the fort, the Union men took possession of Mrs. Alexander's plantation. As the Confederate forces withdrew, Mrs. Alexander had no choice but to stand by as Taylor's men destroyed her cotton consisting of the production from the 1862 growing season. However, she did not inform the men who burned her cotton that she had an additional seventy-two bales stored in the plantation's gin house from the 1861 crop.

On March 26, 1864, the Union gunboat *Ouachita,* under the command of Adm. David Porter, landed at Mrs. Alexander's plantation. The crew of the *Ouachita* explored the plantation and discovered the seventy-two bales of cotton in the gin house. The crew took possession of the cotton, loaded the bales on river transports, and shipped them to Cairo, Illinois, for disposal in the U.S. District Court for the Southern District of Illinois in Springfield. The men of the *Ouachita* reasoned that they were naval personnel and had taken possession of the cotton while on duty as a crew of a U.S. gunboat. Therefore, they requested the U.S. attorneys to libel the cotton as a prize of war in that court. If the gunboat crew succeeded in getting the cotton so classified, they would share personally in the proceeds of the sale, probably to the extent of 50 percent.

As the Federal advance continued up the river, the citizens of the area who had remained loyal to the Union made an effort to organize the loyal state of Louisiana. Elections were held to select delegates to a constitutional convention that was to be held in New Orleans. Mrs. Alexander's plantation would have been part of this loyal state. In addition, she took an oath to uphold the U.S. Constitution as permitted by President Lincoln's December 8, 1863, Proclamation of Amnesty and Reconstruction. Individuals who took this oath were given a full pardon, and their property rights were restored to them except as regarding slaves.

Then the battle of Sabine Crossroads took place on April 8, 1864. This battle effectively halted the Federal advance and forced Banks and Porter to withdraw their forces back down to the mouth of the Red River. Heavy casualties were suffered by both the Federal and Confederate forces. Mrs. Alexander's plantation served as a sanctuary and almost a field hospital to the sick and wounded of both sides. These men had grown fond of the plantation for yet another reason: They enjoyed the company of many pretty young women who lived there with Mrs. Alexander. However, the plantation was soon taken over by forces of the Confederacy that had recaptured Fort De Russy. The Union occupation of Mrs. Alexander's plantation lasted less than eight weeks.

Prior to the reoccupation of the plantation by Confederate forces, Mrs. Alexander had retained attorneys to represent her at the prize hearing in Springfield, Illinois. The hearing took place after she had again become a citizen of the Confederacy because of the reoccupation. The District Court held that the seizure of the cotton was not a prize of war. The court ordered the cotton sold and the proceeds restored to Mrs. Alexander. The United States appealed this decision to the Circuit Court, which affirmed the District Court decision. The United States then appealed to the U.S. Supreme Court, requesting that the court reverse the District and Circuit Courts and hold that the capture of the cotton was a prize of war. The case came to the court under the title of *United States, Appt., v. Elizabeth Alexander, Claimant of Seventy-Two Bales of Cotton.*[4]

The Arguments before the Court
The arguments were made to the court on February 27, 1865. The attorney general, James Speed, represented the United States. J. Hubley Ashton was the attorney who handled the case for the attorney general. The crew of the *Ouachita* was represented by Charles Eames. Mrs. Alexander, still living in the Confederacy, was represented by Richard W. Corwine and W. M. Springer.

The attorneys for the government and crew of the *Ouachita* argued first. Before the District and Circuit Courts, they had insisted that the capture of the cotton was a prize of war. If the courts had agreed with that argument, the proceeds of the sale of the cotton would have gone entirely to the crew, or the crew would have divided the proceeds with the government, depending upon whether the Confederate forces were interpreted to be stronger or weaker than the forces under Banks. Under this interpretation, Mrs. Alexander would have lost the entire proceeds of the sale. Because the District and Circuit Courts disagreed with this argument, the attorneys for the government and crew constructed a very meticulous and carefully contrived argument in the hope of persuading the Supreme Court to overrule the lower courts. This argument consisted of six carefully reasoned points.

The first point argued by the attorneys was that if the country where the capture of the cotton took place was enemy country in the sense of the law of prize, then all commercial property of the inhabitants, without regard to their loyalty or disloyalty, was subject to capture and condemnation as enemy property and as a prize of war, the same as if the property had been captured on the high seas. This was especially true, they argued, in the case of staple commercial products of the soil from that region. The attorneys cited early English cases in support of this view, as well as the *Amy Warwick* case.

Their second point was that the Red River took on the aspects of the enemy country through which it flowed, and therefore it constituted enemy inland water. Thus the cotton, if captured afloat on the river by a duly commissioned naval force of the United States, would have been a lawful prize of war. The attorneys insisted that no text writer had ever intimated that a capture under these circumstances could not be a prize of war. Again, the attorneys cited many maritime cases that they claimed supported their stand.[5]

Their third point was that if the Red River was to be merely considered an internal navigable river of the United States, then it was clear and unquestionable that if the cotton were brought within the jurisdiction of the United States by the enemy, it would have been subject to capture as a lawful prize of war.

In points four and five, the attorneys asserted, again citing a multitude of cases, that the capture of the cotton on land did not change the fact that it was a lawful prize of war, because the cotton was captured during belligerent naval operation and was transported by naval vessels. Their final point reiterated that the controlling factor in their case was the fact that the cotton was captured while the area was enemy country. This had been determined, they claimed, by the legislative, executive, and judicial departments of public authorities, Rebel or legitimate.

The attorneys for the government and the crew concluded that the decrees of the District and Circuit Courts should be reversed, and they requested the Supreme Court to accomplish this.

Corwine and Springer then presented their argument on behalf of Mrs. Alexander. They opened by forcibly insisting that enemy property could not be captured as a prize of war when the property was situated upon land. The captured cotton had never been on waters navigated by the navy, nor had it ever been afloat; it was captured on Mrs. Alexander's plantation, nearly one mile from the river. They argued that there never had been a prize of war on inland waters of the United States where seagoing vessels never had gone, and further, the cases cited by the United States to support this approach clearly did not apply.

The gunboats, including the *Ouachita*, were not part of the navy in the Red River campaign, they argued, but had made up part of the army and had been controlled by the army. The gunboats comprised water batteries for the army, and as such, they trailed the advance of the army. When the gunboats landed at Mrs. Alexander's plantation, it was already in Federal hands. Mrs. Alexander, as a resident in an area so occupied, was a loyal citizen obeying the laws of the United States. Under these conditions, they argued, there could be no such thing as a capture of the cotton being classified as a prize of war. The crew of the *Ouachita* had acted illegally, they maintained, because it was not part of Banks's design and orders for them to capture cotton. Therefore, the capture was null and void.

The attorneys then cited Article I, Section 6, Paragraph 11 of the U.S. Constitution, which declared that Congress had the power "to declare war, grant letters of marque and reprisal, and make rules concerning captures on land and water." They argued that this capture therefore was governed entirely by Congress, and not only had Congress not authorized captures on land by naval forces, but on July 2, 1864, it had passed legislation declaring that no property captured on the inland waters of the United States by naval forces should be regarded as a maritime prize. Property thus captured was required by the new legislation to be promptly delivered to the proper officers of the courts.

Mrs. Alexander's attorneys then asserted that the good faith of the government was involved. She had taken the oath of allegiance pursuant to the invitation of President Lincoln's Proclamation of December 8, 1863. Though there existed a question of whether Mrs. Alexander fell within the class of persons for whose benefit the Proclamation of Amnesty was issued, her attorneys argued that from the moment she took the oath, she was entitled to her rights of property as promised by the proclamation.

The attorneys closed their argument by stating that "the courts have ever regarded such promises and have enforced them." They left this argument with the court: The U.S. government had committed itself to Mrs. Alexander, and others like her, through President Lincoln's proclamation, and the Federal government should uphold its words and promises. They then requested the court to uphold the decisions of the District and Circuit Courts, which had awarded the proceeds of the sale of the cotton to Mrs. Alexander.

The Opinion of the Court

The opinion of the court was given on March 10, 1865, by Chief Justice Salmon P. Chase. The chief justice first reviewed the interesting facts. He then stated that these facts posed the prime question as to whether the capture of Mrs. Alexander's cotton was a lawful maritime prize subject to the prize jurisdiction of the courts of the United States.

To be a maritime prize, he explained, the first requirement was that it be enemy property as set forth in the *Prize Cases*. The chief justice then held that there was no doubt that it was enemy property, noting that the Federal occupation of Mrs. Alexander's plantation was too short to change her status. He set aside her attorneys' arguments that she was loyal to the Union even though she remained in the Confederacy by stating that he felt compelled to follow the principle "so often announced from this Bench" that all people living in an area in insurrection were enemies until some governmental action was taken to change their status. The elections held in a loyal constitutional convention were not such an action. Nor did the amnesty have any effect, because Mrs. Alexander had resumed residency in the Confederacy.

Chase then held that, being enemy property, the cotton was liable to capture and confiscation by the Union forces, again citing the *Prize Cases* as support for the holding. He acknowledged that this seizure on land had very important qualifications, however, based upon previous cases and enlightened legal commentators. He went on to cite the *Commentaries on American Law*, by James Kent, that such a seizure as that of Mrs. Alexander's cotton was limited to special cases dictated by the necessary operations of war, which generally excluded the seizure of private property of noncombatant enemies solely for personal gain. It was not unusual for the court to cite James Kent. Born in the state of New York in 1763, Kent became a well-respected jurist there and was the first professor of law at Columbia University, assuming that post in 1793. His decisions and other writings helped shape the common law in the formative years of the United States. He was also highly respected and very influential in England.

The chief justice, relying on Kent, indicated several factors that would place this seizure as a special case. He indicated that the seizure of Mrs. Alexander's cotton was justified by the character of the property, that being that cotton was the backbone of the Confederate war effort. He made reference to the Confederacy's reliance on cotton to purchase munitions in Europe and discussed the efforts that the Confederate forces made to prevent cotton from falling into the hands of the Union forces.

The capture was also justified by legislation, he said, referring to the act of Congress approved on August 6, 1861, which declared that all property used in aid of the Rebellion with the consent of the owners was subject to prize and capture wherever found. He also cited the Act to Suppress the Rebellion, approved on July 17, 1862, which provided that the property of persons who had aided the Rebellion and who had not reassumed allegiance to the Union should be seized and confiscated. The chief justice held that Mrs. Alexander's aid in the building of Fort De Russy placed her within the spirit and letter of both acts. He then made reference to the Captured and Abandoned Property Act of March 8, 1863, stating that this act provided that there could be naval captures separate from maritime prizes.

Chase then tied all these loose ends together and held that the capture of Mrs. Alexander's cotton was lawful; however, the conclusion that the property captured was a maritime prize did not follow. He stated that the English cases cited by the government to support a prize classification did not support such a classification under these facts. The chief justice then cited the basic law relied upon by the government to establish whether a capture was a maritime prize, the Act for the Better Government of the Navy, pointing out that this act excluded property on land from the category of prize for the benefit of the captors. He held that this act was decisive of the case as far as the claims of the captors were concerned.

With the captors removed as claimants, Chase indicated that the disposition of the property was controlled by the laws discussed. Under the provisions of those laws, and the orders under them, all military personnel were commanded to turn over such property to the Treasury Department, whose agents were required to sell the property for as much money as possible and turn the proceeds over to the national Treasury. Any claimant could then bring suit within two years after the close of the Rebellion and assert claims against the property or its proceeds. The chief justice called this "liberal and beneficent legislation," for it made a distinction between enemies classified under international law and those who remained loyal. The latter could regain their property, or the proceeds from its sale, by proving their loyalty, even if they remained in areas controlled by the Confederacy.

Chase then referred to the law cited by Mrs. Alexander's attorneys that had been passed a few weeks after the capture of the cotton. This law completely abolished the possibility of obtaining a maritime prize on all inland waters. The chief justice acknowledged that this law did not apply to Mrs. Alexander, but it was cited as an illustration of the general policy of legislation.

Chief Justice Chase then decreed that the seizure of the cotton was not a maritime prize, thus defeating the cases of the government and the crew and agreeing with the District and Circuit Courts. But the chief justice went further, holding that the cotton should have been turned over to the Treasury Department to be disposed of under the Captured and Abandoned Property Act of March 8, 1863. He ordered that the proceeds from the sale of the cotton, which had not been turned over, but had been derived from the sale ordered by the District Court, should then be paid into the U.S. Treasury. Chase further ordered that the proceeds be held there for Mrs. Alexander to claim in the Court of Claims when the Rebellion was suppressed or she was able to otherwise leave the area of the Rebellion.

Chief Justice Chase then ordered that the decree of the District Court, as affirmed by the Circuit Court, was reversed, and the cause was remanded to the District Court with directions that the libel should be dismissed.

Technically, Mrs. Alexander lost her case. The District Court had ordered that the proceeds of the sale should have been paid directly to her under one or both of the confiscation acts. However, as a practical matter, this was physically impossible, because Mrs. Alexander was living in the Confederacy. The fact that the court ordered the United States to hold the proceeds from the sale of the cotton in trust for Mrs. Alexander so she could claim them in the future was an improvement in her position, though she would have to file a petition in the Court of Claims and prove her right to the proceeds. Overall, Mrs. Alexander did very well. She appeared before the highest court in the land even though technically she had no standing because she was living in the Confederacy and was classified as an enemy. She preserved her rights and helped establish the doctrine that a maritime prize in the United States could not be obtained on land.

THE *ANDERSON* CASE

The results of a second case reached far beyond the simple determination of the claim itself. The date of the beginning of the war can be fixed to President Lincoln's Proclamation of April 15, 1861, wherein he called the militia to active duty to suppress the "combinations" that were resisting the government. But what was the date of the end of the war, and why was it important beyond a mere date in the history books? These issues were brought to the forefront in a case that was filed under the Captured and Abandoned Property Act of 1863 by another unusual claimant.

That claimant was Nelson Anderson, one of the 1,455 free black men who resided in Charleston, South Carolina, in 1860, according to the census of that year. In the early part of the war, Anderson, a drayman and a cotton sampler, purchased cotton from Daniel F. Fleming, who also resided in Charleston. Later, in the fall of 1864, Anderson purchased another lot of cotton in the same city from Philip M. Doucen.

Following the February 1865 evacuation of Charleston by the forces of the Confederacy, Anderson informed the Federal military authorities about the presence of his cotton. On April 5, 1865, members of the Northern Forces took control of the cotton and turned it over to agents of the Treasury Department. These agents shipped the cotton to New York, where it was sold. After deducting the expenses involved in the transportation and sale of the cotton, the net proceeds from the sale were $6,723.36. This amount was paid into the U.S. Treasury.

Up to this point, the applicable provisions of the law had been carefully followed. Then Anderson took advantage of that part of the law that permitted him to recover the net proceeds of the sale if he could prove that he had remained loyal to the Federal government and that he owned the cotton. These claims were filed with the U.S. Court of Claims, and it was a mandatory provision that claims had to be filed within two years following the end of the conflict. Anderson filed his claim for $6,723.36 on June 5, 1868.

In the Court of Claims, Anderson introduced evidence that he had purchased the cotton in good faith in the usual course of trade long before Charleston had fallen to the Federal forces. He also was able to prove that he had remained loyal to the United States, and that he had not rendered any aid or comfort to the Rebellion or to anyone engaged in seditious activities.

The government argued that Anderson had failed to file his claim within the required two years following the suppression of the Rebellion. It also maintained that Fleming and Doucen were citizens of the Confederacy, therefore enemies, and as such, they could not convey good title of the cotton to Anderson. The government attorneys added that Fleming and Doucen, as citizens of the Confederacy, were incompetent to testify, and their depositions should not have been admitted.

The Court of Claims decided in Anderson's favor and decreed that he should be paid the proceeds from the sale of the cotton. The U.S. attorney general at the time, Ebenezer Rockwood Hoar, was greatly concerned over how the issues were decided by the Court of Claims and how the decision would be applied to hundreds of future cases. Hoar believed that the issues, especially defining the two-year period that limited the time for filing the claims, should be determined by a court with more authority. Therefore, the government appealed the case to the U.S. Supreme Court.[6]

The Arguments before the Court
The United States was represented by Hoar and special counsel Robert S. Hale. T. J. D. Fuller and A. G. Riddle represented Anderson. They were joined by three attorneys who were counsel to the claimants of three other cases

identical with issues that awaited the decision in the *Anderson* case.[7] These attorneys were George Taylor, J. A. Wills, and W. Penn Clarke. Because of these waiting cases, Anderson had the benefit of the work of five attorneys. The claimants in the three cases with identical issues were William Pollard, also a free black, Morris Kohn, and Huldah L. Stanton.

The case was argued before the court on February 10, 1870. Counsel for the government argued first. They insisted that Anderson had not filed his claim within the two-year period required by the act under any of the available tests. The end of the war was not a matter of proclamation or other legislative or executive act, they argued; rather, it was a matter of actual fact as stated in the Prize Cases. There Justice Robert C. Grier had stated that when the courts could not be kept open because of armed conflict in the area, a state of war existed. The government attorneys argued that the test for the termination of the war was the same—that when the courts were no longer deterred from operating because of armed conflict, the Rebellion was suppressed.

Next, the counsel for the government pointed out to the court that Generals Robert E. Lee and Joseph E. Johnston had surrendered in April 1865, Gen. Richard Taylor on May 4, 1865, and Gen. Kirby Smith on May 26, 1865. If the date of the war's termination set by the Court of Claims, August 20, 1866, was to prevail, they argued, the Rebel states remained a hostile and belligerent power until that date. That meant that all the commerce and other intercourse between the states of the North and the former Rebel states that had taken place between the surrender of the armies and August 20, 1866, was utterly void.

The attorneys continued their argument by illustrating to the court that the executive and administrative departments of the government had recognized the restoration of peace by reopening the post offices and letting out contracts for mail service and extending the revenue system throughout the former rebellious states prior to August 20, 1866.

The various proclamations of the president did not create a condition of peace, they reasoned, but only acknowledged that peace had been restored. If, however, proclamations were to be regarded as a requisite to establish a suppression of the Rebellion, they insisted that the Proclamation of June 13, 1865, which removed all restrictions on trade with the insurrectionary states east of the Mississippi, was the proper date for the termination of hostilities in South Carolina. The freedom connected with open trade was the recognition of peace, they argued.

The government counsel then closed their argument by contesting three additional points. They challenged Anderson's title to the cotton because he had purchased it from people who had openly rendered aid and comfort to the Rebellion; they challenged the admission of the depositions of the vendors of the cotton because, they claimed, they were incompetent witnesses; and they argued that the Court of Claims did not have the power to render a judgment for a specific sum. The government's attorneys closed their presentation by requesting that the court overrule the Court of Claims.

The counsel for Anderson and the connected three cases then assumed the podium. Their first assertion was that it was not within the jurisdiction of the court, but rather the legislative branch of the government, to determine the date that the Rebellion was suppressed and when the two-year statute of limitations began to run. They cited three proclamations of the president. The first, dated June 15, 1865, declared that the insurrection, not the Rebellion, was at an end in Tennessee. The second, dated April 2, 1866, declared the insurrection, not the Rebellion, at an end in several enumerated states, but not the state of Texas. The third and final proclamation, dated August 20, 1866, declared that the insurrection had terminated in the state of Texas. That statement in the proclamation was then supplemented, pointed out the counsel, with an additional clause stating that "peace, order, tranquillity and civil authority" then had been established throughout the whole of the United States.

The attorneys representing Anderson argued that this date, August 20, 1866, had been recognized in subsequent congressional legislation as the official close of the Rebellion. This legislation, which had become law on March 2, 1867, continued the wartime pay of noncommissioned officers and privates for three years from and after the close of the Rebellion. The date set as the close of the Rebellion was that announced in the proclamation that fixed the date at August 20, 1866.

Anderson's attorneys then dismissed the arguments of the government that Anderson's title was flawed, and that the sellers of the cotton could not testify in the Court of Claims. They asserted that these arguments did not apply to Anderson, because he had purchased the cotton long before the surrender of Charleston in good faith with no intent to aid the Rebellion in the usual course of trade. The attorneys arguing on Anderson's behalf closed their presentation by requesting that the court uphold the decision of the Court of Claims.

The Opinion of the Court

Justice David Davis rendered the opinion of the court on February 28, 1870, eighteen days after the hearing. Davis first reviewed the facts of the case. In this review, he mentioned that Anderson was a "free man of color," the only reference to this fact made throughout the arguments and court opinion. The justice followed the facts with a brief résumé of the argument made by the government as to why the Court of Claims should be overruled.

Davis then reviewed the background of the Captured and Abandoned Property Act of 1863. As the war progressed, it was expected that forces of the North would capture properties. As the enemy retreated, that property would be without apparent ownership. Provisions were made under the act, explained the justice, for the Northern government to sell the property and pay the net proceeds from the sale into the Treasury. A unique part of the act was that though all citizens in the Confederacy were generally regarded as enemies, the act did not treat them all as enemies. The act recognized the faithful Southern people by providing that the government was a trustee of the funds generated from the sale of their property. Provisions were then made that those who remained loyal to the North could claim the funds by merely proving their ownership of the property and their loyalty. However, the justice explained, these claims must have been filed within two years following the suppression of the Rebellion.

This measure of "great beneficence," observed the justice, was passed by Congress because of its sympathy for the situation of the loyal Southern people. In enforcing this law, he said, the court had to keep in mind the purpose and objectives of Congress that were evidenced by its passage.

Applying this law to Anderson, the justice said that Anderson's loyalty was not questioned, but his ownership of the property was denied. Davis took note of the argument of the government that Anderson had purchased the cotton from persons who were citizens of South Carolina and were therefore classified as enemies. The government argued that enemies were prohibited from conveying title to anything. This argument was not sound, said Davis, in that it imported a provision of the confiscation laws of July 17, 1862, into this law, which was a disability that this law did not contain. If this interpretation of the law were allowed to stand, no loyal person in the South would be able to take advantage of the claim provisions in the captured property law, and Congress had no intent to pass a law that was this restrictive, observed the justice. The law was meant to be broad and comprehensive, and it did not discriminate in favor of the person who could trace his title through a loyal source and against the individual who was not so fortunate.

Davis then distinguished the confiscation act by stating that it provided for the seizure of property owned by Rebels as punishment for their crimes, whereas the Captured and Abandoned Property Act was not criminal in nature and provided that a citizen who remained loyal to the Union in the South could achieve the return of his funds. The justice summed up this part of the court's opinion by stating that the two acts could not be construed together: "One is penal, the other remedial; the one claims a right, the other concedes a privilege." Davis thus held that the government's argument that Anderson had purchased his cotton from enemies of the North, and thus his title failed, was fallacious and did not apply in this case.

Similarly, Davis held that the law prohibiting a claimant, any person who conveyed his claim to a claimant, or any person who had an interest in the result of the suit from testifying in the suit did not exclude Doucen and Fleming from testifying in Anderson's case. With these points taken care of, the justice then got to the major issue in the case: whether Anderson's suit was filed within two years from the suppression of the Rebellion.

There was no doubt that a person could file his claim immediately after the funds from the sale of his claimed property were deposited with the U.S. Treasury, said Davis. Congress realized that Union men in the South, as a general thing, would be unable to prosecute their claims while the war continued; but nonetheless, it was recognized that some persons would be able to do so, so the right to sue was conferred at once. To impute to Congress a design to compel these impoverished people to await the conclusion of the war to file their claims would be inconsistent with the general spirit of the statute and could not be entertained.

Then Davis posed the question that if the right to file a claim accrued as soon as the money reached the Treasury, when did the right to file a claim expire? It was basic, he said, that the two-year period meant to start at the suppression of the Rebellion was to begin to run after the suppression of the entire Rebellion. He referred to the fact that as a practical matter, the fighting had ended at different times in different localities; however, the citizen of a state where hostilities had ceased should not be in a better or worse position in this regard than a citizen of a state where hostilities still prevailed. The inherent difficulty posed by this problem, the justice continued, made it apparent that Congress did not intend that all of the people in the South affected by this act should take notice of the time that the last Confederate general surrendered and start counting the two-year period from that date.

Davis then stated that it was apparent that Congress intended that those whose private rights were affected by the war's ending should be able to rely on some legislative act or proclamation. There were a number of acts of Congress and proclamations of the president bearing on the subject, but in agreement with Anderson's attorneys, Davis stated that it was only necessary to notice the proclamation of the president of August 20, 1866, and the act of Congress of March 2, 1867. President Johnson's earlier proclamation of April 2, 1866, had stated that armed resistance had ceased everywhere except in the state of Texas. The presidential proclamation that followed this on August 20, 1866, stated that the insurrection had ceased in Texas and followed with the statement that "the said insurrection is at an end, and the peace, order, tranquillity and civil authority now exist in and throughout the whole of the United States." Congress had accepted this proclamation as fixing the end of the war by referring to it when it passed the military pay bill on March 7, 1867. The text of that bill fixed the end of the Rebellion as August 20, 1866, as decreed by the proclamation. If August 20, 1866, was set as the end of the war for noncommissioned officers and privates in the military, asked Davis, "can it be supposed that it intended to lay down a harsher rule for guidance of the claimants under the Captured and Abandoned Property Act?" The justice answered his own question by saying that to answer the question affirmatively would require the court to construe two acts relating to the same general subject differently, and this the court was not prone to do.

Justice Davis then concluded his opinion by declaring that August 20, 1866, was the legal date that the Rebellion ended, and there was no reason why this date should not be accepted as settling the question wherever private rights were affected by it. He stated further that this would be the date from which the two-year period for filing claims under the Captured and Abandoned Property Act would begin to run. Nelson Anderson, having filed his claim on June 5, 1868, had filed within the period, and he was therefore entitled to receive the net proceeds from the sale of his cotton of $6,723.36. Thus the decision of the Court of Claims was affirmed. The Court of Claims judgments in the three similar cases awaiting this decision were also affirmed by the court.

The facts in the *Anderson* case were typical of the cotton cases under the Captured and Abandoned Property Act. Over the years, the total amount paid out under the act was $9,864,300.75.[8] Considering that the awards were not large, the award to Nelson Anderson probably being average, and also considering that only one in three claims was successful, it is easy to see that the Court of Claims handled hundreds of claims under the act.

Twelve years prior to the filing of this case by Nelson Anderson, the Supreme Court had determined in the *Dred Scott Case*[9] that a black was not a citizen and therefore had no standing in the courts of the United States. Even though the *Anderson* case had been filed in the Court of Claims prior to the Fourteenth Amendment becoming effective, the Court of Claims handled the case routinely, and the Supreme Court accepted Anderson as a litigant without question, hardly even mentioning that he was black.

The court's determination that the legal date of the termination of the Civil War was August 20, 1866, was in itself a major decision that affected hundreds of citizens who filed cases under the Captured and Abandoned Property Act and other acts where private rights could be asserted and a similar statute of limitations existed.

Many other serious issues pertaining to the status and rights of those whose properties were being confiscated were confronted by the court. For example, what if the owner of the property being confiscated—unlike Mrs. Alexander, who for a short time lived as a loyal citizen—was a permanent resident in the Confederacy but nevertheless desired to enter the case and actively oppose the confiscation of his property? Or what if it could not be shown that the owner of the property being confiscated, living in the Confederacy, had received notice of the confiscation proceeding? Another corollary issue concerned the property itself: Could property that was not capable of seizure, such as intangible property, be confiscated at all?

Two cases addressed the above issues. One dealt with the issue of whether a Confederate citizen could become a party in a case filed in the North and defend his property. The case will be presented here only in summary, as the issue was presented in a very straightforward manner, and the case was very short and direct. The other two issues were treated by a case in which more involved issues came to the fore and intertwined themselves into the decision.

THE *McVEIGH* CASE

The first case involved a man by the name of William N. McVeigh, who was a resident of Richmond. Living within the Confederate lines, he was classified as a Rebel. McVeigh owned certain real estate and other personal properties in that part of the state of Virginia controlled by the Union. Sometime after the passage of the confiscation act of July 17, 1862, government attorneys in the area, acting on behalf of the United States, filed a libel against the properties owned by McVeigh in the District Court of the United States for that area, asking the court to forfeit the properties and sell them. This was done under the provisions of that act, which called for the forfeiture and condemnation of properties of those engaging in armed rebellion, or of those who aided and abetted such rebellion, against the United States and had not returned to allegiance with the United States after notice.

McVeigh could not be served a notice of the forfeiture while in Richmond, so the government brought him within the jurisdiction of the court by a notice by publication. Somehow McVeigh became aware of this notice, and he retained an attorney to represent him in the District Court. This attorney interposed a claim to the property and filed an answer. The U.S. attorney then submitted a motion asking that the court strike McVeigh's claim and answer. This motion stated that McVeigh was a resident of Richmond, Virginia, in the Confederacy, and that as a Rebel, he was ineligible to appear as a party in a Federal court. The District Court granted this motion. A default judgment was then entered against McVeigh, and the property was condemned and ordered sold. McVeigh had no success in an appeal to the Circuit Court, and he then appealed to the U.S. Supreme Court. The case appeared before the court as *William N. McVeigh, Plff. in Err., v. United States.*[10]

The Appeal to the Supreme Court

The case was first argued on January 31 and February 1, 1870. It was reargued one year later, on February 8 and 9, 1871. After the attorneys appeared for both parties, the decision was rendered on March 6, 1871, on behalf of a unanimous court by Justice Noah Swayne.

In just five paragraphs, Justice Swayne made it plain that the court was extremely upset with the U.S. attorneys and the District and Circuit Courts. Reciting that McVeigh's guilt under the statutes—that is, determining whether he had participated in or aided and abetted the Rebellion—was fundamental to the case, he said that McVeigh should have been afforded the opportunity to have a hearing on that subject. The justice stated: "If assailed there, he could defend there. The liability and the right are inseparable." A different result would be a "blot upon our jurisprudence and civilization." To uphold the District and Circuit Courts, the justice continued, would be contrary to the first principles of the social compact, as expressed by the early English and French political philosophers, and of the right administration of justice. Swayne followed by acknowledging that an alien may have a disability to sue in the courts of a hostile country; however, if liable to be sued in those courts, he had a clear right to use all the means available to defend himself in those courts.

Justice Swayne then held that the District Court was reversed, and the cause was remanded to the Circuit Court with directions to proceed in conformity with the law.

Thus it was made abundantly clear by the court that an individual who could be sued in a court in the United States clearly had the right to defend himself in that court, even though, as in the case of McVeigh, he was a resident in the Confederacy and was legally classified as a Rebel and an enemy.

THE *MILLER* CASE

The second case was more involved. It concerned the statutory and constitutional issues raised when there was a claimed seizure of intangible property of a resident of the South, and in addition, it could not be shown that the owner of the property had received actual notice of the confiscation proceeding.

In 1863, Samuel Miller lived in Amherst County, Virginia, and was a Rebel citizen. Miller owned shares in two corporations that were incorporated in Michigan, the Michigan Southern & Northern Indiana Railroad and the Detroit, Monroe & Toledo Railroad. Under terms of the August 6, 1861, and July 17, 1862, confiscation acts, the attorneys acting on behalf of the United States in Michigan caused the seizure of Miller's stock in the two railroad corporations, with the objective of confiscating them and selling them in a public sale.

The stock was seized by the Federal marshal by serving notice upon the vice president of the Michigan Southern & Northern Indiana Railroad and the president of the Detroit, Monroe & Toledo Railroad. A libel designed to confiscate the stock was filed in the United States District Court for the Eastern District of Michigan. At about the same time, an information was filed alleging that Miller was a public enemy and a Rebel citizen residing in the state of Virginia; that he was the owner of the stock named separately in the libel; that he employed and used this stock in the aid of the enemy; and that by owning this stock situated in a loyal state, he had assisted and given aid to the Rebellion against the government.

A libel is in the nature of a complaint in a civil action. An information is the same as an indictment, except that it is issued by a governmental official, here the attorneys representing the government, rather than by a grand jury. The marshal then gave notice by publication to all persons who might have claimed an interest in the stock or claimed that the stock should not be confiscated. The publication notified these individuals that they could appear before the court at a designated hearing date and make their claims known. Miller did not appear at the designated time, and the court entered a default judgment against him and the stock. The court ordered the stock confiscated and sold.

Miller later discovered that this proceeding had taken place. Through his attorneys, he filed a petition with the District Court to reopen the judgment that had condemned and ordered the sale of the stock, and he requested the court to set aside the judgment. The court refused Miller's petition, and he appealed to the Circuit Court of the United States for the Eastern District of Michigan. This court affirmed the District Court. Miller then, in a manner not disclosed by the court, met his death. The executor of his estate assumed the responsibility of preserving the properties owned by Miller. Fulfilling this responsibility, the executor appealed the case to the U.S. Supreme Court. The case came to the docket of the court under the title of *Nathaniel M. Page, Exr. of Samuel Miller, Deceased, Plff. in Err., v. United States.*[11]

The Arguments before the Court

The case was originally argued on February 1 and 2, 1870, and reargued on February 10, 1871. Note that in the *McVeigh* case, the original argument was January 31 and February 1, 1870, and the reargument was February 8 and 9, 1871. Justice Robert C. Grier resigned from the court on January 31, 1870, just as the original arguments in both cases began. This left the court with only seven justices, at least two of whom, Justice Samuel Nelson and Chief Salmon P. Justice Chase, had illnesses that interfered with their full performance on the court. This undoubtedly accounted for the one-year lapse between the original arguments and the rearguments of the cases. When Justices William Strong and Joseph P. Bradley joined the court in March 1871, the court resumed a full complement of nine justices, and the backlog of cases began to diminish.

Handling the appeal for Samuel Miller's estate were B. R. Curtis, William P. Wells, and Samuel T. Douglas. The government was represented by the attorney general, Ebenezer Rockwood Hoar, in the first hearing. Hoar was replaced as attorney general on June 23, 1870, by Amos T. Akerman, who represented the government at the second hearing. B. H. Bristow assisted Akerman. George F. Edmunds made an appearance at the appeal hearing representing the purchasers of Miller's stock at the public sale.

The attorneys for the Miller estate argued first. They reminded the court that this case concerned the seizure, condemnation, and sale of shares of stock in two corporations. Ownership in corporations, Miller's attorneys argued, was an intangible interest. The actual physical certificates of the stock were not the ownership itself, but only evidence of the ownership. Here, the District Court did not even have the certificates in its possession. The supposed seizure of the shares by serving the president and vice president of the corporations with notice of the seizure was obviously faulty, and the court did not acquire jurisdiction over the stock by these means.

The proceedings under terms of the confiscation laws, they maintained, had to conform to proceedings in admiralty and revenue cases as closely as possible. In admiralty and revenue cases, a seizure of property had to be actually or constructively in possession of the court; the property must have been "arrested," according to the popular terminology of the courts. This was usually done by an actual levy upon the property, and thereafter the court's possession must be actual, open, and visible. This could not take place in this case, they insisted, because there could be no actual seizure of corporate stock.

The attorneys then attacked the judgment itself. They argued that there was no valid judgment, because a default proceeding still required a hearing and sufficient proof to support a valid decree, and such a hearing and development of proof never took place. The only justification for the judgment against Miller, they maintained, could be found in the law of nations. That law might not be restricted by the numerous rights given a defendant by the Constitution. But, Miller's attorneys added, though Congress was able to pass laws controlling the capture of property under the law of nations, once they passed penal or criminal statutes, as was done in the confiscation laws, these laws became part of the body of law of the sovereign government of the United States, and the rights to individuals guaranteed by the Constitution applied to them.

The counsel for Miller then read the title of the July 17, 1862, act: An Act to Suppress Insurrection, to Punish Treason and Rebellion, to Seize and Confiscate the Property of Rebels, and for Other Purposes. This act, they argued, applied to all the people of the United States, not just to Rebels. If it did apply only to Rebels, the law of nations could possibly apply. Since, however, it applied to all the people, the rights guaranteed by the Constitution followed, they argued. Since the rights guaranteed to Miller in the Fifth and Sixth Amendments of the Constitution—that is, that the case should have been initiated by an indictment of a grand jury, that a speedy and public jury trial should have been afforded, and that there should have been no taking of his property without due process of the law—were not granted him under provisions of the confiscation laws, those laws were unconstitutional, insisted Miller's attorneys. Therefore, the taking of the stock was totally void, and the decrees of the lower courts should be vacated. Miller's counsel asked the court to reverse the lower courts.

The attorneys for the government and the representative for those who had purchased the shares at the public sale then gave their presentations to the court as to why the decrees of the District and Circuit Courts were constitutional.

Before rebutting the arguments presented by Miller's counsel, the government attorneys first asserted that Miller did not have a legal standing before the court. They argued that the action was against the property, not against an individual. Miller need not have been named in the proceeding, the attorneys insisted. Miller, not having been a claimant in the District and Circuit Courts, had no right to be treated as a claimant in the Supreme Court. The attorneys indicated that this was a doctrine of long standing in Anglo-American law; the only exception was under the English Act of 1797, but that had no application to this case.

The attorneys for the government then brought to the court's attention that Miller could not claim to his benefit that he had not received notice of the hearing, because the law imputed notice to all concerned persons in these cases. They then asserted that if the proceedings that took place were not void, the judgment was conclusive; if the proceedings, on the other hand, were void, the remedy that was available to Miller was not an appeal, but a separate suit to regain his property.

Responding to the assertions that the seizure of the shares was improper, the attorneys pointed out that the allegations contained in the information were complete. The stocks, though incorporeal, were proper subjects of confiscation, they insisted. Not only that, but the property could be transferred only in the state of Michigan, and therefore the property was located within the district where it was seized and proceeded against. The attorneys then cited an old common-law doctrine from debtors' law that held that the situs, that is, the location of the property, became the residence of the debtor, in this case Miller.

The attorneys capped the argument pertaining to seizure by insisting to the court that the power of the legislature and the war-making departments of government to confiscate property of enemies on land could not be questioned. The laws under the July 17, 1862, act carried out this right and duty by authorizing the executive department to seize for the use of the entire nation all properties of public enemies. The appropriateness of the seizure of Miller's stock, they insisted, could be judged only within this power.

As to Miller's challenge to the rightness of the entry of default judgment against him, the government attorneys argued that upon filing the information, the court took control of the property, notice was given to all, and when Miller failed to appear, a default against him was entered and the sale took place. These proceedings were all proper under the law, whether considered under domestic law or under the law of nations. Constructive notice to Miller was just as effectual as actual notice, they argued. Miller's only redress if he claimed hardship was an appeal to open the default, not a general writ of error. The court could not consider the latter, they insisted, because there was no record to form the basis of such an appeal. The attorneys concluded this phase of the argument by revealing their actual personal feelings toward Miller when they argued that based upon settled principles, no trial by jury was required where all of the claimants were in default and were in "contumacy," or were stubbornly resisting authority.

The counsel for the government then stated that if the justices were bothered by the seizure of Miller's property under the confiscation laws as domestic laws tied to constitutional rights, the court should consider the seizure in all respects as a belligerent act under the war powers where the constitutional rights did not apply. The intention of Congress, they pointed out, was to suppress insurrection and carry the war to a successful termination. Congress intended to do this through the confiscation laws by first punishing treason and second seizing the property of Rebels.

It was not necessary, the attorneys argued, for Miller to be found guilty of a crime in order to forfeit his property. The property could be treated in its own right and proceeded against, separate from Miller, as enemy property. Counsel then described to the court that this was true in a civil war as well as an international conflict. They pleaded with the court not to interpret the legislative acts in such a way that the legislature would be guilty of an absurdity. If the main portion of the act providing for the condemnation of property was meant as a penalty for treason, the attorneys pointed out, these provisions would have been placed as a penalty in that section of the law. They would not have been placed elsewhere in the law, where they appeared.

Aside from this, they argued, it was a long-standing doctrine that all property of an enemy found within a country during a state of war could be seized. This was a proposition so well established that no argument was necessary to prove it. This right existed in a civil war as well as in a public war, they said, citing Sir Alexander Cockburn, the lord chief justice of England in a case arising from the domestic tumult in Jamaica in 1865.[12] How far this policy could proceed was a question for the political department of the government to determine, and it was certainly competent for Congress to treat the property of domestic enemies the same as properties of foreign enemies.

The attorneys for the government closed their argument by opening another door but refusing to elaborate what was on the other side. They simply said that one of the enumerated powers of Congress in the Constitution was to support the army. Congress was able to make all laws necessary to carry out this power, they argued, and the confiscation laws were one of the means used. They then requested the court to affirm the judgments of the District and Circuit Courts.

The Opinion of the Court
The opinion of the court was given by Justice William Strong on April 3, 1871. Strong joined the court on March 14, 1870, one month after the original argument was presented by the parties and about a year prior to the reargument and decision.

Justice Strong recited the facts of the case, and then stressed that under a provision of the July 17, 1862, act and the president's proclamation following the act, Miller had failed to respond to the provisions of the proclamation that if he ceased aiding and abetting the Rebellion within sixty days and returned his allegiance to the United States, his property would not be seized. The justice indicated that Miller's continued activity in aiding the Rebellion removed him from the safe harbor provided by the proclamation.

Strong then considered whether the seizure of Miller's shares in the railroads was valid, because if the seizure itself was inappropriate, this was a fatal error in the government's case. The justice began this part of his opinion by stating that it could not be presumed, from the record, that an illegal seizure had been made. Though Congress desired that the seizure provisions in the confiscation laws conformed to those in admiralty and revenue cases, it did not require that the proceedings conform precisely to those cases, but only "as near as may be." In most admiralty and revenue cases, the property was capable of actual seizure. However, the mode of seizure had to vary according to the type of property; lands could not be seized as could movable chattels, and actual possession could not be taken of stocks. But, said the justice, it did not follow that stocks were incapable of being seized within the meaning of the confiscation laws.

A seizure could be actual or constructive, he said; it did not always involve the taking of the object into manual possession. An assertion of control, the justice indicated, was often sufficient. For example, in admiralty cases, certain seizures were by notice. It followed that where property was incapable of seizure, the property could be attached by notice as in admiralty, just as though it were in the hands of a third party. It was in this mode, said Strong, that the marshal seized Miller's stock. The record showed that through the marshal's warrant, there was sufficient seizure of Miller's stock, and Miller could not contradict the marshal's warrant. The stock being held by the marshal, the seizure was complete and jurisdiction of the court attached. To hold otherwise would be to sacrifice spirit to the letter of form, "the substance to the shadow," said the justice.

Holding that the seizure of the stock was sufficient to give the court jurisdiction, Strong then moved on to consider whether the proof presented at the District Court was sufficient to support the decree of condemnation even though Miller was not afforded a formal hearing. He indicated that the record of the case itself would answer this question. The justice stated that the information revealed that the stocks were owned by Miller; that he was engaged in the Rebellion; that the seizure was made and a default was duly entered because no one appeared to show cause why the stock should not be condemned. The information also revealed the marshal's warrant and the publication of notice. This, held the justice, when considered with the deposition submitted by the United States, was sufficient to support the entry of the decree of condemnation, because the effect of the default against Miller was a virtual confession that the allegations contained in the information were true.

Furthermore, Strong held, it was not necessary that the record show affirmatively that there was no irregularity in the proceeding. The justice stated that the burden of showing error was upon the person who alleged it and, citing Justice John Catron in *Erwin v. Lowry*,[13] the District and Circuit Courts were entitled to the presumption that, having jurisdiction, they did everything necessary to warrant the judgment.

Strong summarized his holding by stating that in revenue and admiralty cases, an entry of default established the facts in the information as effectively as they could have been established at a hearing, and the decree of condemnation was therefore warranted.

The justice then tackled what had become the major issue in the case: Miller's attorneys' challenge to the constitutionality of the 1861 and 1862 confiscation laws. Strong stated that the constitutionality had been challenged because it was maintained by Miller's counsel that the purposes of these laws were to punish offenses against the sovereignty of the United States; that they were, in effect, statutes against crimes. If this were the case, the justice admitted, the 1861 act and the vital part of the 1862 act would, indeed, have been contrary to certain provisions of the Constitution. Those provisions were the Fifth and Sixth Amendments, which provided that no person should be held to answer for a capital or infamous crime unless it was based upon an indictment of a grand jury; that no person should be deprived of his property without due process of law; and that in all criminal prosecutions, the accused should enjoy the right to a speedy and public trial before an impartial jury.

However, the justice emphasized, if the confiscation laws were passed as an exercise of the war powers of Congress, those constitutional rights did not attach. Therefore, he said, the issue to be determined was whether the action of Congress in passing these laws was a legitimate exercise of its war powers.

The justice began his analysis of this issue by stating that the Constitution conferred upon Congress the power to declare war, grant letters of marque and reprisal, and make rules respecting captures of properties on land and water. No restrictions were imposed upon these powers, he said. The power to declare war involved the power to prosecute it by all means and in any manner in which war could be legitimately prosecuted. This included the conceded right to seize and confiscate all properties of an enemy and to dispose of the properties as the captors saw fit. The only restrictions to the war powers were to be found in the law of nations, and this law indicated that property could be confiscated, not because of the guilt of the owner, but because of the relationship of the property to the opposing belligerent. Any property that the enemy could use in its war effort was a proper subject of confiscation, the justice maintained. The 1861 confiscation law was aimed exclusively at the seizure of this type of property, and there was no question that this property could be seized.

Strong then discussed the provisions of the 1862 confiscation law. The first four sections of the act were aimed at persons who had committed treason, had engaged in insurrection, or had given aid to the Rebellion. These, said the justice, were domestic crimes and could not be classified under the war powers. However, Section 5 of the 1862 act was devoted to seizing and confiscating property of Rebels. The purpose of this section, observed the justice, was to ensure the speedy termination of the Rebellion. Under the proper interpretation of the law, Rebels and enemies were synonymous, he held, and because the types of people listed in Section 5 were considered public enemies, this brought them under the laws of war and subjected them to the nation's war powers. Strong then stated that the parts of the law declaring that all slaves of persons engaged in the Rebellion who had escaped within the Union lines, or were otherwise captured, were forever free were clearly under the war powers and enforced the idea that these parts of the law were exercised pursuant to the war powers of Congress.

Where the 1861 and 1862 confiscation laws applied directly to the confiscation of property of Rebels, maintained Strong, this was pursuant to the nation's power of war, and the personal rights in the Fifth and Sixth Amendments of the Constitution did not apply. Therefore, held the justice, the confiscation laws were constitutional. The decrees of the U.S. District and Circuit Courts were affirmed. The vote of the court was six to three.

Justice Stephen J. Field, the rugged individualist on the court, wrote a lengthy dissent in which Justice Nathan Clifford concurred.

Justice Field maintained that the confiscation laws were not passed under the war powers. He argued that private property was not ever subject to confiscation under the laws of nations, and that these particular laws applied to persons who had committed certain acts and therefore were domestic crime laws. This was substantiated, he insisted, by the proclamation of the president, and the resolution of Congress, that where real estate was concerned, the confiscation could not extend beyond the life of the offender. The application of the laws by the lower courts here meant that there was double punishment: The usual punishment was given for the commission of the crime, and then the defendant's property was confiscated in addition. This, he stated, made these laws unconstitutional.

As to the seizure of the stock, Field insisted that it must conform to revenue cases, and a great deal more was required than merely a marshal's seizure. In revenue cases, the stock had to be brought under custody of the court, and this could be done only by a court process. Serving notice upon the officers of the railroads fell far short of this requirement, said the justice, because these officers did not have possession of the stock. The fact that no further attempt to seize the stock after the libel was filed confirmed a complete failure of the seizure.

Field then observed that the confiscation laws were highly penal and therefore should have been strictly construed. Miller should have been found by the court to have somehow engaged in the Rebellion, he said. Field then cited Justice Peleg Sprague in *U.S. v. Lion*,[14] where the justice held that in revenue cases, a hearing was required after the entry of default. Finding that Miller had purchased the stock to aid and abet the Rebellion would have been difficult, said Field, because Miller owned the stock before the Rebellion had even begun.

Justice Field closed by stating that he felt that the judgment should have been reversed.

Justice David Davis presented a separate dissent. Davis concurred with the majority of the court that the confiscation laws were constitutional. However, he dissented from the court's conclusion because there were errors in the record that would entitle Miller to a reversal of the District and Circuit Court decrees.

He insisted that in all such cases, including those revenue and admiralty cases, actual notice to the party whose property was affected was fundamental and necessary to the whole structure of this type of judicial proceedings. Davis maintained that notice to officers of the railroad corporations did not give notice to Miller, because these officers were not in any way bound to appear and protect Miller's interests. In fact, said the justice, these officers may have been in direct hostility to Miller's interests. The publication of notice was not sufficient; Miller lived in an insurgent state, and any attempt to convey notice to him was forbidden and illegal.

Davis went on to state that the seizure of the stock did not conform to revenue practice. The stock, said the justice, could be seized only pursuant to a statute. There was no law in Michigan providing for the seizure of stock, and it was not the duty of the court to supply this omission.

The justice then observed that the libel set forth grounds for condemnation under both the 1861 and 1862 acts, but the court's decree condemning the property did not find any fact as grounds for forfeiture. This in itself was grounds for reversal, insisted the justice.

Then Davis made an observation not heretofore mentioned by the court. He stated that under the 1861 law, not the 1862 law, the proceeds from the condemnation were divided with an informer. Here the proceeds were divided,

The justices of the Supreme Court sometime after the death of Justice Catron on May 30, 1865. Even for this photo the court followed its seating tradition by lining up with the justice with the most tenure to the chief justice's right, second in tenure at his left, and so on with the justices alternating based upon tenure. Here, from the left, are Justices David Davis, Noah Swayne, Robert C. Grier, James M. Wayne, Chief Justice Salmon P. Chase, and then Justices Samuel Nelson, Nathan Clifford, Samuel F. Miller, and Stephen J. Field.

observed the justice, which meant that the proceeding was under the 1861 act. The property could be confiscated only under the terms of the 1862 act, he said, and thus the condemnation was improper.

Another fact that bothered Davis greatly was that the court had relied upon an affidavit of an informer, John M. Thatcher, which reflected adversely upon Miller. The affidavit apparently reflected Miller's supposed lack of interest in defending his property and resulted from a conversation Thatcher purportedly had with Miller after Thatcher somehow crossed the Confederate lines, got into Confederate Virginia, hunted up Miller, and talked with him. The justice obviously believed this to be far-fetched and felt that the court should not have placed reliance upon this affidavit. Davis then said that the decrees of the lower courts should have been reversed.

Chapter Thirteen

Property Disputes

When the shooting war came to an end, hundreds of smaller battles were initiated and continued across the nation, North and South, in the form of court cases to determine ownership of properties. These cases involved citizens who had remained loyal to the Federal government, who now battled former Confederate citizens over who owned good titles to the properties in question.

These disputes arose when the parties to a real estate purchase contract, entered into prior to the war, found themselves on opposite sides of the battle lines during the war. A purchaser in such a contract often discovered that he could not continue his payments because lines of battle separated him from the seller. The more serious problem arose when the seller foreclosed against a buyer who was on the other side of the battle lines.

Most of these cases were fought with deep emotion and a great deal of bitterness. The parties hurled allegations at each other, not all of which necessarily pertained to the subjects of the suits. The trial courts did the best they could to sort out these squabbles, apply the law, and arrive at fair outcomes. Several of these cases appeared on the docket of the U.S. Supreme Court.

The Supreme Court had difficulty sifting through the facts of these cases and arriving at fair and equitable legal conclusions. This was reflected in the complexity and obtuseness of several of the court's decisions rendered in these disputes. This chapter considers two cases reasonably representative of this litigation. The first case reveals interesting facts interwoven with wartime intrigue surrounding a historical parcel of property. The second case concerned a property dispute that was more typical of these cases.

THE *BIGLER* CASE

In May 1853, James Bigler, a New York investor with dreams of owning and developing a Southern community, purchased an old Virginia estate named Rippon Hall, which consisted of 2,000 acres along the York River in York County. The estate was sold to Bigler by a Virginian, William Waller. Bigler agreed to pay Waller $30,000 for the estate: $5,000 in cash at the time of sale, and

$25,000 over a period of ten years. These payments were to consist of $2,000 on May 10, 1855, and $1,000 annually on that date until 1863, when the entire balance was due. Interest of 6 percent per annum on the balance owing was to be paid in addition to each payment.

Waller executed a deed on the property to Bigler on May 10, 1853. On June 23, Bigler followed the convention of the time and executed a deed of trust to the property to Robert Saunders, appointing Saunders as the trustee to hold the property until the total consideration was paid. When that amount was paid, Saunders would be expected to reconvey the property to Bigler. However, in the event that any of the called-for payments were not made, Saunders had the duty, when instructed by Waller, to sell the property and pay the balance of the debt owed Waller plus expenses incurred in the sale. The balance, if any, would be paid to Bigler. This was termed a foreclosure, and it was supervised by the court. In the event of such a sale, it was provided in the deed of trust that sixty days' notice of the sale was to be given in the newspapers in Richmond and New York City.

Bigler took possession of the property and immediately had contractors build a wharf, two mills, a hotel, store, church, and schoolhouses. He laid out a village and had a large number of private residences built on the village lots. He also planted an orchard of 30,000 fruit trees. The cost of all these improvements approached $150,000.

Bigler made all the payments called for in the deed of trust up through May 10, 1860. Following this payment, a balance remained on the obligation to Waller of $13,000 plus interest.

When the Civil War approached, Bigler ceased the development of the Rippon Hall estate and returned to the safety of his home in New York. Waller, on the other hand, reported for active duty with the Confederate army.

When the May 10, 1861, payment came due, Bigler was prevented from making the payment because the lines between the North and the Confederacy were closed. When the payment was not made, Waller requested Saunders to sell the property under the terms of the deed of trust. Saunders proceeded to do this but could not, for obvious reasons, advertise the public sale in New York City. The public sale took place on April 1, 1862, and Waller himself purchased the property. He bid the balance owed him by Bigler plus interest, or $17,000. He paid the amount over and above Bigler's obligation to him in Confederate currency. Waller then leased the land and the buildings to the Confederate army, which had already occupied the estate. He also disposed of much of the personal property belonging to Bigler. Waller made arrangements for the mills to be dismantled, moved to Richmond, and sold. The dismantling was to be supervised by a Confederate spy known only as Knapp. Knapp had been instructed to make this appear as a legitimate business, while his main task was to observe the movement of the Federal troops and report these movements to the Confederate officials.

Unfortunately, Rippon Hall was in the path of the Federal advance up the Peninsula under Gen. George B. McClellan. As McClellan completed preparations to begin the seige of Yorktown, the Confederate forces withdrew. As they withdrew, a Confederate colonel named Duke ordered and supervised the burning of the mills and wharf, and the partial destruction of the other buildings that Bigler had so carefully planned and had constructed at Rippon Hall. This destruction took place on May 2, 1862, just two days prior to the fall of Yorktown to the Federal forces. Even though this area remained a war zone until the end of the war, Waller somehow remained in control of Rippon Hall and received benefit of the crops raised on the land, what the record of the case referred to as the "esplees," a now obsolete term used to mean the produce of the land. He also received the amount of $2,000 in Confederate currency from the Confederate government as rent and as compensation for the damage to the property caused by the Confederate armed forces.

When the war came to a close in Virginia, Bigler hurried back to Rippon Hall and was aghast at what he found. All of the construction was destroyed. Waller appeared to realize that the 1862 foreclosure was a nullity because notice had not been given in the New York City newspapers, as required by the deed of trust. He therefore did not attempt to prevent Bigler from taking possession of the land. Waller did, however, go to New York City, and he sued Bigler there in the New York courts for the $13,000 balance owing under the terms of the sale.

As Bigler investigated what had taken place on the land during the war, he became infuriated and began to blame Waller for everything. It followed that he sued Waller and Saunders in the Circuit Court of the United States for the District of Virginia.[1] This suit was filed on June 14, 1866. Sometime after the filing of this suit and before the final judgment was entered, both Waller and Saunders died. Waller's administrator stepped into the shoes of both defendants and thereafter acted in their behalf.

In this suit, Bigler acknowledge that the balance owing Waller on paper was $13,000, but he alleged that, in actuality, he did not owe Waller anything. On the contrary, Waller owed him a sizable amount of money based upon the rent and compensation Waller had collected and the waste and damages that had occurred to the property, for which Waller was responsible. Waller's claim for the balance due under the purchase contract, Bigler asserted, was a cloud on his title, and the court should order this claim absolved from the records.

The court then referred the dispute to a commissioner of the court, George Chahoon, to investigate the claims between the parties and report back to the court. Chahoon filed his report with the clerk of the court on November 2, 1867. Though the commissioner found that there was a balance of $13,000 owed by Bigler to Waller, he also found that the amounts owing to Bigler by Waller exceeded this amount. The net amount due Bigler to compensate him for the damage and waste to the property, and for the rent and compensation paid Waller by the Confederacy, Chahoon reported to be $26,186. Part of these damages resulted from the failure of Waller to release certain lots in the village from the deed of trust, which the commissioner found was part of the original contract.

When the case came to trial, attorney J. K. Hayward represented Bigler, and J. Alfred Jones appeared on behalf of Waller. Hayward gave a detailed, nearly textbook argument to the court on the ancient law of disseisin, which held that any interference with the actual possession of land by an individual, in this case Waller, that was in derogation of the rights of the true owner, here Bigler, created damages to which the actual owner was entitled. In this case, Hayward argued, Waller's assumption of possession of the land by way of an invalid foreclosure, then leasing the land to the Confederate army and collecting the rents, made him liable for the destruction that took place on the land. Hayward used the commissioner's report to back his claim for damages. He asked the court to confirm the commissioner's report; enter a judgment against Waller for $26,186 plus interest from April 3, 1865; order Waller and Saunders to release all of Rippon Hall from the deed of trust; and cancel Bigler's obligation to Waller. There is no record in the report of the case that Jones, Waller's attorney of record, made an oral argument to the court.

The Circuit Court for the District of Virginia was on the court circuit of Chief Justice Salmon P. Chase. In September 1870, he rendered the decision for the Circuit Court. Chase began his opinion by indicating that he did not believe it was appropriate to give an opinion in the Circuit Court until the case in New York had been determined. He acknowledged that the New York case had been discontinued, however, and there remained no reason why a final disposition of the case before him could not be made.

The justice made a quick disposal of the report of Commissioner Chahoon. The court was of the opinion that the damages afflicted upon the property were acts of war. Therefore, the exceptions that Waller had filed to the report were sustained, and the report was not considered by the court. The issues that remained to be determined by the court, said Chase, were three: how the interest should be computed on the $13,000 still owed Waller by Bigler; what credit should be given Bigler from the money received by Waller from the Confederate government; and what damages accrued to Bigler from Waller's refusal to grant property releases.

Again, Chase promptly disposed of the issues. He cited the approach of the Supreme Court that interest should cease between citizens or subjects of belligerent states during war. Taking the date of April 19, 1861, as the beginning of the war, and the date of the movement of the executive department of Virginia from Alexandria to Richmond, May 26, 1865, as the date of the end of hostilities for this purpose, the court suspended interest payments for that period.

Chase then acknowledged that Waller had received from the Confederate government a payment of $2,000 in Confederate currency for the use of the property and as compensation for damages. The court held that at that time, the ratio between Confederate currency and gold was thirteen to one. Chase ordered that Bigler be given a credit in the amount of the specie value of the Confederate currencies for this payment, computed to be $153.84. He then held that as to the releases that Waller had failed to give Bigler, the evidence was much too vague and indefinite to form a basis of part of the decree. This claim for damages was dismissed. Chase ordered that a decree be entered in conformity with the principles set forth in his opinion, that Waller's administrator should be paid by Bigler $17,377.48 in U.S. coin. Bigler immediately appealed this decision to the U.S. Supreme Court.

The Appeal to the Supreme Court

The case appeared before the court two times. The first case appeared on the docket of the court as *James Bigler, Appt., v. William Waller and Robert Saunders.*[2] This was a procedural hearing. The attorneys for Waller's administrator appeared just for the purpose of challenging the citation given by Bigler, notifying the administrator of the appeal and the appeal bond given by Bigler. Because both were addressed to Waller and Saunders, who had died prior to the final decree in the Circuit Court case, the attorneys for the administrator moved that the appeal be dismissed. The citation and the bond, they insisted, were invalid. The citation was not served properly, because it obviously could not be served on deceased persons, and the bond should have been addressed to Waller's administrator.

The motion to dismiss was heard on March 24, 1871, and decided three days later. The opinion was written by Justice Nathan Clifford. The justice observed that the citation of appeal was acknowledged by the attorney for Waller's administrator; therefore, its misdirection was waived. As to the bond, Clifford recited the rules governing it and pointed out that its prime reason was to compensate Waller's administrator for not being able to execute on the judgment of the Circuit Court during the course of the appeal. Then, if Bigler lost the appeal, the administrator would recover the amount of the judgment plus costs and interest from the bond proceeds. Not having a bond under the rules was certainly a basis to dismiss the case; however, in this case, it did not necessarily follow that a dismissal should take place. It was the constant practice of the court, explained the justice, to allow the one who appealed a case to have a reasonable time to file a new bond. The required times for filing the bond were not an issue before the court, he said. The court then entered a decree granting Bigler the right to file a new bond.

The suit was revived with a new bond under the name *James Bigler, Appt., v. William Waller et al.*[3] one year later. Bigler was again represented by the attorney who had given the scholarly textbook argument in his behalf at the Circuit Court, J. K. Hayward, who was assisted by E. L. Fancher. Conway Robinson, who had represented Waller in the bond hearing, also represented him in this revived suit. The arguments were made to the court on March 26, 1872.

The Arguments before the Court

Hayward opened his argument on behalf of Bigler by taking an approach that must have confused Waller's attorney, and certainly it confounded the court. He argued that the case had proceeded on an erroneous assumption from the time that Commissioner Chahoon had submitted his report to the court. That erroneous assumption was that Waller's 1862 foreclosure was a nullity. Hayward argued that the foreclosure was valid—that Waller, and not Bigler, owned Rippon Hall. He followed with the next logical conclusion from this new assumption, stating that therefore Bigler's debt to Waller was paid, because Waller had bid the amount owing as part of his purchase consideration in the foreclosure proceedings. Furthermore, insisted Bigler's attorney, Waller had bid an additional $1,100 over the amount of Bigler's debt and the costs involved, and it was obvious that Waller owed this amount to Bigler and it should be promptly paid to him. Hayward and Bigler let this bombshell rest with the court in silence.

Then Hayward posed a question to the court. He meekly asked that if the court were to compel Bigler to retake title to the property, then what was Waller's relation to the estate following the 1862 foreclosure and during the war? Hayward maintained that it could not be validly argued that Waller's actual relation to the property was not "sufficiently intimate" to not be considered to be in actual possession of the estate. He illustrated this statement by arguing that Waller exercised all the factors of ownership over the property that it was possible to exercise under the conditions that then existed. The attorney then detailed Waller's acts of ownership: He purchased the property, paid for it, and accepted a deed to it; he tried to sell the property as the owner; he disposed of the personality (a legal term for all items not attached to the land) on the property; and he shared in the production from the property for four years.

If the estate were owned by Bigler, Hayward went on, then Waller was a disseisor, a trespasser, and a wrongdoer. As such, Waller was liable to Bigler for all the damages to the property while the property was in Waller's possession. Hayward, as in his Circuit Court argument, cited sources that indicated that a jury could find for Bigler to the extent of three times the actual damages done.[4]

Hayward closed his argument with three additional points. He pointed out that Waller did not have authority to negotiate a settlement for damages with the authorities of the Confederacy, but in so doing, Waller had sacrificed a valuable claim that could have been realized by Bigler. Hayward then argued that if the court would hold that Bigler was the owner of the property and owed the amount found by the Circuit Court, that part of the order that the amount must be paid in coin was improper. Finally, he argued that if the court insisted that Bigler owned the property, he was entitled to releases from Waller's heirs, and they were not made a party to the suit when the court permitted the administrator to enter the case in Waller's behalf.

Hayward then asked the court to decree one or the other of two holdings: that Waller owned Rippon Hall and owed Bigler the amount of the excess that Waller bid on the property in the 1862 foreclosure, or that Bigler owned Rippon Hall and Waller was liable for damages to Bigler for the destruction to the estate, for rentals and compensation received by Waller, and for the produce of the estate for four years. Hayward brought his argument to a close.

It does not appear in the published opinion of the court that Waller's attorney, Conway Robinson, made an oral argument to the court. This would have been consistent with Waller's approach to the case taken in the Circuit Court. If this was in fact true, it was an indication that Waller placed his total reliance upon the appeals brief prepared and filed by Robinson.

The Opinion of the Court

The opinion of the court was given by Justice William Strong on May 6, 1872. The justice began his opinion with the observation that the complaint was "most inartificially drawn." What it amounted to, said Strong, was the allegation that Waller, the holder of note, had taken possession of Rippon Hall, confiscated the rents and profits from land, and committed waste. The argument given to the court by Bigler that Waller's foreclosure in 1862 was valid was indeed strange, said the justice, because it was inconsistent with the arguments in the Circuit Court and the allegations in the complaint itself.

Strong then observed that Waller had denied everything, including that he was even on the property after the war began. Waller did admit, however, that the trustee, Saunders, did not advertise the 1862 foreclosure in New York City because communication with the Northern states was prohibited at that time. The justice then stated that a foreclosure that did not follow the terms in the deed of trust did not convey any title to Waller. Therefore, the property had remained under the ownership of Bigler, and Bigler's assertion that Waller owed him any funds resulting from Waller's supposed purchase of the property in the foreclosure was unfounded.

As to the responsibility of Waller for the rents, profits, and damages done to the property, Strong demonstrated some impatience. He observed that for Waller to have any such liability, it must have been proven to the court that Waller had actual possession of the land. Here there was absolutely no credible evidence that Waller was on the land at all after the 1862 foreclosure. The justice added that a false claim of title, if asserted by Waller, was insufficient to show possession, or even constructive possession, of the property. It was equally unsustained that Waller had any responsibility for the waste and damages. The evidence in the Circuit Court supported the fact that the damages were caused by the Confederate military forces in Waller's absence and without his knowledge, and such damages were not compensable, said the justice.

Regarding Bigler's allegations that Waller had refused to approve releases from the deed of trust for certain of the village lots, Strong continued to demonstrate his impatience with Bigler, questioning why Bigler had not complained about this until he filed his case in the Circuit Court. Furthermore, that agreement did not appear anywhere in the final documents of the sale. Therefore, the court must assume, said the justice, that this provision had been changed or that the agreement was merged into the final documents and from that time on did not exist. He held that no credit should be given Bigler for this claim.

Similarly, the justice disposed of Bigler's claim that Waller's heirs should be ordered to give Bigler releases of the land. He held that at the time the debt was paid and the trustee reconveyed the property to Bigler, any interest of the heirs would have been cut off. In addition, the court could not order the heirs to give releases because they were not parties to the suit. The justice then informed the Circuit Court that it could protect Bigler in this regard by entering a stay of any final amended decree until the heirs conveyed whatever interest they may have had in the property to the trustee.

One thing remained, said Strong—that the amount ordered to be paid by Bigler to Waller's administrator by the Circuit Court was ordered to be paid in U.S. coin. He referred to the ruling in *Knox v. Lee*[5] and *Parker v. Davis.*[6] Strong himself had written the combined opinion in those cases just one year prior to this opinion. There he held on behalf of the court, in a strong opinion, that the Legal Tender Acts were constitutional. This meant that paper money, the so-called "greenbacks," were legal tender, and all debts of individuals could be paid with them. Therefore, the Circuit Court decree stating that Bigler's obligation to Waller must be paid in coin was contrary to the *Knox* and *Parker* cases. For this reason alone, the justice held, the Circuit Court judgment must be reversed.

Justice Strong then ordered the decree of the Circuit Court reversed and he remanded the case to that court, with instructions to proceed to amend the decree in accordance with his opinion rendered this date.

One must peruse Strong's opinion carefully to determine just what the Circuit Court was instructed to do. It was clear, however, that most of the Circuit Court opinion would stand. The holdings would remain that Bigler had owned Rippon Hall from the time of his purchase of it in 1853, and that Bigler owed Waller $17,377, which, however, could be paid with greenbacks. Also, the Circuit Court, if it saw fit and if necessary, could order Waller's heirs to release any interest they might have obtained in the property because of his death. The Circuit Court could stay any decree until such time as this was accomplished.

This ended not only an interesting Civil War legal case, but a little-known phase of Virginia and U.S. history.

THE *LUDLOW* CASE

The facts of the second case are more rudimentary. When the war began, J. G. M. Ramsey owned several properties in Knoxville, Tennessee. Among those properties were a house and lot that Ramsey had rented to a third party. He also owed the amount of a note, the balance of which was $300, to Cynthia S. White, another citizen of Knoxville. Sometime after the organization of the Confederate States of America, Ramsey went on active duty with the Confederate army. White remained in Knoxville.

In 1863, when the small Federal army led by Gen. Ambrose E. Burnside occupied Knoxville, the note that Ramsey owed White remained unpaid. When the courts reopened, she filed a case against Ramsey to collect the note in the Chancery Court in Knoxville. In the complaint filed in that case, White alleged that the note plus interest remained unpaid; that Ramsey had left the state, or was concealing himself in such a manner that she could not serve him; and that Ramsey owned one or more properties in Knox County. She prayed the court to order that so much of these properties should be attached and sold that would be sufficient to pay her note, plus interest and other costs. White posted the requisite bond according to the law and rules of the court, and a publication was made to notify Ramsey to appear and make defense on the first Monday in April 1864.

By the following October, Ramsey had not appeared; therefore, a decree was entered by the court awarding White a judgment in the amount of the note, plus interest and costs, and directing the master of the court to sell the house and lot owned by Ramsey. The master advertised the sale, and when it took place, he accepted a bid submitted by one S. Vail for $5,100. The sale was confirmed by the court, and possession was awarded to the purchaser. However, Vail's possession was vigorously opposed by Ramsey's renter. Following additional court proceedings and negotiations, Vail sold the property to Jacob R. Ludlow, who then took possession of the house and lot.

As the guns became silent, Ramsey returned to Knoxville. He could not believe what had happened. After reviewing the upsetting situation, he retained an attorney and filed a case against Ludlow in the Circuit Court of the United States for the Eastern District of Tennessee, with the objective of regaining the ownership of his property. In the complaint filed in that case, Ramsey alleged that when the notice of the sale of the property was published in the Knoxville paper, he was in no situation to see, or even hear about, the publication. He maintained that he was in an area controlled by Confederate troops, that no newspapers published within the Federal lines were allowed, that there were no mail facilities available, and that the only communication between the opposing sides was a flag of truce. Ramsey further asserted that Knoxville was part of an area subject to martial law, and that the civil courts were open only at the will of the military commanders. Everyone knew that as an enemy, he could not appear in the court to make a defense.

The Circuit Court considered Ramsey's allegations and found that the equities of the case favored Ramsey. The court entered an order that the Knoxville Chancery Court did not have jurisdiction of the attachment proceedings, and that those proceedings were null and void. Ludlow was therefore ordered to reconvey the property to Ramsey. Ludlow, firmly believing that he had paid full value for the property, and not understanding why the Knoxville court did not have the authority to sell it, appealed to the U.S. Supreme Court. The case was entered on the docket of the Supreme Court as *Jacob R. Ludlow, Appt., v. J. G. M. Ramsey.*[7]

The Arguments before the Court

The arguments were made to the court on April 12, 1871. Ludlow was represented by two attorneys, Thomas A. R. Nelson and Horace Maynard. Ramsey also retained two attorneys, J. W. Moore and Edward Lander.

Nelson and Maynard argued first on behalf of Ludlow. Their role was a heavy one. In both their briefs and in the court argument, they tried to convince the justices of the Supreme Court that the proceedings before the Chancery Court in Knoxville were valid, and that the decision of the Circuit Court reversing the Chancery Court should itself be overturned. This argument revolved around, and essentially was caused by, the unique position that the chancery court system occupied within the Anglo-American system of law. Chancery courts were courts that made their decisions based upon equity and fairness. They came into existence when the staid and formalized common-law courts failed to have remedies for persons with serious legal problems. A party who clearly deserved to be compensated for a wrong but could not find a solution in the common-law courts soon found that the only way he could receive a just result was to petition the king or, later, the government of a colony or a state. The petition would explain that the conventional remedies afforded by the courts would not compensate him, and that they should be disregarded and the court should administer his case simply on the basis of truth, fairness, and equity.

From this procedure, over the years chancery courts arose. Even states that did not have chancery courts, as such, set up equity divisions within the common-law system. As these courts evolved, many rules developed governing their function. As might be expected, many of these rules set high standards that had to be met to qualify for jurisdiction. For example, a person seeking equity had to come to the court with "clean hands." He could not be guilty of anything unethical that was even remotely connected with the case he wanted the court to accept.

It was understandable, therefore, that when Ramsey appealed to the Circuit Court as a court to administer equity, he painted himself as someone who did not even have an opportunity to be heard, who had lost a valuable piece of property over a very small debt, and who had had his rights abused with every step that was taken by the Chancery Court in Knoxville. By these arguments, Ramsey succeeded in convincing the Circuit Court that the Knoxville court did not have jurisdiction of the case. This made Ludlow's appeal an uphill fight.

Nelson and Maynard began their argument on Ludlow's behalf by attempting to hit the jurisdiction issue full force. They first pointed out that jurisdiction of the Chancery Court was determined by Tennessee law, and that White had complied with every requirement of that law. When the Chancery Court decided that, under Tennessee law, it had jurisdiction of the case, the Circuit Court could not challenge that finding, they insisted, because this was a state issue. They cited several cases in support of that assertion.[8]

Their next argument was to cite the Tennessee code pertaining to service of process. They pointed out to the court that the publication of service upon Ramsey was legal under that law. The fact that Ramsey was in the Confederate army was totally his doing, they argued, and White had no control over that. Furthermore, the recital in the decree of the Chancery Court that the default judgment against Ramsey was regularly taken was a confirmation of the finding that there was valid personal service upon Ramsey. This was a finding of fact that the Circuit Court had no right to challenge, they insisted.

The counsel for Ludlow closed their argument by reminding the court that the acts of secession by the state of Tennessee were void, and that the long-standing statutes and laws of the state were immediately revived in the areas that were reoccupied by Federal forces. According to these statutes and laws, and considering equity, Ramsey could not hide behind the war. Ramsey had voluntarily placed himself behind the Rebel line, and he could not, they insisted, take advantage of his own wrongdoing.

Moore and Lander then argued for Ramsey. They appeared full of confidence that the court could not possibly reverse the Circuit Court. The record of the case presented facts that showed that an extreme injustice had been committed against Ramsey, they insisted. They pointed out that Ramsey had received a pardon from the president. Ramsey had lost a building and lot worth in excess of $10,000, they argued, thirty times the amount owed to White. At the same time, it was well known that Ramsey had owned properties of lesser value, but still of a value sufficient to pay the debt, close by. The sacrifice of this property would not have been permitted by the government if it had proceeded against the property under one of the confiscation acts.

Ramsey was within Rebel lines, they pointed out, and had no opportunity to defend the suit. He was prohibited from coming within the Federal lines by presidential proclamation, and Ludlow pretended not to have known about this.

The counsel for Ramsey then argued to the court that international law was as much a part of the law of the United States as common law. Under international law, Ramsey had been an alien enemy, and nonintercourse existed between the warring parties, all debts and interest were suspended, and a writ of attachment could not have been issued against the property of an alien enemy, nor could service of that writ have been made. In addition, international law dictated that an alien enemy could not sue or be sued. Having cited cases to support each of these allegations, the attorneys for Ramsey rested their case.[9]

The Opinion of the Court

The opinion of the court was given by Justice Joseph P. Bradley on May 1, 1871. The justice first recited in detail the facts that led to the case, and its history through the Knoxville Chancery Court and the U.S. Circuit Court. Then he indicated that because the case was a collateral proceeding to set aside the sale of property, mere errors or irregularities committed in the Chancery Court would not be sufficient to overrule that court. To overrule the Chancery Court, it would have to be shown that the court did not have jurisdiction of the case. The justice proceeded to examine this question by citing the Tennessee Code on the subject. The code stated that any person could sue out an attachment in Chancery Court for any debts of a legal nature, except those derived from the commission of a tort, if the amount in controversy exceeded $50. White certainly qualified under the code, said Bradley.

The Circuit Court also relied upon the fact that the affidavit given to support the attachment was somehow insufficient. But, said the justice, he had examined the affidavit in the record of the case, and he found that it had more "particularity" than that required by the statute. In addition, the writ of attachment was in due form and was served properly. Bradley then held that the Knoxville Chancery Court had fully possessed proper jurisdiction of the case.

The justice then discussed Ramsey's argument that when the attachment of his property was taking place, he was in country held by Confederate troops and completely unable to receive notice of the proceeding. Bradley observed that Ramsey's home was in Knoxville, and he very easily could have remained there, or he certainly could have found an opportunity to return there if he had so desired. Ramsey had not been forced to leave, and his absence was totally voluntary. If Ramsey had been forced to leave and his return was prohibited, his failure to receive notice would have been much more persuasive, said the justice.

Bradley then made it very clear that the justices of the court believed that there was a legal doctrine that overrode the various international laws cited by Ramsey's counsel as determinative of his case. That was that when a party voluntarily left his country for the purpose of engaging in hostilities against his country, he could not be permitted to complain of legal proceedings regularly prosecuted against him in his absence on the ground of his inability to return to defend himself.

Justice Bradley followed with the holding that Ramsey's inability to defend himself was no excuse. Ludlow had the Chancery Court title and possession of the property, and considering all the equities between Ludlow and Ramsey, Ludlow had the better title to the house and lot. The justice declared that the decree of Circuit Court was therefore reversed, and that the decree of the Knoxville Chancery Court was the final holding of the case. Ramsey lost his property, and Ludlow became the legal owner.

Chapter Fourteen

Business Battles

The Civil War created circumstances that led to yet another category of cases disputing the ownership of properties. These cases determined the ownership of businesses or of interests in businesses. Prior to the war, commerce between the North and South was brisk. As the economy of the South began to expand beyond the confines of agriculture, and Southern entrepreneurs encountered a shortage of venture capital, many people from the North found Southern businesses to be fertile investments. Consequently, when the war began, many Southern businesses of all types had Northern shareholders or partners. Many of these businesses were controlled and managed by their Northern investors.

The battle lines of war often separated these businesses from their owners and shareholders. At times, members of management were split from the businesses they were expected to participate in managing. This created an atmosphere that generated many court battles. Two cases are typical of these conflicts.

THE *DEAN* CASE

The first case occurred six months prior to *Ludlow v. Ramsey*. It concerned a dispute over two blocks of capital stock in the Memphis Gas Light Company, a company incorporated in Tennessee. These shares were originally owned by Thompson Dean of Cincinnati. With the war approaching, Dean worried about the company operating in Memphis in the Confederacy while he was situated in the city of Cincinnati in the North. He tried to solve the problem in May 1861 by transferring all of his shares to James H. Pepper, the secretary of the company, with instructions to sell them on his behalf. Because hostilities came to the area sooner than either of them expected, Pepper hurried to make disposition of the stock under the best terms he could and as quickly as he was able.

On June 11, 1861, Pepper sold and transferred fifty shares of the stock to Thomas A. Nelson at the rate of $100 per share. Thomas A. R. Nelson was co-counsel with Horace Maynard in their victorious representation of Ludlow in the case discussed in the previous chapter. Were they one and the same person?

After the case considered here, Nelson was known as an expert in this type of property dispute, so it is possible.

Nelson paid for the fifty shares purchased from Pepper and Dean by giving Pepper a note for $5,000 with interest at 6 percent per annum. This note was to be paid from the net receipts received as dividends on the stock until the $5,000 was paid, plus interest, on a quarterly basis. In the event any quarterly payment was missed, the entire balance then owing, plus interest, was immediately due.

To secure payment of the note, Nelson gave Pepper a mortgage on his percentage of ownership of the real estate owned by the Memphis Gas Light Company. The mortgage would become null and void when the note was paid. If the note was not paid, Pepper could foreclose upon the real estate. This mortgage was properly recorded in the registry of mortgages in Shelby County. On July 20, 1861, Pepper sold a second block of the stock consisting of 154 shares to Nelson for $15,400 under the same terms as the previous shares. He then hurriedly sold several miscellaneous remaining shares to other persons under the apprehension that the shares would be confiscated by the Confederate authorities, which they had threatened to do. In addition, Pepper desired to leave Memphis for his own personal safety. Nelson purchased the shares in good faith, without any side agreements to hold the shares in trust or promises that the shares would someday be returned to Dean. However, Pepper assigned the notes and mortgages to Dean, who remained in Cincinnati.

Following these transactions, the war became intense. Not only did all intercourse between the states of the Confederacy and the North cease, but it was prohibited by President Lincoln's Proclamation of August 16, 1861. Nelson continued to reside in Memphis, where he received the quarterly dividends on the 204 shares of stock, but he could not make any payments to Dean. By June 1862, these dividends amounted to $3,672. Nelson then transferred ten shares to a man named May for the purpose of qualifying him as a director of the company. On June 1, 1862, Nelson assigned to his wife the balance of 194 shares in order to give her a separate source of income in the event something happened to him.

On June 6, 1862, Federal naval forces captured Memphis. When the Union occupation became secure, Dean visited Memphis and talked with Nelson. Although Dean indicated to Nelson that according to the terms of the notes, the stock had been forfeited back to him because of Nelson's failure to pay, Nelson apparently made no overtures to make payments on the notes. He refused to make any payments because he claimed that he had received some indication that he might have to pay these amounts to the Confederate government.

Then, to add more confusion to an already difficult situation, Confederate guerrillas began to harass the Union forces in the Memphis area as well, raiding the properties and persons of local citizens who had remained loyal to the Union. In retaliation for these outrages, on April 5, 1863, the Federal officials ordered Nelson and his family removed from Memphis beyond the Confederate lines. There was no indication in the written opinion of the case as to why the

Nelson family was so chosen, but they were forced to comply, and further, they were ordered never to return to Memphis. Shortly after this removal took place, Nelson challenged the order by formally requesting permission to return, but his request was refused. Once again, these business combatants found themselves on the opposite sides of the lines of battle.

On April 25, 1863, a special order establishing a Court of Civil Commission was issued by General Veatch, the commander of the Military District of Memphis. This court was given jurisdiction to hear and determine suits instituted by loyal citizens to collect debts, enforce contracts, recover possession of properties, and conduct other matters that could be done by courts that derived their powers from military authority. Dean, realizing that his forfeiture argument was flimsy, and suffering great frustration over the whole arrangement, filed a petition in this court on September 1, 1863. His petition asked the court to foreclose on the 204 shares of stock, sell them, and apply the proceeds to pay the notes that the Nelsons owed him. The defendants—Nelson, his wife, and May—could not be found to serve them the notice of foreclosure. This notice was then published, following the laws of Tennessee as they existed prior to the war.

As expected, none of the defendants appeared to defend against the foreclosure. A decree was then entered by the court in Dean's favor, an execution was issued, and the stock was sold on October 23, 1863, to a man by the name of Hanlin. The shares were transferred to Hanlin by the company secretary, and Hanlin immediately transferred the shares to Dean. From that time on, Dean was paid the dividends attributed to the stock.

Following the collapse of the Confederate lines, the Nelson family and May returned to Memphis. There is no record as to what passed between Nelson and Dean when they finally met; however, one can assume that it was more than just the common pleasantries of the day. Finally, the Nelsons and May initiated a suit seeking to regain ownership of the shares and to force Dean to account for the dividends he had received since the foreclosure in the Court of Civil Commission. The suit was filed in the Circuit Court of the United States for the District of West Tennessee in June 1865.

Dean defended against the Nelsons' allegations by insisting that the forfeiture provisions in the notes—that is, if a payment was not made, the entire balance came due and the shares were forfeited back to Dean—made the sale of the shares a conditional assignment and not a mortgage. It followed, he argued, that once the forfeiture provisions went into effect, he owned the shares, and the Nelsons had no right thereafter to redeem them. He also cited the decision of the Court of Civil Commission. In that commission proceeding, according to Dean, even if the arrangement was a mortgage, all equity of redemption to recover the shares was foreclosed.

The Nelsons insisted that the arrangement was a mortgage, and the forfeiture was merely a penalty that should not have been enforced in an equity proceeding. Furthermore, they maintained that the actions of the Court of Civil Commission were illegal because it did not have jurisdiction over the Nelsons or the stock. The Nelsons argued that their involuntary forced residence in the Confederacy forbade any legal proceeding against them or their property. Therefore, Dean's taking of the shares was illegal, and they were entitled to have the shares returned to them, together with an accounting of the amount Dean had received in dividends.

The Circuit Court took the matter under consideration, and then decided the case in favor of the Nelsons and May. The court ordered that the shares be immediately returned to the Nelsons and May, and that the dividends received by Dean be applied as payments against the notes he held. Dean promptly appealed to the U.S. Supreme Court. The case came to the Supreme Court as *Thompson Dean, Appt., v. Thomas A. Nelson, et al.*[1]

The Arguments before the Court

The arguments to the court were made on November 2, 1870. Dean was represented by William S. Holman. The Nelsons and May were represented by P. Phillips, who was assisted by two gentlemen by the names of Kortrecht and Craft.

Holman argued first on behalf of Dean. His first point was a potent one. He maintained that the agreement between Pepper and Nelson was not a legal contract. A contract, to be a valid and binding legal agreement, must have had consideration, and consideration, he continued, had to impose a clear obligation upon the person whose responsibility it was to pay it. Holman insisted that Nelson's agreement to pay for the stock out of the stock's own earnings was not a valuable consideration that would bind a contract.

He then argued that in Tennessee, stock was personal property. The mortgage on the stock that was given by Nelson placed absolute title of the stock into Pepper's name when the payments were not made. Under Tennessee law, Holman maintained, this was a conditional sale. If Nelson held any right to the stock at all, it was an equitable right to redeem the stock. But Nelson refused to pay anything, including the funds generated from dividends. Nelson did not take advantage of the right to redeem, and that right had certainly expired by the time this suit was filed, Holman contended.

Next the attorney pleaded that Dean had a right to rely upon the decision of the Court of Civil Commission in Memphis. The commission was a valid court in every respect, and after a valid and legal hearing, it had decided the case in favor of Dean. The validity of these courts, insisted Holman, was sustained by writers of international law and in an unbroken series of decisions in the U.S. courts.[2] Holman concluded Dean's argument by requesting the court to overrule the Court of Appeals.

Phillips, Kortrecht, and Craft then presented the Nelsons' argument to the court. First, they admitted that a mortgage could be more than a lien, and that the title could have rested in Pepper when forfeiture took place. However, they contended that it still would have been held by him merely as security for a debt, because Nelson still had the right to redeem. This right of redemption could be extinguished by a sale of the property by Pepper. However, for the sale to be valid, it was absolutely essential that notice of the time and place of the sale be given to Nelson, and this was not done. Even if Nelson had somehow heard about the sale, they argued, the military power had forbade him from appearing, and "the law cannot create a default when the law forbids a performance."

The Nelsons' attorneys then insisted that the Court of Civil Commission in Memphis was not a legal court. Such courts in military-occupied areas, they pointed out, could be set up only by the president as commander-in-chief, whereas the subject court in Memphis was created by the area commander. They also challenged Holman's "unbroken series of decisions" as in reality not supporting the validity of the Court of Civil Commission whatsoever. They closed their argument by pleading with the court to sustain the judgment of the Circuit Court.

The Opinion of the Court

Justice Joseph P. Bradley gave the opinion of the court on December 6, 1870. The justice first reviewed the facts of the case and its history in detail. Before he considered the legal ramifications of the case, he observed that the transaction was an absolute sale. The terms were clear, and the shares were physically transferred to Pepper, then to Nelson. When Dean foreclosed on the shares in the proceeding before the Court of Civil Commission in Memphis, he fore-closed solely as a holder of the notes and mortgages, thus recognizing that a valid sale of the shares had taken place. In addition, in the answer filed in this case, Dean nowhere suggested that Nelson was guilty of bad faith, or that Nelson made any agreement to hold the shares on his behalf. Then the justice held that there was consideration for the contract, because Nelson's agreement to pay the whole amount immediately in case of a failure to pay any installment was an obligation sufficient to constitute consideration. This was not a penalty, held Bradley, but this provision was the substance of the contract. Following this agreement, the stock was the property of Nelson, and the contract was an executed contract and could not now, in this case, be impeached.

The next question that had to be settled, said the justice, was to determine the nature of the security agreements. Was this a conditional sale, or was it a mortgage? Bradley appeared not just a bit annoyed by this argument. He stated that the court had no power to make the transaction different from what the parties themselves had made it, and there was no doubt that they had made it a mortgage. The justice then quoted a legal adage, "once a mortgage, always a mortgage," as applicable to the contractual terms of the agreement. Being a mortgage, said the justice, Nelson possessed an equity of redemption—that is, a right to redeem the shares after foreclosure—unless that right had been extinguished. Bradley then observed that the "great question" of the case was whether this right had been extinguished. Since the only method used to cut off this right of redemption was the legal proceeding before the Court of Civil Commission, an examination of whether these proceedings were valid and effectual could be made. However, this was not necessary, because the proceedings themselves before that commission were fatally defective, as the Nelsons and May were within the Confederate lines at the time. The Nelsons had been expelled from the Union in retaliation of the Confederate guerrilla activities, and they could not return to Memphis even though that was their desire. Published notice to them, held the justice, was a "mere idle form," and they could not lawfully see it or obey it. The Court of Civil Commission's proceedings were therefore wholly void and inoperative. This left the Nelsons' equity of redemption still valid, and they had every right to use it and redeem the stock, said the justice.

Bradley then held on behalf of the court that the entire principal and interest of the notes were due and payable, and a retransfer of the shares to the Nelsons should take place only on condition that the total amount of that principal and interest were first paid. The Nelsons, however, should have received credit for the amounts paid to Dean from the dividends since he had held the stock.

The court then unanimously held that the decree of the Circuit Court should be upheld but modified. In lieu of the Circuit Court holding that the shares be immediately transferred back to the Nelsons and May, it was ordered that the shares be transferred only after the Nelsons and May had paid the total amount determined by the court to be owed on the notes plus interest. Bradley added that none of the parties would be awarded their costs incurred in the proceeding.

The decisions in this case and in the case of *Ludlow v. Ramsey,* in the previous chapter, were made within six months of each other. Justice Bradley wrote the decision in each case, and in each case, the effectiveness of a published notice of the hearing was instrumental in its determination. Bradley made it clear that if the defendant to whom the notice of a hearing was directed had entered the Confederacy of his own free will, as Ramsey had, he could not hide behind the fact that the notice was not received to overturn the court's default judgment against him. If, however, the defendants not only were in the Confederacy against their will, but also could not return, as was the case with the Nelsons, then the fact that notice of the hearing was not received was a factor that would overturn a default judgment against them. These rulings governed thousands of cases that were filed in the lower trial courts of the nation. In addition, they encouraged many prospective litigants to use other means to reconcile their business disputes.

THE *FRENCH* CASE

The next case illustrates how deeply embroiled these business disputes could become. On February 27, 1854, the legislature of the state of Virginia, following the existing Virginia laws pertaining to railroad incorporations, passed a law incorporating a company whose purpose was to construct and operate a railroad between Alexandria and Washington. The name of the company was the Alexandria & Washington Railroad Company.

The promoters of the company were James S. French, who subscribed to 75 percent of the outstanding shares of the company, and Walter Lenox, who subscribed to the remaining 25 percent. These two founders then undertook the supervision of the building of the line. To finance this construction, they took out three large loans. The company secured these loans by executing three separate deeds of trust where Lenox acted as the trustee. These deeds of trust were mortgages that made the properties of the railroad security for the loans.

As the line entered its first stages of operation, the war began. Both French and Lenox, their motives personal and not disclosed, joined the Confederacy and went within the lines of the insurgents. The Federal government took over the railroad and used it for military purposes. While the railroad was being so used and Lenox was in the Confederacy, Joseph Davison, who explained that he was an agent and attorney for the holders of the notes secured by the deeds of trust, applied to the County Court in Alexandria and asked that court to change the trustee of the railroad properties under the terms in the deeds of trust. Davison explained to the court that the then existing trustee set out in those deeds, Lenox, was "incapacitated" and unable to act in a trust capacity.

The County Court was sympathetic; it removed Lenox as the trustee and appointed a new trustee in all three deeds of trust. On April 10, 1862, payments not being current on the notes, the new trustee initiated foreclosure of the notes and sold all the properties of the railroad to a group headed by Samuel M. Shoemaker. Shoemaker organized a new company called the Washington, Alexandria, & Georgetown Railroad Company. A charter was not granted to this company by the state. Legally, it remained a shell, at least at that time. However, when the government relinquished the railroad in 1865, this new company took possession of its facilities. The new company then entered into a contract with Adams Express Company to operate the railroad.

Shortly thereafter, French and Lenox returned from the South. On March 28, 1866, they filed a suit in the same County Court on behalf of the Washington & Alexandria Railroad Company against the new company in order to regain title and possession of the railroad properties. In support of their request, they alleged that the foreclosure and the formation of the new company were both fraudulent and should be held null and void.

In the meantime, both the old and new companies agreed that Adams Express Company had failed to operate the line properly. Both parties approved a new ten-year operating agreement with a different entity owned by Oscar A. Stevens and W. J. Phelps. However, in a short time, this contract was also in litigation.

French and Lenox were destitute when they returned from the South. Their failure to get anything accomplished to relieve their situation prompted them to request a meeting with the men who had formed the new company. In November 1866, the men involved in the controversy all met with Shoemaker's attorney, R. T. Merrick, with the hope that some agreement could be consummated. Following an extended period of negotiation, an understanding was reached. It took time to reduce its terms to writing, but soon this was done, except that the date was left blank. The other parties executed the agreement, but French had misgivings and hesitated. Shoemaker then agreed to make a loan to French of $5,000. How this loan was to be repaid was incorporated into a second agreement.

The agreement provided that French and Lenox would convey their interest in the railroad to the old company, or a new company if one was formed; Stevens and Phelps would transfer their management contract to an old or new company; Shoemaker would compromise or pay all of the liabilities of both companies; 20 percent of the receipts would be apportioned among the owners according to their percentage of ownership; the terms of the agreements would be initiated when the County Court case filed by French and Lenox was terminated, no matter what that court decided; French and Lenox would own 1,250 shares out of 3,000 shares; management was provided for; and Shoemaker would loan the $5,000 to French under the conditions specified. To secure this loan, French agreed to assign all of his interest in the companies to Shoemaker.

Then the County Court entered a decree in favor of French. The decree restored the railroad to French and Lenox, but the only effect of the decree according to the agreements was that it should have kicked off the start of the agreements. Following the agreements, Lenox called a meeting of the people involved for the purpose of initiating the agreed terms. The meeting was held, and a new company with Shoemaker as president was formed. However, French, who obviously had had a change of heart, and claiming to act as president of the railroad consistent with the County Court decree, obtained a writ from the court giving him possession of the railroad. The sheriff of the county supervised the turning over of the railroad to French pursuant to the court decree. French also applied to the County Court for an injunction, hoping to restrain the other parties from holding and carrying through on the agreements reached at the meeting called by Lenox.

Shoemaker did not stand still. He rushed to the Circuit Court of the United States for the District of Virginia and obtained an injunction from this Federal court preventing French from acting as president of the Alexandria & Washington Railroad Company. In this case, Chief Justice Salmon P. Chase, acting as a Circuit Court justice, ruled that jurisdiction of the state court was "ousted" or had to be exercised solely in subordination to the Federal court.

Despite this holding, French filed a complaint based upon equity in the Supreme Court of the District of Columbia against all of the other parties, asking that court to enter a decree that he was the rightful owner of the railroad, and further requesting it to prevent the other parties from interfering with that judgment. At this point, the U.S. Circuit Court that had issued the injunction against French reentered the fray and held a hearing as to why he should not be fined or imprisoned for contempt in that he violated the injunction by filing the District of Columbia case. French was forced to back down. He requested the District of Columbia court to dismiss the case, and that court complied with his request.

French then appealed the Circuit Court injunction case to the U.S. Supreme Court. Before the merits of the case were heard by the court, it considered two motions filed by both French and Shoemaker. French filed a motion with the court asking it to require the Circuit Court to set an appeal bond. Such a bond would have protected Shoemaker if French lost the appeal. More important to French, it would have shielded him from a contempt citation by the Circuit Court while the appeal was taking place. Shoemaker simply filed a motion to dismiss the appeal based upon the assertion that an injunction was not a final decree that would support an appeal. The motions were heard by the court on March 31, 1871, and the court denied them both.[3]

The issues determined by the Circuit Court then came before the Supreme Court on their merits. The issues were extensive in scope. The injunction handed down by the Circuit Court prohibited French from acting as president of the Alexandria & Washington Railroad Company and from interfering with the carrying out of the terms of the agreements arrived at by the parties. The Circuit Court had also agreed that Shoemaker had the right to foreclose upon the interests of French because the $5,000 loan was still outstanding and in default.

The Circuit Court's denial of French's cross-complaint had also raised several issues. In the cross-complaint, French had asked the court to require Shoemaker to give an accounting of the profits received from the operations of the railroad. He had also asked the court to order Shoemaker to return his interest in the railroad to him upon the payment to Shoemaker of the $5,000, and to declare the entire agreement creating a new company and appointing new officers fraudulent and null and void.

All of these issues then came before the U.S. Supreme Court. The case reached the court as *James French, Appt., v. Samuel M. Shoemaker.*[4]

The Arguments before the Court

The arguments to the court were not made until April 10, 1872. French was represented by H. O. Claughton and F. P. Stanton. Shoemaker's attorneys were J. H. Bradley, Thomas J. Durant, R. T. Merrick, and George William Brent. The attorneys for French carefully summarized their arguments to the court as to why the Circuit Court should be overruled. Leaving well enough alone, Shoemaker's counsel advised him to rely solely upon the written briefs, and this advice was followed when oral arguments were not made.

The counsel for French set out their argument in twelve points designed to show that a court of equity had absolutely no basis for entering a decree supporting the main contract among the parties. The initial part of the argument concerned the fact that French had executed the contract on December 6, 1867, and Shoemaker had waited an unconscionable period before seeking assistance of the court. Equity, they argued, does not approve of such a delay. They then claimed that there was a lack of mutuality in the agreement, and this invalidated the contract. The opposing parties had violated their fiduciary responsibilities, they said, in that they were bound as officers and directors of the company to act in its behalf; rather, they had acted solely for themselves.

The attorneys then maintained that not only was there no consideration supporting the contract, but the contract was entered into by French under a mistake and misapprehension. When French signed the contract, they asserted, he believed that the parties would defend his title; on the contrary, they were trying to steal the railroad from him. This, the attorneys argued, was a mistake, as French would not have executed the agreement if he realized this was the case.

French's counsel then combined several points into their main argument. They asserted that the parties with whom French had contracted had possession of the railroad, and the court injunction existed at that time, preventing French from attempting to regain his title. The other parties had received an estimated $100,000 in earnings per year from the railroad's operations, and French had received nothing. These parties, according to French, were well aware of his financial distress, and they obtained his signature under the duress of his financial condition. Such a contract, argued French's attorneys, was not only void, but illicit.

They went on to claim that the contract was therefore inequitable, unconscionable, and tainted with fraud, or as they put it, so polluted with fraud that it was a "fatal infection." French, through his attorneys, requested that the court overrule the Circuit Court's decision.

Shoemaker's attorneys rested their case upon their written briefs.

The Opinion of the Court

Justice Nathan Clifford gave the opinion of the court on April 22, 1872. He began by stating that it would be impossible to understand the grounds of the court's decision without explaining in detail the facts of the case. The justice meticulously took the time to do this. He then said that French's argument to overturn the Circuit Court was based upon the alleged facts that his signature to the first agreement was obtained by fraud and oppression, and that the agreement was therefore contrary to public policy. Further, French asserted that the assignment of all his interests in the railroad that secured the $5,000 loan was obtained by threats and deception. The nature of the fraud was alleged to be threats that if French did not sign both agreements, he would be kept out of possession of the railroad for years. French claimed that because of these alleged threats, deceptions, and his financial situation, explained the justice, he was forced to execute the agreements.

Clifford then stated that a contract procured by means of threats and duress was wholly void; this needed no further discussion. The justice added that actual violence was not required to establish duress, because consent was necessary to a valid contract, and where there was compulsion, there was no consent. The justice went on to define duress as that degree of constraint or danger, either inflicted or threatened, that was sufficient in severity to overcome the mind and will of a person of ordinary firmness.

The justice then closely examined the facts. The court, he said, was convinced that French was in "straitened" circumstances. French's business affairs had become complicated; he was greatly embarrassed with litigation. Further, he was "in pressing want of pecuniary means." But, said Clifford, the court was wholly unable to see that Shoemaker was responsible for the circumstances in which French found himself. Therefore, the alleged fraud was not supported by satisfactory proof. Furthermore, the fraud allegations had been abandoned in the cross-complaint.

There was no showing that Shoemaker had committed any unlawful act designed to deprive French of his property or that in any way created French's

In 1860 the Supreme Court began to hold its sessions in the old Senate chamber in the capitol. The court met there throughout the Civil War. Here is a Harper's Weekly *sketch of the 1888 court in session there depicting a scene that was duplicated many times in the hearings of the Civil War cases.*

problems, stated the justice. French had accepted the $5,000 as a "choice of evils," and he voluntarily signed the agreement and the assignment after ample time for inquiry, examination, and reflection. He was therefore bound by their terms and must abide by the consequences of his acts, Clifford concluded.

Justice Clifford then dismissed French's other bases for overruling the Circuit Court. He stated that the claim of a want of consideration was unfounded; that mistake was not supported, the delay in execution was not sustained by adequate proof, and the contracts did not fall into the classification of being inequitable or unconscionable, because Shoemaker had advanced the $5,000 and paid all the bills of the railroad, which were substantial.

French lost all of his interest in the railroad when Clifford, on behalf of a unanimous court, affirmed the opinion and decree of the Circuit Court.

Chapter Fifteen

Amnesty, Pardons, and Oaths

The individuals who took up arms against the Federal government committed the ultimate acts of treason against their country. Those citizens of the North, and indeed of the South, who dreamed of restoring the Union fully realized that somehow persons guilty of treason would have to be absolved of their crimes and restored as good citizens before a feeling of nationhood could be reachieved. There was no underestimating the magnitude of this problem.

Thoughtful people in the North fully understood that winning the war would not create the essence of one nation and one people. To accomplish this, it was apparent to all who had this concern that the people of the South could not all be dealt with as traitors; the people of the North and South would ultimately have to deal with each other on common ground as equals.

President Lincoln and the people in his administration and Congress grappled with this problem. Early on in the war, they instituted a policy of amnesty and pardons that was designed to bring the people of the South, both those who had remained loyal to the Union and those who were actively fighting against it, back into the Union as good citizens.

The president had the powers to grant reprieves and pardons for offenses against the United States under Article II, Section 2(2) of the U.S. Constitution. Possibly to remind him of this power, on July 17, 1862, Congress authorized the president to pardon or grant amnesty to people who may have participated in the Rebellion, with such exceptions as he may deem expedient. The president did not use the power until December 8, 1863, when he issued a proclamation offering full pardons with restoration of property rights, except as to slaves, to all who engaged in, or aided and abetted, the Rebellion. Those who accepted the pardon did so by taking an oath that they would thenceforth support the U.S. Constitution, abstain from further participation in the Rebellion, and support the acts of Congress and proclamations of the president that had to do with slaves.

Between this pardon and a pardon and amnesty granted on July 4, 1868, the president granted three additional pardons with varying conditions and exceptions. Then, on December 25, 1868, President Andrew Johnson granted full pardons and amnesty to all who had participated in the Rebellion, without exceptions, unconditionally and without reservations. No oaths were required to be taken by those who desired to take advantage of the pardon or amnesty. In addition, thousands of special pardons to individuals were granted by Johnson.

As the war came to a close, many people in the South began to reassume responsible positions in society. However, many of those in the North and South who had remained loyal to the Union had difficulty overcoming the inherent distrust they felt for the Southerners who were returning and attempting to reassume often important positions in society. True, these Southern folks would not be tried for treason, but did they possess the high moral standards normally associated with positions of trust? A majority of the people who wrestled with this problem soon came to the conclusion that positions in society that required high moral standards and trust should be occupied only by people who had remained loyal to the Union. Prior to the war, many people in the South had occupied positions that required them to take an oath to uphold the U.S. Constitution, yet they had joined the Confederacy. If they had violated their oaths once, would they not violate them again?

Legislators in many states and even the Federal government determined that the solution to this problem was to require "test" oaths. These oaths were required before a man or woman could assume a position of responsibility. The persons involved were required to attest that they had not engaged in, or aided and abetted, any armed conflict against the United States before they were eligible to assume the position. Heavy penalties would be administered if the position in question was assumed without taking the oath or if the oath were falsely given. These so-called "test" oaths tended to nullify all the good that was hoped would be accomplished by the presidential pardons and grants of amnesty.

These oaths generated interesting legal cases as those affected fought against them. Three such cases are examined in this chapter: a challenge to a state-created test oath; a challenge to a congressionally authorized test oath; and a challenge to a test oath associated secondarily with a law passed by Congress.

The strictest test oath was created by the people of the state of Missouri in their new constitution adopted in 1865. Article II, Section 3 of that constitution required an oath of loyalty from every person in the state who held an office of honor, trust, or profit as defined by the constitution. Among such offices so defined were that of an attorney, bishop, priest, deacon, minister, elder, or other clergyman of any religious persuasion. The law required that the oath be taken within sixty days after the constitution took effect.

The takers of the oath were required to solemnly swear that they had always been loyal and true to the United States and had never been in armed hostility against the nation, and to uphold the state and Federal constitutions. They also had to swear to an additional thirty affirmations and tests of all types that, it was felt, reflected upon the quality of the oath taker's character. If the individuals required to take the oath should refuse to do so, the position held by that individual was declared to be vacant, and if the type of position so required, it would be refilled according to law.

In the event that an individual required to take the oath refused to do so but still exercised the power of an office or profession, he or she could, upon conviction, be punished with a $500 fine or imprisonment in the county jail for not less than six months, or both. If anyone falsely took the oath and was convicted of doing so, he or she would be guilty of perjury and could be punished by imprisonment in the penitentiary for not less than two years.

THE *CUMMINGS* CASE

Father John A. Cummings, a Roman Catholic priest, preached and taught in the rural Mississippi River country in and around Pike County, Missouri. When the Missouri constitution became effective, and he was told that he was required to take the test oath in sixty days or he would have to give up being a priest, he vehemently objected and refused to take the oath. Father Cummings thought it was wrong for the state to insert itself into his practice as a priest. He continued to serve his church and was ultimately arrested under the test oath provisions of the new state constitution. He was tried under the applicable provisions of the law in Pike County. The Circuit Court there found him guilty and fined him $500. He was committed to jail until the fine was paid. Cummings appealed to the Missouri Supreme Court. In October 1865, that court affirmed the Pike County court's conviction.

Cummings then appealed that decision to the U.S. Supreme Court on a writ of error. The case appeared on the docket of the court as *John A. Cummings, Plff. in Err., v. The State of Missouri.*[1]

The Arguments before the Court

The arguments to the court were made on March 15 through 20, 1866. Father Cummings was represented by an impressive legal trio: Reverdy Johnson, David Dudley Field, and Montgomery Blair. Johnson was an attorney of national recognition. He was a former senator from Maryland and would be mentioned as a possible presidential candidate. Field was also nationally known and the older brother of Justice Stephen J. Field, who ultimately wrote the court opinion in the case. Blair was a member of Lincoln's original cabinet. The state of Missouri was represented by G. P. Strong and J. B. Henderson. Henderson had been a member of Congress representing Missouri.

The counsel for Cummings opened the arguments. They first pointed out to the court what would happen to a Missouri resident if he or she did not take the oath. Such a person could not vote, hold office, be a candidate for office, serve as a juror, practice as an attorney, manage a corporation, teach, be a trustee, be a clergyman or any type of church official, or be an individual who solemnized marriages. They claimed that these disabilities were penal in nature and violated Article I, Section 10 of the U.S. Constitution, which prohibited any state from passing a bill of attainder or an ex post facto law.

Quoting from and citing extensive sources,[2] the attorneys related what the legal texts and cases revealed about bills of attainder. They cited English sources,[3] including the *Commentaries on the Laws of England* by William Blackstone, and the abuses that bills of attainder caused in England. They carefully explained to the court, quoting Justice Joseph Story, that bills of attainder were special acts of a legislature that inflicted punishment upon persons without any conviction in an ordinary court by judicial proceedings.

Cummings's counsel argued that depriving citizens of Missouri of their civil rights and their ability to earn a living because of the failure to take the test oath was a penal punishment passed by the legislature. These citizens were not found guilty of crimes by a court. Therefore, the effect was that the law was a bill of attainder that violated the cited section of the U.S. Constitution.

In addition, they argued that the test oath was an ex post facto law. This referred to a law that made an action done before the passage of the law, that was innocent when done, a criminal act and punished the action. They explained the enlarged definition of ex post facto law to include any statute that made a crime a greater crime than it was when committed, or any law enlarging the punishment or easing the rules of evidence after the commitment of the crime. The attorneys argued to the court that many of the items in the test oath that the taker of the oath was required to state he had not performed were not crimes when done. Therefore, punishing those who had performed those acts made the test oath law a true ex post facto law.

The attorneys then criticized the Supreme Court of Missouri, which had attempted to defend the test oath law. That court, in upholding Cummings's conviction, held that one who refused to take the oath simply violated an existing law after its enactment, and this was not a bill of attainder or an ex post facto law. The counsel for Cummings argued that the Missouri court neglected the fact that the law prohibited him from pursuing his calling on account of his commitment of antecedent acts.

The Missouri court indicated that the constitutional convention had the right to set forth rules to govern who would be qualified to hold office. But, said the attorneys, even the Missouri court did not deny that the test oath laws were "the most elaborately contrived and cruel system of partisan proscription and oppression which political controversy ever invented," and that they were contrived solely to punish political opponents. Cummings's attorneys then posed this question to the court: Could the wartime successful party in the state deprive its opponents of all rights and means of making a living and thus banish them from the state?

Cummings's attorneys then referred to one miscellaneous fact that had been introduced at his trial. They argued that prior to the adoption of the Missouri constitution, it was not a penal act for Father Cummings in 1861 to give cups of coffee to soldiers with Confederate sympathies who were opposing the forces of Brig. Gen. Nathaniel Lyon. But after the passage of the new constitution, such an act was a penal act because of how it was treated in the test oath.

The counsel for Cummings then drove home the point that what Missouri could not do directly, it could not do indirectly. If, in 1865, Cummings could not be found guilty of serving coffee to Confederate troops in 1861 because it was not a crime to do so at that time, neither could he be found guilty indirectly of the crime of aiding and abetting the Confederate troops by penalizing him for his refusal to state this in an oath in 1865. The penalty, the counsel emphasized, was severe—the loss of his profession.

The attorneys for Cummings closed by stating that the laws prescribing the test oath as they applied to Cummings were clearly bills of attainder and ex post facto laws, and these provisions violated the U.S. Constitution. Therefore, the counsel insisted, that part of the Missouri constitution providing for the test oath should be invalidated. The attorneys requested that the court overrule the decision of the Supreme Court of Missouri, which had affirmed the conviction of Cummings.

Strong and Henderson then argued on behalf of the state of Missouri. They did not attempt to meet the arguments of Cummings's counsel with reference to bills of attainder and ex post facto laws directly. Instead, they placed their emphasis upon a higher law based upon states' rights. They insisted that in cases similar to that presented by Cummings, the judicial power of the Federal government was limited to questions arising under the U.S. Constitution and did not extend to issues arising under the constitutions of the states. When it had been requested that this power be used to annul an act of a state legislature because of repugnance to the U.S. Constitution, this power had always, and should be, exercised with great caution, they argued. The conflict between the two should be "clear and palpable."

Each of the original states, the attorneys explained, originally possessed all of the attributes of sovereignty and gave up only portions of it when they formed the U.S. Constitution. They then quoted from *The Federalist Papers,* "The powers reserved to the several states will extend to all objects which, in the ordinary course of affairs, concern the lives, liberties, and properties of the people, and the internal order, improvement and prosperity of the state."[4] Among these rights reserved to the states, claimed the attorneys, was the exclusive right of each state to set the qualifications of voters and office holders and the terms and conditions governing the practice of the professions.

The counsel then argued that the test oath provisions came within the rights reserved to the states. They were neither bills of attainder nor ex post facto laws, but were merely laws designed to define who should be voters, who should hold office, who should exercise the professions, and who should mold the character of people by becoming their teachers. These laws did not relate to crimes and punishments as did the normal laws of bills of attainder and ex post facto laws, they maintained. Every private calling was subject to regulations set by the state, and the private rights associated with occupations were always subordinate to the public good.

The counsel for Missouri closed by asking the court to affirm the Supreme Court of Missouri by finding that the test oath sections in the state's constitution did not conflict with the U.S. Constitution and were therefore valid laws.

The Opinion of the Court

Justice Stephen J. Field gave the opinion of the court on January 14, 1867, ten months after the oral arguments. Following the arguments, the justices of the court had voted to delay the opinion until the following term. The oaths had become not only a seriously debated issue in an election in Missouri itself, but also the subject of dispute throughout the nation. The politics involved in these debates and discussions washed over to the Supreme Court and became a factor in the delay of the opinion, and even generated some hard feelings among the justices themselves.

Justice Field had made known his critical attitude toward test oaths while serving as a circuit judge in California. However, no challenge was made by anyone as to the possible conflict created by Field's older brother representing Cummings.

Field began his opinion by reviewing the facts of Cummings's arrest, conviction, fine, and imprisonment. Then the justice paid attention to the separate parts of the oath required by the Missouri constitution. He stated that an individual taking the oath must have attested that he did not participate in over thirty acts. Some of these "tests" were serious offenses, while several of them had never been classed as offenses in any state. Many of the tests, said the justice, were not even "blameworthy." As an example of the latter, he indicated that an oath taker had to attest that he had never "by act or word" expressed sympathy for the cause of any enemies of the United States, had never engaged in or helped anyone engage in guerrilla warfare against the loyal inhabitants, and had never entered or left a state to avoid the draft or military service.

He then laid out the penalties for not taking the oath or swearing falsely. The severity of the oath and the connected punishments, observed the justice, were without precedent. England and France had test oaths from time to time, but they were always limited to present intent and belief, whereas the Missouri oath was retrospective; it embraced all of the past right up to the day the oath was taken. In this regard, the oath not only was directed to overt and visible acts of hostility toward the government, but was intended to reach words, desires, and sympathies, making no distinction between true acts of hostility and acts based upon charity or affection. Field concluded his discussion of the oath by defining what the court's role was in the case: to determine whether the provisions of the Missouri constitution that set out the oath were in conflict with any provisions of the U.S. Constitution.

The justice then summarized the prime arguments of counsel. The attorneys for the state of Missouri insisted that the requirement to take the oath was merely a necessary qualification to occupy certain offices and practice certain professions, and that the prescribing of these qualifications fell exclusively within the powers of the state. On the other hand, the attorneys for Cummings insisted that the provisions in the Missouri constitution were adverse to that part of the U.S. Constitution that prohibited bills of attainder and ex post facto laws and were therefore void.

Field began his analysis of the issues by agreeing with the counsel for Missouri that states that existed prior to the Constitution, possessing all the attributes of sovereignty, gave up only that sovereignty necessary to form the Constitution. New states, when admitted, occupied the same position. Among the rights reserved to the states, acknowledged the justice, was the right to determine the qualifications for holding office and the conditions that must be met to exercise or practice certain professions and callings.

These qualifications as fixed by the legislatures, pointed out the justice, had to relate to the fitness of an individual to carry out the job or profession. Field then observed that he could find no relationship, for example, between Cummings leaving Missouri to avoid the draft and his fitness to administer the sacraments of his church. The states could not fix the qualifications to hold office in such a manner that they fixed a punishment for a past act that was not punishable when committed, he said. The question, therefore, was not whether the state had the power to fix qualifications for office, but whether that power in this case was an instrument for the infliction of punishment. Many of the matters that the oath taker had to state that he had not done, said the justice, had no relationship to the job. As a matter of fact, the oath was directed to reach the person, not the calling; the designated acts did not relate to the qualifications of the job or calling, but rather to the person, and if they had been committed, the person would be punished.

Field then defined punishment and whether the consequences of having committed one or more of the acts set forth in the oath was punishment. The court did not agree with the Missouri attorneys, he said, that punishment was only the deprivation of life, liberty, or property, and that anything less was not punishment. In this case, the only way that punishment could be administered was to deprive the individuals involved of several of their civil rights and privileges as citizens. Clearly, the deprivation of these rights was punishment. To back this holding, the justice cited old English statutes,[5] Blackstone, and the French Code,[6] which all had indicated that the deprivation of a citizen's rights was punishment.

The theory upon which our political institutions were based, said Field, was that all men had certain inalienable rights, such as life, liberty, and the pursuit of happiness. All avocations, positions, and honors were open to everyone, and in the protection of these rights, all were equal before the law. Any deprivation of these rights for past conduct, held the justice, was punishment and "could be in no otherwise defined." Considering that the subject oath incorporated punishments, Field restated the prime issue of the case: Was there any inhibition against the enforcement of the oath in the U.S. Constitution?

The justice then observed that the Missouri constitution was formulated during a struggle between the friends and enemies of the Union. This struggle, he said, aroused fierce passions, and the resulting constitution reflected the outcome of this struggle. He indicated that it was this type of excited action and strong and sudden passions of the states that the framers of the U.S. Constitution had intended to guard and shield the people and their property against. He then cited the provision in the U.S. Constitution that "no state shall pass any bill of attainder, ex post facto law, or law impairing the obligation of contracts."

Field then agreed with the counsel for Cummings that a bill of attainder was a legislative act inflicting punishment without a judicial trial. The oath required by the Missouri constitution, held the justice, fit precisely within that definition. The provisions requiring the oath were the legislative equivalent of exercising the power of a judge and pronouncing a party guilty without the safeguards of a judicial trial. Field then stated that if the clauses in the Missouri constitution had declared Cummings guilty of armed hostility against the United States, or that Cummings had entered the state to avoid the draft, and therefore he should be deprived of his right to be a priest, there would be no question that the law would be a bill of attainder. The provisions in the Missouri constitution obtained the same result, only it was disguised. "What cannot be done directly, cannot be done indirectly," held the justice.

The U.S. Constitution "deals with substance, not shadows," said Field, and its inhibitions were leveled at the thing, not the name. Holding on behalf of the court that the oath was a bill of attainder, the justice stated that the U.S. Constitution intended that the rights of the citizen should be secure against deprivation for past conduct by legislative enactment under any form, however disguised. If this inhibition could be evaded by form, he said, its insertion in the fundamental law of the land was a vain and futile proceeding.

Field then turned his attention to ex post facto laws. He quoted Chief Justice John Marshall that an ex post facto law was one that imposed a punishment for an act that was not punishable when committed or that imposed additional punishment to that which existed at the time the act was committed.[7] Ex post facto also applied to laws that lessened the standard of evidence necessary to convict an individual of a crime after the crime had been committed, he said. Although the Missouri constitution did not define crimes or prescribe punishment, it produced the same result upon the people affected, those who participated in or sympathized with the Rebellion. The punishment, said the justice, was to bar those people from holding certain public and private offices and from certain professions. This was no less a punishment because it could be avoided by taking an oath, because for people who could not take the oath, the punishment was absolute and perpetual. Field emphasized that it was a "misapplication of terms to call it anything else."

Many of the acts to which the oath was directed were not offenses when committed; others of the acts were offenses; but in both cases, the provisions prescribing the oath added punishment and fell into the category of an ex post facto law. In addition, the clauses of the Missouri constitution subverted the presumption of innocence and altered the rules of evidence, because they assumed a party was guilty and that party had to overcome the burden of guilt.

Innocence, said the justice, could be shown in only one way: by an "inquisition" in the form of an expurgatory oath.

Field then undertook a lengthy summation of the court's opinion. He stated that if the clauses of the Missouri constitution had been enacted as statutes by the legislature, it would be obvious that the statutes would have imposed a penalty without the formality of a judicial trial and conviction; likewise, they would have assessed penalties that did not exist when the crimes were committed. As state statutes, they obviously would have failed; so, too, must the clauses of the Missouri constitution fail. The U.S. Constitution could not be evaded in this form; if it could, said the justice, the U.S. Constitution could be evaded at pleasure.

The justice continued to drive home the point of the court. What if a man was accused of treason, and he was tried and acquitted, or if convicted, he was pardoned? If that defendant did not take the oath stating that he had never committed the acts charged, pointed out the justice, he would be further punished. And further, what if the current minority in Missouri should gain control of the state in the next election? Could they require an oath from the citizens of Missouri as a qualification for certain jobs and professions that they never supported this oath? If the people involved refused the oath, said the justice, they would be permanently barred from all positions and be deprived of all political and civil rights.

Field closed with extensive quotations of statements that supported the court's opinion made by Alexander Hamilton as counsel in a New York case.[8] He also cited *The Matter of Dorsey*,[9] where views similar to those expressed in this opinion by Field were consolidated and presented with great force.

Justice Field then ordered that the judgment of the Supreme Court of Missouri upholding the oaths be reversed, and that the case be remanded to that court with directions to enter a judgment reversing the Circuit Court's judgment that found Cummings guilty. Field further ordered that court to discharge Cummings from prison without delay.

Despite the firm severity and conciseness of the court's opinion, Chief Justice Salmon P. Chase and Justices Samuel Miller, Noah Swayne, and David Davis dissented. Miller wrote a dissent for the minority that applied to both this case and the *Garland* case, which is considered next. Miller's dissent appears at the conclusion of that case.

THE *GARLAND* CASE

Augustus H. Garland was a native of Little Rock, Arkansas. In the December 1860 term of the U.S. Supreme Court, Garland was admitted as an attorney and counselor able to practice before the court. He satisfied the qualifications to practice before the court contained in Rule 2 of the court. These were that he must have been admitted to practice before the Supreme Court of Arkansas for the preceding three years, and that his private and professional character had to be acceptable. The oath Garland was required to take upon his admission incorporated a commitment that he would demean himself uprightly and according to law as an attorney of the court, and that he would support the U.S. Constitution.

In May 1861, the legislature of the state of Arkansas passed an ordinance that withdrew the state from the Union. This was followed by a second ordinance the same year that attached Arkansas to the Confederate States of America. As a citizen of Arkansas, Garland had no choice but to participate in these events. He ultimately became a member of the Confederate Lower House, and later he became a member of the Confederate Senate. He was a member of this Senate when the Confederate forces surrendered to the armies of the United States.

On July 2, 1862, the U.S. Congress enacted a law that required every person elected or appointed to a U.S. government office to take a special oath. That oath incorporated a swearing that the oath taker had never voluntarily borne arms against the United States or given aid or encouragement to anyone who had done so. Anyone who falsely took the oath would be guilty of perjury.

This act applied solely to Federal office holders; however, on January 24, 1865, Congress passed another law providing that no person could practice law before the U.S. Supreme Court without taking the oath set forth in the July 2, 1862, act. This also applied to other courts in the Federal system, taking effect at later times.

Then, on July 15, 1865, President Andrew Johnson granted Garland a personal full pardon and amnesty from all offenses he may have committed in connection with his participation, "direct or implied," in the Rebellion.

When it came time for Garland to resume his law practice in Little Rock, he desired to practice in all the courts to which he had previously been admitted, the Federal court system, including the U.S. Supreme Court, among them. Garland realized, however, that the oath required by the January 24, 1865, Federal act effectively terminated his right to practice in those courts because he could not truthfully take the oath.

Garland resorted to the only alternative available to him. He petitioned the Supreme Court for permission to continue his practice before it without taking the oath required by the January 25, 1865, act.[10] He explained to the court that he was unable to take the oath because he had held offices in the Confederate government. He rested his application upon two grounds: first, the Act of January 24, 1865, so far as it affected his status with the court, was unconstitutional and void; second, if this act were constitutional, he was released from compliance with its provisions by the pardon and amnesty granted him by President Johnson.

Because the court controlled who could practice before it, Garland was able to petition the court directly and not file a formal legal case. Those who were admitted to the court became officers of the court and possessed the right to petition the court directly on matters that affected their status before the court. That status was defined by the court's rules, and in Garland's case, by the Federal law. The petition was argued before the court two times: on March 14, 1866, and on December 15, 1866.

The Arguments before the Court

Garland first argued to the court on his own behalf. His first argument concerned the nature of the president's right to pardon. He stated to the court that though there were no direct case authorities on the subject, it was obvious from the very nature of the Constitution that, except for cases of impeachment, the power to pardon was unqualified. Therefore, Congress could pass no law that could abridge the pardoning powers of the president.

The effect of the pardon granted to him was to absolve him from penalties for the offenses, Garland explained, just as though he had never committed them. Congress, by applying the oath to him, subjected him to penalties for offenses that the president said, in effect, that he had not committed; therefore, the oath fettered the president's right to pardon and was unconstitutional. In support of this analysis, Garland cited Joseph Story in his *Commentaries on the Constitution* and a former U.S. attorney general, John J. Crittenden.

Next, Garland argued that he was being deprived of his property without due process of law in violation of the Fifth Amendment to the Constitution. He defined a penalty from a popular law dictionary of the time as "a punishment imposed by a statute as a consequence of the commission of a certain specified offense." Certainly the January 25, 1865, act imposed a penalty if the acts cited in it were committed. An additional trouble with that, he went on, was that many of the offenses listed in the oath had not been offenses at the time they were committed. Quoting the famed American jurist Chancellor James Kent, Garland insisted that a retrospective statute changing vested rights was founded upon unconstitutional principles and was inoperative and void. The application of this statute to him deprived him of his livelihood without due process of law. Garland lectured the court that this feature of our Constitution was borrowed from the Magna Carta, where "law of the land" was substituted with "due process of law."

Garland concluded his argument by pointing out to the court that the January 24, 1865, act could also be interpreted as a bill of attainder. When Garland completed his argument, Reverdy Johnson, who had previously represented Cummings, and Matt H. Carpenter presented additional arguments to the court in Garland's behalf.

They first reminded the court that the president had given Garland a full pardon of the offenses. The constitutional effect of this pardon, they argued, was to restore to Garland all of his rights, civil and political, fully and in every respect, as though Garland had never committed the offenses. They reminded the justices that prior to the Rebellion, Garland had been a respected member of the Supreme Court bar.

Johnson and Carpenter quoted again the constitutional provision granting the right of pardon to the president. They added as emphasis a quotation of Alexander Hamilton in *The Federalist,* "As the sense of responsibility is always the strongest in proportion as it is undivided . . . the benign prerogative of pardoning should be as little as possible fettered or embarrassed."[11] They quoted

Hamilton a second time to the effect that it was most important that the president's right of pardon extended to the crime of treason.

The attorneys then cited Chief Justice John Marshall that the president's pardoning power should be interpreted similarly to how the pardoning power was interpreted in England because of the close resemblance of the judicial institutions. Quoting from English texts and cases, they argued that the law of England held that a pardon discharged not only the punishment for the crime, but also the guilt of the offense itself, the offender being declared as innocent as if he had never committed the offense.

Quoting the recent attorney general of the United States, James Speed, that a pardon should be liberally construed and that the person receiving it was entitled to all of its benefits, Johnson and Carpenter contrasted this with the January 24, 1865, act, which, they insisted, subjected Garland to punishment for the pardoned crime. This forced Garland to answer for a crime without the presentment of an indictment by a grand jury and to be a witness against himself. This subjected him, they argued, to deprivation of life, liberty, and property without due process of law, all in violation of the U.S. Constitution.

Attorney General Henry Stanbery appeared on behalf of the United States. Either he did not make an oral argument, or if he did so, it was not recorded in the reports.

The Opinion of the Court

The opinion of the court was given by Justice Stephen J. Field on January 14, 1867, the same day he gave the court's decision in the *Cummings* case. The court split by the same five-four vote in both cases, with Justices Nathan Clifford, Samuel Nelson, Robert C. Grier, and James M. Wayne voting with Field in the majority. Chief Justice Salmon P. Chase and Justices Noah Swayne and David Davis voted in the minority with Justice Samuel Miller, whose elaborate dissent, though filed with this case, applied to both cases.

Justice Field first reviewed what he believed to be the true nature of the oath. He acknowledged that Garland could not take the oath; therefore, for him, the oath operated as a legislative decree of perpetual exclusion from his profession. Such an exclusion for past conduct, observed the justice, was a punishment. Being legislatively administered, it was in the nature of the ancient English idea of pains and penalties and was subject to the constitutional inhibition against bills of attainder. Also, insofar as the statute imposed a punishment for acts that were not punishable at the time they were committed, or added punishment for these acts, both of which the statute accomplished, the law was brought within the definition of an ex post facto law, which was also prohibited by the Constitution.

Field then explored the nature of a membership in the Supreme Court Bar. He indicated that the admission or exclusion of an individual from that bar was not a ministerial function, but rather the exercise of judicial power. As such, it was solely within the jurisdiction of the courts as to who could be admitted or excluded. One could not be excluded at the pleasure of the court or the command of the legislature, but only by the judgment of the court based upon moral or professional delinquency. Rather, the question here, said Field, was not whether Congress had the right to prescribe qualifications for admission to the Supreme Court bar, but whether that power had been exercised as a means for the infliction of punishment. This could not be done, held the justice, stating that he had already set out the basis for this in the *Cummings* case. The reasoning there, he said, applied equally to this case.

This point of view was strengthened, said the justice, when the nature of the pardon and the pardoning power of the president were considered. He then quoted from Article II, Section 2 of the Constitution that the president "shall have power to grant reprieves and pardons for offenses against the United States except in cases of impeachment." This power, he said, was unlimited except in cases of impeachment. It extended to every offense known in the law, and it could be exercised at any time after the offense was committed. Furthermore, this power of the president was not subject to legislative control; Congress could neither limit the effect of a pardon nor exclude any offender from its exercise.

Agreeing fully with the arguments presented by Garland and the attorneys who appeared on his behalf, Field said that a pardon reached both the punishment and the guilt of the offender; that when a pardon was full, the offender was as innocent as if he had never committed the offense. Therefore, President Johnson's pardon of Garland relieved him of all penalties and disabilities attached to the offense of treason, and Garland was placed beyond the reach of punishment of any kind.

Field then held that to prevent Garland from practicing his profession by reason of his offense was to punish him for the offense notwithstanding the pardon. The oath provided for in the act of January 24, 1865, in effect indirectly avoided the pardon, and, said the justice, that which could not accomplished directly, could not be accomplished indirectly. Garfield therefore could not be subjected to the oath required by the January 24, 1865, law, Field held on behalf of the court.

Justice Field then ordered that Garland's petition be granted and held that the court rule that followed the law and initiated the oath had been "unadvisedly adopted" and was rescinded. In so doing, the court ruled that the January 24, 1865, act, insofar as it required the subject oath to be taken by members of the Federal bar and punished those who were deprived of their jobs and positions because they could not truthfully take the oath, was unconstitutional.

Justice Samuel Miller then presented a lengthy dissent that applied not only to this case but to the *Cummings* case as well. Approaching his fifth year on the court, Miller had already earned a reputation for a keen intellect and a strong feeling that the Union should be preserved. At times, he was most eloquent in expressing his views, and some of this eloquence together with his sharp wit came through in this dissent.

Miller first lamented the need for such a law as the act requiring the subject oath. He stated that he hoped for a "speedy return of that better spirit, which shall leave us no cause for such laws," and that all good men looked to that time "with anxiety, and with hope, I trust, not altogether unfounded." The justice then referred to the power of the court to declare that Congress, or a legislative body of a state, had exceeded the Constitution, and thus rendered void its attempt at making legislation, as "an extremely delicate power." Such an incompatibility with the Constitution should be so clear as to leave little reason for doubt before the court used this power, he continued. He was unable to see this incompatibility in either the act of Congress or in the constitution of the state of Missouri, and therefore he would place his dissent, and the reasons for it, on the record.

The practice of law was a privilege, not a right, said Miller, and every state had passed laws making this privilege dependent upon good moral character and professional skill. Under these conditions, the justice asked, could not Congress require an oath to show whether an individual possessed the proper qualifications? The oath required by the law was nothing more than the same oath required of every officer of the government. The oath merely required one to swear that he had not committed treason, and that he would bear faithful allegiance to the Constitution in the future. These were the most essential qualifications required of every lawyer, and this seemed too clear for argument, he observed. "To suffer treasonable sentiments to spread here unchecked, is to permit the stream on which the life of the nation depends, to be poisoned at its source," exclaimed the justice.

Miller then discussed bills of attainder. He indicated that he was not aware of any decision of a Federal court that defined a bill of attainder; therefore, to determine just what the Constitution prohibited, it would be necessary to examine what bills of attainder were in the English Parliament. Initially, bills of attainder in that body, explained the justice, were statutes declaring the blood of certain people to be corrupted. They were declared to be attained, and as such, they lost all heritable quality. This, said the justice, was what our Constitution prohibited.

Later, there were other matters that became classified as bills of attainder, the justice acknowledged. These included legislative convictions and sentences that were determined by no fixed rules of evidence. He then observed that neither the January 24, 1865, act of Congress nor the Missouri constitution incorporated a corruption of blood law, and they did not provide for a conviction and sentence of any designated person or group of persons. The justice further stated that the oath applied to all persons, and none were compelled to take it. A statute that did not designate a criminal, declared no guilt, did not pronounce a sentence, and inflicted no punishment could in no sense be called a bill of attainder, he concluded.

Ex post facto laws, unlike bills of attainder, had been well defined by the court and left no room for controversy, said Miller. He then summarized ex post facto laws as laws that made an innocent act when committed a criminal act and provided for punishment, laws that made the punishment greater than when the act was committed, and laws that made the rules of evidence more liberal than when the act was committed. These laws, said the justice, applied to criminal cases only. In nearly all respects, the laws providing for the subject oath created a civil proceeding, not a criminal one. Not being criminal in nature, these oath laws could not be ex post facto laws, Miller concluded.

The justice then made several observations that contradicted the conclusions of the court majority. He indicated that the "fatal vice" in the reasoning of the majority was the meaning they gave to punishment. He said that the majority applied punishment as synonymous with chastisement, or suffering of the party being punished, whereas the legal definition of punishment was a penalty inflicted for the commission of crime.

Those guilty of the offenses listed in the oath were, by the laws in force at the time, liable to be punished by death and the confiscation of their property, said the justice. By a law passed since the offenses were committed, they were liable to the "enormous" additional punishment of being deprived of the right to practice law. This was not punishment, asserted the justice, but merely a qualification that must be met in order to practice law before the court. It was a dictate of good sense, he said, that a person who had borne arms against the government while a citizen thereof should forfeit the right to appear in her courts. Such a person was unfit to be an officer of the court, and his name should be struck from the rolls if it was found there. The purpose of the act was to require loyalty as a qualification of all who practiced law in the national courts, said the justice, not to impose a punishment for past acts of disloyalty.

Miller went on to observe that the majority of the court believed that no requirement could be a qualification to practice before the court unless it was attainable by all, and a qualification that was not attainable by all was, in actuality, a punishment. He explained that there were many qualifications for various positions that could not be satisfied by everyone. For example, the Constitution provided that a candidate for president and vice president must be native-born citizens. Was this, asked the justice, a punishment to those who could never comply with that qualification? The constitutions of all the states specified that one must be a white male citizen to be qualified to vote. Was this, he asked, a punishment to all blacks, who could never be white? Many states prescribed that to be qualified to become a judge, one had to be under sixty years of age; many of our ablest lawyers could never qualify, said the justice. Was this punishment? Furthermore, the history of the act, and the fact that it was passed in the darkest hour of the country's great struggle, clearly showed that the law was purely meant to be a qualification and not to be a punishment for past offenses.

He then discussed the effect of the presidential pardon given to Garland. Assuming he was correct in that the requirement of the oath was a qualification, not a punishment, Garland would not be relieved from taking the oath by virtue of the pardon. The pardon relieved Garland from punishment; however, if the oath was not punishment, but rather a qualification to practice, the pardon could not possibly absolve Garland from the necessity of taking it.

Justice Miller ended what was one of the more eloquent minority opinions up to that time by stating that Chief Justice Chase and Justices Swayne and Davis concurred with him in the opinion.

Thus Augustus H. Garland was restored, or more accurately, remained, an active member of the Supreme Court bar, and he could continue to practice before the other Federal courts. Garland did an admirable job in the preparation of his case and in working with the other attorneys who represented him. This was possibly one of the incidents that launched Garland on his distinguished career. He became governor of Arkansas and was elected U.S. senator from Arkansas. Later, he was appointed the attorney general of the United States in the first administration of President Grover Cleveland.

THE *WILSON* CASE

The Captured and Abandoned Property Act passed by Congress on March 12, 1863, applied to properties seized in the Confederacy by the military authorities of the United States. Although it applied to properties that could aid the Confederate cause, it made no difference whether the owner of the property was an enemy or had remained loyal to the North. The property was turned over to the U.S. treasurer without the necessity of a judicial proceeding.

Treasury agents supervised the sale of the property, but no divestiture of title was made at that time, because the law provided that the United States should be trustee of the sale proceeds for two years following the end of the war. If, within that period, the owner filed a claim for the proceeds in the U.S. Court of Claims and demonstrated to the court that he had remained loyal to the United States, he would be entitled to the sale receipts less expenses.

The showing of loyalty by a claimant was an essential requirement to be entitled to the payment of the funds. If, however, a claimant had received one of the presidential pardons and amnesties, his rights were totally restored. This included his rights to own property or have his property restored to him. The Court of Claims, interpreting the effect of the oaths strictly, began to hold in favor of claimants solely on the basis of their having taken an oath under one of the president's pardons and amnesties or having been subject to the president's blanket pardon and amnesty of 1868.

Many members of Congress began to take a dim view of this approach by the Court of Claims. These members found a way to express their dissatisfaction in the 1871 appropriations act, which provided for the necessary funds to run the legislative, executive, and judicial branches of the government for the year ending June 30, 1871. Those disaffected members of Congress added a proviso that was little noted by the public and even failed to draw the attention of some members of Congress.

This proviso radically changed how the Court of Claims should treat a claimant's proof of loyalty by altering the effect of the presidential pardons and amnesties. Thereafter, if a presidential pardon or amnesty acknowledged that a claimant had committed acts of disloyalty, and the claimant, in accepting the pardon in writing and taking the oath, did not disclaim these acts, this constituted conclusive evidence that the acts had indeed been committed. The Court of Claims no longer had jurisdiction to hear the case, and the case was to be dismissed. This proviso not only disallowed a presidential pardon from being a substitute for proving loyalty, but it also used these pardons themselves as proof that a claimant had been disloyal. Therefore, the proceeds from the sale of the property would be forfeited.

In the summer of 1863, a series of facts began that forced the U.S. Supreme Court to consider the validity of the provisions of this proviso. During that summer, 664 bales of cotton were taken into possession by agents of the Treasury Department under the Abandoned and Captured Property Act of 1863. The cotton was owned by Victor F. Wilson, and the sales proceeds of $125,300 from the sale of the cotton were held in trust for him by the U.S. treasurer as provided in the 1863 act. In the year following the capture of the cotton, Wilson took an oath pursuant to a pardon and an amnesty granted by the president.

Wilson died before he could take any steps toward filing a claim. John A. Klein became his surviving administrator. Klein had a firm belief, based upon past cases, that Wilson was entitled to the proceeds from the sale of the cotton. Therefore, he filed a suit on his behalf in 1866 with the U.S. Court of Claims.

Despite the finding by the Court of Claims that Wilson had acted as surety in 1862 and 1863 on two official bonds of military officers in the Confederate army, the Court of Claims entered a decree that Klein was entitled to the proceeds of the cotton. The decree was entered on May 26, 1869, and was based on the oath taken by Wilson pursuant to the presidential pardon and amnesty in 1864. The Court of Claims subsequently denied a motion for a new trial filed by the attorneys for the United States.

The United States then appealed to the Supreme Court. The appeal was filed on December 11, 1869. Seven months later, the troublesome proviso was passed by Congress as a tag-on to the 1871 appropriations bill. Under this proviso, the fact that Wilson had been a surety on the bonds of the Confederate officers was conclusive evidence that he had aided and abetted the Rebellion. With this finding, a strict interpretation of the proviso would dictate that the Supreme Court did not have jurisdiction to continue with the case. Therefore, the U.S. attorneys filed a motion to dismiss the case as supplementary to the appeal. The case came to the Supreme Court under the title *United States, Appt., v. John A. Klein, Surviving Admr. of Victor F. Wilson, Deceased.*[12]

The Arguments before the Court
The United States as the appealing party was represented by the attorney general, A. T. Akerman; T. H. Talbot, from the attorney general's office; and B. H. Bristow, the solicitor general of the United States. Victor F. Wilson's estate was represented by the firm of Bartley & Carey, R. W. Corwine, T. D. Lincoln, and

J. M. Carlisle. Apparently a man by the name of McPherson assisted on the brief. The individuals listed could have been part of the firm or have been practicing on their own. There was no evidence in the case reports that T. D. Lincoln had any relationship to President Lincoln's family.

The attorneys representing the United States first explained to the court that they were not prosecuting the appeal under the original filing. Since the proviso under the 1871 appropriations act was passed on July 12, 1870, they were filing a motion to dismiss the case under the proviso. Under the terms of the proviso, they argued, the Supreme Court did not have jurisdiction of the case. All the Supreme Court had a right to do, they insisted, was to send the dispute back to the Court of Claims with instructions to dismiss the suit.

The U.S. attorneys went on to argue that the only manner in which an individual could draw money from the Treasury was under the provisions of congressional statutes; the court had no independent authority to authorize such withdrawals. The proviso in the 1870 act, they argued, merely limited some people's ability to draw funds from the Treasury; it had nothing to do with limiting the president's powers of pardon.

The attorneys then explained to the court that only the incidents associated with presidential pardons at the time of the adoption of the Constitution could not be altered or abolished by legislative acts. For example, voting and the ability to testify in court were not rights restored by a presidential pardon in 1789. Likewise, the right to recover the proceeds of an enemy's property captured in war was not restored by a presidential pardon in 1789. Therefore, the attorneys closed, the claims of Wilson's estate that the provisions in the proviso were beyond the powers of Congress to pass were not a valid argument. They requested the court to dismiss the case from the Supreme Court docket and order the Court of Claims to do the same.

The counsel for the Wilson estate then attempted to answer the assertions of the government attorneys plus added further arguments that the U.S. attorneys had failed to treat. First, they asserted that the Constitution provided that the executive authority of the government was vested in the president. Part of this executive authority, they explained, was the power to grant reprieves and pardons for offenses against the United States. The attorneys then quoted from *Ex Parte Garland* that this power was not subject to legislative control.

Wilson's attorneys then argued that the act of July 12, 1870, nullified the amnesty given to Wilson by the president and deprived him of the right to receive the proceeds from the sale of his cotton under the provisions of the Abandoned and Captured Property Act. To sustain the proviso in the July 12, 1870, act, the court would have to hold that instead of Congress and the president being independent coordinate branches of government, the president was merely a dependent and subordinate appendage to a sovereign Congress. If this were the case, the division of powers in the Constitution was a "chimera and a delusion."

The provisions in the proviso were unconstitutional, they maintained. These provisions were ex post facto laws in that they altered the evidence necessary to convict after the commission of the offenses. This could not be challenged because the proviso's provisions did not relate to crimes, they asserted, as *Ex Parte Garland* specifically overruled this claim.

In addition, argued Wilson's counsel, the provisions in the proviso were void because they deprived the claimant of his property without due process of law. They quoted Chief Justice Salmon P. Chase in *United States v. Padelford*[13] that after a pardon, no offense connected with the Rebellion could be imputed to that individual, and that the law made simple proof of a pardon a complete substitute for proof that Wilson gave no aid or comfort to the Rebellion.

Furthermore, the proviso in the July 12, 1870, act was unconstitutional because it was a legislative usurpation of the powers and function of the judiciary, they asserted. If the proviso's provisions were valid, the judiciary would shrink into a mere instrument of Congress. "Congress can neither exercise judicial power nor refuse to vest it in the courts," they pointed out.

The counsel for the Wilson estate wound up their argument by stating that this was a case arising under the Constitution and the laws of the United States in which jurisdiction was given to the Supreme Court. Therefore, the case could not, and should not, be dismissed.

The Opinion of the Court

Chief Justice Salmon P. Chase, who had voted with the dissent in the *Cummings* and *Garland* cases, gave the opinion of the court in a seven-two decision. Chase first identified the question of the case as whether the proviso in the July 12, 1870, statute barred the Wilson estate from recovering the proceeds from the sale of Wilson's cotton.

The chief justice then reviewed the four classes of seized properties and how the owners of those properties could be divested of their titles. This review was a summary of the more detailed explanation set forth in chapter 12. Chase noted that, except for property captured in actual hostilities, judicial proceedings that led to judgments were required to divest owners of their titles. In addition, the United States recognized to the fullest extent the "humane maxims of the modern law of nations" that exempted private property of noncombatant enemies from capture as booty of war. Even the law of confiscation was sparingly applied, he added.

Then the chief justice discussed the Abandoned and Captured Property Act, which governed the determination of the case. There had been no similar legislation in history, he observed. Under the provisions of that act, all property abandoned by its owners or captured by the United States was turned over to agents of the Treasury Department and sold. The United States became trustee of the funds, so there was no change of ownership of the property if the owners were loyal or if they became loyal and followed the procedures set forth in the law.

The government was trustee first to those who never gave aid or comfort to the enemy, said Chase, and consequently the right to recover funds was dependent upon the proof of loyalty. But it was also implied that there may be proof of ownership without proof of loyalty, and whether restoration of funds would be made to others was left to be determined by public policy that would be subsequently developed.

The president's Proclamation of March 26, 1864, said Chase, offered full pardon with rights of ownership of properties to those who voluntarily came forward and took the oath. Wilson took this oath, observed the chief justice, and it was the government's decision to determine whether the proceeds of the sale of the cotton should be returned to him. The promise of the restoration of the rights of property after taking the oath decided that question in the affirmative. As long as those pardoned made application within the two years from the close of the war, as dictated by the statute, they were entitled to the proceeds as an absolute right, the chief justice held on behalf of the court.

Chase went on to elaborate that the return of funds was promised for "an equivalent." That was that the pardon and restoration of political rights were in return for the oath and its fulfillment. The chief justice disclosed the importance that the court placed upon this holding by stating that to refuse the restoration would be a breach of faith not less "cruel and astounding" than an abandonment of the freed people who had been promised their freedom.

He then posed the question of what effect the proviso had on the decision of the court. The substance of the proviso, he said, was that an acceptance by an individual of a pardon without a disclaimer of the unlawful acts that were recited in the pardon would be conclusive proof of the acts pardoned. This would cancel the pardon and remove jurisdiction of the Court of Claims and the Supreme Court to even consider this type of applications for the proceeds.

Congress had complete control over the existence of the Court of Claims, the chief justice explained. Congress had created this court as a true court with jurisdiction over contracts between the government and citizens of the country, with appeal to the Supreme Court. If Congress had simply denied the right of appeal in a designated class of cases, he continued, this would have been a valid exercise of power. The language of the proviso, however, showed very plainly that Congress was withholding the right to appeal as a means to an end. That end, the chief justice continued, was to deny that presidential pardons had the effect in these cases that the Supreme Court had adjudged them to have—that pardons should have the same effect as proof of loyalty. The proviso stated that claims founded upon such pardons had no merit, and the Court of Claims and the Supreme Court were without jurisdiction to even consider them. Indeed, the courts were instructed to accept the pardons as conclusive proof that disloyal acts had been committed, the chief justice wryly observed.

Chase continued his analysis by stating that what Congress had done was not part of its powers to prescribe regulations governing the appellate powers of the courts, but was rather an interference with the court's powers to conduct its trials or appeals based upon the laws and evidence before them. The courts, said the chief justice, were forbidden to give effect to evidence in accordance with their findings, but were required to give effect to the evidence that was contrary to their findings.

The chief justice then held that Congress had inadvertently crossed the limit that separated the legislative from the judicial power. It was extremely important, he held, that these powers be kept distinct based upon the Constitution. He then added an observation that had obviously bothered him throughout his opinion: Congress had provided the Supreme Court with jurisdiction to handle appeals; could it now prescribe a rule that required the court to deny itself jurisdiction because the result would be adverse to the government?

The chief justice felt compelled to add that the rule prescribed by Congress impaired the effect of presidential pardons, thus infringing upon the constitutional powers of the president. It was clear, he said, that the legislature could not change the effect of a pardon any more than an executive could change the law.

Chief Justice Chase brought his opinion to a close with an unusual statement: "It is impossible to believe that this provision was not inserted in the appropriation bill through inadvertence." He then held that the true intent of the legislature would be best fulfilled by denying the motion to dismiss and affirming the Court of Claims, which was accordingly done.

This was undoubtedly the first, and possibly the only, time that the Supreme Court declared a statute invalid and void because Congress really did not intend to pass it. Possibly Chase was moved by Miller's dissent in the *Cummings* and *Garland* cases, in which he announced that the holding of a statute to be unconstitutional was an extremely delicate power that should be restrained in its application. Did the chief justice hope that by holding the statute simply to be inadvertently passed he could win Miller over to the majority? If that had been the chief justice's goal, it was not achieved, because Miller wrote yet another dissenting opinion.

Justice Samuel F. Miller began his dissent by agreeing with the majority but by recognizing the court's action for what it actually was. He indicated that he agreed with the majority that the proviso in the July 12, 1870, act was unconstitutional. He agreed with the court that the presidential power of pardon was firmly based in the Constitution, and whatever may be its limits, Congress could not impair its effect by attempting to regulate how the judiciary approached the subject in its proceedings.

However, said the justice, he had other reasons for dissenting from the majority of the court. He said that the true intent of Congress in the Abandoned and Captured Property Act was that the government should be trustee of the proceeds of the sales of properties that were owned by loyal citizens, not the disloyal.

Miller then cited *United States v. Anderson*,[14] where the court had specifically held that the United States was a trustee for so much of the property that belonged to the faithful Southern people. He also cited *United States v. Padelford*,[15] where a distinction was made between the owner being pardoned before the property was seized versus after it was seized. In this case, said the justice, it was clear that if Padelford had been pardoned after the property was seized, and he had been guilty of aiding and abetting the Revolution, the United States was not a trustee for him, and the proceeds of the sale would have been forfeited to the government. A pardon in that situation could not restore that which had completely passed away. If the views in the current case before the court were sound, said Miller, he was at a loss to explain the reason for the extended argument in the *Padelford* case, which was designed to show that Padelford had availed himself of the pardon before his property was seized. It would have made no difference under the present holding, the justice maintained, if Padelford had been pardoned before or after the seizure of his property.

Justice Miller closed the dissenting opinion by stating that Justice Joseph P. Bradley concurred in the opinion.

Chapter Sixteen

The Wild West

When the war began, the vast majority of the peacetime army of the United States was stationed in the West. This army, prior to defections to the Confederacy, numbered about 13,000 officers and men. The largest number of them were distributed in small detachments to over sixty Federal posts and forts along the prominent trails and close to the initial settlements.

The duty of this army was to protect the settlers and those using the trails from Indian attacks. The Indians were fighting desperately to preserve the sources of their life: the game used for food and shelter, the prairie grasses, and their water reserves. All of these essentials to Indian existence were disappearing with the encroachment of white settlers. As the war began, the Indians became aware that they had allies in their fight against the "bluecoats." Many of them aligned themselves with the South, not because they supported the Southern cause, but for the supposed help they could receive from the South to salvage their civilization.

The military of the Confederacy did not wait long to seize this opportunity. It envisioned the Indian tribes as a force to disrupt Union communications and supply lines. From a tactical standpoint, the Confederates looked upon the Indian tribes as an aid to protect their western flank and for assistance to reach the goldfields of the West. Early on, the Confederacy sent representatives to the Indian tribes, and after several months of negotiations, treaties were consummated that brought many of the tribes into the protective arms of the Confederacy and aligned them in the fight against the North. Not all Indians joined the Confederacy; inexplicably, many maintained their independence and others remained "loyal" to the North.

With the sparse settlement and complete lack of convenient courts, not many cases were generated from the West. Yet there were some, and three that reached the U.S. Supreme Court are examined in this chapter. Two of these cases reflect problems incident to communications and supply in the West's unique environment; the third concerns a prominent Confederate officer whose assignment placed him in the West.

THE *HOLLADAY* CASE

The first case concerns a man who was very popular in the West, and indeed, in the entire country, Ben Holladay. In 1865, Holladay was the owner and proprietor of the main stage line to the Pacific. His overland route was divided into three divisions: Atchison, Kansas, to Denver; Denver to Salt Lake City; and Salt Lake City to Placerville, California. A superintendent oversaw the activities in each division, and an agent of the company called a conductor or messenger, or simply referred to as the express agent, rode with each coach in the front seat next to the driver and acted as the director of each trip. Stations along the route were placed at intervals of ten or fifteen miles. A home station was located every fifty miles. Drivers were changed at the home stations. Even though the home stations were more elaborate and had more facilities, all the improvements along the route were very crude.

During the first phase of the war, the Union troops were withdrawn to the East. This gave the Indians the opportunity to raid the stations and home stations along the routes, and they were not adequately protected again until the Federal territorial volunteers moved in. At one time, the overland routes became so dangerous that the new postmaster general, Montgomery Blair, ordered all mail to California be carried by sea until the Indian raids could be brought under control.

The case concerned an incident that took place on Holladay's stage line. Thomas W. Kennard sent a package of money destined to Central City in Colorado Territory. The package was delivered to the United States Express Company in New York City, from where it was dispatched to Atchison, Kansas. On January 2, 1865, the package was turned over to an agent of Ben Holladay's overland stage line. The money was placed in a safe made of leather and iron and carried in the stage under the protection of the line's express agent. The trip was largely uneventful until the stage reached a point about four miles east of Julesburg, Colorado.

Julesburg was a station on the express line with a log house, a stable, a telegraph office, and a warehouse. The staff at the station consisted of three or four persons. One mile west of Julesburg was a military post where forty Union troops were quartered in a fifty-foot-long adobe building. Several outbuildings also were part of the post. The men there were under the command of a captain by the name of O'Brien. In addition to their personal arms, the men had three pieces of light ordnance. East of Julesburg, about a mile distant, was Bulin's Ranch, which consisted primarily of a mud house.

At 2:00 A.M., as the stage carrying Kennard's money approached within four miles of Julesburg from the east, the stage was fired into by a large contingent of Indians consisting of Sioux, Cheyenne, and Arapaho, who were committing outrages in the area at that time. A mad race ensued, with the agent and driver maintaining what speed they could and the Indians in hot pursuit. When the stage reached Bulin's Ranch, the Indians pulled back. The agent and driver kept the stage at Bulin's Ranch until daylight, and then went on with careful eye and maximum speed to Julesburg.

They changed horses at Julesburg, then went on to the military post, where they informed Captain O'Brien of the attack. The express agent requested a military escort into Denver. O'Brien replied that he could not give them a military escort at that time. He had only forty men on duty, and they were mounting up to go fight the Indians who were in sight and appeared to number close to 1,500 warriors. O'Brien told the agent to keep the stage at the post because he thought it was unlikely that the Indians would attack there.

After the troops left, the express agent delivered and picked up mail at the post. Then, for some unexplained reason, the express agent and driver returned with the stage to Julesburg. They had no more than put the horses in the stable when they, to their horror, observed the troops rapidly retreating to the station, followed closely by the Indians. There was no time to rehitch the horses to the stage; the driver and the express agent hastily mounted horses and rode with the troopers back to the military post. The Indians stopped at the Julesburg station, robbed the stage, and broke open the safe. After rifling the safe's contents, the Indians resumed their pursuit of the troops. Getting back to the post, the troopers had just enough time to bring out their howitzers. They unleashed them on the Indians as they approached and forced them to retire to the hills. O'Brien lost fourteen men in that engagement.

It did not take long for Kennard to learn the fate of his money. He investigated the facts. When he learned that O'Brien had instructed the driver and express agent to remain at the military post and that those instructions were defied, Kennard was convinced that the men operating the stage were negligent. He filed an original suit against Ben Holladay in the Circuit Court of the United States for the Southern District of New York, asserting that Holladay was liable to pay him the money he lost because of the negligence of his stage crew.

The trial came before a jury. When it came time for the trial judge to instruct or charge the jury as to the issues that they should determine, he first told them that the Indian attack was an attack by an enemy with whom the United States was at war. Therefore, said the trial judge, the normal and ordinary responsibility of a common carrier did not apply. It followed that Holladay could be liable for the loss of the money only if the driver and express agent operating the stage were guilty of carelessness, negligence, or want of vigilance or attention that contributed to the loss.

The judge went on to instruct the jury that in making that determination, they were to judge what a "cool, self-possessed, prudent, careful man" would have done with his own property under similar circumstances, and that it was Holladay's duty to provide such a man of good judgment and forethought in such a hazardous business. The trial judge had refused to instruct the jury, as requested by Holladay's counsel, that Kennard had the burden of proving fraud or collusion of Holladay with the Indians; that if the express agent had exercised his best judgment, Holladay could not be charged with negligence; and that the only way Holladay could be found liable would be for the jury to find willful negligence in connection with the stolen property. The trial judge thought that these instructions did not conform to the proper legal standards in this situation, because the standard of care that Holladay had to meet was higher than that indicated in his counsel's request.

The jury found in Kennard's favor under the charges and instructions given to the jury by the trial judge. Kennard was granted a judgment in the amount of his loss; the exact figure was not revealed in the reports. Holladay's counsel promptly appealed to the U.S. Supreme Court. The case came to the Supreme Court under the title *Ben Holladay, Plff. in Err., v. Thomas W. Kennard.*[1]

The Arguments before the Court

The case was argued to the court on October 23, 1871. H. M. Ruggles represented Holladay, and W. W. McFarland and Joseph Larocque represented Kennard.

Ruggles argued on Holladay's behalf that the charge to the jury by the trial judge describing Holladay's standard of care as that of a prudent man was too high. He explained that the law was that a common carrier, which included an overland stage line, was relieved of all responsibility when a loss occurred from an attack of an enemy. The only exception, Ruggles insisted, was that if the express agent and driver were guilty of willful negligence that contributed directly to the loss of the money. It was serious error, he maintained, for the trial judge to refuse to give instructions to the jury in line with Holladay's counsel's request at the trial. He requested the court to overrule the trial court.

McFarland and Larocque then argued the case for Kennard. First, although a common carrier was relieved of a high standard of care if losses occurred because of an attack by an enemy, some standard of care still applied, they said, and the prudent man standard set by the trial judge's instructions to the jury was the correct standard. Under that standard, just plain, ordinary negligence of the express agent and driver would make Holladay liable for the loss of Kennard's money. Certainly, they maintained, Holladay's men were careless and negligent when they left the safety of the military post after being charged by Captain O'Brien to remain there. In addition, unhitching the horses and stabling them after returning to Julesburg only enhanced the negligence. Furthermore, they argued, Holladay was negligent in not hiring a responsible man as the express agent. McFarland and Larocque closed their argument by requesting the court to affirm the judgment of the trial court.

The Opinion of the Court

The opinion of the court was given by Justice Joseph P. Bradley on November 6, 1871. The justice opened his opinion by reviewing the facts of the case in great detail, including the background information and some history of the overland stages and the routes they traveled. He also mentioned the war activities of the Indians and referred to them as "enemies" throughout his opinion.

Bradley then reviewed the charges and instructions to the jury that the trial judge made, including the instructions that were requested by Holladay's attorney, but denied. It was very apparent at this point that the court would affirm or overturn the trial court on the basis of the validity of these instructions and charges.

The justice then summarized the trial judge's charge to the jury. This charge stated, according to the justice, that although a common carrier, such as a stagecoach company running stages on the overland trail, was not responsible for the destruction or loss of goods by the act of a public enemy, the company was, nevertheless, bound to use due diligence to prevent such destruction or loss. If negligence of the company or want of proper attention contributed to the loss, the stage company would be liable. All this charge exacted of the express agent, continued the justice, was that he should have used the care and attention that he would have given naturally to his own goods—that is, ordinary care and attention.

The justice held on behalf of the court that it was not necessary that there should have been fraud or collusion on behalf of the express agent with the Indians, or willful negligence on the part of Holladay's agents, to render Holladay liable. All the trial court required to make Holladay's company liable was the failure to use ordinary care. This was the correct standard, held the justice. Whether or not such negligence was proven, he went on, was properly left to the determination of the jury.

The only doubt as to the accuracy of the trial court judge's charge to the jury was the degree of care and attention required of Holladay in the selection of the express agent, he said. The trial court held that it was Holladay's duty to provide a cool, self-possessed, prudent man of good judgment and forethought to perform his job in those hazardous business conditions. "Now surely," said the justice, "no one would think of employing a man wanting in any one of those qualifications to carry his own goods across the plains at that time."

However, said the justice, ordinary diligence is a relative term. It would not be a want of ordinary care or diligence to entrust the shoeing of a horse to a common blacksmith, but it would have been gross negligence to entrust such a person with the cleaning or repair of a watch. Or a man who would be competent to perform the duties of an express agent on the commodious express car of the new Union Pacific Railroad might have been an unfit and incompetent agent in 1865 when nothing but a small mail coach traversed the prairie and roving bands of Indians infested the route.

Justice Bradley then held that whether the express agent in charge on this occasion was such a man as should have been employed could only be judged by what he did or neglected to do. This was fairly left to the jury to determine this. That jury had determined that Holladay's agents were negligent and that Holladay himself was negligent in his failure to hire a proper agent, and the Supreme Court accepted these findings and therefore affirmed the judgment of the trial court.

Ben Holladay was held to be liable to Thomas W. Kennard for the loss of Kennard's money. The vote of the court was unanimous.

THE *GRANT* CASE

A more encompassing problem than the individual raids upon the overland stages was the supplying of the U.S. military posts in the West. Protecting the people using the trails and in the settlements placed these posts on a war footing. The men stationed at these posts required not only the necessities of life, but also arms and ammunition, as well as feed for their animals. For certain of these posts, this was an overwhelming task.

For example, the posts in Arizona had little or no local sources to provide the needed supplies. These supplies could only be transported from long distances. The California coastal sources were 500 miles distant, Yuma was 240 miles away, St. Louis was approximately 1,200 miles off, and Lavaca on the Texas Gulf coast was a hard trip of 1,400 miles after a lengthy and dangerous sea journey. A comparatively convenient source of supplies was the Mexican ports on the Gulf of California. However, this source became unreliable as the war progressed because of the fighting between the French and Mexican forces in Sonora.

Several of the routes to Arizona were over famous and well-used trails. Shipments from St. Louis joined the Santa Fe Trail in the middle of Missouri. Continuing south from Santa Fe, the trail joined the routes running west from the Texas coast to form the Gila Trail. The route from Lavaca on the Texas coast also joined the Gila Trail at this point. As the war began, terror reigned along these trails because of the impossibility of protecting wagon trains from Indian attacks and from capture by the newly formed Texas militia. No matter how supplies were assigned to reach the Arizona posts, many disputes arose among the government, the supply contractors, the freighters, the Indians, and the new militias. One such dispute reached the U.S. Supreme Court.

This dispute began on March 9, 1860, when the secretary of war issued an order to the quartermaster general and the commissary general of subsistence. This order granted two men, T. W. Tailafero and W. S. Grant, who owned a freighting and supply business in New York, the privilege of furnishing all the needed supplies to the Arizona military posts for a period of two years. The prices of the supplies were stated in the order, and Tailafero and Grant were expected to deliver the supplies to the posts. This order amounted to a contract between these gentlemen and the U.S. government. Shortly after the issuance of this order, Grant purchased Tailafero's interest in the business.

On July 29, 1860, the commissary officer in Arizona requested Grant to ship certain supplies to the posts. On September 22, 1860, the War Department approved the requisition and specified that for the convenience of Grant, the requested supplies would be inspected for approval prior to shipment in New York rather than at the points of destination. The inspection took place under the guidance of a Major Eaton, and the goods were found to be of acceptable kind and quality and were packed in strong, sound, full-hooped barrels and well-secured tierces. Eaton also reported that the barrels were properly marked with the correct destinations. After innumerable delays, the supplies were sent by ship to Lavaca, Texas. The supplies arrived safely at this port and were loaded on a large wagon train owned by Grant for the overland trip to Arizona.

The problem that Grant and his freighters did not foresee was that Texas passed its ordinance of secession on February 1, 1861. Union troops in Texas surrendered, and there was no military protection afforded Grant's wagon train. The wagon train did get as far as Rio Hondo, just beyond San Antonio. At this point, however, it was captured by the new armed forces of the state of Texas. The capture was made without a serious fight on April 20, 1861. Not only were the supplies captured, but the Texas militia also took possession of the wagons and teams that made up the wagon train.

Assessing his position and that he had no control over the start of the war, Grant determined that the War Department remained liable for the supplies and his loss of the teams and wagons. He made demand upon the War Department to pay him on the basis that the government had accepted the goods when it inspected them in New York. This approach did conform to how some other contracts had been handled with his company. Grant took the approach that the actual payment awaited the delivery of the goods, and if, for a reason beyond his control, the goods could not be delivered, he was still entitled to payment. Not only that, Grant reasoned, if the government had not delayed the inspection, the goods would have been transported through Texas prior to the passage of its ordinance of secession. In that case, the trails would have been protected by Union troops.

The government did not agree with Grant and refused to pay him. The War Department claimed that the order would not be consummated until the supplies were actually delivered to the military posts in Arizona. Since the supplies were not so delivered, the government maintained that the loss was Grant's, because the military stationed at the posts never had an opportunity to accept delivery of the goods.

Totally frustrated by the War Department's refusal to pay, Grant filed a legal action in the U.S. Court of Claims, where he claimed payment for the order and reimbursement for his other losses and gave his reasons in support of his allegations. The government rebutted Grant's claim successfully, and the court decided in the government's favor. Grant then appealed to the U.S. Supreme Court. The case came to the court as *William S. Grant, Appt., v. The United States.*[2]

The Arguments before the Court

Arguments were made to the court on February 18, 1869. Grant retained three attorneys to represent him on this appeal: C. B. Goodrich, J. S. Black, and W. H. Lamon. The government was represented by the attorney general, W. M. Evarts; the assistant attorney general, T. L. Dickey; and E. P. Norton, a special counsel.

The attorneys for Grant first argued that the government had accepted the goods when Major Eaton inspected and marked the items and gave a certificate that the supplies were of acceptable kind and quality. At that point, insisted Grant's attorneys, the government had accepted the shipment, and Grant retained possession only for purposes of delivering the supplies. The delivery was prevented by a public enemy, and they maintained that the loss must be borne by the government. They cited several cases, as well as Emmerich de Vattel's 1760 work, *Law of Nations,* in support of their argument.

Reliance upon Vattel was unusual in that Grant's attorneys acknowledged that although Vattel agreed that someone in Grant's position should recover on principle, there did not exist a right of action against the state for "misfortunes of this nature." The attorneys carefully quoted Vattel when he stated that "the sovereign, indeed, ought to show an equitable regard for the sufferers, if the situation of his affairs will admit of it."

Grant's attorneys closed by claiming that he clearly fell within the group described by Vattel and was clearly entitled to that "equitable regard." Therefore, they concluded, Grant was entitled to be paid for the lost supplies and reimbursed for the loss of his wagons and teams. This was well within the jurisdiction of the Court of Claims, they pointed out. They respectfully requested the court to overturn the Court of Claims judgment and order it to pay Grant according to his claims filed with that court.

The attorneys from the U.S. attorney general's office then carefully laid out the government's position. They first felt it necessary to rebut two claims that Grant had asserted in his brief but had not mentioned in his oral argument. The first of these claims was based upon Secretary of War Cameron's rescission of Grant's contract. Grant claimed in his brief that if this rescission was a true severance of the contract, he was entitled to damages equal to the profit that he would have made had the contract been fulfilled. The government's attorneys maintained that this rescission had nothing to do with the case and was not a rescission at all. The rescission took place after the execution of the current order, and since there were not any outstanding orders at the time of the rescission, there was no basis for damages.

They insisted that Grant's contract simply gave him the right to supply the military posts with needed supplies. The supplies were not classified as "needed" until they were ordered, they claimed. Therefore, the rescission of the contract did not rescind anything.

The second claim was that Grant's losses were incurred because of the government's delay in inspecting the supplies in New York. There was no evidence in the case, the attorneys pointed out, as to who delayed the inspections. In fact, they argued, there was no evidence whatsoever of a delay. Further, if there had been a delay, there was no evidence that such a delay caused the damages to Grant, nor was there any finding that Grant himself had not caused the delay.

They then maintained that there was no case law directly in point supporting Grant's position that the government's inspection that approved the supplies was a contractual acceptance of the supplies.

The government's attorneys concluded their argument by insisting that Grant's claim that the government was liable for the loss of private property taken in war by the enemy could not be supported on general principles of law. Furthermore, if there was support for such a claim in the law, the Court of Claims did not have jurisdiction to hear such a case. The attorneys representing the United States asked the court to affirm the decision of the Court of Claims.

The Opinion of the Court

The decision of the court was given in an opinion written by Justice David Davis on March 15, 1869. Justice Davis first reviewed the facts leading to the case and the nature of the contract. He indicated that the obligations under the provisions of the contract were clear. He stated that it was the duty, and exclusive privilege, of Grant to furnish the supplies needed by the troopers based in Arizona. It was the government's obligation to pay for the supplies when received pursuant to the schedule of payments contained in the contract.

Davis then held that according to the terms of the contract, it was too plain for controversy that the supplies did not vest in the United States until delivered. The justice discounted Grant's argument that title to the supplies vested in the government at the time of the inspection in New York. He pointed out that the terms of the contract did not provide for such a title transfer, nor was it in the contemplation of the parties that such a transfer of the title should take place. The inspection of the goods in New York was more to the advantage of Grant than the government, Davis said. Otherwise, the inspection would not have taken place until the goods were delivered in Arizona, and this could have caused a great inconvenience to Grant. The delivery of the supplies to Arizona was agreed to by Grant, and until this was accomplished, said the justice, there was no obligation on the part of the government to pay for them.

As to whether the delay in the inspection in New York made the government liable for the loss of the goods and wagon train, Davis said that the inspection was not provided for in the contract; therefore, Grant could have elected to have the inspection upon delivery. It was up to Grant whether he would submit to the New York inspection. Furthermore, the record reflected that the prime delay in the inspection was caused by the difficulty incurred by Grant's agents in fulfilling the requisition. In addition, said Davis, there was no evidence in the record that the delay in inspection had any connection with the loss, and there was no evidence that a delay was the proximate cause of the loss.

The justice then acknowledged Grant's argument that where private property was seized by a public enemy without default by the owner, the government was bound to indemnify the sufferers. He held that the principles of public law did not sanction such a doctrine. Davis quoted Vattel, as Grant's attorneys had, that no action was available against the state for misfortunes of this nature. The justice held on behalf of the court that where property was destroyed by accident, which covered Grant's situation, the party in whom the title was vested at the time had to bear the loss. If there were equities that favored the reimbursement of Grant for his losses, Davis observed, this should be addressed to Congress; treating equities of this nature was not in the province of the judicial department.

Addressing the remaining issue created by the rescission by Secretary Cameron, Davis said that this issue would not be considered by the court, for Grant had not shown that he would have been entitled to recover damages if the rescinding order had never been made. Grant should have proven that the military posts needed certain supplies after the rescission order was made, and that he had suffered losses for not being able to fulfill that need. The justice held that Grant had failed to meet this burden.

Justice Davis closed his opinion by stating, "We cannot see that this is a case for even nominal damages; but if it is, the Court of Claims was not instituted to try such a case." He then affirmed the Court of Claims decision disallowing Grant's claims. There were no dissents from any of the other justices.

THE *BURNS* CASE

The facts leading to the final case were put in motion by a man whom the general histories of the war describe as one of the more debonair, dashing, and handsome officers of both armies: Henry Hopkins Sibley.

Sibley was a captain in the army of the United States who, before the war, was stationed in several of the western outposts. Sibley's role in the West was routine and not distinguished. However, probably prior to his assignments in the West, he had used his active mind and military experience to invent the famous Sibley conical tent and the Sibley portable stove, which was used in the tent. He succeeded in patenting the tent in 1856.

In 1858, Assistant Quartermaster General Thomas made an offer to Sibley's agent, W. E. Jones, that the United States would manufacture the tent for military use, paying Sibley a royalty of $5 for every tent made. Sibley accepted the offer, and the arrangement was approved by the War Department in February 1858. The arrangement was to last to January 1, 1859, and beyond if no notice of severance was given by either party. The government undertook the immediate manufacture of the conical tent upon the consummation of the agreement.

Just a short time later, on April 16, 1858, Sibley executed an assignment of "one-half interest in all of the benefits and net profits arising from and belonging to the invention" to William W. Burns, a fellow officer in the Union army. The royalty proved to be very profitable. The tent was unique and particularly served its purpose of protecting troopers from the elements.

The tent was round, tepeelike, and twelve to fifteen feet high. It had rope ribs spreading out from the top to hold the canvas sides. The top was conical and could hold a pipe that conveyed smoke from a portable stove, which was also of Sibley's creation. The top had a canvas cover that could be used when heat was not required or removed by a rope arrangement when the stove was in use. The door was a convenient flap that could be tied shut or open, depending on the weather. The tent could sleep up to twenty men.

The agreements among Sibley, Burns, and the War Department functioned without any problems until the war began. At that time, Sibley, having deep Southern ties with Louisiana, resigned his commission on the same day he was promoted to major. Sibley joined the Confederate army and later traveled to Richmond, where he had a long personal conference with President Jefferson Davis. Sibley emerged from that conference as a brigadier general with an assignment to raise an army in Texas, train and use that army to conquer New Mexico, and push north into the goldfields of Colorado. Then he was to advance to California and capture the Pacific Coast for the Confederacy.

Sibley did indeed raise and train an army in Texas. He succeeded in taking possession of New Mexico Territory, except for its Northern portions. There, however, on March 26 and 28, 1862, he suffered defeat when he encountered a combination of Union Regulars and the 1st Colorado Volunteer Infantry Regiment at Glorieta Pass. Sibley and his tattered army retreated ingloriously all the way back to Texas.

When Sibley resigned his commission and joined the Confederate army, the War Department stopped the payment of his half of the royalty. Because Burns remained loyal to the North and continued to serve in the Union army, advancing to a general's rank, his half of the royalty continued to be paid until December 26, 1861, at which time the payments were stopped by an order of Secretary of War Simon Cameron. Quartermaster General Montgomery C. Meigs had called Cameron's attention to a new, confusing provision in the 1861 Revised Regulations of the Army that seemed to indicate that contracts between members of the military service and the government need not be honored by the War Department. This regulation gave the secretary of war the excuse he needed to sever the entire Sibley conical tent royalty, and he took advantage of it. He ordered that no further payments thereafter be made to Burns.

Burns, handicapped by his military service, was unable to persuade the War Department to resume his payments. He delayed until the war was concluded, then he filed a legal action against the government in the U.S. Court of Claims to recover all of his unpaid royalties. At the time of the filing of the case, the United States had not paid Burns royalties on 40,497 manufactured tents. Burns sued for $2.50 on each tent, or $101,242.50.

The Court of Claims heard the case and held that the contract between the United States and Major Sibley was legal. Furthermore, the court held that it was not terminated by Secretary Cameron's order of December 26, 1861. The Court of Claims went on to hold that Sibley's assignment to Burns of half the royalty was valid. It then entered a judgment for Burns, decreeing that he was entitled to receive the amount for which he sued, $101,242.50, from the government. The people in the War Department were very upset and concerned with the judgment. They appealed the decision to the U.S. Supreme Court.[3]

The Arguments before the Court

The arguments to the court were made on October 20, 1871. The United States was represented by the U.S. solicitor general, B. H. Bristow, and Assistant Attorney Generals T. H. Talbot and C. H. Hill. Burns retained James Hughes and M. H. Carpenter.

The U.S. attorneys argued first. They maintained that the contract between Sibley and the government was contained in two letters between the representatives of both parties, and that according to the terms of those letters, when read together, the government had the right to terminate the agreement at any time.

They then set forth their belief that the agreement between Sibley and Burns was not an assignment of the patent. They explained to the court that if it were such an assignment, it should have been filed with the patent office in the manner directed by Federal law. They admitted that a lack of filing did not invalidate the agreement, but it was substantial evidence that it was not an assignment. Therefore, the assignment was in reality an agreement of partnership. If the partnership agreement gave Burns a right to receive one-half interest in the patent, it was not a legal interest owned by Burns until such an assignment of the interest took place. Since the assignment never took place, they maintained, the interest of Burns "was a mere equitable right" and did not operate as an assignment against third parties. An equitable interest, they insisted, was not a sufficient interest to give Burns the right to file a suit against the government.

The attorneys for the government went on to contend that the law was clear that a partnership between Sibley and Burns was dissolved and terminated when Sibley became a public enemy by joining the Confederate army. The dissolution of the partnership suspended the contract between Sibley and the government, and since Burns's interest could be no better than that of Sibley, they argued that any interest that Burns may have possessed was severed also. The secretary of war possessed the right to terminate Burns's rights at any time, and the secretary had every right to withhold payments from Burns, the attorneys concluded. They requested that the court reverse the judgment of the Court of Claims.

The attorneys for Burns then presented a short and concise argument on behalf of their client. They first pointed out to the court that Burns was both an owner and a partner in the tent enterprise with Sibley, and that this ownership had occurred before the patent was filed and prior to the contract with the government. The original contract with the government, they insisted, was with W. E. Jones "as agent for the Sibley tent" and was therefore an agreement with both Sibley and Burns. Thus the case in the Court of Claims filed by Burns was "well brought," they contended.

Following the discontinuing of the payments to Sibley, the act of the government in continuing the payments to Burns, they argued, created a new, separate contract with Burns. To enforce this point, the counsel for Burns brought to the attention of the court the partnership law in the United States that the treason of one partner does not forfeit the rights or property of an innocent partner. The attorneys for Burns then requested that the court affirm the decision of the Court of Claims.

The Opinion of the Court

The decision of the court was given in an opinion written by Justice Stephen J. Field on November 16, 1871. Field began by stating that based upon the facts found by the Court of Claims, the court was of the opinion that the contract between Major Sibley and the government of the United States was not prohibited by the army regulations and was therefore a valid agreement. The justice explained that the contract was properly negotiated by the government agents and approved by the secretary of war. The contract was, in fact and in law, an act of the secretary of war. The secretary was not in the military service, as contemplated by the regulation, but was a civil officer of the government in the executive department. The justice observed that to hold that the War Department could not deal with a military person if that person possessed a valuable asset that the government required would be to carry the army regulation to an "absurd extent."

There was no question as to the ownership of Sibley in the improved conical tent, said Field. The government recognized his right to the patent by dealing with him for its use. Burns had become equally interested in the patent, said the justice, and neither of the parties involved had ever expressed a desire to terminate the contract.

Field then held that the order of the secretary of war to terminate payments to Burns was not intended as a repudiation of the liability of the United States to Burns for the tents previously made or to be made. The order, said the justice, was meant to permit the rights of Burns to be interpreted by the proper judicial tribunals because of the unusual status of Sibley. If the secretary had intended to terminate the contract, Field held, something more would have been required of the secretary of war than a mere direction to withhold payments.

Whether or not Sibley had transferred one-half of the patent to Burns was not important, said the justice. The facts showed that half of the contract was clearly passed to Burns, and Burns was entitled to half of the royalty. The interest of Burns in the contract was severed from the interest of Sibley by the government's recognition of Burns's interest when it paid him the royalty separate from that of Sibley. Furthermore, said Field, the right of Burns in the contract and the compensation stipulated could not be forfeited or impaired by the disloyalty of Sibley.

The justice held that Burns was true to his allegiance to the government, and that he had served loyally in the army of the Union. His claim could therefore be presented in the Court of Claims; however, Sibley's claim was barred by his disloyalty. The claims were effectively severed, allowing that of Burns but denying Sibley's.

The rule of pleading in a common-law court that required a contract held by two to be prosecuted in both names, if they were living, had no application in this situation, said the justice. The Court of Claims was not bound by any special rules of pleading.

Justice Field held that the court could see no error in the ruling of the Court of Claims, and the judgment awarding Burns $101,242.50 was therefore affirmed by a unanimous court.

Supreme Court Justices, 1861–1871

Included here are biographies of the justices and chief justices of the Supreme Court of the United States who served at any time between the December 1861 and December 1871 terms of the court. Beginning in 1844, the opening day of the court was the first Monday of December of each year. The term of any one year included cases of the following year to the opening of the next term. The pictures of the justices are courtesy of The Foundation of the Federal Bar Association.

JAMES M. WAYNE

James M. Wayne was born in Savannah, Georgia, in 1790. He graduated from Princeton University, then called the College of New Jersey, in 1808. He studied law in Connecticut and in 1810 returned to Georgia, where he was admitted to the bar in 1811. Wayne began the private practice of law in Savannah. He was active in politics, and in 1819 he became a judge of the Savannah Court of Common Pleas. In 1822, he became a judge on the Superior Court. He was elected to the U.S. House of Representatives in 1828 and served three terms. President Jackson appointed him to the U.S. Supreme Court in 1835. When the war began, Justice Wayne did not resign from the court. The Confederacy treated him as a traitor and confiscated his property. He served on the court until 1867, the year of his death.

ROGER B. TANEY

Roger B. Taney was born in Calvert County, Maryland, on March 17, 1777. Following his graduation from Dickinson College in 1795, he studied law at Annapolis, Maryland. He was admitted to the bar in 1799. Taney practiced law in Frederick, Maryland. He served in both the Maryland House of Delegates and the Maryland Senate. He moved his practice to Baltimore and was appointed the attorney general of Maryland in 1827. Taney was a supporter of President Andrew Jackson, who appointed him attorney general of the United States in 1831. Later he was appointed secretary of the Treasury, but he was turned down by the Senate. He replaced John Marshall as chief justice of the U.S. Supreme Court in 1836 and served until 1864, the year of his death.

JOHN CATRON

John Catron was born in 1786. He had a difficult childhood, reaching majority in the state of Kentucky. He served under Gen. Andrew Jackson in the War of 1812. Catron was admitted to the bar of Tennessee in 1815 and practiced in Nashville beginning in 1818. He served as the chief justice of the highest court in Tennessee from 1831 to 1836. President Jackson appointed him to the U.S. Supreme Court, and he was sworn in on May 1, 1837. He remained on the court until his death on May 30, 1865.

SAMUEL NELSON

Samuel Nelson was born in Hebron, New York, on November 10, 1792. He graduated from Middlebury College. He studied law in Salem, New York, and was admitted to the bar in 1817. He conducted a private practice of law and became an expert in admiralty law. After serving as an associate justice on the Supreme Court of New York, Nelson became its chief justice in 1836. President Tyler appointed him to the U.S. Supreme Court in 1845. He resigned from the court in 1872 and died the following year.

ROBERT C. GRIER

Born in Cumberland County, Pennsylvania, on March 5, 1794, Robert C. Grier grew up in that state. He graduated from Dickinson College in 1812 and taught there for one year. He studied law while continuing his teaching career and was admitted to the Pennsylvania bar in 1817. He practiced law in Bloomsburg, Danville, and Allegheny City. He was appointed a judge on the Allegheny County District Court in 1833. Grier was appointed to the U.S. Supreme Court by President Polk in 1846. He served on the court for twenty-three years, until January 31, 1870. He died on September 25, 1870.

NATHAN CLIFFORD

Nathan Clifford was born in Rumney, New Hampshire, on August 18, 1803. He was educated at Haverhill Academy, New Hampshire, and at Hampton Literary Institution. He read the law in New Hampshire and began his practice in Maine in 1827. In 1830, he was elected to the legislature in Maine. Later he served as attorney general of Maine and in the U.S. House of Representatives. President Polk appointed him attorney general of the United States in 1846. Clifford returned to Maine and resumed his practice in 1849. In 1857, the president appointed him to the U.S. Supreme Court. Clifford served on the court until 1880. He died the next year.

NOAH H. SWAYNE

Born in Frederick County, Virginia, on December 7, 1804, Noah H. Swayne was educated in Waterford, Virginia, and studied the law in the offices of two attorneys in Warrenton, Virginia. He was admitted to the bar in 1823 at age nineteen. He moved to Coshocton, Ohio, where he opened a law office. In 1830, President Jackson appointed him the U.S. attorney for Ohio, an office he occupied until 1841. He was appointed to the U.S. Supreme Court by President Lincoln in 1862. He resigned from the court in 1881 and died in 1884.

SAMUEL F. MILLER

Samuel F. Miller was born in Richmond, Kentucky, on April 5, 1816. He graduated with a medical degree from Transylvania University in 1838. He conducted a medical practice in Kentucky for nearly twelve years, and then studied law. He was admitted to the bar in 1847. Miller then moved to Iowa, where he became active in politics and supported Lincoln in 1860. In 1862, President Lincoln appointed him to the U.S. Supreme Court. He was reputed to be the intellectual leader of the court. He served on the court for twenty-eight years. He died on October 13, 1890.

DAVID DAVIS

David Davis was born on March 9, 1815, in Sassafras Neck, Maryland. Following his graduation from Kenyon College, Ohio, in 1832, he studied law in the office of an attorney in Lenox, Massachusetts, and at the New Haven Law School. In 1835, Davis opened his law office in Pekin, Illinois. Soon after, he purchased an existing practice in Bloomington, Illinois, where he became a friend of Abraham Lincoln. He served as a judge in Illinois from 1848 until he was appointed to the U.S. Supreme Court in 1862. Justice Davis resigned from the court in 1877. He then served a term in the U.S. Senate. He died on June 26, 1886.

STEPHEN J. FIELD

Stephen J. Field was born in Haddam, Connecticut, on November 4, 1816. At age thirteen, he went to Smyrna, Turkey, and studied oriental languages. He graduated from Williams College in 1837. At that time, he began to read law in the New York office of his brother, David Dudley Field. He entered the bar in 1841 and joined his brother's firm. He later moved to California and opened a law office there in Marysville in 1849. He was elected to the California Supreme Court in 1857 and became its chief justice in 1859. Justice Field took a seat on the U.S. Supreme Court in December 1863, after Congress had created a tenth seat. Although a Democrat, he was a strong Unionist. His knowledge of the land laws of the Southwest was needed to handle the backlog of Mexican land cases that remained before the court. He retired from the court in 1897 and died in 1899.

SALMON P. CHASE

Salmon Portland Chase was born in Cornish, New Hampshire, on January 13, 1808. He graduated from Dartmouth in 1826 and read law in Washington, D.C. He was admitted to the bar and began his practice there 1829. He moved his practice to Cincinnati and became a U.S. senator from Ohio in 1848. He served as governor of Ohio from 1855 to 1861. He was considered as a possible presidential candidate in 1860, when the nomination went to Lincoln. Following Lincoln's election, he became secretary of the Treasury in the president's cabinet, a position in which he ably served. In 1864, he was appointed chief justice of the Supreme Court, replacing Taney. He served until May 7, 1873, the day of his death.

WILLIAM STRONG

Born on May 6, 1808, in Somers, Connecticut, William Strong attended local schools, and then graduated from Yale College in 1828. After a short teaching career, he returned to Yale and studied law. He was admitted to the Connecticut and Pennsylvania bars and began his practice in Reading, Pennsylvania, in 1832. He served on the Pennsylvania Supreme Court from 1857 to 1868. President Grant appointed him to the U.S. Supreme Court in 1870. Strong advocated that Christian principles be applied to all issues before the court. He resigned in 1880 and died in 1895.

JOSEPH P. BRADLEY

Joseph P. Bradley was born in Berne, Albany County, New York, on March 14, 1813. He was self-taught until he entered Rutgers College. He graduated in 1836 and began to read the law after graduation. Bradley was admitted to the New Jersey bar in 1839 and practiced in Newark until 1870. He was appointed to the U.S. Supreme Court by President Grant on February 7, 1870. He served until 1891 and died the following year.

	1862	1862	1863	1864	1865	1866	1867	1868	1869	1870	1871	1872
Nathan Clifford (Buchanan)	██	██	██	██	██	██	██	██	██	██	██	██
Samuel Nelson (Tyler)	██	██	██	██	██	██	██	██	██	██	██	12-1
Robert C. Grier (Polk)	██	██	██	██	██	██	██	██	1-31			
Roger B. Taney Chief Justice (Jackson)	██	██	██	10-12								
Salmon P. Chase Chief Justice (Lincoln)				12-15	██	██	██	██	██	██	██	██
James M. Wayne (Jackson)	██	██	██	██	██	7-5						
John Catron (Jackson)	██	██	██	5-30								
Noah Swayne (Lincoln)	1-28	██	██	██	██	██	██	██	██	██	██	██
Samuel F. Miller (Lincoln)	12-1	██	██	██	██	██	██	██	██	██	██	██
Stephen J. Field (Lincoln)		12-7	██	██	██	██	██	██	██	██	██	██
David Davis (Lincoln)		12-10	██	██	██	██	██	██	██	██	██	██
William Strong (Grant)									3-14	██	██	██
Joseph P. Bradley (Grant)									3-23	██	██	██
John Archibald Campbell (Pierce)	4-26											
John McLean (Jackson)	4-4											

This graph indicates the justices who were sitting on the Supreme Court at any given time. The names of the justices appear on the left of the graph with the names of the presidents who appointed them. The solid black lines indicate when the justices served. The dates to the left of the black lines indicate when a justice joined the court. The dates to the right of the black lines indicate when a justice resigned or died.

For example, to ascertain the composition of the court at the beginning of 1865, select the line between 1864 and 1865 at the top of the graph and follow it down. A black line will be intersected for each justice who served on the court at that time.

Justice John McLean died while a member of the court on April 4, 1861. Justice John Archibald Campbell, loyal to his home state of Alabama, resigned from the court at the beginning of the war. Neither of these justices participated in the Civil War cases.

Appendix B

Civil War–Related
Supreme Court Cases

Supreme Court cases whose facts and issues were generated by the Civil War appear here in alphabetical order. These cases appeared before the court between the December 1861 and December 1871 terms and represent nearly all of the cases connected to the war. The case titles have been shortened and are followed by citations from the *U.S. Supreme Court Reports, Lawyers' Edition*, giving the volume number and page number; the date of the decision; and the name of the justice who wrote the opinion. A short description follows.

Adams, Theodore, The United States v., 74 U.S. 249, 3-12-69, Justice Nelson.
The Supreme Court held that because Adams had submitted certain of his claims to a commission in the Frémont investigations, he was bound by the commission's findings. (See chapter 11.)
Connected cases: 76 U.S. 584, 76 U.S. 808, 79 U.S. 360.

Albury, John H., The Schooner Nonesuch, *United States v.*, 76 U.S. 663, 3-14-70, Chief Justice Chase.
The Supreme Court held that it could not acquire jurisdiction of a case by consent of the parties.

Alexander, Elizabeth, The United States v., 69 U.S. 915, 3-10-65, Chief Justice Chase.
The Supreme Court held that cotton captured on Alexander's plantation along the Red River was not a prize of war. The proceeds should be held in trust so Alexander could sue when she no longer was subject to the Confederacy. (See chapter 12.)

Alicia, *The Schooner, v. The United States*, 74 U.S. 84, 3-25-69, Chief Justice Chase.
The Supreme Court held that an appeal was not valid when the Circuit Court failed to enter a decree.

Anderson, Nelson, The United States v., 76 U.S. 615, 2-28-70, Justice Davis.
Anderson, a free black in Charleston, sued to recover the proceeds from the
sale of cotton captured by the Union forces. To determine the case, the
Supreme Court determined the legal date of the end of the war. (See chapter
12.)

Armstrong, Hibernia, v. The United States, 80 U.S. 614, 3-25-72, Chief Justice
Chase.
The Court of Claims denied Armstrong's claim for proceeds from the sale of
captured cotton based upon her fleeing with slaves ahead of the Union forces
to avoid emancipation. The Supreme Court overruled the decision based
upon the president's blanket amnesty.

Armstrong, John, v. The United States, 73 U.S. 882, 3-25-68, Chief Justice
Chase.
A foundry owned by Armstrong was condemned by the Circuit Court
because it had been used to aid the Confederacy. The Supreme Court
reversed the decision and sent the case back for retrial based upon the common law.

Austin, William, v. The United States, 75 U.S. 394, 11-8-69, Chief Justice
Chase.
The case concerned the condemnation of the schooner *Lucy.* The Supreme
Court held that it could not acquire jurisdiction of a case by consent of the
parties.

Avery, William T., v. The United States, 79 U.S. 405, 11-13-71, Justice Davis.
The United States leased Avery's property in Memphis to a third party when
Avery remained in the Confederacy. The case concerned whether Avery
could offset the lease proceeds against a debt he owed to the United States.
The Supreme Court said no.

Bailey, John, The United States v., 70 U.S. 105, 1-28-66, Justice Clifford.
Bailey owned the schooner *Reform,* which had been captured on a trip from
Baltimore to the Confederacy. Bailey claimed the trip was under the aus-
pices of the government. The Supreme Court disagreed.

Bank of West Tennessee v. The Citizens' Bank, 80 U.S. 514, 1-22-72, Justice
Swayne.
The Tennessee Bank sued the Citizens' Bank of Louisiana for deposits and
collections made in Confederate currency. The Supreme Court of Louisiana
found for Citizens' because these were dealings in unlawful currency. The
U.S. Supreme Court agreed and dismissed the appeal.

Bates, Edward, v. The United States, 74 U.S. 122, 2-15-69, Justice Nelson. Bates purchased a Confederate man-of-war, the *Georgia,* in England and converted it to a merchant vessel. The merchant vessel was captured by the U.S. Navy, and the Supreme Court enforced international law that such a conversion did not protect the vessel. (See chapter 3.)

Battersby, Jos., v. The United States, 70 U.S. 175, 3-5-66, Justice Field. A British vessel, the *Cheshire,* claimed to be headed to Nassau when captured, but its cargo and position indicated that it was running the blockade. The Supreme Court held that it could be condemned without regard to the domicile of the owners.

Bennett, Henry M., v. Alexander Hunter, 76 U.S. 672, 3-21-70, Chief Justice Chase. A third party attempted to pay the land tax of Hunter, a Confederate officer, while he was serving the Confederacy, but the tax authorities refused to accept the payment. The Supreme Court held this to be improper and ordered the land returned to Hunter. (See chapter 8.)

Bethell, Pinckney C., v. Elizabeth Demaret, 77 U.S. 1007, 1-30-71, Justice Nelson. Bethell successfully foreclosed upon land in Louisiana based on a loan made in Confederate currency. The Louisiana court reversed the foreclosure because Confederate currency was illegal. The Supreme Court affirmed the decision. (See chapter 10.)

Bevans, William A., v. The United States, 80 U.S. 531, 2-5-72, Justice Strong. The United States sued Bevans, a resident of Arkansas, for Federal money he had in his possession at the start of the war. The Supreme Court confirmed a lower court ruling for the United States, even though the funds had been confiscated by the Confederacy.

Bigelow, John R. v. Douglas F. Forrest, 76 U.S. 696, 3-28-70, Justice Strong. The Supreme Court held that the forfeiture of property confiscated from a member of the Confederate armed forces could not exceed the life of the offender.

Bigler, James, v. William Waller, 81 U.S. 891, 5-6-72, Justice Strong. During the war, Bigler, a resident of New York, could not make mortgage payments to Waller, who lived in the South, and Waller foreclosed. The Supreme Court sorted out the rights of the parties. (See chapter 13.)

Blakely, Alexander T., v. The United States, 70 U.S. 200, 3-12-66, Chief Justice Chase.
The Supreme Court determined when a neutral ship traveling between neutral ports was subject to capture. (See chapter 2.)

Bragdon, Joshua, v. The United States, 72 U.S. 583, 4-22-67, Justice Clifford.
Bragdon attempted to intervene in the condemnation of the steamer *Wm. Bagaley* because he owned an interest and he lived in the North. The Supreme Court denied his petition.

Brinkly, Joseph B., v. The United States, 72 U.S. 659, 5-6-67, Justice Miller.
The Supreme Court held that when a vessel was condemned as a prize of war, a holder of a mortgage was not entitled to be paid from the proceeds of the sale.

Bronson, Frederick, v. Peter Rodes, 74 U.S. 141, 2-15-69, Chief Justice Chase.
The Supreme Court held that if a contract specified payment in gold or silver, the debtor could not pay with greenbacks, despite the law that made greenbacks legal tender.

Brooks, James, v. The United States, 73 U.S. 933, 4-6-68, Justice Nelson.
The Supreme Court held that the condemnation sale of a vessel as a prize of war overrode all previous liens against the vessel.

Burns, William W., The United States v., 79 U.S. 388, 11-6-71, Justice Field.
The Supreme Court held that when the government severed a royalty owed to Henry Hopkins Sibley because Sibley had joined the Confederate army, that part of the royalty previously assigned to Burns, who had remained loyal, was still valid. (See chapter 16.)

Butler, Thomas C., v. Benjamin Horowitz, 74 U.S. 149, 3-1-69, Chief Justice Chase.
The Supreme Court held that where a contract required payment in gold and silver coin, damages incurred because of the contract should also be paid in gold and silver coin.

Butler, William, v. Josiah Maples, 76 U.S. 822, 4-30-70, Justice Strong.
The Supreme Court determined that the purchase of cotton through an agent who possessed a Treasury license to trade in insurrectionary areas was legal.

Caperton, Allen T., v. William A. Ballard, 81 U.S. 885, 5-6-72, Justice Davis.
By dismissing this appeal because of the lack of a Federal question, the Supreme Court let stand a decision of the Virginia courts that an administrator appointed by Confederate court could not legally convey property.

Caperton, Allen T., v. Philip Bowyer, 81 U.S. 882, 5-6-72, Justice Clifford.
Bowyer recovered a judgment against Caperton in the state courts based upon a suit for unlawful imprisonment during the war. The judgment was maintained when the Supreme Court refused to take jurisdiction of the case on appeal. (See chapter 6.)

Carroll, Lucy H., v. The United States, 80 U.S. 565, 2-18-72, Chief Justice Chase.
The Court of Claims denied Carroll's claim of the proceeds from the sale of seized cotton owned by her husband, because her husband had aided the Confederacy. The Supreme Court reversed the decision because the cotton was owned by the estate when seized.

Caymari, B., v. The United States, 73 U.S. 755, 12-30-67, Justice Nelson.
The cargo of the condemned schooner *Flying Scud* was claimed by British, Spanish, French, and Mexican subjects. The Supreme Court returned cargo to all except the Mexican subjects, because they were in business in Brownsville and were classified as enemies.

Clark, Jared H., v. The United States, 73 U.S. 915, 3-30-68, Justice Grier.
Clark supplied potatoes to the army. The Supreme Court affirmed a lower court's decision that the written agreement providing for the supply of potatoes was binding, not the correspondence prior to the agreement.

Clements, Nehemiah K., v. The United States, 70 U.S. 55, 3-15-66, Justice Davis.
A British vessel, the brig *Isabella Thompson,* was captured while en route from Nassau to Halifax. The Supreme Court affirmed the lower court in restoring the brig and cargo to the claimants and defined when damages could be assessed on behalf of the claimants.

Clyde, Thomas, The United States v., 80 U.S. 479, 12-11-71, Justice Bradley.
Clyde sued the United States for rent from a steamboat and for the loss of a barge that had been destroyed by Confederate forces. The Supreme Court overruled the Court of Claims and returned the case to them for a more fair decision.

Confiscation Cases, 74 U.S. 196, 3-22-69, Justice Clifford.
The Supreme Court ruled that informers had no vested rights in cases that the United States desired to dismiss.

Cooke, David G., The United States v., 69 U.S. 866, 2-27-65, Chief Justice Chase.

The schooner *Venice* and its cargo were ordered returned to Cooke because of Major General Butler's proclamation after the fall of New Orleans that all rights of property would be held to be inviolate.

Cooley, Samuel A., v. Mary O'Connor, 79 U.S. 446, 11-27-71, Justice Strong.

O'Connor claimed that the sale of her land for the nonpayment of taxes was invalid because the notice was given within military lines. The Supreme Court held that whether the notice was sufficient was a matter for a jury and granted a new trial.

Cooper, William F., City of Nashville v., 73 U.S. 851, 3-16-68, Justice Swayne.

This case concerned alleged trespasses by Union forces in Tennessee during the war. The Supreme Court held that Federal laws should be interpreted by Federal courts.

Corbett, V. P., v. William D. Nutt, 77 U.S. 976, 1-9-71, Justice Field.

While a trustee of two married women was in the Confederacy, the land owned by the trust was sold for taxes. The Supreme Court affirmed the lower courts, which held that a successor trustee could redeem the property.

Coxe, M. K., v. The United States, 70 U.S. 58, 1-15-66, Justice Clifford.

Ruling on the capture of the ship *Admiral,* the Supreme Court found that a ship was liable to capture if its intent to violate the blockade could be established.

Cronan, George, v. The United States, 73 U.S. 884, 3-25-68, Chief Justice Chase.

When the St. Louis Street Foundry was condemned by the Circuit Court, the Supreme Court reversed the decision and gave Cronan a new trial so that he could plead the general amnesty.

Crusell, Thomas G. W., The United States v., 81 U.S. 821, 3-25-72, Chief Justice Chase.

The Supreme Court affirmed the Court of Claims decision holding that Crusell was entitled to the proceeds of the sale of cotton under the confiscation laws, even though Crusell could not prove that his cotton was part of the lots of cotton sold.

Cummings, John A., v. The State of Missouri, 71 U.S. 356, 1-14-67, Justice Field.

Cummings, a Catholic priest, was arrested for refusing to take a loyalty oath prescribed by the Missouri constitution. The Supreme Court found the Missouri law unconstitutional. (See chapter 15.)

Currie, John, v. The United States, 67 U.S. 459, 3-10-63, Justice Grier.

This case was part of the Prize Cases. The Supreme Court determined the nature of the conflict and the legality of the blockade and several other issues. John Currie was the listed claimant of the schooner *Crenshaw* and its cargo. (See chapter 1.)

Currie, William, v. The United States, 67 U.S. 459, 3-10-63, Justice Grier.

This case was part of the Prize Cases. The Supreme Court determined the nature of the conflict and the legality of the blockade and several other issues. Currie was the listed claimant of the brig *Amy Warwick* and its cargo. (See chapter 1.)

Davenport, J. H. B., The United States v., 73 U.S. 889, 3-30-68, Chief Justice Chase.

Cotton was libeled under the confiscation acts, which required that admiralty rules be applied. The Supreme Court held that where there were facts that should be determined by a jury, the case should be remanded for a new trial in conformance with the common law.

Dayton, William, v. The United States, 70 U.S. 169, 2-26-66, Chief Justice Chase.

The Circuit Court had condemned the schooner *Monterey* but made no mention of the cargo. The Supreme Court dismissed the appeal and sent the case back to the Circuit Court because the decree was not final.

Dean, Lecil W., v. Robert D. Harvey, 75 U.S. 365, 11-1-69, Chief Justice Chase.

Dean filed a suit to set aside a deed based upon fraud because his payment was in Confederate notes. The lower court dismissed the case, and the Supreme Court affirmed the decision. (See chapter 10.)

Dean, Thompson, v. Thomas A. Nelson, 77 U.S. 926, 12-6-70, Justice Bradley.

When Nelson could not make the agreed payments on the purchase of shares from Dean because he lived in the Confederacy, Dean, who lived in the North, foreclosed. The Supreme Court held the foreclosure invalid because Nelson could not receive adequate notice. (See chapter 14.)

Delmas, John T., v. John Henderson, 81 U.S. 757, 11-25-72, Justice Miller.
The Supreme Court determined that a mortgage held by Delmas against land
purchased by Henderson was valid, even though it was based upon Confederate currency. (See chapter 10.)

Diana, The Schooner, The United States v., 74 U.S. 165, 3-1-69, Justice Field.
The owners of the schooner, captured by Union blockading vessels, claimed
that an unavoidable necessity forced the schooner to violate the blockade.
The Supreme Court overruled the District Court and held that such a necessity did not exist.

Dooley, Jabez, v. Enoch Smith, 80 U.S. 547, 2-5-72, Justice Miller.
Dooley incurred a debt to Smith of $9,843.92 prior to the passage of the
Legal Tender Act. The Supreme Court overruled the Kentucky courts and
held that Dooley could pay the debt with greenbacks.

Duvall, John H., v. The United States, 70 U.S. 252, 4-3-66, Justice Swayne.
The Supreme Court affirmed a Circuit Court decision that the ceasing of the
war did not release goods seized under the confiscation acts.

Falker, William, v. The United States, 70 U.S. 135, 2-5-66, Chief Justice Chase.
The British brig *Herald* was captured on the high seas. The Supreme Court
affirmed condemnation based upon several facts, one of which was the falsification of its destination.

Fallenstein, O. T., v. The United States, 70 U.S. 168, 2-26-66, Chief Justice
Chase.
The case concerned the clear violation of the blockade by the steamship
Douro. The Supreme Court affirmed the District Court, which had condemned both the vessel and cargo, and chastized counsel for filing an appeal
with no expectation of reversal.

Fernandez, Anthony, The New Orleans Mail Co. v., 79 U.S. 249, 1-24-70, Justice Clifford.
The company sued for the return of two steamboats captured by the Union
forces. The Circuit Court issued orders pertaining to the boats, and then dismissed the case. The Supreme Court affirmed the decision.

Filor, Emily J., v. The United States, 76 U.S. 549, 1-24-70, Justice Field.
Tift's wharf was sold to Filor when Tift joined the Confederate forces. The
United States seized the property and then entered into a lease. Filor sued for
the rent. The Supreme Court affirmed the Court of Claims decision against
Filor but stated that compensation should be authorized by Congress.

Flint, John, The Norwich Trans. Co. v., 80 U.S. 556, 2-12-72, Justice Bradley.
Flint was injured by riotous soldiers while a passenger on a steamboat. The Supreme Court affirmed a lower court decision for Flint and ruled that evidence of the company's negligence was admissible.

Francis, James, v. The United States, 72 U.S. 603, 4-22-67, Justice Grier.
Francis, an informer, petitioned the lower court to appear as a party in a cotton confiscation case. The Supreme Court affirmed the lower court's denial of the petition and defined what an informer was.

Fraser, Trenholm & Co. v. The United States, 70 U.S. 200, 3-12-66, Chief Justice Chase.
The British steamship *Bermuda,* claiming to have been traveling between two neutral ports, was captured. The Supreme Court affirmed a lower court's decision to condemn the vessel, and it defined contraband and when such a vessel could be condemned. (See chapter 2.)

Freeborn, William A., v. The Ship Protector, 76 U.S. 812, 4-30-70, Justice Bradley.
The ship *Protector* was libeled by several merchants who were not paid for supplies in 1859. The case was filed in the District Court in Alabama, and that court dismissed the case. The appeal was not filed until July 28, 1869. The Supreme Court held that the war tolled the time for appeal and refused to dismiss the case.

Freeborn, William A., v. The Ship Protector, 79 U.S. 463, 1-29-72, Chief Justice Chase.
This case was connected to the previous one. Here the Supreme Court reiterated the dates of the beginning and the end of the war.

French, James S., v. Samuel M. Shoemaker, 81 U.S. 852, 4-22-72, Justice Clifford.
French and his associate owned and supervised the construction of the Alexandria & Washington Railroad. When the war began, French and his associate joined the Confederacy, and the United States used the railroad for military purposes. Later, a group headed by Shoemaker took over the railroad. French returned after the war and in a series of lawsuits attempted to take back the railroad but failed. The Supreme Court affirmed the decision. (See chapter 14.)

Fry, Charles M., v. The United States, 70 U.S. 197, 3-12-66, Justice Swayne.
The case concerned the capture of the bark *Sally Magee.* The Supreme Court held that the capture and successful condemnation of the property gave the captors the rights of the owners of the vessel, as these rights existed at the time of the initiation of the voyage.

Garland, A. H., Ex Parte, 71 U.S. 366, 1-14-67, Justice Field.
Garland, an attorney in Arkansas, was pardoned by the president for his service with the Confederate government during the war. Later, Congress passed a law requiring a loyalty oath before anyone could practice before the Supreme Court. Garland claimed this oath to be unconstitutional. The Supreme Court agreed. (See chapter 15.)

Garnet, Alexander Y. P., v. The United States, 78 U.S. 79, 3-6-71, Justice Swayne.
The Supreme Court held that Garnet, though a Confederate citizen, had a right to appear in the lower courts and defend against the condemnation of his property.

Garrison, Cornelius K., v. The United States, 74 U.S. 277, 4-15-69, Justice Miller.
Major General Butler entered into a contract with Garrison to purchase 6,000 Enfield rifles. When a dispute arose as to the amount to be paid because of unclear language in the contract, the Supreme Court held for Garrison because Butler had drafted the unclear language. (See chapter 11.)

Gay, Edward J., v. The United States, 80 U.S. 606, 3-18-72, Justice Miller.
In 1864, a steamer headed upriver from New Orleans with a sizable amount of gold coin was seized. The Supreme Court affirmed a lower court decision confiscating the steamer, because it was obvious that it intended to trade with the enemy.

Generes, Louis F., v. Walter L. Campbell, 78 U.S. 110, 3-27-71, Justice Swayne.
In 1861, Generes bought slaves from Campbell and gave a note as consideration in New Orleans. Campbell left the area during the war and did not collect the note. The Supreme Court affirmed the Circuit Court's ruling on behalf of Campbell.

Georgia, State of, v. Ulysses S. Grant, 73 U.S. 848, 3-16-68, Chief Justice Chase.
The Supreme Court determined when and how a complaint could be filed in an equity case of original jurisdiction.

Georgia, State of, v. Edwin M. Stanton, 73 U.S. 721, 5-16-67, Justice Nelson.
The state of Georgia attempted to prevent certain Reconstruction acts from taking effect. The Supreme Court dismissed the case because of the political character of the dispute.

Gibbons, Francis A., v. The United States, 75 U.S. 453, 12-13-69, Justice Miller.

Gibbons had a contract with the United States to supply 200,000 bushels of oats. The United States held up part of the delivery, and then insisted on delivery after the price had increased. When Gibbons sued for the higher price, the Court of Claims decided against Gibbons, and the Supreme Court affirmed the decision.

Graham, James, Ex Parte, 77 U.S. 981, 1-9-71, Justice Swayne.

The United States confiscated certain lots under the confiscation acts. The former owner of the property petitioned the Supreme Court for a writ of prohibition for an accounting. The Supreme Court held that such a writ could be granted only in an admiralty case, and this was not such a case.

Grant, William S., v. The United States, 74 U.S. 194, 3-15-69, Justice Field.

While supplying military outposts in Arizona, goods and wagon trains owned by Grant were captured by the Texas militia. Grant sued for the price of the goods and for damages. The Court of Claims denied his claim, and the Supreme Court affirmed the decision. (See chapter 16.)

Grey Jacket, *The Steamer, v. The United States,* 72 U.S. 646, 5-6-67, Justice Swayne.

The steamer was captured while attempting to run the blockade outbound. The owner claimed that he was loyal and only trying to remove his property from enemy territory. The Supreme Court affirmed the lower court, which condemned the vessel. (See chapter 2.)

Grossmayer, Henry, The United States v., 76 U.S. 627, 3-7-70, Justice Davis.

Grossmayer, a resident of New York, claimed the proceeds from the sale of cotton he had purchased in the South through an agent. The Court of Claims decided in his favor, but the Supreme Court overruled and held that Grossmayer had traded with the enemy.

Haigh, Edwin, v. The United States, 70 U.S. 200, 3-12-66, Chief Justice Chase.

The Supreme Court held that a neutral ship, ostensibly headed for a neutral port, was liable to capture if the cargo was contraband and evidence showed it was destined to a belligerent port. (See chapter 2.)

Hall, H. F., v. George Coppell, 74 U.S. 244, 3-10-69, Justice Swayne.

Coppell, the British consul in New Orleans, attempted to protect cotton he had purchased in the Confederacy from Hall with consular certificates. After the war, when Coppell sued to recover the cotton, the lower court ruled in his favor. The Supreme Court reversed the decision, holding that the transactions were invalid.

Halliburton, John G., v. The United States, 80 U.S. 533, 2-5-72, Justice Strong.
Halliburton, a marshal in Arkansas when the war began, possessed certain funds of the United States, which were subsequently seized by the Confederacy. After the war, the United States sued to recover the funds. The Supreme Court confirmed the decision of the lower court for the United States.

Hallock, Benjamin S., The United States v., 68 U.S. 568, 2-8-64, Justice Grier.
The *Pilgrim* was captured attempting to run the blockade. Its owners lived in the Confederacy and in the North. The Supreme Court held that the interest of the Northern owners could be confiscated because they were dealing with the enemy.

Handlin, W. W., v. G. M. Wickliffe, 79 U.S. 365, 10-30-71, Chief Justice Chase.
As Louisiana was occupied by Union troops, Handlin was appointed a judge by the military governor. When Handlin was replaced by a new military governor, Handlin sued for his salary. The lower court decided against Handlin, and the Supreme Court affirmed the decision.

Hanger, Peter, v. J. S. Abbott, 73 U.S. 939, 4-6-68, Justice Clifford.
Abbott, a resident of New Hampshire, sued Hanger, a resident of Arkansas, on a prewar debt. The trial court held that the statute of limitations had been tolled during the war, and the Supreme Court affirmed the decision.

Hannauer, Louis, v. Alden M. Woodruff, 77 U.S. 991, 1-23-71, Justice Nelson.
Hannauer purchased Confederate bonds during the war and sold them to Woodruff. Part of the payment was a note. When Hannauer sued on the note, Woodruff defended by alleging that the note was invalid because the bonds were illegal. The Circuit Court split evenly and sent the case to the Supreme Court, which also split evenly and sent the case back to the Circuit Court to do "as it may be advised."

Han[n]auer, Louis, v. Samuel H. Doane, 79 U.S. 439, 11-27-71, Justice Bradley.
Hannauer purchased supplies for use by the Confederate army from Doane and gave notes for consideration. When Doane sued on the notes, the lower court gave him a judgment. The Supreme Court overruled the decision, holding that the notes were used to buy supplies used in a crime, and no crime was greater than treason.

Harlan, Samuel, Jr., v. The United States, 71 U.S. 413, 2-4-67, Justice Davis.
Pending a court decision, an alleged prize of war was held in trust by the government. The Supreme Court held that during this period, neither the vessel nor the cargo was subject to be attached by private parties.

Harris, John Meyer, v. The United States, 70 U.S. 220, 3-26-66, Chief Justice Chase.
The schooner *Stephen Hart,* captured while traveling from London to Cardenas, Cuba, was owned by British citizens. The Supreme Court approved its condemnation because of its military cargo, some of which had "C.S.A." markings.

Hart, Simeon, The United States v., 73 U.S. 914, 3-30-68, Justice Nelson.
The Supreme Court of New Mexico Territory held that state courts had no jurisdiction to enforce the confiscation acts. The Supreme Court affirmed the decision. Two connected cases appear at 73 U.S. 915.

Hepburn, Susan P., v. Henry A. Griswold, 75 U.S. 513, 2-7-70, Justice Miller.
This was one of the Legal Tender Cases. The Supreme Court determined that paper money was not legal tender in the payment of debts incurred prior to the passage of the Legal Tender Act. (See chapter 7.)

Hickman, James, v. Jones, 76 U.S. 551, 1-24-70, Justice Swayne.
Hickman was arrested in Alabama during the war and tried by the Confederate courts for treason against the Confederate States. Following the war, Hickman sued the judge and others involved for malicious prosecution. The Supreme Court overruled the lower courts and held that this suit was proper and ordered a new trial. (See chapter 6.)

Holladay, Ben, v. Thomas W. Kennard, 79 U.S. 390, 11-6-71, Justice Bradley.
Kennard shipped money by means of Holladay's stage line from New York to Central City, Colorado Territory. Indians who had aligned themselves with the Confederacy attacked the stage and stole the money. Kennard filed suit for negligence. The lower courts held for Kennard. The Supreme Court affirmed the decision. (See chapter 16.)

Holmes, Henry J., v. Ambrose H. Sevier, 81 U.S. 876, 5-6-72, Justice Swayne.
Holmes filed suit to collect a note that had been consideration for the purchase of slaves. The Circuit Court held that the emancipation of the slaves invalidated the note. The Supreme Court overruled the decision, holding that if the transaction was valid at the time it was consummated, the note could be collected.

Hook, Zadoc, v. Ann Payne, 81 U.S. 887, 5-6-72, Justice Miller.
Payne, a citizen in the Confederacy, sued Hook, who lived in Missouri, for an accounting and distribution of an estate. The trial court appointed a master, who found fraud and ordered distribution to Payne. The Supreme Court affirmed the decision.

Hosmer, Henry J., The United States v., 76 U.S. 662, 3-14-70, Justice Swayne.
Hosmer, a private in a regiment of Massachusetts volunteers, sued for a $100
bonus promised him when he signed up. The Supreme Court affirmed a
lower court decision in his favor.

Hunt, Henry J., The United States v., 81 U.S. 739, 11-18-72, Chief Justice
Chase.
When Congress increased the pay for brevet brigadier generals and below,
Hunt, a brigadier general, applied for the increase. The Supreme Court
denied the increase because a brigadier general was higher in rank than a
brevet brigadier general.

Hunter, Edward, v. The United States, 69 U.S. 796, 1-30-65, Chief Justice
Chase.
The Supreme Court affirmed the condemnation of the British steamship *Cir-
cassian* and cargo, which was captured when it intended to run the blockade.
The Supreme Court held that the blockade was not terminated when a block-
aded port was captured. (See chapter 2.)

Jarman, Stephen, v. The United States, 72 U.S. 564, 4-15-67, Chief Justice
Chase.
The steamer *Peterhoff* was captured while on a trip from London to Matamoros, Mexico. Intensive arguments were made concerning the expansion of
the doctrine of continuous voyage. The Supreme Court condemned the
cargo but released the vessel.

Jenny, *The Schooner, The United States v.,* 72 U.S. 693, 5-14-67, Chief Justice
Chase.
The schooner *Jenny* was captured in 1863 and libeled as a prize of war.
Though the claimants said they were neutrals, the Supreme Court held that
the weight of evidence indicated that the vessel and part of the cargo were
owned by the Confederacy, and reversed the lower court decision for the
claimants.

Justice, Philip S., The United States v., 81 U.S. 753, 11-25-72, Justice Davis.
When Justice agreed to supply muskets to the United States in 1861, he represented that they would be the same as a sample. Troops from Pennsylvania
found the muskets to be dangerous and unlike the sample. The United States
refused to pay the full amount, and the Supreme Court agreed. (See chapter
11.)

Keehler, Orestes A., The United States v., 76 U.S. 574, 2-14-70, Justice Miller.
Keehler, a postmaster in North Carolina, had $330.03 of Federal money on
hand when the state seceded. The Confederate post office ordered him to pay
the money to another carrier. After the war, the United States sued for the
funds, and the Supreme Court held for the United States.

Kentucky, Commonwealth of, v. George S. Boutwell, 80 U.S. 631, 3-25-72, Justice Davis.
Kentucky sued the United States for reimbursement of funds expended in
defense of the Union. Even though the warrant had been issued to pay the
funds, the Supreme Court denied the claim.

Kimbal, John H., The United States v., 80 U.S. 503, 12-11-71, Justice Swayne.
The United States leased a vessel from Kimbal to carry coal from Philadelphia to Port Royal, South Carolina. The vessel was beached due to negligence of the United States. The Supreme Court confirmed the decision of
the Court of Claims, awarding Kimbal the full contract.

Klein, John A., The United States v., 80 U.S. 519, 1-29-72, Chief Justice Chase.
Congress passed legislation that in effect overrode the presidential oaths.
The Supreme Court held that this legislation was inadvertently passed and
approved a decision granting a claimant proceeds from the sale of cotton, as
though the legislation did not exist. (See chapter 15.)

Knox, William B., v. Phoebe G. Lee, 79 U.S. 287, 5-1-71, Justice Strong.
The Supreme Court held that paper money was legal tender in the payment
of all debts incurred before and after the passage of the Legal Tender Acts.
This decision overruled *Hepburn v. Griswold.* (See chapter 7.)

Lane, County of, v. State of Oregon, 74 U.S. 101, 2-8-69, Chief Justice Chase.
The Supreme Court held that greenbacks could not be used to pay state taxes
when the state courts had held that taxes could be paid only in gold or silver.

Lane, George W., The United States v., 75 U.S. 445, 11-29-69, Justice Davis.
Lane purchased cotton in the Confederacy pursuant to a contract with a U.S.
Treasury agent. The U.S. Navy seized the cotton but returned it. Lane sued
for damages and was given a judgment by the Court of Claims. The
Supreme Court overruled the decision, because Lane was trading with the
enemy.

Law, George, v. Wallerstein, 76 U.S. 651, 3-14-70, Chief Justice Chase.
A case that was begun in Louisiana in the Federal court there prior to the
war was transferred to a provisional court created by Lincoln when the
Union forces regained control. The Supreme Court held that the provisional
court was a legal court.

Laws, David O., v. The United States, 77 U.S. 983, 1-9-71, Justice Strong.
A steamer was captured on the Roanoke River 130 miles from its mouth.
The United States asserted that it was a prize of war, and the District Court
agreed. The Supreme Court held that such an inland capture could not be a
prize of war and ordered the United States to proceed under the confiscation
acts.

Leary, Arthur, v. The United States, 81 U.S. 756, 11-25-72, Justice Field.
In 1862, the United States chartered a vessel from Leary to engage in military operations. During the charter, an accident sunk the vessel. The Court of
Claims refused to grant Leary damages, and the Supreme Court affirmed the
decision.

LeMore, Gustave A., v. The United States, 73 U.S. 935, 4-6-68, Justice Swayne.
LeMore, who owned a commercial house in France, purchased cotton from
Confederate agents. The cotton was captured by Union forces in Louisiana
in 1864. LeMore sued for the cotton proceeds, and the lower court denied
his claim because he dealt with the enemy. The Supreme Court affirmed the
decision.

Levy, A., v. A. T. Stewart, 78 U.S. 86, 3-20-71, Justice Clifford.
Following the close of the war, former Confederate creditors sued Levy, a
resident of New York, on three notes that were payable in New Orleans in
1861. The Supreme Court affirmed the lower court, which held that the
statute of limitations was tolled during the war.

Ludlow, Jacob R., v. J. G. M. Ramsey, 78 U.S. 216, 5-1-71, Justice Bradley.
Ramsey, who lived behind the Confederate lines, owed a note to Cynthia
White, who lived in the North. White sued on the note and attached and sold
a house owned by Ramsey in Knoxville. After the war, Ramsey sued for the
return of the house. The lower courts ruled in his favor, but the Supreme
Court reversed the decision. (See chapter 13.)

Mauran, Suchet, 2nd, v. Insurance Companies, 73 U.S. 836, 3-9-68, Justice
Nelson.
The ship *Marshall,* owned by Mauran, was captured in the mouth of the
Mississippi by the Confederate vessel *Music.* The *Marshall* was insured
against the usual risks, including piracy, by one of the insurance companies.
The Supreme Court held that the capture was not piracy and the policy did
not cover the capture.

May, Thomas, v. The United States, 72 U.S. 480, 1-3-67, Chief Justice Chase.
The *Springbok,* a British vessel whose destination was Nassau, was captured on the high seas. The Supreme Court released the vessel but condemned the cargo because it was contraband.

McCardle, William H., Ex Parte, 73 U.S. 816, 2-17-68, Chief Justice Chase.
The Supreme Court held that a right to appeal attaches to all judgments of the Circuit Court, including cases of habeas corpus.

McGlynn, John A., v. Emily W. Magraw, 75 U.S. 531, 2-7-70, Chief Justice Chase.
A debt was incurred prior to the passage of the Legal Tender Acts. The Supreme Court held, following *Hepburn v. Griswold,* decided the same day, that the debt could not be paid with greenbacks.

McKee, John M., v. The United States, 75 U.S. 329, 10-18-69, Justice Davis.
McKee purchased cotton from a resident in the Confederacy. When the cotton was captured, McKee filed his claim. The District Court dismissed his claim because he dealt with the enemy, and the Supreme Court affirmed the decision.

McVeigh, William N., v. The United States, 78 U.S. 80, 3-6-71, Justice Swayne.
McVeigh, a Richmond resident, had his property in the North confiscated. When he tried to enter the case and defend, the Circuit Court held that he was a Rebel and had no right to appear. The Supreme Court reversed the decision, holding that as long as McVeigh could be sued, he had a right to appear and defend himself. (See chapter 12.)

Meaher, Timothy, v. The United States, 72 U.S. 646, 5-6-67, Chief Justice Chase.
The Supreme Court held that where the United States was adequately represented in a case, no counsel may be heard in opposition from any other department of the government. (See chapter 2.)

Merrill, Lewis, The United States v., 76 U.S. 664, 3-14-70, Justice Clifford.
The Supreme Court held that Merrill was not entitled to his three months' pay bonus at discharge, because he had transferred to the Regular army.

Miller, Peter, v. The United States, 67 U.S. 459, 3-10-63, Justice Grier.
The Supreme Court determined the nature of the conflict, the legality of the blockade, and other issues. Part of the Prize Cases. (See chapter 1.)

Milligan, Lambdin P., Ex Parte, 71 U.S. 281, 4-3-66, Justice Davis.
Milligan had been arrested for inciting an insurrection and tried before a military commission. The Supreme Court held that martial law could not be declared when civilian courts are operating, and the trial before the commission was declared invalid. This was James A. Garfield's first Supreme Court case. (See chapter 5.)

Mississippi, The State of, v. Andrew Johnson, 71 U.S. 437, 4-15-67, Chief Justice Chase.
The Supreme Court denied a motion for leave to file a complaint, holding that it did not have jurisdiction to enjoin the president from performing his official duties.

Monadnock, *Ship of War, v. The United States,* 80 U.S. 505, 12-18-71, Justice Swayne.
The case concerned the ship of war *Monadnock* and several other vessels, their officers and crews. The Supreme Court sorted out the rights of the United States and crews of the capturing vessels in instances where the ship was taken by both the army and navy and costs of salvage were involved.

Morgan, Thomas P., v. The United States, 81 U.S. 738, 11-18-72, Justice Davis.
The United States hired a vessel owned by Morgan to transport troops to Texas on a per diem basis. The vessel was damaged because of negligence of the United States. The Supreme Court affirmed an award of the Court of Claims, which covered only part of the per diem and damages.

Morris, Josiah, v. The United States, 74 U.S. 281, 4-15-69, Chief Justice Chase.
Cotton captured by the Union had been sold to Morris, and by Morris to a third party. The District Court entered a judgment against Morris, but the Supreme Court overturned it, stating that the confiscation acts could apply only if there existed specific property.

Morris, Josiah, v. The United States, 75 U.S. 481, 12-13-69, Justice Clifford.
The Supreme Court held that where the seizure of cotton was on land, though in the form of a libel under the confiscation acts, it was an action under common law, and the claimants were entitled to a jury trial.

Murphy, Susan, The United States v., 70 U.S. 217, 3-19-66, Justice Miller.
Murphy was arrested for assaulting an officer while the officer was engaged in enrolling men for the draft. The Supreme Court held that it had jurisdiction of the case, but that interfering with an enrollment was not the same as interfering with the draft.

Murray, Robert, The Justices v., 76 U.S. 658, 3-14-70, Justice Nelson.
A former prisoner of the Federal government sued Murray and another for his arrest in a state court. When the prisoner obtained a judgment, the Federal government attempted to remove the case to the Federal courts. The Supreme Court held that such a removal would have violated the Seventh Amendment to the Constitution. (See chapter 6.)

Netto, Francis, v. The United States, 72 U.S. 618, 4-29-67, Justice Swayne.
The Supreme Court held that a license granted by the Treasury Department authorizing one to trade with an area in insurrection was a nullity; only the president could grant such a license.

The New Bedford Company v. The United States, 81 U.S. 760, 11-25-72, Justice Strong.
New Bedford chartered the steamer *Thorn* to the United States with an agreement that the United States had an option to purchase the vessel for $40,000 less the charter payments. The *Thorn* was sunk by a Confederate torpedo. The Supreme Court affirmed a judgment by the Court of Claims that New Bedford could recover only the option price less the charter payments.

Norris, Samuel, The Providence Tool Co. v., 69 U.S. 868, 2-27-65, Justice Field.
Norris obtained a musket contract for the tool company and sued for a finder's fee.
The lower courts decided for Norris. The Supreme Court overruled the decision and held that such contracts were contrary to public policy.

O'Keefe, James, The United States v., 78 U.S. 131, 4-3-71, Justice Davis.
O'Keefe sued under the confiscation laws to recover the value of cotton owned by him and was awarded a judgment by the Court of Claims. The United States appealed on the basis that O'Keefe was a citizen of Great Britain and had no right to sue. The Supreme Court disagreed with the United States and affirmed the lower court's decision.

Osborn, Henry T., v. Young A. G. Nicholson, 80 U.S. 689, 4-22-72, Justice Swayne.
When Osborn sued Nicholson to recover the amount of a note that resulted from the sale of a slave, the Court of Claims held for Nicholson because the constitution of the state of Arkansas invalidated such notes. The Supreme Court overruled the decision and also ruled that the emancipation of the slave did not violate a warranty that the slave would be such for life.

The Pacific Insurance Co. v. Frank Soule, 74 U.S. 95, 2-1-69, Justice Swayne.
The Supreme Court ruled that the law taxing the income of corporations was valid, and that a corporation could not declare its income in specie and pay the tax in greenbacks. (See chapter 8.)

Padelford, Edward, The United States v., 76 U.S. 788, 4-30-70, Chief Justice Chase.
The Supreme Court held that Padelford's purchase of Confederate bonds was involuntary and could not be classified as aid and comfort to the enemy. (See chapter 9.)

Page, Nathaniel, v. The United States, 78 U.S. 135, 4-3-71, Justice Strong.
Page was the executor of Samuel Miller, a Rebel citizen living in Virginia who had railroad stock he owned confiscated in Michigan. The Supreme Court affirmed a lower court's holding that the confiscation was proper and that the confiscation acts were constitutional. (See chapter 12.)

Pargoud, John Frank, v. The United States, 80 U.S. 646, 4-8-72, Chief Justice Chase.
Pargoud claimed the proceeds from cotton captured from him in 1865. The Court of Claims decided against Pargoud because he had aided the Confederacy. The Supreme Court overruled the decision, holding that the president's blanket pardon qualified Pargoud to receive the proceeds.

Parish, Joseph W., v. The United States, 75 U.S. 472, 12-13-69, Justice Field.
Parish agreed to supply ice to hospitals in the West and Gulf, including New Orleans. The United States deleted New Orleans from the contract when it was executed. Parish sued on the agreed contract, which included New Orleans. The Court of Claims ruled against Parish, and the Supreme Court affirmed the decision.

Pelham, Henry, v. David G. Rose, 76 U.S. 602, 2-12-70, Justice Field.
The Supreme Court held that for property to become within the jurisdiction of the court for condemnation, there must have been an actual physical seizure of the property if it was subject to manual delivery.

Preciat, Rafael, v. The United States, 67 U.S. 459, 3-10-63, Justice Grier.
The Supreme Court determined the nature of the conflict, the legality of the blockade, and other issues. Part of the Prize Cases. (See chapter 1.)

Pugh, Edward, v. The United States, 80 U.S. 711, 5-6-72, Chief Justice Chase.
Pugh sued the United States in the Court of Claims, alleging that Union troops had damaged his plantation in Louisiana. The Court of Claims dismissed the suit, and the Supreme Court affirmed the decision, stating that this was a military action during the war.

Queyrouze, Paul, v. The United States, 70 U.S. 65, 1-15-66, Chief Justice Chase.

The Supreme Court held that the revocation of the blockade in New Orleans did not lift the blockade of the nearby coasts that remained in the possession of the Confederacy.

Rackett, Henry S., v. The United States, 74 U.S. 129, 2-25-69, Justice Field.

Following its capture, and while in the possession of the prize crew (the crew taking the captured vessel to court) the steamer *Siren* collided with and sunk another vessel. The Supreme Court held that the resulting damages should be paid out of the results of the condemnation sale prior to payments to the captors.

Read, John, The United States v., 72 U.S. 625, 5-6-67, Chief Justice Chase.

The cargo of the captured bark *Science* contained Confederate uniform cloth; however, there was no evidence that the bark was destined for enemy territory. The Supreme Court held that the vessel should be restored to its owner.

Reeside, John E., v. The United States, 75 U.S. 318, 4-15-69, Justice Nelson.

Reeside owned rural mail routes in three Southern states. If the postmaster general severed them, Reeside would be entitled to one month's pay. When the postmaster general merely suspended the routes, Reeside sued for the severance pay. The Court of Claims dismissed the suit, but the Supreme Court reversed the decision.

Reeside, John E., v. The United States, 75 U.S. 391, 11-8-69, Chief Justice Chase.

Major General Frèmont contracted with Reeside to purchase and inspect horses. When Reeside sued for the contractual amount, the Supreme Court confirmed a lower court's decision that Frèmont lacked the authority to enter into such a contract, but held that Reeside should be paid for the work actually accomplished.

Renaud, Bernard, v. The United States, 69 U.S. 880, 3-8-65, Chief Justice Chase.

The Supreme Court held that once a blockade was established, it was presumed to continue until formal notice of its discontinuance was given or there was other persuasive evidence of its discontinuance.

Rive, John, The United States v., 72 U.S. 622, 5-6-67, Chief Justice Chase.

The brig *Dashing Wave,* an English vessel destined for Matamoros, was captured off the Texas coast. The District Court restored the vessel to the owners because none of the cargo was contraband and assessed costs to the claimants. The Supreme Court affirmed the decision but modified the costs.

Rogers, John, v. The Steamer Atlanta, 70 U.S. 253, 4-3-66, Justice Field.
This case resulted from a dispute concerning the division of the prize money among the officers and crews of the vessels that had captured the steamer *Atlanta*. The Supreme Court determined that half of the prize money should go to them. (See chapter 3.)

Roosevelt, James J., v. Lewis H. Meyer, 68 U.S. 500, 12-21-63, Justice Wayne.
The Legal Tender Acts were declared constitutional by the New York Court of Appeals. The Supreme Court held that it did not have jurisdiction to revise that judgment and ordered the dismissal of the case.

Russell, John H., The United States v., 80 U.S. 474, 11-27-71, Justice Clifford.
Three steamboats owned by Russell were appropriated by the United States for use in the war as transports. No contract existed. When Russell did not receive adequate pay, he sued, and the lower court held that that there was an implied contract that full compensation would be paid. The Supreme Court affirmed the decision.

Ryan, William, The United States v., 76 U.S. 663, 3-14-70, Chief Justice Chase.
The Supreme Court held that it could not obtain jurisdiction of the case by consent of the parties.

Scott, George Y., The United States v., 70 U.S. 218, 3-19-66, Justice Miller.
The Supreme Court held that a statute declaring that a death occurring in opposition to enrollment was murder did not apply to the draft.

Sea Witch, *The Schooner, The United States v.,* 73 U.S. 786, 1-13-68, Chief Justice Chase.
The *Sea Witch* was restored to its owner because the owner and the vessel's cargo were neutral and the vessel had been cleared to New Orleans by the U.S. vice consul.

Semmes, John T., v. The City Fire Insurance Company, 80 U.S. 490, 12-18-71, Justice Miller.
The Supreme Court held that a requirement in an insurance policy that a claim must be filed within two years of a loss was waived when the insured lived in the Confederacy and was unable to file a claim.

Sevier, Ambrose H., v. Langdon C. Haskell, 81 U.S. 827, 4-1-72, Justice Swayne.
Haskell sued Sevier to foreclose four notes that Sevier had given him to purchase slaves. The trial court held that the notes were invalid, and the Supreme Court of Arkansas reversed the decision. The U.S. Supreme Court dismissed the appeal because there was no Federal question.

Simonson, John, v. The United States, 70 U.S. 93, 1-29-66, Justice Miller.
The schooner *Elmira Cornelius* was captured running the blockade to Charleston. The owners of the vessel and cargo were from New York and claimed that the vessel was forced to beach itself because of serious leakage. The Supreme Court confirmed a lower court decision of condemnation.

Sir William Peel, *The Schooner, The United States v.,* 72 U.S. 696, 5-16-67, Chief Justice Chase.
The steamship *Sir William Peel,* an English vessel, was captured while traveling from London to Matamoros. The lower court dismissed the case, and the Supreme Court affirmed the decision.

Speed, J. Smith, The United States v., 75 U.S. 449, 11-29-69, Justice Miller.
Speed and his partner entered into a contract with the United States to slaughter and pack 50,000 hogs, which were to be supplied by the government along with cooperage and salt. The United States failed to supply the hogs, as agreed. The Supreme Court approved the Court of Claims judgment against the United States for the full amount of the contract.

Stewart, Alexander T., v. S. Bloom, 78 U.S. 176, 4-10-71, Justice Swayne.
The U.S. Supreme Court overruled the Supreme Court of Louisiana and held that the Federal statute that tolled the statute of limitations was constitutional and that it also applied to the states.

Stiles, Edward C., v. The United States, 73 U.S. 876, 3-23-68, Justice Nelson.
The steamship *Wren,* owned by a British subject, successfully ran the Galveston blockade and headed for Havana. When the vessel left Havana destined for Liverpool, the crew mutinied and claimed the vessel as a prize of war. The Supreme Court held that once the ship had reached its destination of Havana, the guilt of running the blockade was absolved. The ship was returned to its owner.

Swift, Eben, The Hannibal & St. Joseph Railroad Company v., 79 U.S. 423, 11-20-71, Justice Field.
Two companies of Union artillery troops were transferred on the Hannibal line from Fort Randal, Dakota Territory, to Cincinnati. The car containing the supplies mysteriously burned. The Circuit Court held that the railroad was liable. The Supreme Court affirmed the decision.

Teresita, *The Bark, The United States v.,* 72 U.S. 627, 5-6-67, Chief Justice Chase.
The bark *Teresita* was captured when an excessive wind blew it into Texas waters. The vessel and cargo were owned by Spanish and Mexican citizens. The lower court returned the vessel and cargo to the owners, and the Supreme Court affirmed the decision and assessed damages to the captors.

Thomas, James P., v. The City of Richmond, 79 U.S. 453, 12-11-71, Justice Bradley.
In 1862, the state of Virginia made currency issued by the city of Richmond redeemable. The Circuit Court held that the issuance of the currency was against Virginia law and the state action was void because it was in aid of the Rebellion. The Supreme Court affirmed the decision.

Thorington, Jack, v. William B. Smith, 75 U.S. 361, 11-1-69, Chief Justice Chase.
The Supreme Court held that the balance owed on a contract that was consummated in the Confederacy could be enforced by the Federal courts and could be paid in Confederate currency. (See chapter 10.)

Trebilcock, Frank, v. Benjamin Wilson, 79 U.S. 460, 1-22-72, Justice Field.
Wilson gave Trebilcock a note payable in specie prior to the passage of the Legal Tender Acts. The Supreme Court held that the language in the note required Wilson to pay in gold or silver despite the act.

Turner, David, v. James M. Smith, 81 U.S. 724, 11-11-72, Justice Miller.
Smith abandoned his home in Alexandria, Virginia, and went to the Confederacy. The property was sold for nonpayment of taxes, but Smith regained the property after the war in the courts of Virginia. The Supreme Court overruled the Virginia courts.

Tweed, John P., Benjamin F. Flanders v., 76 U.S. 678, 3-21-70, Justice Nelson.
Tweed sued Flanders, an agent of the U.S. Treasury Department, for the return of cotton that had been confiscated under the confiscation acts. Procedural problems caused a mistrial in the trial court, and the Supreme Court reversed and returned the case for a new trial.

Tyler, Henry B., v. John D. Defrees, 78 U.S. 161, 4-10-71, Justice Miller.
Tyler sued Defrees to recover a real estate lot that had been confiscated by the United States. The lower courts decided for Defrees, holding that the seizure complied with the law. The Supreme Court affirmed the decision.

The Union Insurance Company v. The United States, 73 U.S. 879, 3-25-68, Chief Justice Chase.
Property in New Orleans that had been leased to a Confederate arms factory was condemned. Union held a mortgage on the property. The Supreme Court took this opportunity to establish standards for this and similar cases, including the role of a jury, and ordered a new trial.

Vallandigham, Clement L., Ex Parte, 68 U.S. 589, 2-15-64, Justice Wayne.
Vallandigham was arrested by the military in Ohio and tried before a military commission for maliciously disrupting the war effort. The Supreme Court held that a military commission was not a court, and that it could not take jurisdiction of an appeal or issue a writ of habeas corpus. (See chapter 4.)

The Veazie Bank v. Jeremiah Fenno, 75 U.S. 482, 12-13-69, Chief Justice Chase.
The Supreme Court held that a 10 percent tax upon the circulation of bank notes of national and state banks was constitutional. (See chapter 8.)

Virginia, The Commonwealth, v. State of West Virginia, 78 U.S. 67, 3-6-71, Justice Miller.
The Supreme Court dismissed this case filed by Virginia, which alleged that the counties of Berkeley, Jefferson, and Frederick were part of Virginia, not West Virginia.

Volant, *The Brig, v. The United States,* 72 U.S. 626, 5-6-67, Chief Justice Chase.
The brig *Volant,* a neutral vessel, was captured off the coast of Texas with a cargo of Confederate army cloth. The Supreme Court held that the cargo justified capture, but since there were no facts that proved it was destined to the Confederacy, it overruled the District Court and returned the vessel to its owner.

Walker, James, v. The United States, 73 U.S. 821, 2-10-68, Chief Justice Chase.
The steamship *Adela,* owned by neutrals, was captured in British waters. The Supreme Court affirmed a decree of condemnation because the evidence revealed that the vessel intended to run the blockade.

Ward, William, v. Francis Smith, 74 U.S. 207, 3-29-69, Justice Field.
Ward purchased land in Virginia from an estate administered by Smith. He paid for the land with cash and three bonds that were to be redeemed at a bank in Alexandria. Smith deposited the first bond at the bank, but he went to the Confederacy when the war began and could not deposit the remaining two bonds. The Supreme Court explained how the bonds should be taken care of and affirmed a lower court decision for Smith.

Watchful, *The Schooner, The United States v.*, 73 U.S. 763, 4-13-68, Justice Miller.
   The schooner *Watchful* was captured when it was headed for Juarez, Mexico, with a cargo of guns. It was not able to land in Juarez because of the French occupation. The District Court dismissed the libel and restored the vessel and cargo to the owner. The Supreme Court affirmed the dismissal of the libel but reversed the restoration of the vessel and cargo, and it gave the United States time to file a new libel.

Watson, Gerald T., v. The United States, 69 U.S. 849, 2-13-65, Chief Justice Chase.
   The Supreme Court set the standards that must be met to successfully condemn a vessel and cargo as a prize of war.

Weed, C. A., The United States v., 72 U.S. 531, 2-18-67, Justice Miller.
   The Supreme Court held that a vessel and cargo under the control of the loyal military was not subject to prize of war and ordered it returned to the claimants.

White, George W., The State of Texas v., 74 U.S. 227, 3-12-69, Chief Justice Chase.
   The state of Texas filed an original suit to regain control of bonds sold by the Confederate state of Texas. The Supreme Court held that Texas never ceased being a state and could recover the bonds. (See chapter 9.) Connected cases: 75 U.S. 532, 77 U.S. 839, 77 U.S. 971, 77 U.S. 992, and 80 U.S. 550.

White, William, Sr., v. John R. Hart, 80 U.S. 685, 4-22-72, Justice Swayne.
   White sued Hart to collect a promissory note. The lower court decided against White because the consideration for the note was a slave. The Supreme Court reversed the decision based upon constitutional grounds.

Wigg, George, The United States v., 72 U.S. 677, 5-13-67, Chief Justice Chase.
   Wigg, a British subject, was the claimant of the steamer *Pearl*, which was captured as a prize of war. The District Court restored the vessel and cargo to him. The Supreme Court reversed the decision because of the nature of the cargo and evidence that the vessel was a blockade runner.

Wiley, John E., The United States v., 78 U.S. 211, 5-1-71, Justice Strong.
   The Supreme Court held that a Federal statute that tolled the statute of limitations between citizens applied with equal force to the government.

Withenbury, W. W., v. The United States, 72 U.S. 613, 4-29-67, Chief Justice Chase.
   The Supreme Court held that a dismissal of the claim and the levying of costs was a final decree and appealable.

Wormer, Daniel, The United States v., 80 U.S. 530, 2-5-72, Justice Bradley.
Wormer entered into a contract with the United States to deliver 1,200 cavalry horses that met certain inspection standards. The inspection standards were changed by the United States after the contract was signed. Wormer sued and won in the Court of Claims. The Supreme Court overruled the decision, holding that the inspection standards were reasonable.

Worthy, John D., v. Henry Marston, 81 U.S. 826, 4-1-72, Justice Swayne.
An estate sued on a note executed by Marston in 1863. Marston claimed that the balance owed was for the purchase of a slave. The Supreme Court of Louisiana held that the note was given before its new constitution and was collectable. The U.S. Supreme Court affirmed the decision.

Zellner, Benjamin H., Ex Parte, 76 U.S. 665, 3-15-70, Justice Nelson.
Cotton owned by Zellner was seized under the confiscation acts. Zellner's claim was denied by the Court of Claims. When Zellner attempted to appeal, the Court of Claims held that the law passed in 1863 did not provide for appeals. Zellner petitioned the Supreme Court for a mandamus forcing the Court of Claims to permit an appeal. The Supreme Court so ordered.

ENDNOTES

Endnotes to the *U.S. Supreme Court Reports* are for the *Lawyer's Edition*

CHAPTER ONE:
DEFINING THE CONFLICT: THE PRIZE CASES
1. Bern Anderson, *By Sea and by River: The Naval History of the Civil War* (New York: Da Capo, 1962), 27.
2. 67 *U.S. Supreme Court Reports,* 459.
3. The case of the *Gerasimo,* Morris's *English Privy Council Cases,* vol. 11, 101.

CHAPTER TWO:
RUNNING THE BLOCKADE
1. J. G. Randall and David Donald, *The Civil War and Reconstruction,* 2nd ed. (Boston: D. C. Heath and Company, 1961), 440.
2. 5 *Federal Cases,* Circuit and District Courts, 712.
3. 69 *U.S. Supreme Court Reports,* 796.
4. 70 *U.S. Supreme Court Reports,* 200.
5. Ibid., 202.
6. The *Polly,* 2 C. Rob. 369 (English Cases).
7. The *William,* 5 C. Rob. 3195 (English Cases).
8. 72 *U.S. Supreme Court Reports,* 646.
9. Ibid., 651.

CHAPTER THREE:
SEA ENGAGEMENTS
1. 2 *Federal Cases,* 116.
2. 70 *U.S. Supreme Court Reports,* 253.
3. See R. Thomas Campbell, *Southern Thunder: Exploits of the Confederate States Navy* (Shippensburg, PA: Burd Street Press, 1996), chapters 7 and 8, for the exploits of the *Georgia.*
4. Anderson, *By Sea and by River,* 210.
5. 10 *Federal Cases,* 239.

6. 6 C. Rob. Adm. (Christopher Robinson Admiralty) 396 (English Cases).
7. 25 *Federal Cases,* 1025.
8. 74 *U.S. Supreme Court Reports,* 122.

CHAPTER FOUR:
POLITICAL RADICALISM

1. Frank L. Klement, *The Limits of Dissent: Clement L. Vallandigham and the Civil War* (Lexington, KY: University Press of Kentucky, 1970), passim.
2. 68 *U.S. Supreme Court Reports,* 591.
3. 28 *Federal Cases,* 874.
4. 3 Pet. (28 U.S.), 193.
5. 7 *Cushing Reports of Massachusetts* 285.
6. 28 *Federal Cases,* 920.
7. 68 *U.S. Supreme Court Reports,* 589.

CHAPTER FIVE:
COMBATING INSURRECTION

1. 71 *U.S. Supreme Court Reports,* 281.
2. Ibid.
3. Ibid., 282.
4. Ibid., 290.
5. Ibid., 291.

CHAPTER SIX:
PRISONER RETALIATION

1. 76 *U.S. Supreme Court Reports,* 552.
2. Ibid., 658.
3. 1 Wheat. (14 U.S.), 346–50.
4. 14 Mass., 420.
5. 76 *U.S. Supreme Court Reports,* 660.
6. *The Federalist Papers,* No. 82.
7. 81 *U.S. Supreme Court Reports,* 882.

CHAPTER SEVEN:
FINANCING THE WAR: LEGAL TENDER CASES

1. 68 *U.S. Supreme Court Reports,* 500.
2. 75 *U.S. Supreme Court Reports,* 513.
3. 74 *U.S. Supreme Court Reports,* 101.
4. Ibid., 141.
5. Ibid., 149.
6. 4 Wheat. (17 U.S.), 316.
7. 79 *U.S. Supreme Court Reports,* 287.
8. Ibid., 289.
9. Ibid., 291.

10. Ibid., 306.
11. 74 *U.S. Supreme Court Reports,* 141.
12. Ibid., 318.
13. Ibid., 324.
14. Ibid., 339.

CHAPTER EIGHT:
FINANCING THE WAR: TAXATION CASES

1. 74 *U.S. Supreme Court Reports,* 95.
2. Ibid., 97.
3. Ibid., 95.
4. Ibid., 96.
5. Ibid.
6. 3 Dall. (3 U.S.), 171.
7. 75 *U.S. Supreme Court Reports,* 482.
8. 11 Pet. (36 U.S.), 257.
9. 76 *U.S. Supreme Court Reports,* 672.
10. 11 Illinois Reports, 428.

CHAPTER NINE:
FINANCING THE WAR: BOND CASES

1. 76 *U.S. Supreme Court Reports,* 788.
2. 69 *U.S. Supreme Court Reports,* 866.
3. 76 *U.S. Supreme Court Reports,* 615.
4. 74 *U.S. Supreme Court Reports,* 227.
5. 2 Cranch (6 U.S.), 452.
6. 69 *U.S. Supreme Court Reports,* 857.
7. 77 *U.S. Supreme Court Reports,* 992.

CHAPTER TEN:
CONFEDERATE CURRENCY

1. 75 *U.S. Supreme Court Reports,* 362.
2. Ibid., 365.
3. 77 *U.S. Supreme Court Reports,* 1,007.
4. 81 *U.S. Supreme Court Reports,* 757.

CHAPTER ELEVEN:
PROCUREMENT PROBLEMS

1. Randall and Donald, *Civil War and Reconstruction,* 311.
2. 74 *U.S. Supreme Court Reports,* 249.
3. 69 *U.S. Supreme Court Reports,* 868.
4. 74 *U.S. Supreme Court Reports,* 250.
5. Ibid.
6. Ibid., 256.

7. Ibid.
8. Ibid.
9. Ibid.
10. Ibid.
11. 79 *U.S. Supreme Court Reports,* 360.
12. 74 *U.S. Supreme Court Reports,* 277.
13. 81 *U.S. Supreme Court Reports,* 753.

CHAPTER TWELVE:
CAPTURED PROPERTY

1. *U.S. Stat. at Large,* XII, 319.
2. Ibid., 591.
3. Ibid.
4. 69 *U.S. Supreme Court Reports,* 915.
5. Ibid., 916.
6. 76 *U.S. Supreme Court Reports,* 615.
7. Ibid., 616.
8. James G. Randall, *Constitutional Problems under Lincoln* (Urbana, IL: University of Illinois Press, 1964), 338.
9. 19 How. (60 U.S.), 393.
10. 78 *U.S. Supreme Court Reports,* 80.
11. Ibid., 136.
12. Ibid., 140.
13. 7 How. (48 U.S.), 181.
14. 78 *U.S. Supreme Court Reports,* 151.

CHAPTER THIRTEEN:
PROPERTY DISPUTES

1. 3 *Federal Cases,* 364.
2. 79 *U.S. Supreme Court Reports,* 260.
3. 81 *U.S. Supreme Court Reports,* 891.
4. Ibid.
5. 79 *U.S. Supreme Court Reports,* 287.
6. Ibid.
7. 78 *U.S. Supreme Court Reports,* 216.
8. Ibid.
9. Ibid., 217.

CHAPTER FOURTEEN:
BUSINESS BATTLES

1. 77 *U.S. Supreme Court Reports,* 926.
2. Ibid.
3. 79 *U.S. Supreme Court Reports,* 270.
4. 81 *U.S. Supreme Court Reports,* 852.

CHAPTER FIFTEEN:
AMNESTY, PARDONS, AND OATHS

1. 71 *U.S. Supreme Court Reports,* 356.
2. Ibid., 357.
3. Ibid.
4. Alexander Hamilton, James Madison, and John Jay, *The Federalist Papers, No. 45.*
5. 71 *U.S. Supreme Court Reports,* 362.
6. Ibid.
7. Ibid., 364.
8. Ibid., 365.
9. Ibid., 366.
10. Ibid.
11. Alexander Hamilton, James Madison, and John Jay, *The Federalist Papers, No. 74.*
12. 80 *U.S. Supreme Court Reports,* 519.
13. 76 *U.S. Supreme Court Reports,* 788.
14. Ibid., 615.
15. Ibid., 788.

CHAPTER SIXTEEN:
THE WILD WEST

1. 79 *U.S. Supreme Court Reports,* 390.
2. 74 *U.S. Supreme Court Reports,* 194.
3. 79 *U.S. Supreme Court Reports,* 388.

BIBLIOGRAPHY

Anderson, Bern. *By Sea and by River: The Naval History of the Civil War.* New York: Da Capo, 1962.

Campbell, R. Thomas. *Southern Thunder: Exploits of the Confederate States Navy.* Shippensburg, PA: Burd Street Press, 1996.

Donald, David Herbert. *Lincoln.* New York: Simon & Schuster, 1995.

Federal Cases, Circuit and District Courts, 1789–1880. St. Paul: West Publishing Co., 1896.

Hall, Kermit L., ed. *The Oxford Companion to the Supreme Court.* New York: Oxford University Press, 1992.

Josephy, Alvin M., Jr. *The Civil War in the American West.* New York: Random House, 1991.

Klement, Frank L. *The Limits of Dissent: Clement L. Vallandigham and the Civil War.* Lexington, KY: University Press of Kentucky, 1970.

Koenig, Louis W. "The Most Unpopular Man in the North." *American Heritage* XV, 2 (February 1964): 12–14, 81–88.

Musicant, Ivan. *Divided Waters.* New York: HarperCollins Publishers, 1995.

Niven, John. *Salmon P. Chase: A Biography.* New York: Oxford University Press, 1995.

Randall, James G. *Constitutional Problems under Lincoln.* Urbana, IL: University of Illinois Press, 1964.

Randall, James G., and David Donald. *The Civil War and Reconstruction.* Boston: D. C. Heath and Company, 1961.

Richardson, James D. *Messages and Papers of the Presidents.* Vol. 5. Washington, DC: Bureau of National Literature, 1912.

Schwartz, Bernard. *A History of the Supreme Court.* New York: Oxford University Press, 1993.

The Statutes at Large and Treaties of the United States of America. Boston: Little, Brown and Company, 1863.

Thomas, Benjamin P. *Abraham Lincoln.* New York: Barnes & Noble Books, 1994.

U.S. Supreme Court Reports, Lawyers' Edition. Vols. 66–81. Rochester, NY: Lawyers Cooperative Publishing Company, Vols. 66–73, 1926; Vols. 74–81, 1901.

INDEX

Page numbers in italics indicate illustrations.

317